New Germans, New Dutch

New Germans, New Dutch

Literary Interventions

Liesbeth Minnaard

Amsterdam University Press

Foundation Palimpsest

Foundation Palimpsest supports the publication of excellent scientific research in the academic discipline of cultural analysis, among other things by subsidizing the book series *Palimpsest: Disorientation*.

The book series *Palimpsest: Disorientation* addresses the culture of war, civil war, violence and conflict. It aims to rethink the discourse of war and enmity, and in doing so it hopes to contribute to the undermining of the stereotyping frames, without which no war can be waged.

The book series first term, *Palimpsest*, (the scraped-off parchment roll) suggests the layeredness, opacity and density of cultural objects and processes, and therefore also their rich possibilities towards rereading and revision. The second term, *Disorientation*, refers to the need to explore and subvert the expediently enforced boundary between East and West, a violent borderline that was incessantly addressed in the work of Inge E. Boer, in whose honour this book series is established. *Disorientation*, in its more common sense, is also a productive force. For disorienting forms of rereading disable the stereotypical ways of reading, which are so seamlessly evoked by dominant worldviews.

Cover design: Studio Jan de Boer, Amsterdam
Lay out: JAPES, Amsterdam

ISBN	978 90 8964 028 4
e-ISBN	978 90 4850 235 6
NUR	617

© E. Minnaard / Amsterdam University Press, Amsterdam, 2008

In loving memory of my open-minded grandmother
Cornelia Spruit-Smallegange (1913-2008)

Contents

Acknowledgements

New Germans, New Dutch began as an adventure stirred by wonder. Wonder about the familiar that all of a sudden seemed unfamiliar, uncanny. Coming home to the Netherlands after the NOISE Summer School in Madrid in September 2001, the world seemed to have changed. The boundaries of Dutchness were hastily being redefined – and in a manner that made me feel extremely uncomfortable. It was the rhetoric of division, which was suddenly dominating public discourse, that triggered the basic questions of this book.

The adventure then began with my departure for Berlin, that enthralling city of challenges and contradictions. A generous gift from the Dr Catharine van Tussenbroek Fund enabled me to transform my astonishment at the self-justified turn towards intolerance within Dutch society into a comparative investigation of the complexities of national belonging. I am grateful to my colleagues at TransAct and to all the friends who encouraged me to embark on this adventure. Djoke Dam, Christel Kohlmann, Deirdre Mol, Janienke Sturm and Janine Willemsen reassured me in my doubts about giving up my tenure job position and supported my decision to set out on the slippery paths of academic research. I have never regretted this step: it has brought me new homes, new worlds, new perspectives.

I thank Gloria Wekker and Rosemarie Buikema at Utrecht University for their guidance at a very early stage of the project – they gave me their trust even before I had actually begun. Inge Boer I thank posthumously, for her careful readings and valuable comments on preliminary research proposals. Although we have never met in person, I will always remember the warm enthusiasm and intellectual generosity that she conveyed to me by telephone or per e-mail. My special gratitude goes to Birgit Lesch, a warm-hearted and good-humoured spirit like no other: she taught me the many ins and outs of the German language and made Berlin feel like home in next to no time. The *Deutsche Akademische Austauschdienst* (DAAD) and Anselm Haverkamp enabled me to extend my stay in the German capital and to continue my research at the Heinrich-von-Kleist-Institut für Literatur und Politik at the European University Viadrina in Frankfurt/Oder. I thank them for offering me this opportunity.

After one year in Berlin I joined the DFG-*Graduiertenkolleg* "Identity and Difference. Gender Constructions and Interculturality (18th-21st century)" at the University of Trier, where a wonderful group of people engaged in true interdisciplinarity. Bernd Elzer, Denise Daum, Thomas Ernst, Anne Friedrich, Hillaria Gössmann, Christine Hanke, Alexandra Karentzos, Ruth Kersting, Stefani Kugler, Nina Möllers, Viktoria Schmidt-Linsenhoff and Melanie Ulz are only some of the interlocutors within this research community with whom I was privileged to

discuss my material. I thank all the participants for the lively exchange and productive sharing of ideas on a broad variety of topics. I am grateful to the *Deutsche
Forschungsgemeinschaft* (DFG) and the *Forschungsreferat* of the University of Trier for
their financial support of my research. Special thanks are owed to Kea Wienand
and Silke Förschler, inspired and gifted woman-warrior-collaborators. Discussions with these two friends were always happily fruitful. With them I share a
deep interest in the intersection of politics and aesthetics, and the belief in an
academia that can and needs to be transformed as well as transformative. I would
like to thank Anna-Lena Sälzer for her spontaneous and accurate help in the final
stage of writing. My dear friends Matthias Brunn and Britta Wegner made an
indispensable contribution to the project by distracting me with evenings of
laughter and leisure. I am thankful for their gift of friendship.

Mieke Bal's Theory Seminar at ASCA, the Amsterdam School of Cultural Analysis, became my second intellectual laboratory. I thank the participants in this
thought-stirring seminar, especially Roel van den Oever and Sonja van Wichelen,
for the lively exchange of ideas, the feedback on presented material, and the
Dutch *gezelligheid* during drinks afterwards. Mieke Bal is the seminar's indefatig-
able and multi-talented guide from whose ideational originality and bright enthusiasm my work and I profited enormously. Her work continues to inspire me. The
same counts for the work of Leslie Adelson, who enabled me to spend some time
at Cornell University at a crucial stage in my writing. Her superb feedback on my
analyses and her encouragement to probe deeper and to not settle with easy answers were of determinative impact on my work. I thank her for her generosity in
sharing critical insights that have kept me thinking ever since. I thank Gizem
Arslan for the vivid and valuable late-night library conversations, her marvellous
sense of humour and her lasting friendship.

This book would not have attained the intellectual depth and rigour that it has
without the guidance and support of my two supervisors, Herbert Uerlings and
Ernst van Alphen. Although they have never met in person, in their comments on
my work they complemented each other amazingly well. I could always count on
both of them for meticulous readings of preliminary chapters, insightful criticism
on lines of argumentation, and probing questions that prompted me to delve deeper and to ask further. Conversations with Herbert Uerlings helped me to balance
my personal and political wish to make a difference and the more subtle (aesthetic) difference provided by the literary texts. Ernst van Alphen taught me how
to make theory productive for literary analysis without it becoming dominant.
Additionally, hc stimulated me to take up more space to unfold my arguments –
advice that has transformed my writing style with powerful effects. I am indebted
to both for their intellectual generosity and I thank them for the trust that they
placed in me and my work.

Shortly after finishing writing this book in 2007, I joined the staff of the Literary Studies Department at Leiden University. I could not have been more fortu-

nate. Not only can I carry on with my analytical work on the multiple cultural effects of interculturality and globalisation, I can do this in a wonderfully inspiring and supportive atmosphere. For this I thank my dedicated and knowledgeable colleagues as well as our highly motivated students: I have worked in many places, but the creative dynamic that I have encountered in the Leiden department is extraordinary. And what counts for the department in general counts for my 'partners in PoCo' in Leiden in particular. Never was planning postcolonial sabotage more thought provoking and delightful than with Maria Boletsi, Isabel Hoving and Sarah de Mul.

Throughout all the stages of writing this book I could rely on the unconditional support (and the necessary distractions) of my down-to-earth family in Zeeland. I cannot express in words how much their warm interest in my well-being means to me. I thank them deeply for being there: whenever, wherever, however. My most heartfelt gratitude goes to Cornelia Fischer, critical companion in wonder and adventure from beginning to end. Without her, this project would not have come into being and this book would not exist. I thank her for posing the most challenging life questions and for exploring possible answers together with me.

Introduction

'But imagination changes mentalities, however slowly it may go about this'
(Glissant 1997: 183).

I started a first draft of this manuscript with the statement that 'migrants' have more and more become part of German and Dutch societies. In the course of writing this book this statement has become increasingly disputed. In both German and Dutch societies, several dramatic incidents – the murders of Pim Fortuyn and Theo van Gogh in the Netherlands, and 'smaller' instances of specifically gendered violence in Germany – have caused a rapidly growing polarisation between several parts of the German and Dutch populations, in particular between the indigenous majority and the (homogenised) 'Muslim' minorities.[1] The global increase of culturally and/or religiously motivated acts of terror has further contributed to a new emphasis on matters of cultural conflict instead of on processes of cultural encounter. This worrisome development has also affected the public discourses that serve both as the context of this book and as its frame for interpretation.[2]

The starting point of *New Germans, New Dutch* is the idea that people of migrant background, in their capacity as 'new Germans' and 'new Dutch', engender new meanings for the contested concepts of Germanness and Dutchness, and of German and Dutch national identity. In the changing German and Dutch ethnoscapes traditional and monolithic definitions of national Self and Other no longer hold.[3] National identities were never static, nor homogenous, but under the influence of transnational migration and other forms of globalisation this (false but influential) assumption has become absolutely untenable. The extensive public interest in issues of national identity in relation to the increased multiculturality of German and Dutch societies underlines the symbolic importance of the question of national boundaries. The two parallel and national public debates on the German *Leitkultur* and the Dutch 'multicultural drama' in the year 2000 can be considered symptomatic for the heightened, and often conflicting, discursivity of this question.

It is clear that the unmistakable transformation of German and Dutch society enforces a thorough rethinking and renegotiation of these national boundaries on several levels of public life. One of these levels is that of literature: in the process of rethinking and renegotiating national identity literature proves of particular significance. *New Germans, New Dutch* investigates the significance of the *literary* imagination in the age of globalisation. It considers literature as an alternative source of (aesthetic) knowledge and as a privileged sphere of reflection and contemplation on the contested issue of national identity. What counts for literature in general, counts for 'migrants' literature' or 'literature of migration' in an exceptional way.[4] In her path-breaking study *The Turkish Turn in Contemporary Literature: Toward a New Critical Grammar of Migration* Leslie Adelson (2005), describes this particular significance of literature of migration as follows: '[T]hese literary narratives provoke us to ponder the historical intelligibility of our time, to become more historically literate by reading against the grain of existing categories, concepts and statistics of migration in order to ask what worlds we inhabit as the millennium turns' (Adelson 2005: 13/14). *New Germans, New Dutch* investigates the imagination of transforming German and Dutch worlds in the literature by four writers in particular: the Turkish-German Emine Sevgi Özdamar and Feridun Zaimoglu, and the Moroccan-Dutch Abdelkader Benali and Hafid Bouazza.[5] It examines how their literary works rework the cultural matter of which German and Dutch national identities are made, and scrutinises in what ways this literature of migration intervenes in public discourses that still very much maintain exclusionary definitions of Germanness and Dutchness. *New Germans, New Dutch* discusses how this literature of migration negotiates the boundaries of these national categories and shows the space it opens up for new imaginaries of belonging.

I. National Identity

The Discursive Production of Germanness and Dutchness

'[T]he nation state is a machine that produces Others'
(Hardt and Negri 2000: 114).

'Increasingly, "national" cultures are being produced
from the perspective of disenfranchised minorities'
(Bhabha 1994: 6).

National Identity under Globalisation: Controversies

The central concept in *New Germans, New Dutch* is that of national identity. For over two centuries scholars and intellectuals in 'the West' have been trying to define this concept under a number of headings such as, for instance, *Volksgeist* or *volks-aard*, national character, national spirit, national consciousness or national Self (-understanding).[1] Its conceptualisation varied according to the circumstances, or, more precisely, according to its function in a matrix of power and interests. The concept was defined and redefined, appropriated and reappropriated, as were its symbols, its myths, and its (invented) traditions. In 'The Question of Cultural Identity' (1993) Stuart Hall describes national identity as a particular kind of cultural identity.[2] He argues that in the modern world the nation state constitutes a prime source of identification, not only as a political entity, but also as a signifying system of cultural representation:

> National cultures are composed not only of cultural institutions, but of symbols and representations. A national culture is a *discourse* – a way of constructing meanings which influences and organizes both our actions and our conception of ourselves (...). National cultures construct identities by producing meanings about 'the nation' with which we can *identify*; these are contained in the stories which are told about it, memories which connect its present with its past, and images which are constructed of it. (Hall 1993: 292/293)

National identity thus combines the membership to a particular nation state and identification with and feelings of belonging to a national culture. It is especially this second dimension of symbols and representations that Benedict Anderson addresses in his influential study *Imagined Communities. Reflections on the Origin and Spread of Nationalism* (1986).[3] His famous conceptualisation of nations as 'imagined communities' has encouraged numerous scholars to study the different (narrative) forms of these imaginations, the (collective as well as individual) processes of national identification, and the affective orientations in respect to national belonging.

Central to the (symbolic) production of national identity is the construction of inner- and outer-boundaries, the definition of the national Self by means of exclusion of a national Other that functions as its 'constitutive outside'. Lauren Berlant and Elizabeth Freeman (1993) refer to these various discursive patterns that together produce both the nation and its subjects with the term 'National Symbolic'.[4] Historically, the conceptualisation of the National Symbolic in a specific nation state was closely linked to the coming into existence, maintenance, threat or expansion of the various other (neighbouring) nation states. The technology of Self and Other, the construction of national (and often cultural) sameness as naturally opposed to a fundamentally different and often demonised Other continues to contribute to an (exclusionary) dynamics of symbolic identity construction. In contemporary Europe the national Other is predominantly an Other that resides *within* the borders of the nation state: ethnic or religious minorities, migrants, illegal aliens and so on.

Whereas in times of stability and continuity people generally aren't too concerned about national identity as a determinant of who they are and where they belong, in times of economic pressure, insecurity or change, national identity returns on the public agenda as a topic of vehement discussion and strong emphasis.[5] The increased crossing of national borders – be it as migratory movements and diasporic dislocations, for reasons of work on the global market, or simply for leisure – immerse people in situations that require a reconsideration of conventional constructions of national identity. The rapid global transformation pressurises national boundaries and prompts a reassessment of many people's national orientation.[6] Migrants appear as icons of this rapidly transforming world. As such they often feature as intruders that pose a threat to cohesion, social order, and stability in worlds that still define themselves as national. It is in these worlds and their ideological and affective frames of reference that national identity comes to function as a discursive means of exclusion, an exclusionary discursive boundary. In its strong intersection with issues of citizenship, national identity sustains a regulating metadiscourse with far-reaching consequences on a social, economic and personal scale for the people defined (or excluded) by it.[7]

Taking all of this into account, it is no surprise that national identity also appears in academic work as a highly politicised and contested concept. On one side of this polarised discourse, more conservative defenders of 'the national' urge for a return to and a (new) appreciation of a national definition of the Self. This (often rather romantic) longing is partly pushed forward by current feelings of uncertainty, insecurity and even threat in a world determined by change and seemingly limitless global expansion. Discourses and practices around international terrorism further contribute to a reification of the national, in particular of its borders. In the German and the Dutch contexts, developments of increasing European cooperation and integration as well as the – until recently – growing numbers of resident aliens and asylum requests constitute two other factors that motivate a protective reorientation on national identity. To a certain extent scholars on the more liberal side of the polarised spectrum of opinions acknowledge these motivations. In the preface to the wide-ranging volume *Unpacking Europe. Towards a Critical Reading*, Gilane Tawadros, for instance, affirms that:

> national identities are in a state of constant turbulence, unsettled from below by the complex, transnational identities of Europe's shifting citizenship and, at the same time, overshadowed from above by the forces of globalisation that stride across the world's continents with little regard for the discrete borders of the nation states. (Tawadros in Hassan and Dadi 2001: 8)

However, instead of persistently holding on to national identities as they were, Tawadros and others propose to take up the challenge posed by the process of global transformation.[8] In their eyes this process opens up a field of possibilities to renegotiate established and suppressive structures of Western hegemony. They put national identity aside as an exclusionary concept that reinforces thinking in dichotomies of 'us and them', of people who belong and those who do not. These scholars imagine a future of transnational communities that transcend national borders and move beyond the hierarchies established by these. In this postnational world, national identity loses its value. Its problematically polarising and divisive fiction becomes obsolete.

Although I agree with much of this critique, including the latter assertion of national identity's divisive and exclusionary qualities, I see no possibility to dismiss the concept altogether: its ongoing influence as a discursive category and as a factor of legal determinacy in issues of citizenship is unabated. As Nora Räthzel insists in her study *Gegenbilder. Nationale Identität durch Konstruktion des Anderen [Counter-images. National Identity by Construction of the Other]*: 'The uniform nation exists to the degree to which a majority of individuals contributes to the image of the uniform nation and defines itself and others that way, i.e. including itself, excluding others' (1997: 41).[9] National identity remains a central factor in any reflection on the (future of the) contemporary globalising world, both as a discursive concept and as a field of contesting discourses. In that sense we need an approach to national identity that includes a critical interrogation of the exclusionary and divisive dimensions of the concept, as well as an open-minded consideration of its particular positive qualities.[10] Any proposal to simply do away with national identity underestimates the connective potential that national identity also possesses. Conceptualised in a non-monolithic way, national identity can, in my opinion, function as a factor of (multi-)cultural integration and social cohesion for the multiethnic communities of this time.[11]

This last opinion feeds in with the influential questioning of transnational and cosmopolitan alternatives to national identity by Timothy Brennan (1997), as laid out in his critical work on cosmopolitanism. In his article 'Cosmo-Theory' Brennan (rather cynically) defines cosmopolitanism as a 'friendly' *cultural* discourse of 'the West' that is on the one hand blinded by the 'euphoria of a good will' (2001: 673), and on the other (inevitably) entangled in the dynamics of the global market. In his opinion the blind spot in the intellectual propagation of the cosmopolitan idea – including the understanding of the nation state as obsolete – is its own (profitable) implication in a particular nation state system: cosmopolitanism 'makes sense only in the context of a specific national-cultural mood' (ibid. 661):[12]

> Among the issues forgotten here are those key advantages nations provide the global subalterns they ['cosmopolitanists', LM] wish to free from the tyranny of the national state – advantages that are particularly condemned by the humanists who are hostile to the myths of national belonging. And yet, any progressive vision today depends on such myths. For, outside cosmopolis, they represent the only basis for organizing opposition to the corporate carnivalesque (…). (Brennan 2001: 672)

Brennan emphasises that the decision to give up on national identity can only be made from the privileged position of having a national identity that is recognised and undisputed. Those who make the claim that national identity has lost its relevance in the present world mostly have no need to worry about questions of national acceptance and national belonging. In a world in which many individuals are still struggling to become national, this claim appears rather precipitate and premature.[13] As Geoff Eley and Ronald Grigor Suny put it:

> Being national is the condition of our times, even as the nation is buffeted by the subnational rise of local, regional and ethnic claims, and the transnational threats of globalization, hegemonic American culture, migration, diasporization, and new forms of political community. In one way nationalism, like racism, becomes the protective cover to resist the uncontrollable transformations of our time. In another, nationalism and belonging to a nation may be

the kind of 'cultural recovery' that could potentially lead – not to a politics of the blood – but to acceptance, even celebration of difference. (Eley and Suny 1996: 32)

National identity thus comprehends both a problematic and a challenging dimension. It appears as the subject of an ongoing and multidimensional process of negotiation and redefinition. In this process the growing multiculturality of national communities features as an important factor of influence and acceleration. The changing German and Dutch ethnoscapes effect a heightened public discursivity of the National Symbolic and its future. In Germany and the Netherlands two strikingly vehement public debates that evolved parallel to each other in the year 2000 testify to this heightened discursivity. In Germany the debate revolved around the idea of a *deutsche Leitkultur* ['German guiding culture']; In the Netherlands it went down in history as the 'multicultural drama' debate. In both debates the question of national identity explicitly intersected with the issue of multiculturality.

The following sections offer a discussion and contextualisation of these parallel debates. Starting with a historical overview of the phenomenon of organised labour migration in both countries and continuing with the socio-political discourses that developed in the wake of this phenomenon, they position the two debates within the larger discursive complex on the multiculturalisation of German and Dutch national identity.

A Shared Moment of National Transformation: German and Dutch Histories of Labour Migration

The historical phenomenon of organised labour migration evolved almost simultaneously in Germany and the Netherlands.[14] It was officially propagated in the years between 1955, when the first agreement of this kind was signed (between Germany and Italy), and 1973, when the international oil crisis resulted in a complete ban on foreign recruitment in both countries.[15] The Federal Republic of Germany was the first western European country that drew up an official bilateral agreement for the temporary importation of foreign labour after the Second World War. With this agreement the West German government responded to the economic boom that is commonly known as the German *Wirtschaftswunder*, the 'economic miracle'. As a result of this economic miracle, the Federal Republic urgently needed more manpower for production work in the heavy industry that profited in great measure from the expansion of the international trade. In the early 1950s most shortages on the expanding West German labour market could still be annulled by workers from the German Democratic Republic (especially in Berlin) as well as by the many postwar refugees from the former German territories in the East. To fill the still-remaining shortages the West German government signed a bilateral agreement with Italy on 22 December 1955. This agreement enabled Italian workers to come to the Federal Republic for work. Bilateral agreements with Spain and Greece followed in 1960. However, after the erection of the Berlin Wall in August 1961 and the further closing off of the German-German border, the labour supply from the East stopped and the labour shortage in West Germany was aggravated seriously. To handle this problem the West German government expanded the labour migration system and also started recruiting in non-European countries. In October 1961, only two months after the erection of the Berlin Wall, the German Federal Republic signed an agreement with the Republic of Turkey that settled the West German employment of large numbers of Turkish labourers. Another agreement with the Turkish Republic followed in 1964.[16]

The first and rather provisional recruitment contracts appointed the labourers for a relatively short, restricted period of time. The labour migrants fulfilled a buffer function on the labour market and their temporary presence rested on a small legal basis. After the stipulated period they were expected (and mostly also planned) to return to their countries of origin. Soon it became clear, however, that the booming West German economy demanded foreign manpower for a longer period of time. The contracts were renewed for a period of up to two years, often at the request of employers who did not want to lose trained, experienced personnal. The increase of numbers of foreign workers was taken as instigation to improve the legislation in respect to foreign recruitment. On 28 April 1965 the first German 'foreigners' law' [Ausländergesetz] was passed, which stipulated that foreign workers needed both residence and work permits. In fact, this law was mainly a means of control that relegated foreign workers to a catch-22 situation: it determined that without a work permit they could not get a job and without a job they could not get a work permit.[17]

The Dutch government followed the German example and also started the institutionalised recruitment of foreign workers in order to meet the demands of the expanding Dutch postwar economy. The Netherlands had to contend with similar problems of labour shortages; manpower was needed particularly for the unskilled and heavy physical labour in mines and in other labour-intensive areas such as shipyards, the textiles industries and blast furnaces.[18] In comparison with the German situation labour migrants came to the Netherlands more often by way of direct recruitment by the personnel departments of these industries. More than in Germany contracts were fixed outside of the institutional frameworks for recruitment (and selection). At a certain point, however, the Dutch government interceded and started to act as a partner in the foreign recruitment agreements as well. In 1968 this governmental mediation became obligatory.

Labour migration was not a new phenomenon for either of the two countries, nor was it their first experience with migrants, as popular public discourse sometimes seems to suggest. It was the official, institutionalised character of the 'guest labour' [*Gastarbeit/gastarbeid*] migration that distinguished it from other, earlier forms of labour migration, aside the larger numbers of migrants and the relatively low social positions available to them. The more striking cultural and, in some cases, religious differences between the migrants and the host society contributed to the novel character of the situation as well.[19] The then-popular term for these foreign workers – 'guest workers' – indicates the assumed temporariness of their presence.[20] In the Netherlands this idea of impermanence distinguished labour migrants from migrants from the former colonies (Indonesia, the Moluccas, Surinam and the Dutch Antilles), who often already had Dutch citizenship and were able to speak the Dutch language. In Germany as well as in the Netherlands the government policy built on the assumption that the labour shortage was temporary and that these 'guests' would at a certain point, after the work had been done, return to their home countries. Most migrants themselves shared this assumption: they saw the foreign work as an investment in a better future in their countries of origin. As a result the integration of these foreign workers into the host societies was not an issue. The migrants mostly lived in (very low standard) accommodation close to their workplace and had no access to health care or education facilities. Both the German and the Dutch governments emphasised that their countries were not migration countries, like the US, Canada or Australia. Foreign labour, they argued, would only be profitable if it remained a short-term proposition.

In 1973, the year of the international oil crisis, both Germany and the Netherlands officially terminated the foreign recruitment programmes. This oil crisis marked a time of severe economic hardship and growing unemployment in which the public discourse on foreign workers also changed. As a consequence of the economic recession they were no longer seen as contributors to economic prosperity; instead they were now discussed in terms of problems and economic burden. The 'guest workers' suddenly appeared as rivals on the dwindling labour market or, after the mass layoffs that hit this group even harder than it did the indigenous workers, as freeloaders of the German and Dutch welfare systems. In the public opinion the idea that the time had come for the 'guests' to leave gained impetus. The growing awareness that, for several reasons and despite the myth of return, a large group of these migrants no longer intended to go back to their countries of origin, but instead planned to stay and bring their families over to Germany and the Netherlands, added to a negatively pitched discourse.[21] The popular demand for a limit on the number of foreign workers became louder, and the social pressure on migrants to return increased.

In the years after the official termination of the foreign labour agreements, however, the number of the migrant population did not diminish. New legal restrictions made it impossible for migrants to return temporarily to their home countries. For that reason, and as a result of an overall state of economic insecurity, also in the countries of origin, many labour migrants opted for a future in

Germany and the Netherlands.[22] After the end of the recruitment phase in 1973, a phase of consolidation began in which many foreign workers brought their families over and settled down in Germany and the Netherlands on a long-term basis.

The ways in which Germany and the Netherlands responded to these developments and the transformation of the national ethnoscapes are quite different. The German government kept refusing to perceive of itself as a country of migration. It even tried to get rid of its foreign worker population by means of a *Rückkehrförderungsgesetz* (10 October 1983), a law that promoted the voluntary return of unemployed foreign workers to their country of origin.[23] The Dutch government, on the contrary, dealing with the consequences of both labour migration and decolonisation simultaneously, chose to acknowledge the Netherlands' new multicultural character and the permanent presence of what it called 'ethnic minorities'. In 1983 the Dutch parliament agreed on an inclusive 'minorities policy' known as the *minderhedennota* that aimed to improve the legal status of ethnic minorities, to diminish their social and economic disadvantage, to fight discrimination and prejudice, and to develop a tolerant multicultural society. A central characteristic of this policy was the idea that ethnic minorities could and should integrate into Dutch society while 'retaining their own identity' [*met behoud van eigen identiteit*].

Ruud Koopmans and Paul Statham assert that the Dutch cultural-pluralist approach of that time perceived of integration as 'best accomplished through confident subcultures, thus making the preservation of minority cultures an essential part of incorporation' (2001: 79). In line with the Dutch tradition of 'pillarisation' the new policy granted ethnic minorities cultural group rights.[24] These rights involved a large degree of autonomy in the cultural sphere, promotion and subsidisation of representative (self-)organisations and inclusion in policy deliberations and implementations (including local voting and the opening up of civil service positions). Koopmans and Statham speak in this respect of a 'Dutch multiculturalism *avant la lettre* adding foreigners on as another pillar in the polder' (ibid. 80). Anita Böcker and Kees Groenendijk also emphasise the extraordinariness of this early migration policy:

> It was not a matter of course that the Dutch government determined on a policy of integration already at the beginning of the 1980s. In Germany one was still discussing the introduction of a return bonus at that time to prevent foreign employees from staying permanently. The Dutch transition to a policy of integration was a result of pragmatic compromises between the large political parties. The violent actions of young Moluccans (1975-1977) served as a catalyst.

> Es war nicht selbstverständlich, dass sich die niederländische Regierung schon Anfang der Achtzigerjahre zu einer Integrationpolitik entschloss. In

Deutschland diskutierte man damals noch über die Einführung einer Rück-
kehrprämie, um zu verhindern, dass ausländische Arbeitnehmer dauerhaft
blieben (...) Der niederländische Entschluss, zu einer Integrationspolitik über-
zugehen, war das Ergebnis pragmatischer Kompromisse zwischen den gro-
ßen politischen Parteien. Die Gewaltaktionen molukkischer Jugendlicher
(1975-1977) wirkten dabei als Katalysator. (Böcker and Groenendijk 2004:
322)

In the comparison with Germany, Böcker and Groenendijk not only assess a more
pragmatic way of dealing with the topic in Dutch politics, but they also point out
the postcolonial pressure that the (radicalised youth of the) Moluccan minority
brought to bear on the Dutch government. The presence and integration of several other minority groups from the Netherlands' former colonies definitely
raised the social demand and urgency to come to a satisfying solution in dealing
with these different cultural groups. Whereas in Germany the discussion on migration and integration policy focused almost exclusively on the Turkish population, in the Netherlands it concerned people of Moluccan, Indonesian, Surinamese and Antillean origin in addition to the labour migrants from the various
European and non-European Mediterranean countries.[25]

After the 1983 change of Dutch policy, ethnic minority groups were encouraged
and expected to participate in Dutch politics as ethnic minorities. To this end a
network of several ethnic advisory boards and participation institutes [inspraakor-
ganen] was established. In comparison to the German foreigner councils [Auslän-
derbeiräte] on a local level, the Dutch representatives of ethnic minorities had considerably more influence on a national level. Comparative research on social
integration and political participation in Germany and the Netherlands makes
clear that these distinct policies also resulted in striking differences in the claims
made by ethnic minorities.[26] Whereas German 'foreigners', for whom it was substantially more difficult to become full-fledged German citizens, kept looking
predominantly in the direction of their home countries, Dutch 'allochthons'
made use of the better claims-making opportunities in the Netherlands, which
increasingly became their country of citizenship as well.[27] Thom Duyvené de Wit
and Koopmans draw the following conclusion from this assessment:

German ethnic minorities obviously feel much more insecure in their position
in their country of residence. The greatest part of their demands concerning
their situation in Germany has to do with immigration and racism, and only
little more than ten per cent with their rights and their position as permanent
inhabitants of this country. Contrary to this in the Netherlands nearly four
times as many demands of ethnic minorities are related to questions concerning their integration into the country of their residence. That seems to be an

indication of a stronger confidence in their legitimate presence as an integral part of the Dutch society.

Deutsche ethnische Minderheiten fühlen sich offensichtlich viel unsicherer in ihrer Stellung in ihrem Aufenthaltsland. Die große Mehrzahl ihrer Forderungen in Bezug auf die Situation in Deutschland betrifft Immigration und Rassismus, und nur wenig mehr als zehn Prozent hängen mit ihren Rechten und ihrer Stellung als ständige Einwohner dieses Landes zusammen. Im Gegensatz dazu beziehen sich in den Niederlanden fast viermal so viele Forderungen ethnischer Minderheiten auf Fragen, die mit ihrer Eingliederung in das Aufenthaltsland zu tun haben, und das scheint ein Anzeichen für ein stärkeres Vertrauen in ihre legitime Anwesenheit als integraler Bestandteil der niederländischen Gesellschaft zu sein. (Duyvené de Wit and Koopmans 2001: 38/39)

Almost all comparative studies on migration in Germany and the Netherlands connect such discrepancies to the (long-term) difficulties German 'foreigners' had in acquiring German citizenship.[28] In addition to the tradition of 'pillarisation', which enabled Dutch 'allochthons' to incorporate relatively easily in Dutch society, the more liberal citizenship and naturalisation laws were also an important distinguishing factor. Since 1953, the Netherlands has had a restricted ius soli citizenship law, a variation on the French civic model that automatically grants citizenship to third-generation immigrants. In 1985 this law was liberalised by means of the option clause that enabled second-generation immigrants between eighteen and twenty-five years of age to acquire Dutch citizenship by declaration. In 1992 the Dutch government also provisionally permitted dual citizenship, but the amendment allowing this was withdrawn in 1997. Numerous exceptions, however, still keep this possibility open.[29]

The Dutch naturalisation law used to be noticeably more liberal than the German one. In order to obtain citizenship, both countries stipulated a permanent residence permit, a 'certain' measure of integration – most importantly fluency in the German or Dutch language – and a clean civil record.[30] In the Netherlands, aliens need to prove five years of residence instead of the German requirement of eight years. Moreover, different from the German law, Dutch law does not have a financial clause that requires a particular minimum income. The effects of these differences in German and Dutch citizenship legislation are still visible in the discrepant numbers of (legal) aliens among the Dutch and German population.[31]

Despite the recurrent protest against the German citizenship law and its rootedness in the 1913 Blood Law, the discussion about the renewal of the migration policy and citizenship legislation in Germany was not resolved until the year 2000.[32] In that year, after a long and difficult political process, the SPD-Green Party government finally settled some of the most urgent issues and a liberalised citizenship law took effect. This new law stipulated that second-generation immigrants obtain German citizenship at birth when at least one of the parents has been living in Germany for eight years or more and possesses an unrestricted residence permit. These children often also receive their parents' nationality; in this case they are compelled to choose between one or the other before their twenty-third birthday. As this law offered a considerable extension of the possibilities to become German for people of migrant background, the year 2000 marks an important transformative moment, both in legal terms as well as in a symbolic respect.

In the same year that Germany liberalised its citizenship law, the Dutch government decided on several restrictions in its naturalisation policy. This more restrictive approach coincided with a strong questioning of the actual success of the celebrated 1983 cultural-pluralist approach. Several violent incidents polarised the debate on the Dutch multicultural state of affairs and enforced a critical reconsideration of the idea of integration in Dutch society while retaining one's own identity. A growing dissatisfaction about Dutch migration policy among large parts of the population incited a vehement debate on the actual profit of the 1983 approach and on the question whether retaining one's cultural identity was not in fact an obstacle for integration into Dutch society. The emphasis in the public discourse on integration shifted from voluntariness to obligation. One incentive for critique was the miserable position of migrants within the Dutch labour market. Comparative research on the socio-economic position of migrants in Germany and the Netherlands reveals a better integration of migrants in the German labour market.[33]

All in all, a continuous discussion on the topic of migration and processes of multiculturalisation resulting from this migration characterises the time between the first foreign recruitment agreement in 1955 and the changes in citizenship legislation in 2000. These discussions vary in terms of intensity and socio-political scale. Peak intensity levels generally coincide with other kind of tensions as economic hardship or the threat of terrorism. At such times, general feelings of insecurity in the autochthonous populations are often causally projected on the presence of people of other ethnic origins. As we will see in the following two sections, discussions about migration and multiculturality are also always discussions about national identity, and about the transformation or preservation of a particular national self-understanding.[34]

Dutch National Identity and the 'Multicultural Drama'

'We cannot keep the alien out and we do not want to keep it out'
(Huizinga [1934] 1946).[35]

Conservative Dutch politicians and scholars such as Frits Bolkestein and S.W. Couwenberg often argue that national identity is more disputed in the Netherlands than in any other (western) European country.[36] A similar statement appears rather suggestive and ahistorical, especially in comparison with a 'burdened' and 'belated' nation state such as Germany. It hints at the Dutch lack of interest in, and even conscious neglect of, its own national identity – a regrettable national trait in the eyes of these 'culture-nationalists'.[37] Bolkestein, for example, criticises: 'Nation leads to nationalism and the Dutch do not join in there. At least that is what they say themselves' (2003: 485).[38] He himself is of the contrary opinion: 'the Dutch' do have an outspoken and particularly Dutch identity and it is important to valuate and protect this identity, especially in the present times of globalisation and European integration.

Culture-nationalists generally agree that it is 'typically Dutch' to feel and behave in a morally superior way in respect to questions of nation and nationalism. 'The Dutch' look down on people or national entities that give proof of or even celebrate national pride, speak about national identity in a patriotic mode or foster nationalist sentiments. According to Bolkestein *cum suis*, the disturbing lack of interest in the Dutch national history is causally connected to this 'typically Dutch' attitude of moral superiority. Many scholars of Dutch national identity subscribe to this observation (but leave out the depreciative judgement) and root this attitude in the specific Dutch history of nation-building. The Netherlands counts as a textbook example of the situation in which the erection of the state precedes the imagination of the nation. The reason for this exemplary status lies in the fact that, in comparison to many other European countries and especially in comparison to its neighbour, Germany, the Dutch state originated from an early and (in retrospect) rather uncomplicated process of unification. In 1648 the Netherlands became the first civil republic in Europe. After a long period of (changing) foreign occupation of the several smaller states, the joint 80 years' war of liberation against Spain (1567-1648) resulted in the pragmatic establishment of the Republic of the Seven United Netherlands.

Taking this historical moment as a starting point, historians often speak of the Dutch 'glorious' and 'continuous' national history, and of a gradual development of a very moderate Dutch identity. They refer to the prosperous years of the 'Golden Age', the humanist and liberal intellectual climate and the freedom of religion after the Reformation, as historical markers of Dutch openness and tolerance. They argue further that the relatively stable borders of the Dutch nation state made the promotion of a strong national consciousness superfluous.[39] Instead of strong national sentiments, a shared history and heritage functioned as the unifying 'cement' of the Dutch nation state and became the foundation for a Dutch national identity.

A conservative scholar such as Couwenberg comments on this representation in worrisome terms. In his introduction to the edited volume with the telling name *Nationale identiteit: van Nederlands probleem tot Nederlandse uitdaging* [National Identity: From Dutch Problem to Dutch Challenge], he writes:

> It is therefore not so much our moral superiority, but the happy circumstance that we delivered ourselves from foreign domination at an early stage that has kept us free from ethnic-nationalist sentiments, and for a long time we did not need to bother about our identity as nation. But that latter situation is changing now that our society is rapidly acquiring a multi-ethnic character and has to process an increasing number of European and global influences.

> Het is derhalve niet zozeer onze morele superioriteit, maar de gelukkige omstandigheid, dat we ons al zo vroeg ontworsteld hebben aan vreemde overheersing dat we gevrijwaard zijn gebleven van etnisch-nationalistische sentimenten en dat we ons lange tijd niet druk hoefden te maken over onze identiteit als natie. Maar dat laatste verandert nu onze samenleving in snel tempo een multi-etnisch karakter krijgt en steeds meer Europese en mondiale invloeden te verwerken krijgt. (Couwenberg 2001: 37)

Couwenberg's rhetoric oscillates between warning and encouragement. On the one hand he maintains that Dutch identity is exposed to two kinds of threats: the multicultural society and Europeanisation. On the other hand he presents these two developments as challenges, as moments in which 'the Dutch' get the opportunity to care for their identity by protecting it against these foreign influences. He uses the idea of a historical lack of national consciousness as a warning against threats currently overlooked.

This polarising line of reasoning, not uncommon among culture-nationalists, easily slides off into a discourse of a disputable (essentialising) quality. Bolkestein, for instance, assumes a similar rhetoric when he asks himself: 'What remains of the Dutch identity when in the big cities, a country's carriers of culture, autochthonous Dutch comprise a minority?' (2003: 493).[40] In this remark 'Dutch culture' is exclusively linked to the so-called 'autochthonous' Dutch population. Dutch national identity is connected to a Dutch origin and is thus inaccessible for Dutch 'allochthons', the Dutch citizens who have at a certain (undefined) moment in history come from elsewhere.[41] During the late 1980s and 1990s, culture-nationalist arguments such as these became more and more accepted and even moved into the mainstream.

The first to publicly address the influence of ethnic difference in and on Dutch society was the sociologist Herman Vuijsje. In his study *Vermoorde onschuld. Etnisch verschil als Hollands taboe* [*Murdered Innocence. Ethnic Difference as Taboo*] (1986) he develops the argument that a strong taboo in Dutch society, especially among the leftist intellectual elite, has determined the Dutch way of dealing with ethnicity and ethnic issues. This taboo, he argues, can be linked back to the Second World War and to the collective, postwar feelings of guilt and shame about the huge number of Dutch Jews that did not survive the Holocaust. It is a well-known fact that in comparison to other occupied western European countries such as France, Belgium and Denmark, the number of Dutch Jews that were arrested and trans-ported to concentration camps is shockingly and embarrassingly high. According to Vuijsje this 'Dutch war myth' (1986: 8) explains the important influence of the ethnic taboo on the Dutch morality. When Vuijsje's study was published, his ar-gument caused considerable indignation, especially among leftist intellectuals whom he accused of being too circumspect in their treatment of and speaking about ethnic Others. However, the controversy settled relatively swiftly and the topic disappeared from the public agenda. Almost 20 years later, Vuijsje main-tains that, in retrospect, the fear of the 'racism-bug' was too strong at that time (Sanders and Schutte 2003: 32). Several other key figures in the discourse on Dutch multiculturality state that the Netherlands just was not ready for this sort of openness yet.[42]

About five years after the appearance of Vuijsje's study, Bolkestein, who was a Commissioner of the European Union at that time, reopened the debate on Dutch ethnic minorities. In a public lecture in Lucerne, published as an article in *de Volkskrant* (12 September 1991), he urged for a much more rigorous approach in respect to the integration of ethnic minorities, in particular of those professing to be Muslims. He called for a defence of European liberal values against the world of Islam that in his eyes yet had to go through a phase of enlightenment after a Western example. His appeal particularly considered issues of gender emancipa-tion and the protection of sexual minorities against the intolerance and suppres-sive ideology that he associated with Islam. In response to Bolkestein's controver-sial statements, the Dutch government organised a national debate on minorities [*Nationale Minderhedendebat*] to discuss the 'obstacles' that hampered the integra-tion of minorities in Dutch society. This state-organised debate was an attempt to actively rethink and (re-)formulate requirements and rules for integration in order to improve multicultural coexistence. The debate appealed to a growing concern among large parts of the ('autochthonous') population about the rapidly increas-ing numbers of refugees seeking asylum in the Netherlands. This refugee issue in many ways obfuscated the discussion about the integration of long-term minori-ties. At that time, however, the Dutch government did not answer the populist call for a more restrictive (European) policy. Abiding feelings of public dissatisfaction thrived under the public surface.

With the publication of Paul Scheffer's by-now notorious article titled 'The multicultural drama' in NRC Handelsblad of 29 January 2000, these sentiments erupted with unexpected vehemence. The telling and provocative title of this article immediately set the terms of the debate: multiculturality and drama were grouped in one semantic field. Paul Schnabel, director of the SCP (Social and Cultural Planning Office) and, in this capacity, an influential intellectual voice in Dutch society, took sides with Scheffer and underlined his warning message. About two weeks later, on 17 February 2000, he published an article in another well-respected Dutch newspaper, de Volkskrant with a headline cast in a similar dramatic vein: 'The multicultural society is an illusion'. References to failure, drama and alarm came to determine the national 'multicultural drama debate' that evolved after these publications.

Central in both articles is the concern for the genesis of an ethnic underclass. Both of these white male intellectuals fear for an impending social segregation along ethnic lines. Scheffer argues that, instead of constituting a national community, people live alongside each other in Dutch society. The Dutch policy of integration while retaining one's own identity hampers the pursuit of emancipation and social participation. He compares the blindness for what he sees as the failure of the Dutch multicultural society to the politics of neutrality on the eve of the German invasion of the Netherlands in 1940 and concludes that because of this negligent attitude the multicultural 'house of cards' is about to collapse.[43] He connects this collapse to the (assumed lack of a) Dutch national identity:

> The culture of toleration that has now reached its boundaries joins with a self-image that is inaccurate. (...) The dismissive way in which the Netherlands has dealt with national consciousness does not have a very inviting effect. We rule the national roost because we think we do not have one.

> De cultuur van het gedogen, die nu op haar grenzen stoot, gaat hand in hand met een zelfbeeld dat onwaarachtig is. (...) De wegwerpende manier waarop in Nederland is omgesprongen met nationaal besef werkt namelijk niet uitnodigend. We slaan onszelf op de nationale borst omdat we denken er geen te hebben. (Scheffer 2000)

Like Vuijsje before him Scheffer seems to assert a remedy for the Dutch 'multicultural drama' in a revaluation of the Dutch national identity. His main critique concerns the moral indifference of the political establishment, as well as the cultural relativism among the leftist intellectual elite. It is their fault that the Netherlands is 'a country where processes of integration have failed' (ibid.). Besides this assessment and the alarming analysis of what he labelled 'a drama', his article also functioned as a call for social engagement. However, this dimension – the plea for social engagement – was largely lost in the debate that developed in the wake of the article.

Many opinion makers responded to Scheffer's article, a majority of them in appreciative agreement. They praised Scheffer's critique of multiculturalism and often connected their approval to a call for stricter rules for integration and even assimilation. The discussion in no way restricted itself to the printed press: the 'multicultural drama' turned into a dramatised multimedia event. A broad variety of reports on problems and deficiencies in respect to the migrant part of the population came to determine the image of the Dutch multicultural society in the media. They corroborated a correlative between ethnic background – especially Moroccan and Antillean – and negative issues as criminality, school dropout and unemployment. This particular media representation resulted in a rather one-sided image of a lost generation of Dutch 'allochthons' and their failing integration.[44] Scheffer's article and the subsequent public discourse also engendered an official debate on the 'multicultural drama' issue in the Dutch parliament. In this debate the 'pillarisation' system and its effects on ethnic minorities' integration and participation in Dutch society were heavily questioned.

In contrast to the earlier discursive interventions by Vuijsje and Bolkestein that were met with indignation, now the public responses were tuned more positively. Scheffer's article fed into a general dissatisfaction with the perceived 'shadow sides' of Dutch multiculturality and worries about a lack of integration of ethnic minorities. Especially the discussion-opening quality of the article was appreciated. In her insightful study, *Voorbij de onschuld. Het debat over integratie in Nederland* [*Beyond Innocence. The Debate on Integration in the Netherlands*] (2004), the philosopher Baukje Prins carefully analyses this development of what she labels a 'new realism' in the Dutch public arena.[45] She argues that it is not so much particular political ideas that became popular in this period, but that a specific way of speaking gained ground in broad layers of Dutch society:

> New realists (...) offer their listeners a self-image that is hard to resist. They construct an image of a Dutch identity that on the one hand, as far as the Dutch are supposed to be modern, tolerant and open, is a sort of non-identity, but that on the other hand contains several specific ethnic, cultural and gendered characteristics. This construction of identity is so attractive because it appeals to a longing for purity, for a form of political and moral innocence from which people would be able to represent reality in the way it really is.

> Nieuw-realisten (...) bieden hun toehoorders een moeilijk te weerstaan zelf-beeld aan. Ze doen dat middels de constructie van een Nederlandse identiteit die enerzijds, voorzover Nederlanders geacht worden modern, tolerant en open te zijn, een soort non-identiteit is, maar die anderzijds tal van specifieke etnische, culturele en geseksueerde eigenschappen bevat. Deze identiteitscon-

structie is zo aantrekkelijk omdat ze een appel doet op een verlangen naar zuiverheid, naar een vorm van politieke en morele onschuld van waaruit mensen de werkelijkheid zouden kunnen weergeven zoals ze werkelijk is. (Prins 2004: 24/25)

New realists often present their discourse as one of honesty and straightforwardness. They portray their opponents as advocates of a discourse of political correctness and cultural relativism, a discourse that in their opinion erects and consolidates discursive taboos, especially in concern to ethnic minorities. New realists promise to bring about a new openness in a public discourse that is assumedly determined by evasiveness. This new attitude is supposed to be true to the Dutch national identity: 'To be Dutch means to be open, straightforward and realistic' (Prins 2002: 244).[46]

The 'multicultural drama' debate caused considerable polarisations among the Dutch population: the old left as opposed to the new right, political correctness as opposed to new realism, and also, sadly, 'autochthonous' Dutch as opposed to 'allochthonous' Others. The dominant public voice was white and male and spoke in the vein of Scheffer's article. Dissonant voices and/or 'allochthonous' speakers – such as, for instance, Anet Bleich, Troetje Loewenthal, Anil Ramdas, and Sawitri Saharso – sounded rather faint and did not manage to refute the basic assumption that something *was* wrong with Dutch society and that the grounds for this wrong had to do with its multiculturality.[47] One of the most ardent responses from the left rephrased the idea of Schnabel's multicultural illusion into the title formula 'Nederland bestaat niet meer' ['The Netherlands No Longer Exists']. Peter van der Veer, its author, another white male and director of the Amsterdam School for Social Studies, published his outspoken piece of critique in the long-standing Dutch journal, *De Gids* (2000). In opposition to conservative culture-nationalists such as Bolkestein and Scheffer, he asserts that it is not the character of Dutch identity that is the subject of discussion, but the assumed threat posed by Muslim migrants in a transforming world. The necessary but resisted assertion that the Netherlands *is* a country of migration and that this migration has structurally changed Dutch social relations lies at the bottom of the exclusionary and polarising discussion. He writes: 'Generally these kinds of conservative ideologists are more conspicuous in describing what threatens the particularly Dutch character than in what determines the particularly Dutch character' (Van der Veer 2000: 744).[48] Moreover, he assesses that '[t]he discussion about Dutch culture is in fact a negative one. Its central concern is the rejection of cultures (and in fact only the Islam) that migrants have brought into the Netherlands and not the definition of Dutch culture' (ibid. 746).[49] According to Van der Veer culture-nationalists cling to an outdated message for fear of change. However, whereas the culture-nationalist statements took centre stage, Van der Veer's important counter-claims remained rather marginal.

Another issue of socio-political significance that came up around the same time was the call for recognition and commemoration of the Dutch involvement in and (co-) responsibility for the history of slavery. In 1999 the National Platform for the History of Slavery [*Nationaal Platform Slavernijverleden*] started an initiative to create a Dutch slavery memorial. The slavery monument was officially opened to the (selected) public in the Amsterdam Oosterpark on 1 July 2002.[50] Emotional discussions about, among other things, the many disappointments about persistent structures of denial and a continuing disavowal of this prominent stain on Dutch national identity marked the years in between. The Dutch cultural memory fails when it comes to accountability for the burdens of slavery and Dutch colonialism. The positive, contemporary Dutch self-image as open, tolerant, and multicultural leaves no space for an acknowledgement of the atrocities against (black and colonial) Others perpetrated in the name of the Dutch nation. In this sense it is extremely bitter that in the contemporary Dutch self-image, colonialism features almost positively as an enabling condition for a happy multiculturality. The discussion on this aspect of national memory and identity remains marginal, especially in comparison to the 'multicultural drama' debate in which the (migrant) Other is made accountable for Dutch problems.

Further Polarisation: The Murders of Fortuyn and Van Gogh

The 'multicultural drama' debate dominated Dutch public discourse throughout the summer of 2000. After that time it lost some of its vehemence, but not its sense of urgency. The debate revived in all its intensity about a year later after the terrorist attacks on 9/11. A series of incidents followed varying from verbal violence and vandalism to arson attacks on mosques and Islamic schools. Despite the appeal for tolerance from both the Dutch government as well as several representatives of Muslim and other religious groups, Dutch society got stuck in a state of interethnic, interreligious and/or intercultural tension. In this social climate of polarisation and mutual distrust, the political newcomer Pim Fortuyn rose to fame with a populist-right discourse with strongly divisive aspects. In both the public and the political arena he staged himself as the voice of the 'autochthonous' underdog and as the ultimate representative of the character trait of 'standing up for oneself'. His particular personality seemed to embody the taboo-breaking quality of his discourse: an extravagant gay dandy who claimed to say what he thought and to do what he said – his political ideology in a nutshell. This notorious slogan is just a mild example of Fortuyn's provocative critique aimed at the politicians in charge of the Dutch nation state. Fortuyn radically dissociated himself from the political establishment, which he blamed for being completely out of touch with the 'common people', especially the indigenous Dutch working class. He accused this political elite of concealing truth for the sake of maintaining a comfortable but disastrous status quo. Fortuyn's primary appeal seemed to lie in his radicalised new-realist discourse, what Prins calls 'hyperrealism' (2004: 42/43). His hyperrealist rhetoric was attractive to a large part of the Dutch population that felt neglected by Dutch politics and was dissatisfied with Dutch migration and integration policy.[51]

In 2001 Fortuyn published a revised second edition of his study *Tegen de islamisering van onze cultuur. Nederlandse identiteit als fundament* [Against the Islamisation of Dutch Society. Dutch Identity as Foundation] (1997). The revision comprised the addition of an introduction and an epilogue in which Fortuyn asserted that the tide had turned in the time between the first and this second edition. In the introduction he writes how he was accused of racism after the work's first publication in 1997. Now, he maintains, the common opinion seems ready for 'the truth' and finally acknowledges the pertinence of his statements. The key term in his plea is 'modernity':

> Whether we like it or not, modernity cannot escape at least an ideological battle with Islam. The battle begins with a conscious experiencing of our own identity, with knowledge of the core norms and values of modernity and with the conscious experiencing and knowledge of our own (national) history.

> Of we het nu leuk vinden of niet, de moderniteit ontkomt er niet aan op zijn minst de ideologische strijd met de islam aan te gaan. De strijd begint bij een bewuste beleving van de eigen identiteit, van het weten wat de kernnormen en -waarden zijn van de moderniteit en bij het bewust beleven en kennen van de eigen (vaderlandse) geschiedenis. (Fortuyn 2001: 9)

In conclusion of his appeal for more national consciousness (and a Dutch 'guiding culture') Fortuyn pleads for more commitment in the defence of 'our own culture': what is needed is 'the effort to protect this [culture], armed to the teeth against excavations or attacks from the inside and the outside' (ibid. 11).[52] On the one hand he accuses the progressive political elite of squandering Dutch achievements as well as Dutch identity. On the other hand he warns for an 'inside enemy': the new Dutch of Islamic background.[53]

In the general elections of 2002 Fortuyn performed as a populist candidate.[54] His charisma, his rhetoric (including some well-placed 'slips' of the tongue) and his media performances, which were of great entertainment value, soon resulted in an amazing popularity. His plea for a complete closure of the Dutch borders for newcomers surely added to his popularity as well. The pre-election polls predicted an incredible rise to political power for him. In Fortuyn's presence the leading politicians of the other, more sedate political parties looked dull and rather helpless, unable as they were to respond adequately to his unremitting provocations. The cat-and-mouse game that developed between Fortuyn and his political opponents ended in a dramatic finale, shortly before the elections. On 6

May 2002 a radicalised animal rights activist murdered Pim Fortuyn just after the recording of yet another radio performance. Despite the country's national state of shock, it was decided that the elections should take place as planned. Fortuyn gained a major post-mortem victory. After the first euphoria this victory soon evaporated, however. Internal party conflicts, unprofessionality and the loss of a charismatic and authoritarian leader caused a fall that was as sudden and media-centred as the rise of Pim Fortuyn himself.

The phenomenon of Fortuyn in general caused a further polarisation and hardening of the Dutch discourse on multiculturality. As a result of the evident success of Fortuyn's hyperrealist discourse, other politicians also started to dissociate themselves from 'evasive' political correctness. A new mode of speaking out freely settled in the mainstream. Prins critically describes the excrescences of this new 'discursive openness':

> In [Fortuyn's] *performance* of the new realism the daring to speak frankly about problems and their solutions changed into the daring to simply speak frankly, to express one's *gut feelings*. (...) Straightforwardness no longer served a higher cause, namely the truth, but turned into a cause in itself.

> In [Fortuyns] *performance* van het nieuw realisme veranderde het lef om vrijuit te spreken over problemen en hun oplossingen, in simpelweg het lef om vrijuit te spreken, uiting te geven aan je *gutfeelings*. (...) Openhartigheid stond niet langer in dienst van een hoger doel, namelijk de waarheid, maar werd een doel in zichzelf. (Prins 2002: 252)

In the time after Pim Fortuyn, this new realist ideal of being open and straightforward no-matter-what remained en vogue and was even aggravated after another tragic murder two-and-a-half years later, on 2 November 2004. On this day the Dutch film director Theo van Gogh was murdered in the streets of Amsterdam by a 26-year-old son of a labour migrant from Morocco. The open letter that the murderer, a convert to Islamic fundamentalism, attached to the corpse made clear that his actual target was someone else: the Somali-born Dutch politician and prominent critic of Islam, Ayaan Hirsi Ali, with whom Van Gogh had produced the short film *Submission* (2005).[55]

The Islamist murder transferred the Netherlands into a state of shock, and internationally it was perceived as a scratch on the (self-)cherished image of the small multicultural, idyllic country on the North Sea. In the German public discourse, the Dutch neighbour lost its previous status as a multicultural role model. The German media covered the cultural and social chasms behind the idyllic Dutch façade extensively.[56] In his much-discussed work, *Murder in Amsterdam. The Death of Theo van Gogh and the Limits of Tolerance*, Ian Buruma connects this idyllic façade to an idealised Dutch self-image:

[In the Netherlands] things often happened earlier than elsewhere: tolerance of recreational drugs and pornography; acceptance of gay rights, multiculturalism, euthanasia, and so on. This, too, led to an air of satisfaction, even smugness, a self-congratulatory notion of living in the finest, freest, most progressive, most decent, most perfectly evolved playground of multicultural utopianism. (Buruma 2006: 11)

In his critical analysis of the Dutch postwar discourse on multiculturality, Buruma, a native Dutchman himself, argues that this cultivated (self-)image collapsed after 11/2, the murder of Van Gogh: 'The Netherlands never was a utopia, but the world had indeed changed since 9/11, and that world had caught up with Amsterdam, just as it had with New York, Bali, Madrid, and London' (ibid. 17). Indeed the global discourse on the war against terrorism in combination with a growing fear of Islam(ism) had now violently entered the Netherlands and inflamed a fierce anti-Islam discourse.

The actual or assumed Islamic threat to the enlightened, liberal, and emancipated values and achievements ascribed to Dutch society became a central topic of discussion. Hirsi Ali became both an (international) icon and an important contributor to an Islam-critical discourse that especially revolved around issues of gender and sexuality. Islam and suppression formed a popular pair in public discourse. The discourse of new realism, already amplified to hyperrealism by Fortuyn, now radicalised even further and became saturated with (moralising) emotions.[57] For many, the protection of an absolute freedom of speech (against Islam) gained utmost urgency, as the murder of Van Gogh was interpreted as evidence of its vulnerable and endangered status. The outcries of violence in response to the Danish cartoons mocking the Prophet Mohammed functioned as a reconfirmation of this necessity. Besides, they instigated the propagation of 'the right to insult', the radical consequence of an absolute freedom of speech that does not stop at taboos.[58] Buruma aptly describes this radicalised new-realist attitude as 'offensiveness projected as a sign of sincerity, the venting of rage as a mark of moral honesty' (ibid. 228).

The described process of polarisation obviously worries many Dutch, and not only the ones who would prefer to cling on to the cherished self-image of the Netherlands as a harmonious, tolerant and open multicultural society. However, this polarisation process fits into a global scheme of growing antagonism between the Western world and its (Islamic) constitutive outside. The non-Western world increasingly resists Western hegemony by resorting to violent and destructive actions. This global pressure adds urgency to come to a more integrative conceptualisation of Dutchness as a counterpoise to the thinking in Western/non-Western or 'autochthonous'/'allochthonous' dichotomies.[59]

German National Identity in a Multicultural Society

Whereas the Netherlands is often regarded as a result from an early and relatively unproblematic process of nation-state building, Germany counts as an example of the opposite situation. Germanness – German national identity – appears as a disputed concept marked on the one hand by the difficult road towards a German nation state and, on the other, burdened by Germany's violent history *as* a nation state. Unlike countries such as France, England and the Netherlands, Germany did not enter the nineteenth century as an established nation state. Although the birth of the *idea* of a German nation is generally located in the time of German Romanticism, it was not until 1871 that the erection of the German Empire – the first predecessor to the contemporary German nation state – became a fact.[60] This first institutional, nation-constitutive moment was preceded by 'the long nineteenth century' with its German-French wars and several earlier failed attempts to establish a national German union. The menace posed by archenemy France consolidated feelings of community spirit and togetherness among the several (loosely confederated) German states. The idea of a shared enemy threatening the territorial borders of this becoming nation was of important influence on the imaginations of Germanness in the public sphere. Culture and the arts in particular provided 'powerful languages of prestige and legitimation' for the German national project (Eley and Suny 1996: 23/24). Folk songs, myths and literature contributed to and confirmed the (gendered) construction of a natural and originary national unity. 'Invented traditions' helped to establish the idea of the distinctive states as historically belonging together, sharing heritage, language, religion and culture.

The erection of the German Empire demanded a definition of membership. After an earlier attempt to come to a comprehensive definition of German citizenship had failed in 1849, the tendency within the confederated states moved into the direction of the – at that time 'modern' – Prussian model of descent-based citizenship: the idea of the nation state as a family-like community.[61] After a twenty-year-long process, this principle of descent (*ius sanguinis*) favouring an ethnocultural definition of German citizenship over a civic one based on factors such as birth and prolonged residence (*ius soli*), was laid down in the 1913 'citizenship law of the Empire and the federal states' [*Reichs- und Staatsangehörigkeitsgesetz*]. On this basis scholars often denote Germany as a *Kulturnation* or a *Volksnation*.[62] Birgit Rommelspacher (2002: 47) maintains that the 1913 citizenship law, very much the result of a compromise between the different states, already comprised the risk of its violent totalitarisation later that century, as it made the ideal of ethnic homogeneity into an absolute principle. This risk was actualised with the 1935 establishment of the Nuremberg Laws that distinguished between 'full citizens of German or related blood' and 'plain citizens' of secondary status. In the time between the Weimar Republic and these Nuremberg Laws, the focus shifted from an ethnocultural to a racial conceptualisation of German citizenship.

The principle of descent and the idea of the German nation as a 'community of descent' [*Abstammungsgemeinschaft*] survived the various exceptionally violent ruptures in Germany's troubled twentieth century history. With the West German Basic Law of 1949 – supervised by the Allied forces – the definition of citizenship became based on civil equality again. However, in the infamous Article 116 this Basic Law (astonishingly) retained the principle of German 'ethnic affiliation' [*Volkszugehörigkeit*]: Germanness remained a matter of ancestry, and German citizenship was attributed on the basis of an ethnoculturally defined German origin.[63] The only time in history that the German nation actually came close to the realisation of its constitutive 'ideal of ethnic homogeneity' was around 1950, as a result of the utterly destructive politics of fascism. It was only *after* the Second World War that the devastated and defeated German nation state was made up of a fairly homogeneous mono-ethnic population. However, this exceptional, atypical situation of the 1950s often still functions as an agreed-upon point of reference in debates on German identity and on the postwar ethnic transformation of German society.

As a result of the Second World War, German national identity obviously suffered a considerable blow. The Holocaust, the German National Socialist project of total destruction of the Jewish Other, counts as the ultimate symbol of evil and inhumanity. After these horrors executed in the name of an ethnically homogenous German nation, pride in the German nation state seemed no longer possible. As Rommelspacher observes: 'the majority of Germans cannot perform their traditions in an uninhibited way and most of them have problems with their Germanness. The nation as a means of integration and stability has turned into a source of uncertainty. The *Heimat* has become uncomfortable' (2002: 48/49).[64] The successful reconstruction of the German states and the economic miracle in West Germany constituted important alternative moments in the establishment of a 'new' German pride after the moral and material defeat of National Socialism. Dieter Haselbach (1998) maintains that the achievement of rebuilding a country from ruins to wealth and respectability offered an opportunity to suppress the (latent) feelings of guilt and shame about the War and to establish a new form of self-respect.[65]

The 'new' Germany carefully invested in international relations and cooperation in order to rebuild the ruined reputation of the 'previous' Germany.[66] An inclusive welfare state, the German success as a trade nation, a pacifist style in international politics and an active role in the process of European unification provided new aspects for positive national identification (and helped many to 'forget' about the Nazi past). Foreign labour contributed considerably to the economic boom; foreign workers functioned as the backbone of the flourishing economy. Their presence, however, was kept hidden from the public sphere. Social integration was out of the question. The first economic crisis in the mid-1960s made clear that there is also a danger to a national consciousness grounded on economic achievements. The economic hardship constituted a blow to the new German self-confidence and caused strong feelings of existential insecurity for indigenous German labourers as well as for the foreign workers. As a result of this crisis, the public discourse on foreign recruitment slowly changed and the previously welcomed foreign workers increasingly became targets of scapegoating. This economic crisis, however, was overcome and the following years the economy flourished again – until the international oil crisis of 1973.

In response to this second economic crisis the German government put a ban on foreign recruitment. In his 1973 government policy statement, Chancellor Willy Brandt (SPD) argued that the limits of Germany's 'ability to absorb foreigners' had been exhausted (Sollors 2005: 1). Again and again, politicians from both the Social-Democrats (SPD) and the Christian-Democrats (CDU) emphasised that Germany is not a country of immigration and that it also should not become one.[67] Populist slogans about Germany being full and the foreign threat to German identity were no longer the exclusive 'intellectual' property of the (extreme) right, but became more and more part of the mainstream discourse. Xenophobic, at times downright racist, sentiments were directed mainly towards Germany's Turkish minority, the largest and most visible group of ethnic (and religious) Others.[68] This singling out went quite far, and one argument that was used by politicians and the media was that 'Germany' had no problem with 'foreigners' in general but only with the Turkish part of the population. On 30 July 1973, the magazine *Der Spiegel* headlined an issue on labour migration with 'The Turks are coming – Save yourself if you can!', thus suggesting a Turkish invasion. Labour migration, initially welcomed as a solution to a problem, was resignified as a problem itself: a Turkish problem.

The discourse on migration that evolved intersected with a renewed interest in the question and history of Germanness. Sabine von Dirke maintains that this 'turn towards national self-exploration via the past represents one attempt to cope with an experience of crisis after the flagship of West German pride – technological and economic progress – had run aground' (1994: 517). In addition to these economic roots Von Dirke also links the debate on migration to the new social movements of 1968 and their critique of the authoritarian (and silencing) structures in German society. These movements prompted a critical questioning of the course of 'Western civilisation' at large. They insisted on a crisis that went much deeper than the economy, and connected this insistence with a call for self-reflection.

In the years after the international oil crisis the discourse on 'guest workers', or 'foreigners' as they were called more and more frequently, hardened considerably. In this respect the *Der Spiegel* article is representative of both the new tenor and the 'Turking' of public discourse. Media and politicians alike presented a fearful image of the German Federal Republic being flooded by 'foreigners' that were mainly of Turkish origin.[69] The publication of the 'Heidelberger manifesto' in 1981, signed by fifteen university professors, constituted a provisional climax in this increasingly problematic discourse.[70] The at times downright racist manifesto pleads for the restoration, revaluation and, above all, protection of the German national culture and identity: 'Jedes Volk, auch das deutsche hat ein Naturrecht auf Erhaltung seiner Identität und Eigenart in seinem Wohngebiet' (*Heidelberger Manifest* 1982: 59). With the formulation of this plea in the name of a German *Volk*, a term that refers to the blood relationship of its members, the manifesto appeals to the constitutional framework of the 1948 Basic Law. Referring to this law it argues that multiculturalism, a concept that had recently entered the German discourse, is of an unconstitutional character.[71] The manifesto caused great public indignation and for a short while gave some impetus to a positive propagation of German multiculturalism.[72] However, this moment didn't last long, and positive and also benevolent approaches to the German multiethnic society continued to include the idea of a fundamental cultural difference. In general, the public opinion remained critical of the presence of – especially Turkish – Others.[73]

The discursive correlation between 'foreigners', 'Turks' and 'problems' grew, and a general shift to the right cannot be disavowed. The refugee issue that also gained urgency in Germany in the early 1980s increasingly featured as a major argument in the discourse on the 'foreigner problem' [*Ausländerproblem*]. In this discourse Turks and asylum seekers were conflated into one homogenised category.[74] The demonisation of this category especially thrived in the run-up to the 1982 elections. The political instrumentalisation of the refugee issue and the propagation of a racist logic of the number during the election campaigns contributed in a considerable measure to the radicalisation of 'anti-foreigner' sentiments among the German population. The CDU/CSU profited most from these sentiments and won the 1982 elections. In 1983 the new German government under the leadership of Chancellor Helmut Kohl responded to the 'problem of the number' and to the ethnicisation or, more precisely, the 'Turking', of several economic and social problems with the *Rückkehrförderungsgesetz*.

Räthzel maintains that the term 'foreigners' on the one hand and the terms 'nation' or 'national identity' on the other mostly appear as separate and even opposite semantic fields in German public discourse. Whereas the discussion on national identity revolves around the positive need for a shared German self-consciousness, debates on 'foreigners' predominantly focus on social conflict, economic burden and cultural threat. Räthzel convincingly argues that the artificial separation of these discourses functions as a means of mutual stabilisation and as an insurance of their discursive boundaries. The 'Historians' Debate' [*Historikerstreit*] (1985-1987), the national debate on the singularity of the Holocaust and the significance of fascism to the German identity, is an insightful example of such artificial separation. According to Räthzel's argument the discourse on 'foreigners' functioned as a catalyst for the Historians' Debate. However, in this debate a juxtaposing reflection on the Jewish Other and the Other of the discourse on 'foreigners' remained taboo. 'Foreigners' were kept resolutely outside of the debate on German identity – both as subjects and as participants.[75]

The Historians' Debate in itself counts as a central moment in the construction of (a post-Holocaust) German identity. The relatively sudden fall of the Berlin Wall on 9 November 1989 and the (so-called) German reunification one year later on 3 October 1990 signify two other constitutive moments of contemporary German identity.[76] As a pivotal moment of historical transformation, the *Wende* required a new orientation on the future and involved a reconsideration of the semantics of German national identity, both on a national and international level. Rommelspacher argues that

> the relatively broad identification with a German nation has supported the unification in both parts of Germany. At the same time, however, the corresponding ideas of homogeneity, together with a strong asymmetry between West and East, have blinded people to factual differences.

> die relativ breite Identifikation mit einer deutschen Nation in beiden Teilen Deutschlands die Vereinigung unterstützt hat. Gleichzeitig haben aber die entsprechenden Homogenitätsvorstellungen, zusammen mit der starken Machtsasymmetrie zwischen West und Ost, blind gemacht für die faktische Differenzen. (Rommelspacher 2002: 60)

After the *Wende* the dominant (political) discourse expected (indigenous) Germans to identify with the 'myth' of a shared, ethnoculturally defined Germanness. At the same time the elements that this discourse offered for identification – democracy and economic success – actually emphasised the differences between East and West Germans.[77] This contradiction makes clear that 'German identity' in the East and 'German identity' in the West had developed in different directions and, at the time of reunion, proved to be historical discursive constructs of a different kind. The process of integration of the two states, in which East Germany was the *de facto* second-class partner, relegated 'foreigners' to a third-class position in the symbolic hierarchy of this new Germany.[78]

The explosion of actual violence against (ethnic) Others in 1992 and 1993 – the towns of Hoyerswerda, Rostock, Mölln and Solingen count as the symbolic markers of this violence – in combination with the newly inflamed discussion on asylum politics, intersected with and simultaneously radicalised the question of (exclusionary) definitions of German identity and Germanness. Andreas Huyssen provides an explanation for this eruption of xenophobic violence that occurred so shortly after reunification in the particular triangulation of West Germans, East Germans and 'foreigners':

> My hypothesis is that the astonishing levels of real and verbal violence against foreigners, including wide-spread populist fellow-travelling in xenophobia, result to a large extent from a complex displacement of an inner-German problematic which right-wing ideologues are successful in exploiting. (...) [W]hat is at stake is rather the displacement onto the non-Germans of forty years of an inner-German hostility where another kind of foreign body was identified as the source of most problems: the other Germany. (...) Only this triangulation of foreigners, East Germans and West Germans fully explains the intensity of the escalation in xenophobia since unification. (Huyssen 1995b: 80/81)

Huyssen's idea of triangulation is an attempt to do justice to more complex, multiple webs of relation and to move beyond a mode of thought caught in static binaries. As a model of thought or as an analytic concept it prompts a more differentiating mode of reflection that complicates the thinking in opposites in a productive way. As such, triangulation is not only helpful for the interrogation of the web of relation between 'foreigners' and East and West Germans, but it is also useful for investigating the relationships between Germans, Turks and Jews, or between Germans, Jews and 'other Others'. Triangulation takes into account multiple webs of relation that are only seldom acknowledged, let alone analysed.

Conversely, Bade (1994) locates the responsibility for the erupting xenophobia in the early 1990s more on the side of politics. He decidedly interprets the violent attacks as the aggressive result of the continuing ethno-cultural definition of German citizenship and the lack of clarity in respect to migration and integration policies. In his compilation of texts *Die multikulturelle Herausforderung. Menschen über Grenzen – Grenzen über Menschen* [*The multicultural challenge – People across borders. Borders across people*], Bade repeats and corroborates these charges against the German government:

> [The political disorientation of the population] resulted from the political refusal to acknowledge the unmistakable social fact that for over more than a decennium the Federal Republic had become a new type of immigration country – not in a legal sense, but in a social and cultural one.

> [Die politische Desorientierung der Bevölkerung] hatte ihren Grund in der politischen Erkenntnisverweigerung gegenüber der unübersehbaren gesellschaftlichen Tatsache, dass die Bundesrepublik seit mehr als einem Jahrzehnt ein Einwanderungsland neuen Typs geworden ist – nicht im rechtlichen, aber im gesellschaftlichen und kulturellen Sinne. (Bade 1996: 247)

Despite the factual ethnic diversification as a result of migration, minorities such as the Turkish-German community remained largely outside of the evolving discourses on 'German' memory, 'German' unification and the 'German' future. It seemed as if these hyphenated Germans did not partake in this historical moment of national transformation. Additionally, after the alarming outcries of racist violence, German politics dodged the long-overdue realisation of appropriate migration and, especially, integration measures. Its main concern remained stopping the flow of the large numbers of asylum seekers.[79] On 26 May 1993, the German government modified its asylum law, put heavy restrictions on the annual number of 'late forced evacuees' [Spätaussiedler] who were allowed entry into the country, and rigorously cut back migration rates. The then-dominant line of political reasoning was: Germany is not a country of migration and thus it has no need for an integration policy.

The 'German Leitkultur'

'In no other country is there so little joy and so much
suffering from one's identity. 'Being German'
aggravates 'becoming German' considerably'
(Şenocak 2001: 45).[80]

The debate on German identity on the one hand and the discussion of German multiculturality on the other remained artificially divided and mutually constitutive at one and the same time. The first strand of discourse struggled with the in many ways contradictory question of (a 'restored') German national identity, a question that had been effectively put aside during the German-German division.[81] The second line of discourse deliberated over concepts of integration within a national framework that still defined Germanness as a matter of blood and culture.[82] Legal issues determined this discourse. The protest against the ethnocultural framework became more and more persistent; it was only after the 1998 change of government from CDU/CSU to a coalition of SPD and the Green Party (the Red-Green coalition) that the way toward actual modernisation was opened up. In the same year, this new government presented a position paper that aimed for a major reform in immigration regulations. After a long-lasting political tussle, a compromise law finally took effect on January 2005. Changes in respect to German citizenship regulations preceded the immigration law: the renewed German citizenship law had taken effect five years earlier. Several scholars criticise the strong emphasis on the legal aspects of migration in the German public discourse on multiculturality. Ulrich Preuß, for instance, warns that this emphasis distracts from the actual 'cultural work' that still lies ahead: 'the negotiation between forms of cultural pluralism and social integration' (Preuß, cited in Sollors

2005: 6). In agreement with Preuß, Sollors assesses that German authorities have no clue 'how a non-assimilationist – or post-assimilationist – pluralist-but-not-balkanizing integration of indigenous and foreign-born minorities should proceed at this point' (Sollors 2005: 6).

In 2000, the same year that the Netherlands controversially discussed the pros and cons of Dutch multiculturality under the label 'multicultural drama', Germany staged a vehement debate on German multiculturality. This German discourse revolved around the formula *deutsche Leitkultur* ['German guiding culture']. Like 'multicultural drama' in the Dutch situation, this phrase has gained a situation-exceeding significance and has come to indicate the precarious controversy around the future of the German multicultural society in general. The concept of a guiding culture was proposed by the political scientist Bassam Tibi in his study *Europa ohne Identität. Die Krise der multikulturellen Gesellschaft* [*Europe without Identity. The Crisis of the Multicultural Society*] (1998). In this study he discusses a European culture of modernity and Enlightenment. Germany, he argues, should reposition itself at the democratic heart of this modern and enlightened Europe by acknowledging and accepting this 'European *Leitkultur*'. Very much in line with Jürgen Habermas' concept of 'constitutional patriotism' [*Verfassungspatriotismus*] (Habermas 1995, 1998) Tibi pleads for a set of European core norms and values which should be accepted and followed by every person living in Germany – indigenous or non-indigenous.[83]

Friedrich Merz, at that time the chair of the CDU in the German Federal Parliament, appropriated the concept in a public speech in autumn 2000. In this speech he redefined *Leitkultur* as 'the putative essence of national culture to which immigrants must assimilate' (Cheesman 2004: 84 n. 8).[84] In his propagation of a 'liberal German *Leitkultur*' [*freiheitliche deutsche Leitkultur*], Merz nationalised and culturalised the concept, suggesting that these core norms and values are (to be) rooted in (a superior) German culture. His provocative propagation of a German *Leitkultur* was framed by the critical discussion of the plans for a new immigration law by the Red-Green coalition. Klaus Ronneberger and Vassilis Tsianos maintain that by way of the demand for a German *Leitkultur* the Christian Democrats tried to 'regain their lost hegemony in the political field of migration' (Ronneberger and Tsianos 2001: 92) as well as to recharge the discursively contested theme of the nation.[85]

Merz strategically played the 'national identity card' during the run-up to the elections. In his article 'The politics of identity in Germany: the *Leitkultur* debate', Hartwig Pautz (2005) comments on these successful tactics as follows:

> Whereas the Süßmuth Commission's intention was to provide practical guidelines for immigration and integration (...), the CDU and CSU managed to shift the focus of debate to questions of national identity and to question the loyalty of non-European immigrants in particular. All attempts to draw up a new idea

of citizenship and a new concept of German society were stalled by the success of this debate. (Pautz 2005: 47)

Pautz subsumes the CDU/CSU-directed debate under a more general 'culturalisation of politics' (Pautz 2005: 41) in accordance with Huntington's best-selling study *The Clash of Civilisations and the Remaking of World Order* (1996). He argues that the *Leitkultur* debate was in fact a neo-racist debate in which the definition of Germanness based on ethnic affiliation shifted to an essentialist and exclusionary notion of culture: 'The notion of "race" was replaced by that of culture, as cultural belonging was essentialised. Culture, as a vague and broadly interpretable changing cluster of meanings, was able to perform the same exclusionary function as race' (Pautz 2005: 40).[86] The idea of a superior German *Leitkultur* encouraged a division in German Self and cultural Other and ultimately legitimated the social marginalisation and exclusion of 'foreigners' on the basis of cultural criteria. At the same time the appeal for a German *Leitkultur* that in concordance with Tibi's original concept is rooted in European civilisation suited the discourse that aimed to 'normalise' German history (and identity). After the Historian's Debate, the *Leitkultur* debate was another attempt to 'overcome' the idea of German exceptionality and to reestablish national self-confidence as detached from the national Holocaust legacy.

Merz's propagation of a German *Leitkultur* was heavily criticised from various positions on the political spectrum. Repeatedly, Germany's National Socialist past was invoked as a warning against what was criticised as a plea for cultural homogeneity and cultural superiority. However, despite its swift 'discursive contamination', the contested concept remained influential in the discussion on the integration of 'foreigners'. Every now and then, especially in times of multicultural turbulence, the concept turns up again as a marker of the cultural norm of Germanness. An example is its attempted rehabilitation by Norbert Lammert, who was the CDU president of the German Federal Parliament at the time. In October 2005 he tried to reopen the *Leitkultur* debate with an appeal for an 'open' and in his opinion long-overdue discussion of the concept. The response to his call, however, was minimal. The edited volume *Verfassung, Patriotismus, Leitkultur. Was unsere Gesellschaft zusammenhält* [*Constitution, Patriotism, Leitkultur. What Holds Our Society Together*] (2006), which Lammert published one year later, confirms this impression.[87] Many contributors to the volume contradict Lammert's call and decidedly argue against the *Leitkultur* concept. They emphasise its contraproductive discursive dimensions and point out its polarising effects in the discourse on German multiculturality.

An interesting moment of (delayed) intersection of the phrases of the Dutch 'multicultural drama' and the 'German *Leitkultur*' debates occurred during the 2004 Humboldt lecture by the Dutch liberal-right politician Bolkestein in Berlin. Contrary to the tendency in German public discourse to avoid the problematic concept, Bolkestein encouraged its further conceptualisation and suggested the Dutch follow the German example. He claimed:

> The debate on the Leitkultur is in fact a debate on the core values that should hold our whole society together. How can we enter into a dialogue with other cultures if we are afraid to stand up for our own culture? How can we understand others, if we do not know who we are ourselves anymore? (...) Europe needs a self-confident German culture in its middle, an inviting, recruiting and integrating culture. This modern Germany should not have any complexes about this. On the contrary, the German *Leitkultur* has a lot to offer newcomers from other cultures.

> Het debat over de Leitkultur is in wezen een debat over de kernwaarden die onze hele samenleving moet binden. Hoe kunnen wij een dialoog aangaan met andere culturen als wij niet meer durven uit te komen voor onze eigen cultuur? Hoe kunnen wij anderen begrijpen als we zelf niet meer weten wie we zijn? (...) Europa heeft in zijn midden een zelfbewuste Duitse cultuur nodig, een uitnodigende, wervende en integrerende cultuur. Dit moderne Duitsland moet daar geen complexen over hebben. Integendeel, de Duitse Leitkultur heeft nieuwkomers uit andere culturen veel te bieden. (Bolkestein 2004)

Bolkestein provocatively expresses solidarity with the contested German *Leitkultur* concept in his plea for a more 'self-confident' – if not self-satisfied – Europe. He invokes a German-Dutch, Western European 'we' that should foster and perpetuate its highly commendable cultural identity in opposition to an Other and his/her Other culture. It is this commendable guiding culture that represents the (static) norm into which 'we' should convince newcomers from other cultures – German 'foreigners' and Dutch 'allochthons' – to assimilate.

In recent years the positive image of a happy and uncomplicated multiculturality in the Netherlands as opposed to the negative image of a persistently xenophobic Germany no longer holds. With the 2000 changes in the migration and citizenship legislation, Germany not only caught up with Dutch liberalism, it even surpassed it: the legal liberalisation in Germany coincided with a tightening of the rules in the Netherlands. Obviously, these recent changes cannot make up for the many previous years of legally sanctioned exclusion of long-term German residents of other ethnic origins, but at least on a legal level they open up a perspective for the possibility of a more integrative future.

Whereas the political murders of Fortuyn and Van Gogh contributed to a hardening and polarisation of Dutch public discourse, in Germany the effects of these instances of violence just across the border were twofold. On the one hand they worked to relativise the idealised German image of the Netherlands as an exemplary multicultural society. The Dutch adversities encouraged a more confident

German multicultural self-reflection, out of the shadow of the assumedly more tolerant neighbour.[88] On the other hand, in Germany (as in many other places) the Van Gogh murder especially caused an intensified level of discussion of issues as parallel societies, gender and Islam, and the threat of Islamist intra-state terrorism. As in the Netherlands, Islam became the central category of difference in a discourse of division. This discourse makes ample use of the symbolic opposition of civilisational values attributed to the West, which is seen as needing to be protected against (Islamic) barbarism or, more precisely, against men associated with Islamic fundamentalism.[89] The generalising tone of this discourse fosters suspicion, and turns all men of Turkish origin into assumed suppressors of their female relatives. To the indigenous majority of the German population, which the discourse constitutes as enlightened and emancipated, this is an appeal to protect these females against the dangers of an all-determinative, anti-Western Islamist patriarchy.

A central factor in this discourse, in Germany as well as in the Netherlands, is the actual or perceived Islamist threat posed by the global Al-Qaeda network. Shortly after the terrorist attacks of 9/11 it appeared that these did not have half the polarising and counter-violent consequences in Germany as they had in, for instance, the Netherlands.[90] Siegfried Jäger (2004) confirms this assessment, but differentiates its interpretation by framing 9/11 within the larger German discourse on migration and multiculturality. His clarification hinges on the notion of 'increase'. A broad analysis of the print media coverage of migration during the period 1983-2004 makes clear that the terrorist attacks enforced the image of Islam as threat, but that the discourse on migration did not change its relatively moderate character. Jäger explains this assessment by referring to the preceding political debate on the new migration law and to the normalisation, even institutionalisation, of a harsher and at times even racist tone of discourse that took place during this debate.[91] Both the proposed law and the migration report by the Commission Süßmuth (named after its chairwoman) adapted their discourse to visions and formulations that used to be the exclusive domain of populist and extreme right ideologists. This adaptation included a shift from the migrant's perspective of migration to what Jäger labels 'German self-interest' (Jäger 2004: 185). The strong emphasis on the 'successful' reduction of the number of accepted appeals resulted in a decrease of public racism and in a positive public stance towards the new migration legislation. By way of the new migration law, a hardened tone, inscribed on an institutional level, had already found its way into the German discourse on migration and multiculturality *before* the 9/11 attacks.

However, irrespective of the measure of discursive polarisation, in Germany the question of national identity has gained interest and urgency again after the various instances of Islamist violence in the wake of 9/11.[92] The fact that one of the 9/11 hijackers was a student from Hamburg, or the shock of the failed suitcase bombing attempts in German trains in the summer of 2006 have brought the feeling of threat within the German borders, and raised the fear for German equivalents of the Madrid or London attacks. These feelings of existential insecurity, however, coincide with appeals for a more positive German self-image by various actors in society. Appeals for pride in German achievements and for confidence in a self-made German future were, to a large extent, responses to the negative-pitched public discourse after the *Wende* euphoria. This discourse focused on persistent economic troubles, high unemployment rates and feelings of disappointment in respect to the post-*Wende* situation. The controversial and widely discussed nationwide 'social-marketing-campaign' *Du bist Deutschland* [You Are Germany] that started in September 2005 and was funded and initiated by 25 media concerns, constituted a remarkable and overwhelmingly visible example of this new call for a positive identification with (an assumedly inclusive) Germany.[93]

Less publicly conspicuous was Zafer Şenocak's contribution of a Turkish-German perspective on this discourse on German national identity.[94] In his article 'Dunkle deutsche Seele' ['Dark German Soul'] in *Die Welt* (7 October 2005), Şenocak criticises the taboo on a constructive attitude towards German identity and points out the paradoxical difficulties that this taboo involves for the integration of 'foreigners' in German society. Using provocative rhetoric, he writes:

> The Germans increasingly wish the Turks to become German patriots, Anatolians are to become professing Germans (...). But, ironically, this insistence on Germanness is in no way indicative of a patriotic attitude. Because German behaviour is not worth copying. They try to imagine the Turk who is about to be naturalised as a better German. He is supposed to display what the German himself misses so painfully and is unable to name – German identity and the profession of allegiance to Germany. If this project fails, as is to be expected, one can once again lean back and bewail the suffering of Germany. One part will do this by condemning xenophobia and racism, the other part by condemning the Turks' inability to integrate.

> Die Deutschen wünschen sich zunehmend die Türken als deutsche Patrioten, bekennende Deutsche sollen die Anatolier werden. (...) Doch ironischerweise deutet dieses Pochen auf das Deutschsein keineswegs auf eine patriotische Haltung hin. Denn die Deutschen verhalten sich dabei nicht wie Vorbilder, die nachzuahmen es sich lohnt. Vielmehr versuchen sie, sich den einzubürgernden Türken als einen besseren Deutschen vorzustellen. An ihm soll sichtbar werden, was man selber so schmerzlich vermißt und zu benennen nicht imstande ist, deutsche Identität und Bekenntnis zu Deutschland. Wenn dieses Projekt, wie zu erwarten ist, scheitert, kann man sich wieder getrost zurück lehnen und über das Leiden an Deutschland lamentieren. Die einen werden es

tun, indem sie den Fremdenhaß und den Rassismus geißeln, die anderen die Unfähigkeit der Türken sich zu integrieren. (Şenocak 2005)

Şenocak has published broadly on aspects of (Turkish-)German national identity. Generally his multilayered and eye-opening opinions prompt a more differentiating mode of reflection. Like Huyssen he too insists on the idea of triangulation or, in his own terminology, on the specific 'trialogue' between Germans, Jews and Turks.[95]

Şenocak's insistence on a 'trialogue' touches on a particularly complex situation in German society and public discourse. Jews – with good reason – constitute an exceptional minority in the German socioscape. Uerlings describes this situation:

> The most important 'other culture' in the German-speaking world is the Jewish one. The Holocaust has nearly made it disappear. This extinction still determines the interaction with Jewish and presumably with other minorities in Germany, namely and above all in the shape of prevailing 'blind spots' in the debate. Every relationship between the majority and minorities in Germany will have to be measured against German-Jewish history, i.e. also with the achieved state of political, literary and artistic discussion.

> Die wichtigste 'andere Kultur' im deutschsprachigen Bereich ist die jüdische. Der Holocaust hat sie fast zum Verschwinden gebracht. Diese Auslöschung prägt auch heute noch den Umgang mit jüdischen und, so steht zu vermuten, mit anderen Minderheiten in Deutschland, und zwar auch und gerade in Form fortwirkender 'blinder Flecken' in der Auseinandersetzung. Jede Beziehung zwischen einer Mehrheit und Minderheiten in Deutschland wird sich und der deutsch-jüdischen Geschichte, d.h. aber auch an dem auf diesem Feld erreichten Stand der politischen und literarisch-künstlerischen Auseinandersetzung, messen lassen müssen. (Uerlings 2006: 22/23)

As a consequence of the Holocaust, Germans and Jews are historically caught up with each other in an extremely complicated way. The position of all other minorities in Germany is measured and negotiated in relation to this German-Jewish trauma. In contemporary socio-political discourse this situation often has the – logical as well as complexly problematic – effect that the Jewish voice and the Turkish or Afro-German voice do not have the same weight in contemporary discussions on German (multicultural) identity. The precarious symbolic importance of the Jewish voice (and experience) within German discussions on structures of Othering and exclusion tends to establish an intricate hierarchy and affects the voices (and experiences) of other Others. Addressing this problem often results in the discussion-killing accusation of 'downplaying the Holocaust'. Nina Glick

Schiller, Data Dea and Markus Höhne (2005) address this extremely complicated constellation in a study written on the occasion of the 'African Village' controversy in which African and Afro-German minorities appeared as the object(ified) Other of discourse and of a highly problematic cultural practice.[96] They argue that

> while the discussion in Germany about the times of Nazism reached a high level of reflection and openness in recent years, the discussion of problems of discrimination and racism not directly linked to the 'Third Reich' is still considered to be of minor or even no importance. And it is this tendency to dismiss as unimportant processes of racialization that are not on the level of Nazi crimes that explains the belief that it is acceptable to profit by placing African culture in a zoo. (Glick Schiller, Dea and Höhne 2005: 39)

The concept of triangulation (or trialogue) attempts to break away from this limiting structure and urges us to take multiple relations into account in order to achieve a more differentiated reflection of (xenophobic, anti-Semitic or racist) structures of Othering and discrimination.

Şenocak's article 'Dunkle deutsche Seele' not only criticises the contradictory and hypocritical dimension of the public and political demands for a 'Germanisation' of the Turkish minority to become more German than the Germans, but also ponders about future developments of the German way with multiculturality. Şenocak states that national pride that restricts itself to the football field does not suffice for a German identity that unites the diverse ethnic and cultural communities that live in contemporary Germany. In 2006 the World Cup football championship indeed seemed to bring about a temporary new impulse for a more positive and fraternal German self-definition. However, the alarming increase of racist violence in 2006 and 2007 as well as the dissemination of discriminatory and racist opinions in the political and public mainstream forestalls any premature conclusions about inclusive, multiethnic notions of German national identity.[97]

Conclusion: The Ongoing Construction of Germanness and Dutchness

The ongoing discussion on what Germanness or Dutchness is or should be that is described in this chapter once again underlines the contested character of the concept of national identity. The recurrent discursive eruptions, moments in history in which national identity appears as an issue of heightened sensitivity, work to confirm its ongoing relevance in the contemporary German and Dutch worlds in flux. In both the German and the Dutch situation migration is a phenomenon that prompts a reconsideration of the boundaries that both include and exclude, unite and divide, in the name of a national entity. The presence of 'new Germans' and 'new Dutch' in the transformed ethnoscapes of the two nation states requires a reorientation of dominant discourses on national identity, and a reimagination of concepts of national affiliation and national community.

Caren Kaplan observes that '[i]mmigrants, refugees, exiles, nomads, and the homeless (...) move in and out of these discourses as metaphors, tropes, and symbols but rarely as historically recognized producers of critical discourses themselves' (1996: 2). Simultaneously this heterogeneous group features prominently in alarming social studies on growing xenophobia – in particular Islamophobia – in both Germany and the Netherlands.[98] Here again, however, migrant Others mainly appear as objects of discourse and as anonymous and passive instigators of a hardening and increasingly hostile social climate.

This study offers a different outlook on the (productive) presence of migrant Others in German and Dutch discourse. The following chapters discuss nine literary works of migration in their capacity as critical cultural interventions in dominant discourses on migration and multiculturality. These chapters aim to oppose the stereotypical image of the 'inarticulate migrant' who does not participate in these discourses him- or herself. The studied works, in all their diversity, appear as forms of cultural labour. In a variety of ways and by use of multiple strategies they – and their 'migrant authors' – contribute to the ongoing discursive construction of national identity from the perspective of migration.

II. Literature of Migration

Aesthetic Interventions in Times of Transformation

'[T]here is a peculiar new force to the imagination in social life today'
(Appadurai 2005: 50).

'Borders have been drawn around both nations and literature;
to some extent they are the same borders'
(Bal 2003: 185).

Introduction

A study that is often mentioned when it comes to the role of the imagination in times of global change is Arjun Appadurai's *Modernity at Large: Cultural Dimensions of Globalization* (1997). In this study, Appadurai claims the imagination has a key role in contemporary social life: 'The imagination is now central to all forms of agency, is itself a social fact, and is the key component of the new global order' (1997: 31). Although Appadurai is not referring to literature as a product of the imagination par excellence here (on the contrary: he focuses on the imagination as part of the logic of ordinary life, of the everyday), his influential statement has conferred a new prominence to the field of the imagination at large.[1] *New Germans, New Dutch* aims to contribute to this field further by investigating the literary dimensions of globalisation.

A central premise of this book is the idea that in contrast to a conflicted public discourse in which the issue of national identity is mostly positioned in a simplifying field of hierarchised binaries, literature fashions alternative modes of understanding. Herbert Uerlings uses the term 'aesthetic difference' (1997: 8) to indicate the specific potential of literature in a world characterised by intercultural encounters, global cultural exchange and the confusion, disputably even dissolution, of cultural boundaries. In his article 'Das Subjekt und die Anderen. Zur Analyse sexueller und kultureller Differenz' ['The Subject and the Others. About the Analysis of Sexual and Cultural Difference'] he explains:

Aesthetic difference enables art to 'perform' the dichotomies that structure one's own culture and to render the polyglossia (Bakhtin) of the social and cultural worlds audible or visible in a different way than dominant discourses do.

Die ästhetische Differenz ermöglicht es der Kunst, die Dichotomien, die die eigene Kultur strukturieren, zu 'inszenieren' und dabei die Vielstimmigkeit (Bachtin) der sozialen und kulturellen Welten anders zur Gehör bzw. vor die Augen zu bringen, als es herrschende Diskurse tun. (Uerlings 2001: 21)

The dynamic and polyvalent complexity that sustains literature's aesthetic difference – its literariness – effects a postponement of meaning that makes it possible to qualify more nuanced modes of representation and understanding. In addition, the semantic time-space 'in between', resulting from aesthetic difference, may prompt a reconsideration of questions of identity and difference.[2] Literature of migration is of particular significance when it comes to (alternative) modes of representing and understanding globalisation as well as its transformative impact on the issue of national identity.

Leslie Adelson recognizes literary narratives of migration as entailing a particular 'labor of imagination'; by means of literary strategies of transformation, these narratives perform 'the reworking of cultural matter' (2005: 14). Literature of migration – and this counts for the German literature of Turkish migration that Adelson discusses, as well as for Dutch literature of Moroccan migration – 'functions as a kind of cultural archive, where changing perceptions and phantasms of sociality are both tracked and imagined. By means of this archive, questions about the historic contours of our time may be variously entertained, depending on which methods one brings to the task if one considers the material at all' (ibid. 14-15). In the particular frame of New Germans, New Dutch the question of how the selected works of literature track and (re-)imagine national identity – Germanness and Dutchness – in the current time of national transformation is the central topic of interest.

Literary Effects of Labour Migration

Although literature of migration is not necessarily authored by writers of migrant background, in this study this is decidedly the case: the four writers whose work I discuss in this book all share a migrant background. As a result it might seem as if the criterion of experience – a problematic, but generally undertheorised concept as Dominick LaCapra (2004) points out – lies at the basis of the selection and grouping of these writers in this study.[3] This is only true to a certain, indirect extent: the migrant background of these writers largely determines their marginal position in German and Dutch societies at large as well as in the respective literary fields. Their (imposed) migrant status functions as a central factor in the discursive processes of national Othering to which both the writers themselves and their literature are subjected.[4]

The four selected writers – the Turkish-German Emine Sevgi Özdamar and Feridun Zaimoglu and the Moroccan-Dutch Abdelkader Benali and Hafid Bouazza – entered the literary field in the 1990s and have been successfully productive as writers ever since. Their presence in Germany and the Netherlands is connected to the shared German-Dutch historical phenomenon of labour migration of the 1960s that I discussed in the previous chapter. Whereas Özdamar's first encounter with and longer stay in Germany directly resulted from this organised labour migration, the three other writers followed their labour migrant parents as children and thus can hardly be considered labour migrants themselves.[5]

The decision to restrict the scope of *New Germans, New Dutch* to writers of Turkish and Moroccan backgrounds has several reasons. The main reason is the symbolic (token) position that these particular minorities occupy in the German and Dutch public discourses on migration and multiculturality. This 'representative' position of (ethnic and cultural) Otherness is partly a result of numbers. In Germany the Turks constitute by far the largest group among the migrant population. In the Netherlands the minorities of Turkish and Moroccan origin are almost equal in number, but Moroccan migrants 'outweigh' the Turkish migrants due to a heightened symbolic status in public discourse;[6] discussions of multiculturality and cultural conflict in the Netherlands often focus on the (male part of the) Moroccan minority. The fact that dominant discourse associates both groups with Islam further adds to their discursive visibility as Other. It homogenises internally diverse groups of Turkish-Germans and Moroccan-Dutch into one religious category: Muslim.[7] Mechanisms of (strongly gendered) religious Othering have dramatically increased since the terrorist attacks of 9/11 and the following Islamist violence under the name of the global Al-Qaeda network. In this process of Othering, the distinction between Islamic and Islamist, as well as that between the numerous variations of Islam, is often lost. 'The' aggressive Islamist male appears as a threat to both the Western world and to 'the' suppressed Muslim female.

None of the selected writers has the German or Dutch language of the literary writing as their mother tongue. Here is a difference between Özdamar, who migrated into another language as an adult, and the other three writers, who more or less grew up and were educated in the German and Dutch languages. For each of these writers, the act of writing in German or Dutch functions as a means to enter the dominant culture. It does not, however, automatically guarantee them a place in the literary centre. Their literary work is not automatically accepted as German or Dutch literature. All four writers have to cope with ethnicised expectations and with several reductive and marginalising modes of reading their work. Central to these modes of reading is the tendency to overlook the literariness of this writing, its aesthetic difference. Aesthetic complexity is mostly neglected in favour of strongly referential readings. Such readings reduce the literary works either to documents of social evidence or politicise them into (resisting) products of dominant discourse, into pamphlets for social recognition within a politics of identity.[8]

New Germans, New Dutch resists these reductive and marginalising modes of reading literature of migration without, however, giving up on this literature's socio-political relevance. It considers the selected works of literature as literary interventions into their dominant discursive contexts of writing as well as into the larger 'narrative of the nation'.[9] These works reflect on and question the socio-political and literary contexts in which they (and their writers) are compelled to occupy a position of Otherness. At the same time they imaginatively work to negotiate the boundaries that determine national structures of inclusion and exclusion, of national identity, alterity and belonging in the rapidly transforming world of today.[10] The analyses of these works focus on the various literary – narrative, stylistic, performative, thematic and commercial – strategies that they develop and deploy in order to negotiate discursively dominant constructions of national identity and to imagine alternative forms of (national) belonging.

By considering these German and Dutch works of literature as interventions into dominant constructions of Germanness and Dutchness *from within* rather than from Turkish, Moroccan or hybrid cultural realms, I reject the idea that these works and their writers in and of themselves inhabit a position 'in between', a 'third space', or a more or less happy hybridity. In this sense I subscribe to Adelson's 'Against Between: A Manifesto' (2001) in which she fiercely criticises the spatial configuration of separate (Turkish and German, but the argument obviously also counts for Moroccan and Dutch) cultural worlds. She writes: '"Between Two Worlds" is the place customarily reserved for these authors and their texts on the cultural maps of our time, but the trope of "betweenness" often functions like a reservation designed to contain, restrain, and impede new knowledge, not enable it' (Adelson 2001: 245).[11] By relating the strategies deployed in the selected works to the German and Dutch contexts in which they originate, this study generates new knowledge on Germanness and Dutchness and offers insight into the German and Dutch specificities of this literature of migration.

Levels of Comparison

An important methodological aspect of New Germans, New Dutch concerns the issue of comparison. The study moves between and connects several levels of comparison (and juxtaposition): inter-national, between literature and public discourse, and between various distinct literary works. Although I discuss these various levels of comparison separately, they are in fact closely intertwined and often mutually constitutive.

The idea of literary or cultural comparison has increasingly come under contestation in a globalising world in which the interplay between power and cultural differences moves more and more to the fore. In the collection *Comparative Literature in the Age of Multiculturalism* (1995), edited by Charles Bernheimer, a select group of renowned literary scholars reflects on the 'anxieties of comparison'.[12] In their contributions they address the political and ideological implications of comparison as well as question the idea of *national* literatures in a world and (global) cultural field that have drastically changed since the beginnings of comparative literature. Deconstruction, New Criticism, literary politics of identity, several forms of ethical criticism, gender and postcolonial studies have reshuffled and disoriented the 'original' discipline in such a way that Gayatri Chakravorty Spivak even argues the *Death of a Discipline* (2003) in the contemporary globalised world.[13] At stake in most of the contributions is the contested relation between text and context, as well as the focus on matrices of power and the patterns of in- and exclusion that sustain (the study of) this relation.

In her article 'Versions of Incommensurability' Natalie Melas criticises the fact that 'the comparison of the cultural expressions of different languages, nations, peoples in practice seems always constrained by an invisible binary bind in which comparison must end either by accentuating differences or by subsuming them under some overarching unity' (1995: 275). A comparison, however, that takes care not to end up in one of these positions, remains worthwhile. As long as it neither entails a homogenisation or a synthesisation into one norm, nor insists on a qualifying or moral measurement that results in a hierarchical ordering of the distinct cases, a comparative frame can yield valuable insights into the specificities of the terms involved in the comparison. It can direct the attention to particularities of constellations that would have remained unnoticed when studied in isolation.

Pheng Cheah even goes a step further and claims the current pertinence of careful and informed comparison: 'The gradual defamiliarization of our daily lives by globalizing processes has made comparison an inevitable and even unconscious perspective' (1999: 3).[14] International comparison offers a critical and differentiating view on what on the one hand is often considered natural or self-evident, and on the other highly particular as well as original. As Seyla Benhabib maintains in her work *The Claims of Culture. Equality and Diversity in the Global Era*: 'A comparative perspective sensitises us to how movements and demands of the same kind in one country may bear quite different meanings and yield different results in another' (2002: x).

This book comprises two main levels of comparison. On the first international level of comparison it focuses on German and Dutch literature of (Moroccan and Turkish) labour migration. Simultaneously, on the same level, it compares the more or less parallel public debates on national identity and multiculturality in both countries. These two dimensions come together in the analyses of the selected works of literature in their particular capacity as literary interventions into these parallel discursive contexts. *New Germans, New Dutch* scrutinises and compares the interaction and mutual constituency between these two particular semantic fields – literature and public discourse – in two neighbouring Western European nation states.

The grounds for the comparison of Germany and the Netherlands are manifold. Both countries share a geopolitical position in the West and several traits that come with this position of power, including capitalism, a colonial history, and a considerable (economic) attraction as geographical destination for migrants.[15] Partly following from this position of power, the Netherlands and (West) Germany also share a history of institutionalised labour migration. Besides these factors, they also share similar public discussions on the (threatened) boundaries of national identity that to a large extent result from these migratory movements.[16] Finally, the emergence and the persistent discussion about the categorisation of 'migrants' literature' in both countries' cultural fields offer another ground for comparison. In his seminal study *The Location of Culture* Homi K. Bhabha warns that '[t]he very concepts of homogenous national cultures, the consensual or contiguous transmission of historical traditions, or 'organic' ethnic communities – *as the grounds of cultural comparativism* – are in a profound process of redefinition' (1994: 5, italics in original). Also national identity as a historical formation can no longer function – if ever it could – as a stable *tertium comparationis*. Taking this idea to heart, *New Germans, New Dutch* conceptualises German and Dutch national identities not as homogenous entities but as two complex fields of meaning in continual transition. This conceptualisation offers a space for juxtaposition and even comparison, but at the same time it acknowledges the temporal and process-oriented character of all statements or assumed parallels resulting from these technologies of research and reading.

The second level of comparison concerns the actual literary works and their specific imaginations of Germanness and Dutchness. The character of these imaginations as well as the points of reference and association to their dominant discursive contexts differ considerably from one work to the other. Whereas one work actually imagines a Self as German or Dutch (or precisely the opposite, a Self as national Other), another indirectly reflects on Germanness or Dutchness by (critically) describing the present society and its patterns of in- and exclusion, or by a roundabout route of imagining alternative and even post-national forms of community. The analysis of the nine pieces of literary writing in this study make it clear that there is no single way of or strategy for imagining Germanness and Dutchness. Although this book positions all of them in the same frame of interpretation, this does not mean that they also all respond to similar key issues by means of similar literary strategies. On the contrary: an important aim of *New Germans, New Dutch* is to make clear that the shared migrant background of the selected writers is no guarantee whatsoever for equivalences in and of their literary writing. The analyses show the diversity and multiplicity of German and Dutch literature of Turkish and Moroccan migration.

Approaching Literature of Migration

Three approaches have inspired my investigation of literature in relation to its particular discursive frame of research, the public discourse on national identity and multiculturality. The first approach concerns the conceptualisation of literature as a source of aesthetic knowledge. In his study *Art in Mind. How Contemporary Images Shape Thought* (2005) Ernst van Alphen discusses the critical function of (visual) art and proposes to consider art as a mode of thinking or as a form of critical understanding. His argument about art's ability to reinterpret historical norms and conventions and, following from this, its capacity to contribute to the production of an alternative form of knowledge applies to works of literature as well. Van Alphen writes:

> The crucial function of aesthetic disruptions of understanding consists precisely in triggering efforts to form new signifiers. It is only through such efforts that the aesthetic enactment of understanding achieves a dissociation or distancing from conventional assumptions. It is in this sense that art is 'autonomous' – not in the sense that it is independent of context but in that it has an agency of its own. (Van Alphen 2005: xvi)

Literature – in particular the aesthetic disruptions of understanding that the literary text brings about – in this sense produces a form of aesthetic knowledge that requires a differentiated as well as contextualised mode of reading in order to fully understand its implications. What counts for literature in general, counts for 'literature of migration' – the topic of this study – in a particular way: the aesthetic knowledge that this literature conveys in its affiliation with the respective national contexts of migration, concerns an alternative understanding of the social and cultural transformations brought about by this migration. As such, German and Dutch literature of migration constitutes a kind of 'cultural archive'.[17] It provides an alternative mode of insight in a pivotal historical moment of national transformation.

The second approach concerns the possibility of art's resisting or even subversive character. If literature of migration is read in the interpretive frame set by the discourses on national identity and multiculturality mentioned above, it can (but not necessarily does) offer a literary counter-discourse on the relation between these two disputed concepts. Bhabha describes the disruptive potential of such literary counter-discourses – he speaks of 'counter-narratives' – as follows: 'Counter-narratives of the nation that continually evoke and erase its totalising boundaries – both actual and conceptual – disturb those ideological manoeuvres through which "imagined communities" are given essentialist identities' (Bhabha 1990: 300). In this capacity, literature appears as resistance to limited and exclusionary definitions of 'the national' and of national identity. It deploys various literary strategies to engage in what Petra Fachinger calls an 'oppositional aesthetics' (Fachinger 2001: 112): these literary works write back to or rewrite dominant constructions of national identity, or they record and reflect on aspects of transforming national worlds that history and cultural memory tend to forget or erase. In this way literature destabilises the suppositions and assumptions that underlie constructions of Germanness and Dutchness and prompt the reader to think 'other-wise'.

In his insightful study *Story Logic. Problems and Possibilities of Narrative* (2002) the narratologist David Herman proposes the term 'boundary work' for the particular interference between texts and their contexts.[18] He claims that 'stories not only assume a relation between texts and contexts but sometimes work to reshape it' (Herman 2002: 336). This idea enables a third approach to literature that takes its controversial, productive dimension – what literature can bring about, the effects of literature – seriously in a 'modest' way. It discusses the changes that literary texts can bring about in contexts of reading, without claiming any earth-shattering socio-political impact. It carefully applies narratological tools of analysis to the literary text in order to scrutinise the way in which the text questions and, sometimes remodels the boundary between itself and its context. Theories on the performativity of language that enable us to conceive of literary texts as acts are helpful here as well.[19] In his article 'Philosophy and Literature: The Fortunes of the Performative' Jonathan Culler writes about the performativity of literature: 'like the performative, the literary utterance does not refer to a prior state of affairs and is not true or false. The literary utterance, too, creates the state of affairs to which it refers, in several respects' (2000: 506). The 'creative' possibilities of the performative, however, are strongly dependent on their specific contexts of utterance and on the social conventions that determine these contexts. The assessment of the act that a literary text in a particular time-space performs again requires the study of this literary text in *context*.

A combination of these approaches – literature as a mode of thought, literature as counter-discourse and literature as (performative) boundary work – enables the multidimensional interpretation of literature in context that the focus on a complex concept as national identity requires. With this combination of approaches *New Germans, New Dutch* explicitly dissociates and distinguishes itself from the already-mentioned modes of reading literature of migration (or 'migrants' literature') in solely sociological or biographical terms, or reducing this literature to a form of identity politics. Neither of these modes takes literature's aesthetic difference and dynamic complexity into account, and the following two sections on the emergence, (academic) reception and discussion of literature of (labour) migration in the German and Dutch cultural fields make it clear that the latter is not self-evident.

Literature of Migration in the German Cultural Field

While first-generation labour migrants appeared on Germany's literary scene in the early 1980s, in the Netherlands, it was only during the 1990s that writers of labour migration background entered the Dutch cultural field in any considerable measure. Several factors intersect in this striking discrepancy. Obviously, national, social and educational backgrounds of the labour migrants are important determinant factors.[20] Similarly important is the specific cultural climate that the host countries offered: the particular possibilities for cultural participation in the dominant cultural fields as well as those for the retainment of the native language and the culture of origin. In this respect, Germany and the Netherlands display salient differences that, according to my hypothesis, predominantly result from the distinctive legal and political frameworks – and the ideas and expectations connected to these – in respect to migration and the new migrant population.[21] Irrespective of the ethical or political valuation of these different laws and policies, it seems that the Dutch's early acknowledgement of cultural pluralism and the official support for cultural activities within minority groups (and in native languages) resulted in a striking absence and silence of the first-generation migrant group in the dominant culture and language. In Germany, where migrants' participation in society was independent of state support, several quasi-private or semi-institutional initiatives had a stake in stimulating the contribution of first-generation labour migrants to the dominant cultural field. These initiatives resulted in a cultural production by labour migrants in the German language that is considerable in comparison to the Dutch situation.

In the late 1980s, US-based literary scholars Arlene A. Teraoka (1987) and Heidrun Suhr (1989) both wrote an overview article on this early migrant writing in Germany.[22] These articles organise the literary production into several 'groups' and locate the emergence of this literature in the early 1980s. The publication of the programmatic article 'Literatur der Betroffenheit. Bemerkungen zur Gastarbeiterliteratur' ['Literature of Being Moved. Remarks about Guest Worker Literature'] (1981) by Franco Biondi and Rafik Schami counts as an important early moment of visibility and speaking out. Biondi and Schami criticise the social situation of guest workers in German society and plead for a multinational literature in service of the improvement of this situation. The publication of this article more or less coincided with the founding of the emancipatory *PoLiKunst-Verein* [Poly-national Literature and Art Society, 1980-87] and a publication series for foreign writers called 'Südwind Gastarbeiterdeutsch' ['Southwind Guest Worker German']. As a politically inspired collective the writers participating in the *PoLi-*

Kunst Society propagated a literature that fosters solidarity among workers of all nationalities.

A second 'group of spokesmen' gathered around the Ararat Publishing House in Berlin; among them were the authors Yüksel Pazarkaya and Aras Ören. These writers operated less as a group, but agreed on the perception of literature as an important source for intercultural exchange, mutual understanding and even cultural synthesis. In his programmatic article 'Literatur ist Literatur' ['Literature Is Literature'] (1986), Pazarkaya explicitly dissociates himself from the socio-political demands on literature made by Biondi and Schami. According to Pazarkaya such demands reduce literature to the level of manuals and cooking recipes, and neglect literature's main aesthetic dimension (1986: 62-63).

A third perspective is represented by the Institute for German as a Foreign Language (IGFL) at Munich University which provided perhaps the best known and – in terms of visibility – most successful initiative in the German cultural field.[23] It played a prominent role in the promotion, dissemination and reception of 'guest worker literature'. The engagement of Irmgard Ackermann and Harald Weinrich in particular enabled the publication of several anthologies of writing by 'foreigners' and raised a considerable amount of academic interest in the social and literary aspects of this writing. Moreover, Ackermann and Weinrich established the Adelbert von Chamisso Prize, a prize for original work in the German language written by authors for whom German is not the native language.[24] Retrospectively, the work of Munich's IGFL is often discussed in negative terms. The ideological thrust of its engagement is fiercely criticised as paternalistic and exoticist, and indeed appears as well meant but extremely patronising in the eyes of the contemporary critic.[25] The Chamisso Prize raises similar ambivalent feelings, as the prize marginalises at the same moment that it celebrates writing by non-native German writers. The main criterion of selection for the award of the prize concerns a biographical feature and not a literary one. The aesthetic complexity of the writing is only secondary as a factor of distinction.

The discussion about the work of Munich's IGFL often intersects and mingles with the discussion on the most appropriate terminology to describe the literature in question. As time goes by and the position of the 'foreign worker' transforms into that of a new, hyphenated German – and 'guest worker literature' into German literature – the (political) question of categorisation and naming becomes increasingly difficult. This counts for the German as well as for the Dutch situation, although in line with the later appearance of 'migrant's literature' in the Dutch cultural field, this discussion also evolved after considerable delay and – importantly – skipped the 'guest worker' terminology.[26] In Germany, Biondi and Schami more or less opened up the discussion on terminology with the article already mentioned. In this article they consciously use the 'stigma "guest worker"' (Biondi and Schami 1981: 135) as a self-referential epithet in order, as they explain themselves, to reveal the 'irony' inherent in the particular combination of guest and worker. Their use of the term *Gastarbeiterliteratur* is strategic in a similar way as Zaimoglu's later, re-signifying use of the term *Kanake* is strategic.[27] Both function as tools in a literary performance of social resistance. Whether in imitation of Biondi and Schami and in recognition of their resisting project or not, in the 1980s scholars also made general use of the term.

Teraoka (1987) importantly asserts that it is quite a different situation whether labour migrants themselves strategically name their work 'guest worker literature' and claim a position in the dominant cultural field, or if (academic) members of the dominant group do the same. She writes: 'It is one thing for those in power – as Weinrich is – to claim *Gastarbeiterliteratur* as German literature, and quite another when the claim is made by the *Gastarbeiter* themselves. One position is that of cultural hegemony, the other, that of critique and resistance' (Teraoka 1987: 100/101). In 1990 Adelson maintained that the debate about the appropriate terminology for literature by migrant writers in fact obscures what is really at stake: 'not the appropriate category for the foreign "addendum" but the fundamental need to reconceptualize our understanding of an identifiably German core of contemporary literature' (1990: 383). However, the search for the most appropriate term for writing by authors of migrant background continued throughout the 1990s.[28] Many proposals – foreigners' literature, minority literature, migrants' literature, migration literature, hyphenated literature, diasporic literature, intercultural literature – were brought forward and most of them were – for various reasons – rejected again.

The *Gesellschaft für interkulturelle Germanistik* [Society for Intercultural Germanistics], founded in 1984, made an important contribution to the academic reflection on concepts as identity and alterity, intercultural dialogue, and German multiculturality, and encouraged the critical interrogation of the significance of these concepts for the study of (German) literature.[29] Ultimately the awareness settled in that literature authored by writers of migrant background – like literature in general – resists categorisation and hardly ever fits prefabricated moulds.[30] Most scholars now acknowledge the prime importance of aesthetic aspects such as style, language and theme in the study of this German (and Dutch) literature. It is not the writers' experience of migration that determines the distinctive quality of their work, but the cultural and aesthetic dimensions of their work that are *possibly* related to migration. Nevertheless, it seems that the need to emphasise the Germanness of this German literature still exists. The title statement of a 2005 interview with four writers from migrant backgrounds in the German magazine *Literaturen* is telling in this respect. There the writer Navid Kermani insists: 'I am a part of the German literature, as German as Kafka' ['Ich bin ein Teil der deutschen Literatur, so deutsch wie Kafka'].[31]

Literature of Migration in the Dutch Cultural Field

The situation of literary marginalisation and responsive defence is very much alike for both German and Dutch writers of migrant background. In the Netherlands these writers struggle with similar processes of (ethnic) categorisation, although national specificities – as for instance the contribution of (post-)colonial writing to Dutch literature or the legacy of early 'guest worker literature' in Germany – influence the modes of discourse.[32] On the basis of comparative research on the reception of 'migrants' literature' in Germany and the Netherlands in the 1990s, Ralf Grüttemeier (2001, 2005) concludes that the Dutch cultural field is more open to this literature than its German equivalent.[33] Scholars and critics of 'migrants' literature' in Germany often assume a role as advocates for the sociopolitical case that this literature is supposed to make, whereas in the Netherlands this literature is judged according to literary conventions. Dutch critics and scholars presumably apply similar standards to 'migrants' literature' as to literature by indigenous Dutch writers. Grüttemeier asserts that 'in the Netherlands "migrants' literature" got through to the centre of the position-determining debates in the literary field, while in Germany it still constitutes more of a subcategory that strives for recognition' (Grüttemeier 2005: 1).[34] The analyses of the work of Abdelkader Benali and Hafid Bouazza in this book question and modify this supposition. Although both writers have managed to become acknowledged 'Dutch writers', they are the first 'of their migrant kind' in this league, an ethnic attribution to writer and work that both Benali and Bouazza by necessity had to come to terms with. In a critical response to Grüttemeier, Herbert van Uffelen (2006) also stops short of too-resolute statements about the more or less open character of literary fields that are complexly different. As the analyses in the following chapters prove, many factors interfere with the reception of 'migrants' writing' and in the (national) acceptance of its authors.

An early example of an initiative that acknowledges and encourages the transformative process of multiculturalisation in the Dutch cultural field is the E. du Perron Prize.[35] This prize, founded in 1986, aims to reward groups or individuals working in the cultural field who have made an extraordinary contribution to the good relations and understanding between the various ethnic groups living in the Netherlands. The prize is neither exclusively restricted to literature, nor does it prescribe any (ethnic) identity characteristics of the laureates. Prizewinners vary from individual ('allochthonous' and 'autochthonous') writers and their oeuvres, to particular works of literature, to culture-educative projects. What is rewarded is the positive social effect of a certain cultural activity. Another important initiative in the Dutch cultural field, especially in respect to the literature of (labour) migration, is the El Hizjra Prize. Since 1992 the El Hizjra Foundation organises an annual writing contest for original work in the Dutch, Arab or Tamazight language written by Dutch people of Moroccan and Arab backgrounds. The awarded work is published in a small anthology. The El Hizjra Prize counts as an important springboard for a literary career and functioned as such for by now well-known writers as Mustafa Stitou, Abdelkader Benali, Mohammed Benzakour, Rashid Novaire and Khalid Boudou.

As I have mentioned before, the academic discussion on 'migrants' literature' in the Netherlands developed quite a bit later than the one in Germany, and did not profit from input from US-based scholarship like the German discussion did.[36] In 1994 the Dutch magazine *Literatuur* presented a special issue with the focus: 'How Dutch is Dutch literature?' ['Hoe Nederlands is de Nederlandse literatuur?']. In this issue neither E.H. Kossmann, who wrote the introductory article, nor any of the other contributors in any way refers to processes of multiculturalisation in Dutch society or in the cultural field. Their main concern is much more the future and retention of 'the Dutch identity' in the process of European unification and the general representation of 'Dutchness' across the Dutch borders. Kossmann writes: 'It is especially in the arts that a population can express something that is characteristic of itself; when foreign countries recognise, appreciate and imitate this characteristic, then it shows its nationality – it is, in other words, a nation' (1994: 4).[37] Kossmann's focus on art as the face of a nation in a European context leaves any transformations *within* this nation – for instance in the composition of its population – unmentioned. The absence of ethnic diversity as a factor of change in respect to Dutch identity in general and in the field of Dutch literature in particular is typical for that time. In my opinion it should be interpreted in the context of the Dutch tradition of 'pillarisation' and the institutionalised cultural pluralist approach that I discussed in the previous chapter.

The publication of the poetry collection *Mijn vormen* by Mustafa Stitou in 1994 is generally agreed to be the first appearance of literature of (Moroccan) migration in the Netherlands. The volume was granted a very positive welcome and stirred the public interest in work by writers of migrant backgrounds. Several writers followed in Stitou's footsteps, among them Hans Sahar, Naima el Bezaz, Hafid Bouazza and Abdelkader Benali. The sudden interest in literature by the ethnic Other was not restricted to literature of labour migration, but also concerned work by writers of colonial or refugee background. Almost all works by 'ethnic Other writers' – at that time generally labelled 'allochthonous literature' – shared in a hearty welcome and a growing public interest. In retrospect several critics maintain that at that time all major publishing houses were eagerly searching for 'allochthonous' writers to include on their list.[38] They criticise that this interest to bring these writers into the spotlights mainly stemmed from marketing reasons: they were hyped as 'exotic fruit' on the Dutch literary scene. The literary merits of the work of these new, ethnicised celebrities often appeared only of secondary importance, after the 'fascinating Otherness' of their literature and, even more so, of themselves. Their work was supposed to represent the (Dutch) world from the critical and refreshing perspective of the outsider.

In this sense the Dutch cultural field eagerly participated in what Graham Huggan in his study *The Postcolonial Exotic* describes as the booming 'alterity industry' (2001: 22) of the 1990s. Huggan argues that this alterity industry successfully trades literature by the ethnic Other as a cultural commodity.[39] This literature is subjected to a 'domesticating process through which commodities are taken from the margins and reabsorbed into mainstream culture' (ibid.). Huggan emphasises that the critical study of this literature often contributes to this process of commodification in the same moment that it resists it.

Many of the 'allochthonous' writers themselves were not too happy with the mostly well-meant, but, in fact, rather derogatory attitude of the Dutch cultural field. However, the available means of protest were rather limited: ethno-marketing simply established opportunities and publicity that they wouldn't have had without the emphasis on their 'Other' ethnic identity. A practical dilemma, for instance, consisted in either publishing in one of the numerous anthologies of writing by 'allochthonous' writers, or not publishing at all. The positioning of Ayfer Ergün, the editor of *Het land in mij* [*The Country within Me*] (1996), one of these anthologies, illustrates this dilemma. She strongly opposes the categorisation 'allochthonous literature' in the preface to the volume:

> In fact the term 'allochthonous' literature only says something about the origin of the authors and nothing about the content of their stories. For that reason the authors themselves are not unequivocally pleased with this imposed categorisation. They emphasise that they want to be regarded as Dutch writers and that they do not want to be grouped under one label.

> Het begrip allochtone literatuur zegt eigenlijk uitsluitend iets over de herkomst van de auteurs en niets over de inhoud van hun verhalen. De auteurs zelf zijn dan ook niet onverdeeld gelukkig met dit hokje waarin ze zichzelf geplaatst zien. Zij benadrukken dat ze beschouwd willen worden als Nederlandse schrijvers en willen niet onder één noemer worden gebracht. (Ergün 1996: 8)

The anthology in itself, however, contributes to exactly the categorisation that she opposes in its preface.

In 1997 Henriëtte Louwerse published the first analysis of this 'new phenomenon' – described as 'The Emergence of Turkish and Moroccan Migrant Writers in the Dutch Literary Landscape' in the article's subtitle – in the journal *Dutch Crossing*. This analysis was an exception in academic circles, despite the public popularity of multicultural literature. In 1998 Elisabeth Leijnse and Michiel van Kempen edited a volume titled *Tussenfiguren. Schrijvers tussen de culturen* [*Intermediary Figures. Writing between the Cultures*], but, here again, literature of (labour) migration is strikingly absent among analyses that mostly focus on (post-)colonial literature. The same is true for the literary journal *Armada* that, one year later, in 1999, dedi-

cated a special issue to the theme 'Migrants'. Here, too, either Dutch (post-)colo-
nial literature or foreign 'migrants' literature' feature as objects of study. Dutch
literature of migration is conspicuous by its absence.

The introductory articles to these two publications, however, offer several
points of reference for the reflection on Dutch literature of migration. The question of categorisation and the search for an appropriate terminology, for example,
are prominent topics of discussion. In *Armada*, guest editor Van Kempen maintains that '[e]xcept for their moving house, migrant writers do not have that
much in common; the individual imagination wins by far from the shared experience' (1999: 6).[40] Nevertheless, he simultaneously assesses that these writers
share a particular characteristic: the perspective of the outsider on the dominant
Dutch Self. He writes: 'They screen society in a way that is out of reach of the
'autochthonous' writer' (ibid.), thus suggesting that this outsider position involves a certain scrutinous view on Dutch society.[41]

In the same year, 1999, the journal *Literatuur*, co-edited by Odile Heynders and
Bert Paasman, presented an issue devoted to 'Literaturen in het Nederlands' ['Literatures in Dutch']. This issue finally discusses literature of (labour) migration,
which by that time had achieved an amazing popularity. This popularity – and the
questioning thereof – is the subject of several of the contributions. In her preface
to *Literatuur*, Heynders writes: 'The Netherlands changes (...) Dutch literature
changes (...) The contours of one Dutch literary tradition fade and at the same
time the canon becomes larger and more colourful, because 'allochthonous'
authors obtain their own place' (1999: 322).[42] She argues that in these times of
globalisation and migration, 'national definitions of literature' no longer apply,
and for this reason she uses the term 'multicultural literature'. In the opening
article of the issue, Paasman proposes the term 'ethnic literature' for a very diverse field of literature by writers who share the fact 'that their roots lie in another
country with another culture, that they are to a larger or lesser degree bi-cultural'
(1999: 329).[43] He adds that 'ethnic literature' often shows signs of political engagement, as it is generally written from a position of social marginalisation. In
his opinion its writers by necessity redefine their identities in a process of negotiating both the country and culture of origin, and their new home. Like Van
Kempen, Paasman connects the minority position of these writers to expectations
of a particularly critical view on Dutch society in their literature.

In his contribution 'Fatal Success. About Moroccan-Dutch Writers and Their
Critics' ['Fataal succes. Over Marokkaans-Nederlandse auteurs en hun critici']
Ton Anbeek explicitly discusses literature of Moroccan migration and addresses
the hype that encompasses its writers.[44] Anbeek decisively rejects the label 'allochthonous writers' as concealing and homogenising in favour of the more specific 'Moroccan-Dutch writers'.[45] He argues that the literature by these writers
generally encountered a 'politically hypercorrect reception' (Anbeek 1999: 336).
In their abundant praise for the Moroccan newcomers reviewers regularly disre-

garded the (sometimes limited) literary qualities of the hyped works of literature. Anbeek rejects the 'condescending benevolence' (ibid. 342) that is solely attached to the writers' Moroccan origin. Instead he recommends approaching this literature by talented beginners in the same way as that of indigenous Dutch writers of the same age. He assumes that – anno 1999 – the hype was passed its highest peak, not knowing that there was still the 'ethnic' National Book Week of 2001 to come.

This 2001 National Book Week was organised around the theme 'Het land van herkomst. Schrijven tussen twee culturen' ['The Country of Origin. Writing between Two Cultures'] and very much figured as the apotheotic 'grande finale' of the extraordinary public interest in writing by the ethnic Other.[46] Numerous events and publications focused on multiculturality in Dutch literature. The pros and cons of the book week's 'ethnicising focus' were controversially discussed. In their 'reconstruction' of the debate on 'migrants' literature' Marnel Breure and Liesbeth Brouwer bring the main issues in this debate back to 'the dilemma between retracing literary works to [questions of] identity on the one hand and denying the difference and differentiation as a result of social origin on the other' (2004: 383).[47] They criticise the romantic idea that literature by ethnic Others contains some sort of authentic essence that literature by indigenous writers assumedly has lost, and claim a transnational orientation instead. In respect to the discussion on the definition of 'Dutch literature' Breure and Brouwer insist that it is more important to question why which boundaries are being watched over, and by whom. The new Dutch ethnoscape might well demand an adjustment of traditional boundaries of Dutch literature.

After the extreme visibility effected by the book week, the public interest in 'multicultural literature' waned. The hyped celebration of a happy Dutch multiculturality was over. Alongside this decline of interest in the literary field, the public discourse on multiculturality changed dramatically, a development that I have discussed extensively in the previous chapter.[48] Only few of the hyped writers managed to maintain their visibility in the cultural field; many others disappeared silently from the literary scene. In the preface added to the 2001 edition of the volume *Tussenfiguren*, Gert Oostindie suggests that, in terms of literary quality and serious attention, this decline is, in the end, a good thing. In his opinion, the theme of 'writing between the cultures' had almost become too popular.[49] Now, he encourages, there is time and need to critically scrutinise the various cultural transformations that processes of migration and globalisation have brought about – without either hyping or marginalising these.[50]

Conclusion: Aesthetic Interventions

By now, the four writers whose work is central to this study are generally considered German and Dutch writers. Their continuous (and acclaimed) literary production in the German and Dutch cultural fields guarantees this, as does their 'long-term' residence in Germany and the Netherlands.[51] National identity, however, that complex combination of active and passive identification with a national culture, remains a more difficult question – both in respect to their people and their literary work. A divisive politics of representation, a discourse that tendentiously speaks in terms of cultural conflict, as well as several structures of in- and exclusion, continue to split the German and the Dutch populations into those who belong and those who – for various reasons and to a greater or lesser extent – do not.

Imaginations of Germanness and Dutchness in literature of migration constitute forms of cultural labour that rework and in various ways transfigure dominant patterns of national belonging. One must use interpretation to understand and mediate these literary reworkings and alternative figurations of national identities. The importance of (nuanced) technologies of reading can hardly be underestimated.

III. Emine Sevgi Özdamar

'I Didn't Know that Your Passport Is also Your Diary'

'I don't like the feeling of belonging to a nation'
(Özdamar in Wierschke 1996: 258).[1]

'Home and abroad are not opposites when travelling
is not set against dwelling and staying home. In a creative context,
coming and going can happen in the same move, and travelling
is where I am, where you are, where your identity is;
that's your place, your home and your being now'
(Minh-ha 2005: 8).

Introduction

In 1991 Emine Sevgi Özdamar was the first writer of non-German (i.e. Turkish-Kurdish) origin to win the prestigious Ingeborg Bachmann Prize. The award-winning writing – an excerpt from her (later) novel *Das Leben ist eine Karawanserei hat zwei Türen aus einer kam ich rein aus der anderen ging ich raus* [*Life Is a Caravanserai Has Two Doors I Came in One I Went Out the Other*] (1992) – caused a controversial discussion about the German identity of Özdamar's literature as well as about the German identity of the Ingeborg Bachmann Prize itself. In her article '"German" literature contested: The 1991 Ingeborg Bachmann Prize Debate, "Cultural Diversity", and Emine Sevgi Özdamar' (1997), Karen Jankowsky offers an extensive analysis of this discussion. She describes an ambivalent contradiction in the specific argumentation used to support Özdamar's election. On the one hand, contributors to the discussion argued that ethnic diversity was to be acknowledged as a constitutive part of contemporary German literature. As a result, national literary awards should be opened up to include writing by 'ethnic Others'. On the other hand, the appreciation of Özdamar's work mainly hinged on exactly this ethnic Otherness. A strong ethnicisation of her work seemed to distract attention from its literary quality.

This persistent ethnicisation positions Özdamar's work – despite the 'German' prize – at the margins of German mainstream culture. The Ingeborg Bachmann

Prize is a public platform for the 'negotiation of ethnicity and culture' (Jankowsky 1997: 262). The election of Özdamar's text as winner of the award brings the Germanness of German literature up for discussion. In this discussion the appreciation for Özdamar's awarded literature is repeatedly attached to features and particularities of her work that are marked as typically Turkish or typically oriental. Many of its multiple dimensions disappear in the reading and categorisation of her work in the storytelling tradition of *One Thousand and One Nights*.

Today, an increasing number of literary scholars resist this orientalising technology of reading Özdamar's literature, and positively acknowledge – and sometimes look beyond – the 'accent' of her literary work. Their studies take this accent as a particular aesthetic quality of Özdamar's literary language and work, and investigate this quality as a symptom or figure of migration. Many point out its (disputatively disruptive) effects on exclusive standards of German literature. They focus on (linguistic) concepts such as 'hybrid writing' (Boa 1996, 2006), 'accented writing' ['Schreiben mit Akzent'] (Konuk 1997), 'modes of writing migration' ['Schreibweisen der Migration'] (Bay 1999), 'nomadic language' and 'feminine writing' (Ghaussy 1999), 'androgyne text' ['Zwittertext'] (von Flotow 2000) or 'borderland writing' (Seyhan 2001). Despite the appreciation of the original and different quality of Özdamar's language, however, this focus again exoticises and ethnicises her work: now Özdamar's hybrid language works to confirm her literary Otherness. In this sense Özdamar's 'German' literature remains categorised as 'accented' German literature. Her literary 'accent' again indicates a deviation from the norm, an 'abnormality'.[2]

Despite the obvious importance of an approach that scrutinises the aesthetic difference of Özdamar's language and writing, the following analysis turns away from Özdamar's 'accent' as a sign of her Otherness, and concentrates on her literary re-negotiations of Germanness. By focusing on the German instead of on the Turkish dimensions of Özdamar's literature of migration, it provides a counterweight to interpretive localisations of her work – whether of positive or of negative judgment – that re-inscribe and consolidate an orientalist tradition of exoticising the (female) migrant Other.[3] I consider Özdamar's work as a reflective contribution to German cultural memory, and read her works of literature as particular interventions in the discursively dominant, monolithic construction of German national identity. As we will see, her work challenges the dominant rhetoric of German Self and ethnic Other and playfully negotiates its stereotypical dichotomous division.

Özdamar's literature seems obsessed with conceptions of (national) space and even more so by the boundaries that constitute, mark and separate these spaces. In her writing she performatively crosses and often disrupts these (discursive) boundaries and questions their static and divisive character. Her particular 'obsession' with (re-)mapping spaces can be interpreted as an example of what Sigrid Weigel in her article on the 'topological turn' in cultural studies describes as the 'unfolding of counter-discourse in the gaps of a colonised respectively euro-centric topography' (2002: 155).[4] Özdamar's literature contributes to such a 'counter-discourse' that perceives of space as a negotiable web of relations and connections rather than as a predetermined stable entity. The autobiographical literary mode that Özdamar deploys functions as a particular form of resistance against what Azade Seyhan calls a 'cultural amnesia that denies the historical legitimacy of different identities' (2001: 150). In her discussion of Özdamar's *Das Leben ist eine Karawanserei hat zwei Türen aus einer kam ich rein aus der anderen ging ich raus*, Seyhan argues that this novel 'is about the power and endurance of communal and cultural memory as an antidote against censored history. It is a personal story firmly embedded in social history, a gem of the genre I term "autobiography as unauthorized biography of the nation"' (ibid.).[5]

Whereas Seyhan is referring to the Turkish nation here, the first section of this chapter scrutinises how Özdamar uses an autobiographical mode to write an alternative biography of the German nation in a very specific and complicated period in its history: the separation into two Germanies between 1949 and 1990. It concentrates on two short stories with the particularly geographical titles 'Mein Istanbul' ['My Istanbul'] and 'Mein Berlin' ['My Berlin']. Both stories were published in the collection of short prose *Der Hof im Spiegel* [*The Courtyard in the Mirror*] (2001).[6] The second section of the chapter complicates the outcomes of the first comparative analysis of these two 'city stories' with an analysis of the longer narration 'Fahrrad auf dem Eis' ['Bicycle on Ice'] from the same collection. This story is mainly located in Amsterdam, the capital of the Netherlands, thus opening up yet another national space. Together these three stories with their specific and connected time-space constellations set the beginning of Özdamar's personal cartography of memory that critically intersects with official narratives of history. They interrogate dominant notions of national space and belonging, and reflect on new and alternative forms of community.

Özdamar's Unauthorized Biography of the Two Germanies

The short prose collection *Der Hof im Spiegel* forms a representative literary landscape of Özdamar's oeuvre. It not only covers a broader period of time as well as a larger geographical space, but it also displays most of the central themes in Özdamar's work. Most stories in the collection connect to Özdamar's three major novels, *Das Leben ist eine Karawanserei hat zwei Türen aus einer kam ich rein aus der anderen ging ich raus* (1992), *Die Brücke vom Goldenen Horn* [*The Bridge of the Golden Horn*] (1998a) and *Seltsame Sterne starren zur Erde* [*Strange Stars Stare toward Earth*] (2003), as well as to her literary debut *Mutterzunge* [*Mother Tongue*] ([1990] 1998b).[7] These connections are established by means of narrative themes and tropes, through chains of associations, and on a linguistic level through repetitive use – both literal and slightly altered – of expressions, phrases and sentences. Both the novels and the shorter pieces of prose refer to, and even pre- and re-tell, each other. Together they can be seen as a complex web of oeuvre-immanent intertextualities.

This interwovenness is a conspicuous characteristic of Özdamar's work. The intertextual cross-references establish her particular narrative universe of fictional continuity, offered in a rather discontinuous form. The fact that most of her work is written in an autobiographical mode – assumedly the ideal genre for identity construction – functions as the glue that holds the different pieces together. However, the hold that this quasi-autobiographical glue offers is delusive and soon enough deconstructs itself. On the one hand the autobiographical mode, with its female first-person narrator who is regularly addressed as 'Sevgi', provides an impression of unity and continuity. The biography of one person, one lifeline being (re-)told, constitutes the narrative frame for the fragment-like stories and novels. On the other hand Özdamar's particular mode of autobiography – its disrupted and disruptive fashion, its fantastic and ironic elements, its playful use of time and space of memory – simultaneously resists all too narrow definitions of unity and continuity. The quasi-autobiographical narrations constantly shift in temporal, spatial and thematic terms, thus refusing any suggestions of chronological order or transparent stability.

Despite real-life correspondences with its author, the autobiographical Self presented in Özdamar's writings is clearly a fictional construction: in a playful way this Self is 'almost-Sevgi' – invented, unfathomable, elusive.[8] In her study *Writing Outside the Nation* (2001) Seyhan argues that the particular possibilities of autobiography as a genre make it into a preferred mode of writing for 'writers of the diaspora'. She postulates that autobiography is an 'out-of-bounds genre that captures the fluid character of memory, migration and transition in an appropriately nuanced fashion' (Seyhan 2001: 96). Although strongly dependent on which definition of autobiography is used, I daresay that this claim applies to an even larger extent to Özdamar's autobiographical mode, to her playful quasi-autobiography. Özdamar's shifting and fragmented writing refuses any 'simple' stories of identity. The questioning potential of her work's temporal and spatial disruption critically annotates her literary representation of personal memories of (life after) migration. Despite its quasi-autobiographical character it undermines any one-dimensional determinations in terms of Self and Other, German and Turkish, or oriental and occidental.

The narrative strategy most characteristic of Özdamar's quasi-autobiographical work is that of naïve surprise. This strategic naïveté is often praised as a sign of authenticity, but in fact it should not to be taken at face value. Claudia Breger (1999) points out that naïveté is in fact a problematical trope in an orientalist tradition of knowledge. She argues that Özdamar re-inscribes this trope of the 'naïve oriental woman' in a playfully critical way.[9] The naïve pose of Özdamar's protagonist functions as a form of mimicry, a '*partial* instalment of the first-person narrator in the form of the autobiographical novel' (Breger 1999: 42, emphasis LM).[10] This mimicry disturbs a strictly autobiographical reading in the same way as it hampers the determination of the narrator's identity as oriental. Breger writes:

> A closer look shows that none of the positions remain intact. From a narratological perspective the impenetrable mutual 'contamination' of the narrated and narrating first person can be seen as a parodic restaging of the always latently present hybridity of the autobiographical first person.

> Bei näherem Hinsehen zeigt sich, daß keine der Positionen intakt bleibt. Aus erzähltheoretischer Perspektive ließe sich die unauflösliche gegenseitige 'Kontamination' von erzähltem und erzählendem Ich als parodistische Reinszenierung der latent immer gegebenen 'Hybridität' des autobiographischen Ichs lesen. (Breger 1999: 43)

This argument of the repetitive (and according to Breger also parodic) performance of the fundamentally hybrid autobiographical Self not only applies to the novel that Breger discusses, but it is easily extended to Özdamar's complete oeuvre. The autobiographical Self that is produced in Özdamar's literary web of intersecting narratives, is multiple and shifting and seems to make a game out of its own changing poses of quasi-naïve wonder. Throughout Özdamar's writing the narrative 'I' observes the world as if, time after time again, all is new to her and open for her personal interpretation.

  In Özdamar's quasi-autobiographical narrations the protagonist's identity strongly depends on the specific chronotopes, the time-place constellations of the particular moments of narration.[11] This identity appears relational. It adapts to the role that the female protagonist plays or represents in a certain chronotope, and it re-adapts to actual or possible other roles that she plays or might play in other chronotopes. Dependent on the temporally and spatially localised perspective and the different (national, familial, lingual) contexts presented in the narrations, Özdamar's autobiographical Self consists of multiple personae in a complex web of relations: she is simultaneously a labour migrant, a German writer, a political activist, a child, an artist, a returning migrant, a daughter, a granddaughter, a friend, a lover. The same counts for her ethnic and national identity: she is simultaneously Kurdish, Turkish, East German, West German and German, depending on place, time and perspective, both hers and that of others. In many of the mentioned chronotopical identities the experience of migration is of determinant importance. Migration often functions as an *enabling* movement for a differentiation in several roles and several Selves. Whereas on the one hand it demands an unlimited and by times painful flexibility, on the other hand it opens up the possibility of a 'nomadic subjectivity' in return.[12]

In Özdamar's work boundaries – between Turkey and Germany, East and West, Orient and Occident – are presented as shared as well as divisive constructions. These boundaries simultaneously operate as ambivalent zones of contact and as sites of contestation (Boer 1996: 16). Rather than stable lines of demarcation, they are dynamic spaces where positions of power and powerlessness are being negotiated and where 'different and contrasting visions, more often than not unequal in terms of power, come into play' (ibid.). Özdamar's two city stories present the protagonist's multiple crossing of several of these boundaries – temporal, spatial, but also political and ideological. She travels from Turkey to Germany, from West to East Berlin, and back again, in actual or imaginary, past or present movements. Welcome and goodbye, Orient and Occident, life and death: all these dimensions intersect and fuse in Özdamar's city narrations. At the end of this confusion, it is often hard to distinguish between home and away, Self and Other. The continual boundary-crossing puts monolithic and homogeneous notions of (national) identity up for discussion. Besides, by pointing out several transnational parallels and similarities between Turkey and Germany (as well as between East and West Germany), Özdamar's work questions the assumedly neutral – *geographical* – but in fact artificial – *ideological* – division into an East and a West.

The stories 'Mein Istanbul' and 'Mein Berlin', with their specific and connected chronotopical constellations, offer an alternative trajectory of identity that is coloured and signed by the personal markings of their protagonist's experience and memory. They establish a specific tension between official 'geographies of history' and a personal 'cartography of memory'. Whereas these first often assume (or pretend the existence of) stable, natural boundaries (if not borders) between for instance East and West, Orient and Occident, German and non-German, the personal cartography of memory that Özdamar's stories offer connects places and locations that from the perspective of these official geographies appear rigidly separated.[13] In her city stories, Özdamar offers an exceptional perspective on (German and Turkish) history and public memory. The trajectory of identity that her literature imagines represents a fascinating and resisting counterweight to dominant notions of national identity.[14] It not only determinedly resists orientalising readings, but also writes 'a new subject of German remembrance into being' (Adelson 2002: 333). Özdamar's literature performs a subtle rewriting of dominant national history – German as well as Turkish – from the perspective of Turkish-German migration.

Mapping Memories: Istanbul-Berlin Connections

The two stories 'Mein Istanbul' and 'Mein Berlin' build on several striking parallels. First of all both stories represent 'personalised metropoles'. They offer descriptions of the cities of Istanbul and Berlin as experienced by the stories' female protagonist and first-person narrator. This protagonist is familiar to the experienced reader of Özdamar's literary work: the stories again use the autobiographical mode discussed above. Other than in her earlier novels, fantastic elements (that hamper autobiographical identification) are missing here. The narrative tone of naïve wondering and associative surprise, however, is the same. It is this travelling, nomadic protagonist that establishes the first link between Berlin and Istanbul: the personal, experiential link of migration. As the stories proceed, the two metropoles – generally conceived of as very different and far apart from each other – turn out to have more in common than usually acknowledged. They are not only connected by developments of globalisation, by labour and other migrations as exemplified by the case of Özdamar's protagonist, but they also share a comparable history of division: both metropoles were once rigidly separated (by a wall and a waterway) in an East and a West part. In the case of Berlin the political character of the boundary – the Berlin Wall, erected in 1961 – is undisputed. In the case of Istanbul, Özdamar's story makes clear that the contentious decision to (*not*) build a bridge connecting the Muslim and non-Muslim parts of the city is just as political. Özdamar's literary cartography unites these two problematic histories of division in a transnational comparison. Her cartography of memory critically questions and compares the meaning of these histories in terms of global hegemony and the geopolitical division of power. The 'geographic' variables East and West are revealed as locally specific, ideological constructs. Their semantic value varies between Asian and European, communist and capitalist, Orient and Occident.

In both the Istanbul and the Berlin story the protagonist recalls travelling between the two separated parts of the cities, collecting and connecting locations on both sides of the division on her 'personal city map' (HS 85). In the Berlin story, references to many train and underground journeys testify to her nomadic existence.[15] The Istanbul story narrates a parallel wandering, this time by boat or ship, from the one side of the Bosphorus to the other.[16] Spatial tropes of separation and connection abound in Özdamar's city stories. The main activity of the protagonist is the crossing of boundaries, and thus the establishment of moments and spaces of contact that subvert the strict divisions. In the specific narrative contexts offered by the stories, her boundary crossing constitutes an undermining activity on a socio-political level. At the same time, on a more personal level, this continuous crossing forecloses the protagonist's homecoming, and it disables enduring feelings of belonging.

The story 'Mein Berlin' opens with the sentence 'In 1976 I returned to Berlin after an absence of nine years' (HS 55).[17] This sentence immediately situates the narration in both temporal and spatial terms, introducing and connecting three distinctive chronotopes: Berlin in 1976, Berlin nine years before and the timespace of nine years 'elsewhere', in the period between the two dates mentioned. That this elsewhere is to be located in Turkey, the protagonist's 'homeland', becomes clear from the next sentence that refers to the politically precarious situation in Turkey after the military putsch of 1971.[18] In the novel *Die Brücke* (1998a) Özdamar extensively describes the experiences of the female protagonist in Istanbul in this period in between, as well as her repeated migration to Germany. In the first case of migration, in the mid-1960s, the young woman travelled to Germany in the company of other recruits to work as a labour migrant. Özdamar's literary depiction of this experience as an exciting adventure breaks with stereotypical representations of labour migrants as passive victims of fate: the young girl 'Sevgi' confidently tries her luck abroad. She seeks freedom from familial and traditional constraints – mainly exercised by the (nevertheless) beloved mother and grandmother – that bind the young woman to strongly gendered expectations and responsibilities. The protagonist's second migration in 1976 further disturbs dominant expectations in respect to labour migration. At this time the protagonist travelled to Berlin for an internship in the theatre field. To her delight and excitement she has been invited to work as a production assistant for director Matthias Langhoff and Bertolt Brecht's student, Benno Besson, at the renowned East German *Volksbühne*. The novel *Seltsame Sterne* (2003) provides a fascinating impression of this period of the protagonist's life.

The first sentence of 'Mein Berlin' brings these two moments together in one story and installs a certain feeling of continuity, of repetition. Berlin is connected to Istanbul through and in the moment of narrating migration. The second migration is in fact a return and inspires feelings of familiarity and homecoming. Istanbul, on the contrary, as well as Turkey as the left behind country of origin, is remembered in the emotional terms of sad separation and dissatisfactory goodbyes. As a result of her migration the protagonist has to leave her dear grandmother behind, who begs her granddaughter – and even makes her promise – to return to Istanbul after two days. The recollecting character of the first-person narration makes clear that this promise has been broken, an actuality that fills the granddaughter with sadness. Migration in this sense also stands for an experience of loss – a loss that might well be of a definitive nature, considering the grandmother's old age. Another sad reference to the Turkey she left behind, this time through a lens of socio-political critique, evokes a goodbye associated with violence: migration as a painful and traumatic repetition of a *final* separation. It concerns a parting from dear dead: the leaving behind of assassinated friends who have fallen victim to the Turkish military dictatorship.

Despite the sadness about saying farewell, the protagonist's departure is not involuntary, however. Migration is primarily an enabling movement in Özdamar's literary work. The protagonist's transnational travelling brings about loss as well as gain, just as her continual commuting between the separated parts of the divided cities does. The contrary emotions attached to both leaving and arriving result in a game of balancing. In 'Mein Berlin' the sadness evoked by the farewell to beloved ones, dead and alive, is more or less neutralised by the encounter with the also once left behind Berlin. The tone of this re-encounter is happily excited. The city is held as a dear and warm memory; in the perception of the protagonist, the animated Berlin itself seems positively expectant of her return. The protagonist relates of an encounter with a city that has been waiting for her, waiting for her return. She describes this encounter as follows:

> At Zoo station I greeted all the passing buses. I was in liberty and was glad about the rain. I thought: Berlin has been waiting for me for nine years. It was as if at that time, when I had gone back to Istanbul, Berlin had petrified into a photo in order to wait for me – with the tall, high trees, with the Gedächtniskirche, with the double-decker buses and with the pubs at the corners.

> Am Bahnhof Zoo begrüßte ich alle Busse, die vorbeifuhren. Ich war in Freiheit und freute mich über den Regen. Ich dachte: Berlin hat neun Jahre auf mich gewartet. Es war, als wäre Berlin damals, als ich nach Istanbul zurückgegangen war, zu einem Foto erstarrt, um auf mich zu warten – mit den langen, hohen Bäumen, mit der Gedächtniskirche, mit den zweistöckigen Bussen, mit den Eckkneipen. (HS 56)

At the same time Berlin's attitude constitutes an interesting contrast to the often-proclaimed (and experienced) rejecting, and even hostile attitude of the city's population towards Turkish (labour) migrants. In the protagonist's experience of place, on her personalised map of Berlin, liveliness and motion are connected to the protagonist's arrival, to her being present again. She imagines how the places that she once abandoned before and now revisits later have all petrified into photographic images at the moment of (de-)parting. In her narration they appear as projections on the screen of her mind, as souvenirs that she can take around with her and preserve as memories held dear.

A similar perception of a particular time-space, a personalised chronotope caught in a photographic image, appears in the parallel story 'Mein Istanbul'. Here the protagonist recalls the Istanbul that she has left behind, using exactly the same formulation as in 'Mein Berlin':

> I look for my former friends in the faces of the people, but I look for them in the faces of the young people of today, as if my friends had not become older within these twenty-two years, as if they had been waiting for me with their faces of that time. As if Istanbul had been petrified at that moment when I went to Europe, as if it had been waiting for me with all its baths, churches, mosques and sultans' palaces. (...) As if Istanbul had been waiting for me with its millions of shoes that are waiting in the houses for the following morning, with its millions of combs lying in front of the shaving cream-flecked mirrors. I am here, now all windows will open up.

In den Gesichtern der Menschen suche ich meine Freunde von damals, aber ich suche sie in den jungen Gesichtern von heute, als wären meine Freunde in den zweiundzwanzig Jahren nicht älter geworden, als hätten sie mit ihren damaligen Gesichtern auf mich gewartet. Als wäre Istanbul in dem Moment, in dem ich nach Europa gegangen war, zu einem Photo erstarrt, um auf mich zu warten – mit all seinen Bädern, Kirchen, Moscheen, Sultanspalästen (...). Als hätte Istanbul auf mich gewartet mit seinen Millionen von Schuhen, die in den Häusern auf den Morgen warten, mit seinen Millionen von Haarkämmen, die vor den mit Rasierseife befleckten Spiegeln liegen.

Ich bin da, jetzt werden sich alle Fenster öffnen. (HS 74)

As this passage illustrates, moments in time blend together here. They condense as it were in the protagonist's web of memories. Her reflections end on an expectant, but at the same time rather unrealistic, utopian note: now that she – the nomadic migrant – has arrived again, the windows that in her photographic perception remained closed during her absence, will open up again and let life in, let life continue. The passage conveys the impression that her absence from the cities causes their standstill: nothing happens, as she is not there to notice and to observe what is happening. The juxtaposed images of the metropoles, both passively waiting for the protagonist's presence, for her return, stress both her central and parallel position in the city narrations. The titles of the stories also emphasise this subjective dimension: these stories imagine 'Mein Berlin' and 'Mein Istanbul'. These are the metropoles as the protagonist has experienced them; these are the metropoles as preserved in her memory and as revived at her return.

An 'Other's' Perspective on German National History

The protagonist's memories of Berlin and Istanbul, her personal histories of these cities, intersect in significant ways with national histories of Germany and Turkey. 'Sevgi's' memories appear as comments on and additions to German and Turkish cultural memory. They contribute to the larger frame of institutionalised history from a very specific perspective, namely that of a female migrant of Turkish origin.

Most of Özdamar's Berlin writings concern a particular period (and place) in the German history of division.[19] However, as I have pointed out before, the German particularity of these writings is often overlooked in favour of the Turkishness or the Turkish 'accent' of her writing. Leslie Adelson encourages us to acknowledge the fact that many cultural effects of migration and those of German unification 'share the same historical moment' (2002: 327). In this sense Özdamar's stories can be read as a particular kind of Wende literature.[20] They offer a very particular after-1989 view on the pre-1989 period of German-German division. Andreas Huyssen states that although the 'focus of German memory culture is in flux, (...) it remains rigorously focused on things German' (2003: 156). The impact of the *Wende* for the Turkish-German community remained largely out of view, and so did their opinions on its significance and meaning. Özdamar's stories break this silence. They cover the far-reaching moment of national transformation in German history from the perspective of Turkish-German migration, and as such represent unusual as well as exceptionally insightful sites of German memory.[21] The stories constitute instances of cultural counter-memory that effectively provide nuances for and adjust 'official' accounts of this particular phase of transition in German national history.

In the story 'Mein Berlin' the narrating protagonist offers a colourful image of what in another story ('Ulis Weinen' ['Uli's Tears']) she calls 'both Berlins' ['beiden Berlin'] (HS 63): the two parts of the divided Berlin of the after-war period. She presents impressions of daily street life on both sides of the border by combining slogans and political statements written on the western side of the Berlin wall with the old-fashioned shop inscriptions still visible on the house façades in Berlin's eastern part of the city. Slogans varying from 'In dreams everything forgotten cries for help', 'We need no tear-gas, we have enough reasons to cry...' to 'GDR: German trash' and 'Attention! You are entering the Axel Springer sector...' (HS 58) are juxtaposed to (out)dated advertisements as 'Firewood – potato peelings' and 'coffins at all prices' (HS 59).[22] In this way Özdamar sketches a personal as well as a political image of this specific chronotope: Berlin as a combined city, an alloyed city, in the year 1976.

The story's images of Berlin establish a condensed archive of memories. 'Mein Berlin' integrates personal impressions and experiences of a female Turkish migrant into a historical frame of socio-political division. The remarkable fact that the personal dimension contradicts the historical one – integrated memories of both parts of Berlin despite their rigid division – lends these memories an unusual and even disruptive quality. This disruptive quality is strongly related to the protagonist's status as an outsider (in national, lingual and visual terms) on *both* German sides of the Wall.

As Huyssen discusses in his important study on German memory, *Twilight Memories. Marking Time in a Culture of Amnesia* (1995b), the 'ultimate Other' in the 1976 situation of political tension between the two antagonistic Germanies was prescriptively located at the other side of the inner-German border. He writes: 'When Germany was divided, the question of German nation had become increasingly theoretical (...). East and West Germans came to live with separate identities. They became even somewhat exotic to one another and recognised each other in their differences' (Huyssen 1995b: 73). Huyssen's use of the term 'exotic' for the other, antagonist German is striking and unaccustomed. Özdamar's story, however, seems to confirm its applicability.[23] The inner-German border was generally kept closed for German citizens of either German state and while crossing was subject to rigorous restrictions, the protagonist's daily routine actually consists of crossing this German-German border. Her 'double' Otherness provides her with an outsider position that in this exceptional case enables rather than disables movement. On both sides of the border the protagonist is positioned as coming from elsewhere, from 'faraway'. She is perceived as having neither part nor interest in the German-German conflict. Despite the fact that in and after the moment of travelling from East to West and from West to East she in a way represents the respective opposite German side, this antagonist-German representativity is reassuringly neutralised by her ethnic Otherness. In the West she is the Turkish woman working in the East; in the East she is the Turkish woman living in the West. Her boundary-crossing practice in this particular situation of German-German division complicates her imposed identity as exotic Other. The fact that the label 'exotic' is already reserved for the *German* Other, confuses this discursive dichotomy. It works to subvert the (still efficacious) orientalising discourse that attributes this label to the Arab-looking (female) Other, in this case the Turkish-German migrant.

Crossing Borders, Trespassing Politics

In his *Twilight Memories* Huyssen observes a reluctance to address the question of post-*Wende* national identity in German public discourse. He expresses his concern about this negligence and warns for the danger of leaving the question to the populist (or extreme) right. As he insists: 'The question is not if, but how and to what extent identificatory memories will be reshaped' (Huyssen 1995b: 82). Özdamar's writing reshapes such identificatory memories. Her contemporary literary descriptions of a pre-1989 Berlin open up an unexpected angle for German self-reflection.

In the story 'Mein Berlin' Özdamar's protagonist observes and registers many instances of division, but leaves most of them uncommented upon, at least, *explicitly* uncommented. In fact, her subtle commentary is the narrative mode of tactful wondering that often touches upon the sad and tragic absurdities of the situations of separation described. The listed selection of 'West slogans' on the Wall signal the politically heterogeneous, partly radicalised West German society. They convey a political image without, however, taking a political standpoint. The protagonist's experiences on the eastern side of the Wall give insight into the limited margins of freedom in East Berlin. This is for instance the case in a registered dialogue between the protagonist and the character of playwright Heiner Müller. He explains to her why the East Berlin theatre audience holds back its spontaneous responses to politically significant scenes in a play. Özdamar writes: 'Heiner said: "They know that the play will be forbidden when they laugh too much. That's why they do not laugh, they agree on not laughing"' (HS 59).[24] Müller's explanatory defence of the East German audience clearly reveals a situation of state coercion. In the GDR, laughing is a political act. The work of art necessarily moves within a narrow state-determined frame. Özdamar's story, however, does not elaborate on this situation describing a lack of freedom. Its first-person narrator refrains from adding explicit political statements or judgements.

Germany – and more specifically East Berlin – appears through the protagonist's personal lens of 'recognition' – in both meanings of the term. On the one hand, her observations mediate a delighted, recognising identification of Germany as the country that she tried to imagine in Istanbul, before coming to Berlin. There she read and performed German drama by Bertolt Brecht and Georg Büchner, and became fascinated by the German society that this drama represented. On the other hand, her narration attributes recognition in the sense of acknowledgement and respect to those German intellectuals that inspired the (repressed) Turkish oppositional student movement of which she was once part. She writes:

> Every time I was pleased anew about the names of the stops at the Volksbühne: 'Rosa Luxemburg Square'. I was also pleased about the tube stop 'Marx Engels Square'. In Turkey people had been arrested for the books of Marx, Engels and Luxemburg. I was also pleased that cucumbers were of the same price at every grocery store: 40 groschen. In contrast to West Berlin, there were no slogans on the walls of the houses or on the Berlin Wall.

> Jedes Mal freute ich mich über den Namen der Haltestelle an der Volksbühne: 'Rosa-Luxemburg-Platz'. Ich freute mich auch über die U-Bahn-Haltestelle 'Marx-Engels-Platz'. Wegen der Bücher von Marx, Engels und Luxemburg hatte man in der Türkei Menschen verhaftet. Ich freute mich auch, dass eine Gurke in jedem Laden gleich viel kostete: 40 Groschen. Im Gegensatz zu West-Berlin gab es an den Hauswänden oder an der Mauer keine Sprüche. (HS 59)

The last two sentences of this passage offer another example of the effective combination of positive wondering and quasi-naïve surprise, combined with a latent comment on the political situation. Her quasi-neutral assessment that in East Berlin no slogans appear on the Wall, contains a critique on the lack of freedom of speech without, however, explicating this critique directly. Her comment seems nothing more than an observation, but is in fact a meaningful reference to the situation of limited freedom in East Germany. The Wall on this side is set off with the 'death strip' [Todesstreifen] and dissent against the GDR state ideology is forbidden.

Several reviewers of Özdamar's Berlin writings (especially of her novel Seltsame Sterne) criticised her observing narrative mode as a problematic downplaying of a repressive political regime.[25] They repudiated her naïve, apolitical stance in respect to GDR politics as an irresponsible attitude. Here, however, it is important to distinguish between narrator and narration. While Özdamar's narrating protagonist can be considered as apolitical and uninvolved, this is not the case for her narration.

It is the exceptionality of the protagonist's outsider position that by contrast foregrounds the inescapable complicity of *all* other German positions, of all *indigenous* German characters. The protagonist's ethnic Otherness enables an alternative perspective on a situation of polarised division. This perspective does not carry the burden of German complicity, but instead addresses and questions this untenable situation. In an analysis of Özdamar's debut stories 'Mutterzunge' ['Mother tongue'] and 'Großvaterzunge' ['Grandfather tongue'] Stephanie Bird argues that German identity, just like Turkish identity, appears as a 'historically, politically and culturally contingent' (2003: 164) *ethnic* identity. She maintains:

> This is why [Özdamar] appears not to 'take sides'. Not because she is adhering to notions of fair play where each nationality has something to offer, but because she is questioning the very notion that identity is immutable, defined and constrained by national borders. There are no 'sides' to take, but there are specific explorations to be made. (Bird 2003: 164)

In my opinion this same argument bears on 'Mein Berlin'. In the described situation of German-German division the Turkish protagonist explores the various national identities in process without, however, installing a personal or political hierarchy.[26]

In the story 'Ulis Weinen' the semantic intersection of several markers of identity – East and West, German and non-German, Orient and Occident – culminates in a situation of insightful identity confusion. In an encounter with an East Berlin woman that for the first time visits the (now again geographical) west part of Berlin, Özdamar is interpellated as the legitimate representative of this West. The East Berlin woman takes the position of a visitor that now occupies West Berlin space. By her modest self-positioning, the East Berlin woman reveals spatial and national hierarchies in a manner that puts them into perspective, and even challenges them. Her unbiased acceptance of Özdamar's protagonist as West German successfully disrupts the dominant rhetoric of (in this case West) German Self and Other. In the encounter between the two women the dominant web of national positionalities shifts: it is the 'visiting' Turkish protagonist that is positioned as 'naturally' at home here, at home in this part of the city.

Özdamar's registering narration of 'both Berlins' offers a perspective that juxtaposes its East and West part as the complementary (instead of antagonist) counterparts of the one city that they used to be, and in a particular way still are. By assessing similarities and shared histories between Berlin and Istanbul Özdamar moreover evokes a multilayered web of transnational connections.[27] Categories of geographic division as East and West, Orient and Occident, are divulged as relative and arbitrary, their boundaries as permeable. However, in spite of the narrative connection of 'both Berlins' through the mapping of memories of a travelling outsider, the city's lived division is nevertheless clear, also for those readers who are not able to locate 'Kino Steinplatz' or 'Café Käse' (HS 56) at either the eastern or the western side of the Wall. References to '[d]ead rails with grass growing in between' (HS 56/57), to desolate platforms of East Berlin railway stations that the West Berlin underground passes without stopping, and to the searchlights of the East Berlin police establish an atmosphere of political tension and discomfort.[28] The same is true for the repeated instances of border-crossing formalities: the strictly regulated money exchange and the intimidating interrogations by border control officers. This tense atmosphere reaches a climax, when at a certain point in the narrative the border crossing protagonist is allowed a longer stay in the GDR. She has been invited for an internship at the East Berlin *Volksbühne*, and for this reason she is issued a residence permit for a period of three months. This permit obliges her to actually *stay* in the GDR and prohibits further border crossing. The practical gain of not having to go through the daily, time consuming money exchange fades against the feeling of being locked up.

This experience, the loss of the freedom to perform her identity-constituting travelling, is of great impact on the protagonist. She has to give up on her self-chosen nomadism (and even her not-belonging) that she enjoyed and celebrated so intensively. Trapped as it were in the Berlin East, she develops a longing desire for the other side, a feeling that she tries to alleviate by visiting the Friedrichstraße railway station:

> Sometimes, on Saturdays or Sundays I went to Friedrich Street station. There the trains with West Germans stopped and then continued to West Berlin. Here *even* I had an ardent desire for the West. I phoned Kati. 'Is it snowing on your side, too?'

> Manchmal, am Samstag oder Sonntag ging ich zum Bahnhof Friedrichstraße. Dort hielten die Züge, in denen Westdeutsche saßen, und fuhren dann weiter nach West-Berlin. Hier bekam *sogar ich* eine große Sehnsucht nach dem Westen. Ich rief Kati an. 'Schneit es bei euch auch?' (HS 60, emphasis LM)

The phrasing 'even I' stresses her 'other' position, other from the East German citizens who, as the text suggests, also long for the cut-off part of their city, for the former unity of their 'homeland'. The limitation of the protagonist's initial freedom again increases the ambivalence of the offered (apparently apolitical) GDR impression. With the GDR residence permit the protagonist more or less loses her outsider position and is forced to temporarily become part of, and so complicit in, one of both German national spaces, in this case, the GDR.

The question 'Is it snowing on your side, too?' in the citation above addresses another mutuality that connects both parts of Berlin. Özdamar's Berlin of 1976 is imagined as a city of both separation and unity. Whereas the separation is under-lined every time that the Özdamar's protagonist crosses the border, the city's unity is established and emphasised through repeated references to its 'natural oneness', symbolically represented by the weather. The wondering surprise about the weather that is the same across and despite a rigid division recurs in both city stories. In 'Mein Berlin' the protagonist relates: 'This way during the day I lived at the theatre in East Berlin, and at night I went back to West Berlin to Kati and Theo. Every time when I left the tube I was astonished: "Oh, it has rained here as well"' (HS 57).[29] In the story 'Mein Istanbul' a similar unifying assessment is attached to a shared sky: 'And the moon was always there both over Europe and Asia' (HS 68).[30]

The naïve emphasis on a shared sky and moon, and similar weather across the divisions, not only underlines the natural commonality between the complemen-tary parts of the two divided cities. It also directs the attention to the artificiality of their division. The historical anecdote in the story 'Mein Istanbul' about the build-ing of the Bridge of the Golden Horn that finally connects the two parts of the city, emphasises the ideological dimension of the (religiously and ethnically moti-vated) decision to build this bridge. Its juxtaposition with the divisive Berlin Wall further endorses the perception of Bridge and Wall as ideological border con-structs. Their establishment is decided within a complex matrix of power rela-tions. Both the opening of the Berlin Wall and the crossing of the new Golden Horn Bridge in Istanbul are described as transgressive events.[31] In the act of boundary crossing the consolidated order is challenged and established struc-tures are opened up for renegotiation. In Özdamar's stories these moments of life in rupture are metaphorically portrayed as scenes in an alienating theatre play – a play with an uncertain outcome. The boundaries become spaces of contact and interrogation: exceptional spaces, performatively reimagined in the transi-tional moments of their crossing.

In 'Mein Istanbul' the newly built bridge between the Asian and the European part of the city is described as a fascinating and lively stage of encounter. The very diverse population of Istanbul meets on the new Golden Horn bridge: 'The bridge became like a stage: Jews, Turks, Greeks, Arabs, Albanians, Armenians, Eur-opeans, Persians, Tserkessians, women, men, horses, donkeys, cows, hens, ca-mels, they all crossed this bridge' (HS 71).[32] In the Berlin story 'Ulis Weinen', the protagonist witnesses the first days of border crossing euphoria after the opening of the Berlin wall in 1989. She remarks:

All of a sudden the whole of Germany was like a stage, nobody knew which play was performed, but everyone wanted to play a role. In West Berlin you saw many people from the East on the Ku'damm, their clothing didn't fit in West Berlin, their costumes looked worn out on the posh West Berlin stage. Those people from the East looked like actors from a Maxim Gorki play who had suddenly lost their stage and had landed on another stage on which a completely different play was performed.

Ganz Deutschland war plötzlich wie eine Bühne, zwar wusste man nicht, welches Stück gespielt wurde, aber jeder wollte darin eine Rolle haben. In Westberlin sah man viele Menschen aus dem Osten auf dem Ku'damm, ihre Kleidung passte nicht zu Westberlin, ihre Kostüme sahen in dem schicken Westberliner Bühnenbild so verbraucht aus. Die Menschen aus dem Osten sahen aus wie Schauspieler aus einem Maxim-Gorki-Stück, die plötzlich ihre Bühne verloren hatten und auf einer anderen Bühne, in der ein ganz anderes Stück gespielt wurde, gelandet waren. (HS 63/64)

In the comparison with a play, the significant historical moment of transition and change becomes a fictive product(ion). Whereas the Istanbul stage is represented as a celebratory encounter, the Berlin stage of reunion is much more marked by feelings of insecurity. The overwhelming, sometimes outright comical, happening makes people seem out of place, lost in this moment of history.[33] Their coming together resembles a scriptless performance in which people play roles of which they are themselves not sure, that have to be invented in the moment of their performance. This scriptless performance results in an atmosphere of uncertainties: what will the future of the performed, and thus more or less self-directed, reality look like?

The resultant situation of alienation or estrangement is strongly reminiscent of Bertolt Brecht's theories of the epic theatre, a link that is supported by Özdamar's own, well-known interest and involvement in the Brechtian theatre tradition. Brecht's theory of the V-Effekt, the alienation or estrangement effect, involved both the audience of and the actors in the theatre performance (Brecht 1968). Easy identifications with characters should be prevented for both. Instead, epic theatre should make people aware of their own position, and encourage, if not force, them to rethink this position in a responsible way. In the scene depicted in Özdamar's story, audience and actors melt into one in a situation in which everything is different from what it was like before. All characters are part of an open-ended transformative play. This situation causes an anxious mixture of expectations and insecurity, but simultaneously opens up a range of possibilities.[34]

Özdamar's stories thus conceive of boundaries as exceptional spaces that have a special, disruptive status. At the end of the Berlin story the protagonist visits another exceptional boundary space: the Dorotheenstädtischer cemetery in Berlin's Chaussee Street. Several famous German writers are buried in this cemetery, among them Bertolt Brecht and Heiner Müller.[35] The cemetery is a boundary space par excellence, a 'heterotopian space' in the terminology proposed by Michel Foucault. In his 1967 lecture 'Des Espaces Autres', Foucault maintains that heterotopian spaces 'have the curious property of being in relation with all the other sites, but in such a way to suspect, neutralize or invert the set of relations that they happen to designate, mirror or reflect' (1986: 24). Foucault discusses several kinds of heterotopian spaces: psychiatric hospitals, prisons, gardens, brothels and ships. What these spaces have in common, he argues, is that they are 'real places (...) formed in the very founding of society', but that they are simultaneously 'outside of all places' and 'absolutely different' (ibid.). On the one hand they are part of official geographies of public space, on the other they simultaneously withdraw from its prescribed order and regulation. In Özdamar's story the cemetery is the place where her protagonist visits the dead, seeking both their comfort and advice. In her imagination there is no rigid boundary that separates life from death: the cemetery constitutes another boundary space of contact.

In the Berlin cemetery, at Hegel's tomb, a young boy approaches Özdamar's protagonist. He spontaneously tells her that it was Hegel's wish to be buried next to Fichte. 'Fichte died of typhoid, Hegel of cholera' (HS 61), the boy casually adds to this information, reinforcing the connection between the two German intellectuals on the level of illness and death.[36] The narrative web-weaving of people, places and time, characteristic of Özdamar's writing, continues. This time it results in a specific intellectual genealogy as well as in a political-ideological map. From Hegel's grave the protagonist, accompanied by the boy, precedes to Brecht's grave, while softly singing the first sentences of his famous *Dreigroschenoper* lyrics 'Die Moritat von Mackie Messer': '...und der Haifisch, der hat Zähne...' (ibid.). This one phrase instigates the protagonist to establish an anecdotal link to her grandmother in Istanbul who, as related earlier in the story, had commented on this song with musings on her own death. The same flowers that the grandmother used to grow in Istanbul adorn Brecht's Berlin grave. In Özdamar's transnational cartography Brecht is connected to the grandmother, and the cemetery in Berlin is connected to reflections on dying in Istanbul. The protagonist's storyworld narration of a dream connects her fantastic visit to Brecht's deathbed to the appearance of Turkish fascists on a sailing ship. By means of the narrative strategy of juxtaposition – threading together death, grandmother, Brecht, Turkish fascism – not only fascism appears as a shared Turkish-German problem, but 'the world in general' features as a web of multiple relations and interconnections.

The story ends with a direct reference to geography: the young boy interestedly asks the protagonist where she comes from. This benevolent question, inquiring for the protagonist's origin, determines the protagonist as visibly Other. At the same time it encourages 'Sevgi' to position herself. On her answer 'from Turkey' the boy responds with a following, specifying question: 'where is Turkey?'. Her response, 'Close to Bulgaria' (ibid.)[37] – a reference to a country with which an East German schoolboy assumedly is familiar – locates Turkey on a specifically *East* German map of 'the world'. Just as with the current controversy on Turkey's future EU membership, this specific localisation makes clear that positioning

Turkey on the map of 'the world' – East or West, Europe or Asia, Orient or Occident – is a highly political act; the map itself is an ideological construct. The protagonist's answer indicates the relativity and arbitrariness of space, and underlines the historical situatedness of positionings.

When the two characters take leave, the boy assures the protagonist that he will look up her country of origin in his father's atlas. Whereas the protagonist's associative wandering in time and space has created a personal map of narrated memory, the boy redirects the attention to the 'official' map of history. Both maps come together in Özdamar's stories that critically interconnect them in an imagined trajectory of identity.

German Self-Orientation Abroad

'And [Can Yücel] said that the search for identity in a foreign country
is somewhat different from trying to find one's identity in an alien country'
(Özdamar in Wierschke 1996: 253).[38]

In the story 'Fahrrad auf dem Eis' (2001) the protagonist's map of relation as well as her trajectory of identity is extended with yet another national space: the Netherlands.[39] The imaginative project of renegotiating national boundaries and questioning monolithic conceptions of Germanness is further complicated by a journey abroad. Like the stories discussed in the previous sections, 'Fahrrad auf dem Eis' is told retrospectively by a quasi-autobiographical first-person narrator. In this story, the only previously unpublished piece included in Der Hof im Spiegel, the narrating female protagonist leaves behind the geographical spaces that generally frame Özdamar's writing: Germany and Turkey. As a professional writer, she travels to the Netherlands to spend some time in Amsterdam. In the story she explains that the 'Foundation Cultural Exchange The Netherlands-Germany' (HS 78/79) has invited her for a stay in the Dutch capital as a 'writer in residence,' an honour that is regularly awarded to German 'workers in the cultural field'.[40] This invitation, based on national criteria pertaining either to her personal background or to her writing, yields a certain tension with my earlier argument about the protagonist's transnationality. The honour determines 'Sevgi's' identity in national terms.

The following analysis reflects on the return of national identity as an abiding factor of influence that cannot be easily left behind. It argues that the story 'Fahrrad auf dem Eis' reveals several difficulties inherent in the nomadic position that the protagonist so elegantly and effectively took up in the city stories discussed in the previous sections. Some of these difficulties could already be sensed in these stories; others only evolve from the specific situation that arises when the protagonist travels abroad.[41] As will become clear the story makes use of exactly these national specificities in order to question both the German and the Dutch status quo in respect to national traumas. Özdamar's German-Dutch juxtapositions prompt a reflection on the affective dimensions of these traumas in the present. The foreign Dutch context confronts the protagonist with her German identity and prompts a new instance of self-reflection. The question of national identity obviously poses itself differently for a German writer of Turkish origin in Dutch residence. In this story the imagination of a transnational identity as well as of a transnational web of relations gains yet another dimension. Art – visual and verbal – proves to be of central significance in the reflection on a future, transnational community.

Like 'Mein Berlin', the story 'Fahrrad auf dem Eis' opens with a chronotopical localisation.[42] A flashback of twenty years transports Özdamar's protagonist to her first visit to Amsterdam. It is the protagonist's second visit to this Dutch metropolis – twenty years after the first – that triggers the memory of her first encounter with the city. She recollects an image connected to the first visit, an image of a bicycle lying on a frozen canal. In the context of the story this unusual image, which is also captured in the title, contains several layers of meaning and opens up several levels of interpretation. First, the image combines three stereotypical Dutch national symbols – a bicycle, the canals and the ice on the canals – and becomes emblematic for the Dutch world that the protagonist presents to the reader. The fact that the chosen combination of the things seen as typically Dutch is so uncommon and clearly, because of its dependence on winter weather, of a very temporary nature, makes the emblematic image into an ephemeral one: an image at the edge of transformation. When read for this emblematic quality the temporality and extraordinariness of the image invoke Dutch society as a transitional society where traditional national symbols appear in new and innovative constellations. Here the national future appears open for reimagination.

On a second, more personal level, the image of the bicycle holds a certain guiding quality for the protagonist as a marker for orientation. She tags the depicted situation on her 'personal city map' (HS 85) as a significant place to which to return. That twenty years later this marked spot cannot be found in exactly the same way turns the image into a particular motivation for the protagonist's wandering through the city during the second visit. The disappeared bicycle adds an element of searching to her city strolls. The possibility that this specific bicycle might turn up again and the hope for this moment of recognition and reunion remain present in the background of the story as an 'entertaining idea'.[43] The central position of the bicycle in the story title underlines the importance of such a temporary station in the protagonist's meandering.

The guiding quality of the bicycle image (the early actual one as well as its memory image) recurs on a third level, where it functions as an incentive for the process of imagination. In the remembered situation of actually seeing the unusual constellation, the image fascinates the protagonist and sets her wondering about the bicycle's story: why is the bicycle lying there, to whom does it belong, what has happened? She suggests several versions in propositional narrative constructions of possibility without favouring or dismissing any of them.[44] This non-hierarchical mode of making up possible stories prompts the reader to wonder along with the protagonist, to identify with her wonderment on an egalitarian basis. The image unites narrator and reader in a situation of not-knowing and in a shared search for possible stories where one is as good as the other. This same wondering imagination appertains to the protagonist's second visit to Amsterdam.

Uniting these three levels of meaning – an image of Dutchness, a personal marker for orientation and an instigation for the imagination – the bicycle image is of symbolic significance for the story.[45] The bicycle functions both as a station on the protagonist's wandering way and at the same time, in the form of a memory image, as a metaphoric vehicle for imaginary transportation of both protagonist and reader. The image contains a promise of movement that in its given situation on the ice is rather improbable, but that in its capacity as metaphor is actualised in the protagonist's imagination. This way stagnation and movement come together in one and the same image.

After presenting this first rich bicycle image as an explorative opening figure of thought, the story proceeds by leaps and bounds in time to the memory of the second visit to Amsterdam. Here the protagonist immediately sets out to check on what used to be her personal Amsterdam city centre:

> When I arrived in Amsterdam on 7 October, I went straight to the canal where I had seen the bicycle on the ice twenty years ago. It was not there anymore. It was raining on the canal. Perhaps this bicycle had sunk after the ice had melted and has been lying at the bottom of the canal for twenty years. And since I am here again, I thought it might suddenly come up again, even jump out of the water onto the road and start riding without an owner, take sharp turns and I would run after it. It would show me the canals and bridges until I knew them all.

> Als ich in Amsterdam am 7. Oktober ankam, ging ich sofort zu dem Kanal, auf dem ich vor zwanzig Jahren das Fahrrad auf dem Eis gesehen hatte. Es war nicht mehr da. Es regnete auf den Kanal. Vielleicht ist dieses Fahrrad, nachdem das Eis geschmolzen war, versunken und liegt seit zwanzig Jahren unten. Und weil ich jetzt wieder da bin, dachte ich, es wird plötzlich hochkommen, sogar aus dem Wasser zur Straße springen und ohne einen Besitzer losfahren, Kurven nehmen, und ich werde hinter ihm herrennen. Es wird mir die Kanäle, Brücken zeigen, bis ich sie alle kennengelernt habe. (HS 79)[46]

The bicycle has disappeared, but as a memory image it nevertheless continues to stir the protagonist's imagination. As in the Istanbul and Berlin stories, the protagonist expectantly connects her return and renewed presence to fantasies of change and, more particularly, of recovery of a previously existing situation. She imagines herself as the central instigator of the bicycle's sudden return to the spot where it had been before. In this personifying imagination the bicycle transforms into an independent, animated city guide that immediately sets out to guide the protagonist on a familiarising tour through the city. 'Sevgi' relates how '[t]he bicycle was riding and telling' (HS 79), a phrasing that is followed by a colon and the citation of a typographically marked intertext.[47] The source of the citation that follows appears ambivalent. Although its descriptive, explanatory content suggests that its origin lies in the Berlitz travel guide listed in the story's source bibliography, the use of the dated term 'Zuiderzee' in the first sentence of the citation immediately unsettles this assumption. As the water that this term refers to was renamed IJsselmeer after its successful draining and embankment in 1932, its use in a contemporary travel guide (the listed Berlitz dates from 1998) seems rather improbable. The reappearance of the term 'Zuiderzee' in a later citation from one of Vincent van Gogh's letters – another important source text listed – seems to direct the reader to an interpretation of the bicycle as impersonating this artist's voice. I will discuss the implications of this suggested correspondence between the guiding bicycle and Van Gogh in the following section.[48]

While the bicycle is not present as an actual point of orientation anymore, the protagonist feels the need to determine another palpable marker for orientation on her 'personal city map' of Amsterdam. She explains this bare necessity in a general mode: 'In a foreign city you must hold on to some point' (HS 86).[49] This time she appoints two chairs standing in front of a café as the new centre of her daily wanderings. They constitute a new point of orientation, which provides her with a feeling of stability and grounding in her exploration of the alien city: 'When I'm standing in front of these chairs, I can lose myself in the city, but when I re-find these chairs, I am simply at these chairs' (ibid.).[50] The chairs supply the basis that enables the protagonist to get lost in the city without feeling lost. This does not mean that she gives up on re-finding the bicycle. As she has fixed another location to temporarily ground her trajectory of identity, this is not an acute necessity anymore. Nevertheless her determination to retrieve the bicycle and to reestablish a feeling of stability as well as of continuity connected to her first spatial anchor remains vivid throughout the story.[51]

The Ethics of Seeing

'You have to make your characters speak in such a way
that their feelings become visible to the reader'
(Özdamar in Horrocks and Kolinsky 1997: 51).

One of the possible bicycle stories that the narrator proposes in the first paragraph of 'Fahrrad auf dem Eis' introduces the figure of the Dutch painter Vincent van Gogh (1853-1890). Van Gogh's collected correspondence constitutes an important intertext in the story. Throughout the story, citations from this correspondence appear as marked instances of intertextuality. At the first mention of Van Gogh, the narrator suggests: 'If Van Gogh had painted it, maybe one could have learned the story of this bicycle' (HS 77).[52] In this suggestion the narrator establishes a conjunction between a visual image and a narrative story. In immediate succession she elaborates on the 'maybe' construction with a citation from John Berger, a writer and an art historian who also features prominently in the dedication of the prose collection.[53] In the passage cited Berger explores Van Gogh's artistic process as one of collecting individual items and making them real through their combination. He maintains that Van Gogh, more than any other painter, has managed to capture the labour involved in the production of the specific objects depicted in his paintings. In Van Gogh's visual representation of a shoe or a chair, according to Berger, the creative labour of the cobbler or the carpenter is revived and, in a certain sense, repeated: '*[Van Gogh] put all the different parts together for the final product: legs, radial wood, armrests, seats. Or: soles, uppers, heels – so as if he indeed wanted to put them together and as if they became real by this act of being put together*' (ibid., italics in original).[54] This artistic process of bringing objects together in such a way that they appear in relation to one another, as a particular kind of (comm)unity, resembles the narrative technique that Özdamar herself deploys in her literature.[55] For both artists, artworks perform a unifying act and make those elements visible that were not consciously visible before. Their careful observations direct the attention to aspects and details of day-to-day scenes that are easily overlooked, but nevertheless constitute nodes of meaning in a web of relation.

By establishing the intertextual link to the oeuvre of the visual artist Van Gogh, Özdamar foregrounds aspects of seeing and visibility. Like in several other stories in *Der Hof im Spiegel*, acts of looking and observing are of central importance in 'Fahrrad auf dem Eis'.[56] Characteristically the protagonist directs her and the reader's gaze – by means of narrative focalisation – to objects, people, situations and circumstances that hardly ever appear in master narratives of collective memory and that are generally not considered of great cultural value. Her objects of attention are taken from the everyday and her detailed characterisations of people and places depict aspects of this everyday. An example from her text can demon-strate this alternative regime of looking. At a certain point the protagonist relates that immediately after her first encounter with the bicycle on the ice, she visits the Van Gogh Museum. There she engages in a practice of looking that is rather unusual when one is visiting a museum: 'I was sitting in front of one of [Van Gogh's] self-portraits and did not look at the painting but at the museum guard. A man. He was the guardian of waiting. (...) I wept for him and believed that Van Gogh looks at him from a painting every day' (HS 77/78).[57] The text presents us with the unusual situation in which the museum visitor, who is now simulta-neously narrator and spectator, watches the museum guard instead of looking at the painting hanging on the wall in front of her. As focalisation and gaze in this particular moment overlap, the reader is prompted to visualise the same image: not Van Gogh's painted self-portrait, but instead the ostensibly actual person of the museum guard. This redirection of the obvious or culturally expected gaze constitutes a disruptive moment in the common regime of looking at culturally valorised things on display in a museum. Not the painting, but the person be-comes the object of attention.

In a later, similar situation during her second visit to Amsterdam and the Van Gogh museum, the protagonist offers an explanation for her tears and sadness in the previous museum situation. Referring to this museum guard and to museum guards in general, she tells the friend who is with her this time: 'This is a profes-sion that makes me sad. They are like a blurred image. So many people are here and no one is looking at him' (HS 107).[58] The protagonist's sadness concerns the social invisibility or mis-recognition of this person in a space in which people habitually direct their gaze to the art objects on display.[59] Obviously, the museum guard falls outside a museum's dominant regime of looking. In the first museum visit described, the protagonist proceeds to imagine how Van Gogh, present in the scene in the appearance of his self-portrait, resists this regime as it were and actually looks at the museum guard. This imaginative act, whereby Van Gogh perceives the museum guard on days when the protagonist cannot be there her-self, has a comforting quality for her. She reads Van Gogh's painted, imagined look as an affirmative look, even what Silverman (1996) calls a 'productive look': a creative opening up of the (conscious and unconscious) look to that which nor-mally falls out of the culturally dominant screen.[60] In respect to their artistic prac-tices this productive look is something that Van Gogh as a painter and the prota-gonist as a writer have in common. Whereas Van Gogh captures connections and relations that mostly remain unnoticed in his paintings, Özdamar adopts a pro-ductive look in the narration of the daily experiences of her protagonist. Her writ-ing makes the reader aware of connections and relations that fall out of the domi-nant *narrative* frame: the frame of national history.

In the example above this act of productive looking might seem specifically connected to the occupation of a museum guard. However, Özdamar's emphasis

on the (productive) look as a practice of recognition is more general and resonates meaning in culture-critical ways. The protagonist's concern for ethnic diversity and her interest in the colonial thematic are important here. Read in this
frame of (ethnic) difference her comments on social invisibility allude to structures of marginalisation and historical forgetfulness. In its typical wondering
mode Özdamar's writing directs the reader's attention to the blind spots and moments of trauma in national memory. She prompts a search for webs of Relation
with a capital R, Relation as the concept that Édouard Glissant's proposes in his
work *Poetics of Relation* (1997). Glissant defines Relation as a process of changing
mentalities and transforming communities, a process that is propelled forward by
the imagination. Referring to Gilles Deleuze and Felix Guattari's theory of the
rhizome as discussed in their study *A Thousand Plateaus. Capitalism and Schizophrenia*
([1980] 2004), Glissant writes: 'Rhizomatic thought is the principle behind what I
call the Poetics of Relation, in which each and every identity is extended through a
relationship with the Other' (1997: 11). Özdamar's writing follows a similar line of
reasoning. Her transnational web of memory appears as a rhizomatic structure of
Relation.

Before turning to the aforementioned German and Dutch blind spots and moments of trauma, I will discuss one other constellation in the story, in which an
act of looking sustains an important step in the production of Relation. In this
particular constellation the protagonist observes a typing man in the neighbouring apartment through the window of her own Amsterdam apartment, her
temporary 'home'. Through the double framing – the two curtainless windows
that separate protagonist and neighbour and also direct the former's gaze – this
image gains a highly artificial quality. In its tranquil and framed quality the scene
again resembles a painting: the protagonist is not partaking, but only observing
in a slightly voyeuristic way as she intrudes on the writing neighbour's private life
unnoticed. The presence of a mirror in the other apartment adds to the directed
mediation of the protagonist's gaze.[61] In a certain sense the observed, concentrat-
ing man himself also constitutes a mirror image: he represents a writer with
whose occupation the protagonist can and does identify. In contrast to a similar
situation of observing in the collection's title story 'Der Hof im Spiegel', where at
a certain moment a gesture of pointing confirms the recognition of the other and
establishes a moment of (imagined) communication, here the gaze is returned
seemingly without any emotions attached to it.[62] The situation is described as
follows: 'He was standing at the window, naked, and looked at me. He saw that I
cried. He did not move a bit' (HS 91).[63] The nakedness of the neighbour and the
tears of the protagonist underline the vulnerability of the two people involved in
this intersubjective act of looking. When the protagonist shows him her book in
order to demonstrate that her tears result from her act of reading, this gesture
remains unanswered or, at least, a possible response is not registered in the text.

The story moves on to the next scene of city wandering without further elaboration on the moment of contact.

In this way the text remains opaque and the given situation remains open for interpretation. The protagonist's attempt to establish a moment of mutual recognition and affective intimacy by pointing out the emotions brought about by reading neither results in a confirmative reaction from the neighbour, nor in a gesture of rejection. The two characters enter in relation, but this relation is not a relation of sharing, of community. It seems as if the insuperable distance that characterises the act of reading is preserved in the window-mediated contact scene between the writer-neighbour and the reader-protagonist. The protagonist's remark that because of her tears she could only see a blurred image of the neighbour can be read as a reference to mediation and hindrance in the attempt to establish contact. The sense of 'blurredness' as a negative condition for the process of recognition and relation already appeared in a metaphorical way earlier in the text, in respect to the museum guard: '[museum guards] are like a blurred image' (HS 107).[64]

In the next window scene in the story the situation has normalised again, as if nothing had happened. The protagonist watches the neighbour working at his computer and continues to identify with his concentrated writing. It seems now that, more than a partner in affective relationship, the neighbour, like the chairs, functions as yet another figure for orientation.[65] His constant presence supplies another image of comforting continuity in the protagonist's daily wanderings. At the same time his image suggests the *possibility* of Relation; Relation, however, that is not *yet* realised as a substantive emotive connection.

A Poetics of (Affective) Relation

The story 'Fahrrad auf dem Eis' not only establishes several webs of relation as, for instance, the narrative triads between Berger, Van Gogh and the protagonist, and between the last two and the museum guard. It also continues its drawing of geographic, transnational lines of Relation. This time the metropolitan cities of Amsterdam, Berlin, Istanbul, New York and Paris are connected in the protagonist's personal web of visited, meaningful places, in her cartography of memory. Making extensive use of temporal and spatial deixis as a means of locating herself, she relates:

> Ten years later, after I had seen this museum guard and the original paintings by Van Gogh for the first time, my mother died in Istanbul. It was November in Berlin. I was lying in bed in a studio apartment and was very sad, didn't eat, didn't drink and wanted to die as well. (...) I read all Van Gogh's letters, his voice helped me. When I started crying again, I embraced one of these books and read a letter aloud.

Zehn Jahre später, nachdem ich diesen Museumswächter und zum ersten Mal die Originalbilder von van Gogh gesehen hatte, starb meine Mutter in Istanbul. Es war November in Berlin. Ich lag in einer Atelierwohnung im Bett und war sehr traurig, aß nicht, trank nicht und wollte auch sterben. (...) Ich las alle Briefe von van Gogh, seine Stimme half mir. Wenn ich wieder zu weinen begann, umarmte ich eines dieser Bücher und las einen Brief laut. (HS 78)

This passage again links Özdamar's protagonist to Van Gogh. It not only establishes something that could be described as *(Seelen)Verwandtschaft*, congeniality of spirit or affinity between the two artists, but it also depicts what could be called narrative intimacy. Reading Van Gogh's letters – a very particular form of autobiography, strongly determined by the complex person deixis of the narrative 'you' – comforts the protagonist in her mourning about the death of her mother. Moreover it reinforces her feelings of loneliness and displacement. The description of the artist's studio room – with the bed in its centre – reminds one of Van Gogh's painting of his bedroom in Arles, also already described in the citation by Berger. The textual image of the protagonist, lying in the bed in the centre of this image, surrounded by a great sadness, evokes another associative connection between this lonely artist-writer in Berlin and the lonely, misunderstood artist-painter Van Gogh.

A parallel image of Van Gogh, also lying in bed, actually appears in the text twice in citations from his edited letters. The first of these images is provided by another Dutch painter in the French village Auvers, Anton Hirschig, who remembers Van Gogh in this particular situation, agonised by horrible pains (HS 110). The other letter fragment represents Van Gogh just before his death. In this piece the painter Paul Gauguin remembers the last letter that he received from his painter friend and comments: 'He shot a bullet of his revolver in his stomach and some hours later he died in his bed smoking his pipe, totally clear-headed, full of love for the art, without any hatred against others' (HS 97).[66] Despite the horrible given of blood-ridden, self-exercised violence leading to Van Gogh's death, the image provided here is more an image of bliss and peace than it is of terror and fear.

Van Gogh was well known as an eccentric, a social outsider of his time. Several of the presented quotations of responses to his person by others testify to this perception: Van Gogh was considered different, his behaviour extraordinary.[67] In 'Fahrrad auf dem Eis' Van Gogh by no means appears as a lunatic, however, nor as a character tormented by suffering. On the contrary, his letters and his voice console the nomadic protagonist, who after the death of her mother feels sad and lonely. In her specific situation this passing away of someone dear is of extra emotional impact. It confronts her with the fact that she is faraway, distant from the place that used to be home and that was in a certain way represented in its original form by the mother. A substantial part of the protagonist's identification and feelings of interrelatedness with Van Gogh depends on the situation of dis-location that they share. Both are (or feel themselves to be) a particular kind of outsiders in the story-worlds they inhabit: as visitors, as migrants, as artists. Especially this last aspect of their alterity is constitutive of their affinity: they share a talent for productive looking and communicate what they see to others by means of their art.[68] Both the intensely observing writer and the letter-writing painter manage to incorporate and sublimate their affection for the world in their artworks. Their careful – visual and verbal – seeing and observing resemble acts of affection that are mediated in and through their work.

In the specific letter that the narrative 'I' reads after the eruption of sadness caused by the loss of her mother, Van Gogh presents an atmospheric description of an Amsterdam cityscape in the setting sun.[69] He writes that this unspeakably beautiful image – '*I cannot tell you how beautiful it was there in the dusk*' (HS 78, italics in original) – brings about a particular '*mood*' ['*Stimmung*'] in which an unspeci-fied 'we' feels encouraged to speak freely.[70] Özdamar's reader does not know whom the 'we' in the fragment refers to, with whom Van Gogh begins to speak '*of all sorts of things*' (ibid.).[71] The double deixis of the narrative 'you' addresses both the narrative 'I' and the reader. In the context of the story the idea that an image can prompt people to speak about topics that they normally eschew or even avoid is important. Van Gogh's letter presents a situation in which the affective impact of an image simultaneously *disables* speech and *enables* communication. Van Gogh's letter itself, presenting this visual image in the form of a narrative image, appears in the story as a soothing voice comforting the sad protagonist. By her reading his letter aloud to herself a pseudo-dialogic situation arises in which the two given situations mingle and Van Gogh is imagined to be actually speaking to her. The phrasing that Van Gogh's voice – 'his voice' (ibid.) – helps her, constitutes a moment in which the letter transforms into the actual person by way of synecdoche.

This narrative foregrounding of Van Gogh's voice (in its sonic and soothing quality) supports the interpretation of the narrative 'we' as Van Gogh and the protagonist. In the given situation of the protagonist mourning her mother the boundary between verbal and visual images blurs. The affective intimacy between the two characters – the 'I' and Van Gogh – originates in an act of reading that results in a questioning crossing of several boundaries: the soothing voice of the text, the tears of reading, the embrace of the book and the narrative image. Again the establishment of relation, of affective connection is central. In the case of the museum guard the feeling of relation or even intersubjectivity depends on a pro-ductive way of looking. In the case of Van Gogh it is especially the mediating act of reading and the processes of visualisation in the text and in this act of reading that establish an affective intimacy. However, in both cases the dialogic aspect of the contact, the mutuality or commonality, remains part of the protagonist's story-world imagination. The intersubjective relation is – for the time being – a product of the protagonist's imagination.

The Problematic of 'Where Are You From?'

Aside these *imagined* relations the story also describes various actual encounters and moments of interaction in the story's virtual world between the protagonist and Dutch (as well as other) inhabitants of Amsterdam. The protagonist is in no way isolated in this foreign metropolis, as my discussion of her quest for contact with these non-responding figures in the text might suggest. On the contrary. She establishes friendships with several characters, two of which – with the German Rudi and the Dutch masseur Harry – are described extensively.[72] In general Amsterdam appears as a friendly *citta aperto* on the protagonist's wanderings, an open city where people spontaneously approach each other and show interest in each other's stories. She relates how several people address her and – in English – ask her for her origin: 'I went into many shops. The shopkeepers asked: "Where are you from?"' (HS 84).[73]

This repeated question reminds her of her visit to another metropolitan port, New York, and she quotes the writer Thomas Brasch, who commented: 'In New York everyone is a stranger' (ibid.).[74] She tentatively elaborates on this statement and the possible connection between a port and (ethnic) diversity: 'Seaports. New foreign people always came down the stairs of these ships. Can a city become addicted to foreign people?' (ibid.).[75] This question is immediately followed by a description of the colonial toys and household goods that Dutch children grow up with, suggesting the abundant availability of traces of the foreign in Dutch everyday life.[76] The rhetoric of the question in combination with this reference to the Dutch everydayness of the foreign suggests that Amsterdam is indeed 'addicted to the foreign'. In the text the supposition of an addiction functions as a clarification for the ethnic diversity of the Amsterdam population. At the same time it has the function to explain the recurring question about her origins.

In the protagonist's perspective – and in the story's narrative linkage of German and Dutch multiculturalism – the question predominantly carries positive connotations. It signals an open interest in non-native others and an acknowledgement of their presence by means of appellation. The welcoming and non-judging responses to her answers to this question add to this positive impression. However, the unmistakable colonial overtone of the assessed Dutch diversity complicates a solely positive interpretation of the use of the term addiction. In the postcolonial Dutch context the term also conveys a semantic dimension of violent coercion that the text certainly does not try to cover up. The predominantly positive marking of the particular question in Özdamar's story-world also contrasts with the actual Dutch context where this same question is subject to fierce critique. Especially the Dutch zmv-women's movement has taken great pains to disqualify the question about origins that it considers prejudiced and exclusionary.[77] In their contribution to the important Dutch volume *Caleidoscopische visies. De zwarte, migranten- en vluchtelingenvrouwenbeweging in Nederland* [*Kaleidoscopic Visions. The Black, Migrant and Refugee Women's Movement in the Netherlands*] (2001), Garjan Sterk and Halleh Ghorashi argue that the self-positioning is asked only of those who are perceived as not belonging, of visible or verbal Others.[78]

Despite the fact that the protagonist never explicitly answers the question by identifying herself as German, German national identity is a central theme in the story. It is the German language in particular – as an important marker of this identity – that on several occasions indirectly defines the protagonist as German. Language first figures as an explicit issue of interest, when the protagonist imagines how the bicycle on ice, in the guise of a guide and speaking in the voice of Van Gogh, suddenly asks her – in Dutch: 'Good morning. Do you speak German?' She continues – in German: 'I will run after it. "Yes"' (HS 79).[79] Both the bicycle's question and the protagonist's affirmative answer – 'ja' in the original text, denoting yes in both the German and the Dutch language – are of a strikingly simple nature. Despite the use of two different languages there is no misunderstanding. The 'ja' appears convinced and accepting: 'ja, ik spreek Duits', 'ja, ich spreche Deutsch'. Amsterdam features as a city of fluidly shifting languages.

In correspondence to a well-known Dutch characteristic – if not stereotype – several Dutch characters easily switch from one language to the other. This characteristic capacity is often taken as proof of the idea that the Dutch deem their language of little national relevance.[80] Flexibility and communication are considered more important. The protagonist experiences this linguistic flexibility in her conversations with Dutch interlocutors. They all smoothly continue the conversation in German or in several other West European languages as soon as they find out that the protagonist does not speak Dutch. For example, when she addresses two people on the street to ask for directions: 'I asked her: "What languages do you speak?" "What you want: English, German, Dutch, French, Spanish"' (HS 90).[81] In another instance she visits a book presentation and mingles with the people present. A Jewish friend introduces the protagonist to her uncle: 'He could speak German, but we talked in French. The famous football player Cruyff was also there. "Sorry, I can't speak Dutch." Cruyff said: "Let's talk German"' (HS 92).[82] On these occasions it is the German language that positions the protagonist as a member of a German national realm. Her Dutch conversation partners accept her German fluency without further ado. This uncomplicated and unconditional acceptance of 'Sevgi' as German-speaking supports the story's depiction of the Netherlands as an open, tolerant and multicultural society. In the Dutch story-world's way of thinking, ethnic diversity is represented as an accepted given, a matter of fact.

It is the German language – the protagonist's acquired second language – that confronts the protagonist with her German identity. However, when she speaks

German abroad in the Netherlands, this language proves problematically marked by the German history of fascism. In addition to the subtle, implicit example of the Jewish uncle cited above, the text offers two other instances in the story where people solicit the protagonist to speak a language other than German: 'do you only speak German, can't you speak French?' (HS 88) and 'I don't want to talk in German. Can't you speak Dutch?' (HS 106).[83] In both cases the characters who request that the conversation continues in another language have explicitly introduced themselves as being Jewish. In the conversations between the German writer-protagonist and these Jewish-Dutch characters German appears as a taboo language, scarred by the horrific history of the Holocaust. The protagonist's 'new' language, the language of her writing, turns out to resonate traumatic experiences: It is neither innocent nor ahistorical, nor is her use of it. Abroad in the Netherlands the German language loses a considerable part of the playful and quasi-naïve pleasure that she associated with it before. The confrontation urges the protagonist to reflect further on German national history, and on the powerful, traumatic implications that come with this history. Simultaneously it prompts the reader to reflect on the position of the Turkish-German population in respect to this history of their new 'homeland' (or current country of residence).[84]

For the protagonist the experience of 'being German abroad', of representing Germany abroad, constitutes a particular form of becoming German, of realising and acknowledging the multiple dimensions – both in positive and negative terms – of what it means to identify and be identified as German. The confrontational experience of becoming German in negative terms is addressed only indirectly. Several subtle references to Germany's fascist history occur throughout the text, but they address its transnational rather than its national implications. In one of these references the protagonist remembers reading the postwar novel *Und sagte kein einziges Wort* (1979) by Heinrich Böll while she was still living in Turkey. She recalls thinking: 'That country has got a drama' (HS 94).[85] Another reference concerns another Istanbul experience. As a young girl the protagonist played the role of Anne Frank in a theatre performance of Frank's famous diary. This memory is revived by the proposal of the Dutch character Christany to visit the Anne Frank Museum in Amsterdam. The German-Dutch history of Nazi occupation and the Holocaust becomes transnational history here. The Holocaust appears as an awkwardly connecting node in a shared, transnational web of memories.

Juxtaposing German and Dutch Traumas

Whereas German national history is implicitly presented as problematic – mostly through the refusal by Jewish characters to use the German language – Dutch national history is explicitly addressed as problematic by almost all the Dutch characters in the story. One after the other mentions the atrocities perpetrated by the Dutch during their dominion as a colonial power. All comment on the violent

Dutch past in ethical terms and in a self-blaming mode.[86] This preoccupation with the own role as colonial perpetrators amazes the protagonist and she addresses the topic in a conversation with one of her self-critical Dutch interlocutors: 'Christany, you know, you are already the third person in Amsterdam today who tells me about the colonial time. Sometimes this also happens in Germany. There I sometimes also hear my friends say "bloody Nazi's" three times a day' (HS 89).[87] In this comment the protagonist juxtaposes the, in her eyes, salient Dutch pose of self-blame in respect to the colonial past to the repeated instances of outspoken conviction of fascism by friends in Germany. Dutch colonialism and German fascism feature as historical contact narratives in this passage, revolving around the question of guilt.[88] In the encounter with the Turkish-German woman, the behaviour of both the Dutch and the German characters testifies to what might be called an obsession with historical guilt and self-blame. Especially the triangular constellation, linking the German and the Dutch to the Turkish-German protagonist in their expressions of affect, is interesting here. Her sole presence seems to function as a silent encouragement to address these national traumas in a self-blaming manner.[89]

The reflective eloquence of the Dutch self-blame in respect to colonialism seems to outdo the angry and upset but verbally rather insufficient German conviction of the Nazi past. The contrite Dutch attitude adds up to the strikingly positive image of Dutchness, and of Dutch men in particular, that the protagonist creates on the basis of her impressions and experiences in Amsterdam. She maintains this image despite the critical differentiations that the Dutch characters provide themselves. On several occasions she romanticises these Dutch men as gentle 'children of the water' ['Kinder vom Wasser'] (HS 82), and naïvely wonders whether they have addressed girls in foreign countries overseas in a similarly kind tone. Her conversation partners, however, keep emphasising the extremely problematic aspects of Dutch history. One of them, Christany's father who refers to himself and other Dutch, using the first-person pronoun 'we', as 'old colonialists' ['alte Kolonialisten'] (HS 86), replies to her inquiry about Dutch men's apparent gentleness as follows: 'When you think of our ancestors, they are not [gentle]. In the seventeenth century Dutch men bled dry whole colonies. I hope that now everything in Holland will intermingle' (HS 87).[90] With the previous juxtaposition of German and Dutch self-blame in mind, a discrepancy between the two becomes clear. In contemporary Germany it is unthinkable that Germans would appellate themselves as 'we old Nazis'. This discrepancy in modes of self-blame, however, is brought to the fore through juxtaposition without measurement or judgement. The Holocaust and colonialism circulate in the text as historical references that trigger distinctive, nationally specific, affective dimensions.

Another German-Dutch juxtaposition appears in the following dialogue between the protagonist and the German Rudi, one of her new male friends:

'The Dutch took their language to the colonies ages ago, that's why many foreigners speak Dutch so naturally.'
'And in Germany the German language spoken by foreigners had to go a long way, to bend, to be broken and then to stand straight again. Rudi, what was your first feeling when you came here?'
'Cold.'

'Die Holländer haben ihre Sprache vor langer Zeit in die Kolonien gebracht, deswegen sprechen viele Ausländer so selbstverständlich Holländisch.'
'Und in Deutschland mußte die deutsche Sprache, die von Ausländern gesprochen wird, einen langen Weg machen, sich biegen, gebrochen werden und wieder geradestehen. Was war dein erstes Gefühl, Rudi, als du herkamst?'
'Kälte.' (HS 95)

Several transnational connections come together in this passage. The sudden transition from the statement on German language acquisition by 'foreigners' to the personal question addressed to Rudi is striking, as there is no apparent logic connecting them. The dialogue on the Dutch and German language spoken by 'foreigners' ends in indeterminacy, juxtaposing the two statements without further comment.[91] This indeterminacy prompts readers to reflect on the statements themselves and encourages them to keep thinking about the stated historical difference between the two neighbouring countries. Rudi's answer about his first impression of the Netherlands is meaningful in this respect as it seems to hint at a particular aspect of German-Dutch relations. The one-word phrase – 'Cold' – opens up a field of ambivalence, as semantically it can refer either to the weather or to the interpersonal climate that Rudi encountered in the Netherlands. The first meteorological possibility is not very probable – although not impossible – as the German weather climate tends to be either similar or colder than that of the Netherlands, depending on the regional location. A more plausible interpretation reads Rudi's answer as an experiential reference to the negative and condescending attitude that many Dutch tend to adopt in regard to their German neighbours.[92] The abiding and vital memory of the German occupation during the Second World War, as well as the – by now diminishing – public perception in the Netherlands of Germany as hostile towards ethnic Others, continues to feed Dutch feelings of superiority toward their German neighbours.[93]

The cited dialogue, or, maybe better, the exchange of statements, both connects to and complicates this last idea. It describes the long and painful process of acquiring, 'bending and breaking' a new language.[94] Germany's 'foreigners' (still) have to go through this process that is described in strikingly forceful, almost violent terms. Rudi's contention that Dutch 'foreigners' – those from the former colonies – speak Dutch 'self-evidently' is, however, problematic. Taking the first part of the sentence into account the apparently innocent term 'self-evidently' acquires a signalling as well as a cynical function. It simultaneously obscures and highlights the violent process of 'colonial education' or, more precisely, forced assimilation to the colonial reign that sustains this fluency in the Dutch language. Again two historical dealings with Otherness – Dutch colonialism and German labour migration – are juxtaposed and connected in their implication in language coercion. In the juxtaposition of the measures of fluency of German and Dutch 'foreigners', the Dutch situation appears further advanced. The ostensibly self-evident fluency of the Dutch 'foreigners' sets the exemplary standard for the not-yet-so fluent German 'foreigners'. The structures of colonial force and violence that undergird this fluency remain implicit in the dialogue, but nevertheless resonate meaning in the larger text, as a result of the repeated gestures of self-blame by the Dutch characters.

All in all, the nomadic protagonist experiences the Netherlands as a successful multicultural society. She sketches a harmonious ethnoscape of befriended citizens, mellow and open in accordance with the Dutch landscape. A Dutch idyll of tolerance: the autochthonous Dutch father praises the Turkish girlfriend of his lesbian daughter, whose best friend is Jewish, whose partner is of Moroccan origin.[95] The self-critical statements of these very diverse Dutch characters, however, work to modify an all-too-positive image. One character after the other points out the important process of coming to terms with the traumatic aspects of the past. All insist on the enduring necessity of working through national 'misbehaviour' in respect to the ethnic – in the particular Dutch case, the colonial – Other. It is in this aspect that the repeated juxtapositions of the German and the Dutch situation resonate meaning: both nation states attempt and have difficulties with integrating histories of violence against Others into the national memory. The Holocaust, colonialism and labour migration feature in Özdamar's story, not as comparable histories, but as histories that complicate both the German and the Dutch identity in similar ways. They share their heightened discursive sensitivity.

Özdamar's protagonist is the narrative figure, or even medium, in which these histories come together. She enables both their juxtaposition and the subsequent reflection of Self and Other in a transnational frame. Like in the stories 'Mein Istanbul' and 'Mein Berlin' the protagonist's quasi-naïve narration seems to trivialise these historical moments of great complexity, for instance in the following reflection:

The men seemed so soft to me. They stood by the sea and saw that the world was large. And Germany is a forest. The colonial time had come to an end by the time they had found the way out. People say that for that reason the Germans have created colonies in their own country, the guest workers.

Mir kommen die Männer so weich vor. Sie haben am Meer gestanden und haben gesehen, daß die Welt groß ist. Und Deutschland ist ein Wald. Bis sie

den Weg raus gefunden hatten, war die Kolonialzeit vorbei. Man sagt, deswegen haben die Deutschen die Kolonien im Land selber geschaffen, die Gastarbeiter. (HS 95)[96]

The protagonist's trivialising parallelisation lends this passage a certain light and
humoristic effect, representing Germans as incapable scouts who did not manage
to find their way out of their forest 'in time'. The Dutch on the contrary, determined by their proximity to the wide horizon of the sea, had a broader vision of
the world with results that are only hinted at. The narrative juxtaposition connects
the assessment that kind and open-minded Dutch men are aware of the size of
the world to colonial history, as well as to the German forest people who – assumedly – came too late to have a share in colonialism's pie.[97] Another narrative
juxtaposition follows when guest workers are described as being colonised within
the German borders.

The protagonist, however, does not judge on these juxtapositions; she only
brings the historical references together in a suggestive and thought-stirring way.
Her trivialising combinations trigger critical reflection on both the mentioned
histories and their transnational connections. The quasi-naïve tone of narration
sort of resizes the traumatic purport of these histories and makes them thinkable
in alternative ways.[98] The protagonist's positive representation of Dutch society
and its open-to-the-world attitude functions as an extra encouragement for the
reader to imagine alternative forms of diverse, multiethnic community. The larger
text, including the self-reflective Dutch objections to any idealisation of Dutch
history, prompts wondering as well as reflection about the possibilities and the
need to acknowledge and work through the affective dimensions of traumatic
national histories in the present.

Conclusion: Storytelling as Transnational Web-Weaving

The first part of this chapter focused on the city stories 'Mein Istanbul' and 'Mein
Berlin'. In these stories Özdamar not only connects these two metropoles on the
personal cartography of her travelling protagonist's memory, but she also evokes
a multilayered web of historical transnational connections. By pointing out and
establishing several parallels between Istanbul and Berlin, the stories resist the
common divisions in East and West, Orient and Occident, and divulge these as
relative and arbitrary. The protagonist's continuous travelling exposes the boundaries of these symbolic categories of division as artificial and permeable. The notion of a symbolic separation of space in two parts reappears on city level:
whereas Istanbul appears divided in a European and an Asian part, Berlin is divided in a capitalist and a communist half. Özdamar's registering narration of
'both Berlins' and of the divided Istanbul offers a perspective that juxtaposes its

East and West or European and Asian part as complementary (instead of antagonist) counterparts of one city.

In the case of Berlin the protagonist's border-crossing activities as well as her
quasi-naïve performative establishment of unity and continuity across this border,
undermine the city's ideological East-West separation. In a wondering way, the
narrating protagonist questions the historical division in two German national
identities and puts this division up for discussion. The fact that the protagonist is
of Turkish origin is important here. As a result of her other ethnic origin she is
not automatically implicated in the German-German conflict and possesses a
freedom – spatial as well as discursive – that is extraordinary for the stories' specific time-space. The protagonist's national identification – both active and passive – appears strongly relative: situated and dependent on perspective. As a nomadic migrant she switches between Turkish, West and East German national
identities, and reflects on identity issues such as displacement and national belonging from a perspective of movement, travelling and boundary crossing. By
persevering in this switching habit, Özdamar's protagonist ultimately rejects any
fixed identity. She gives preference to transnationality as her personal, alternative
and dynamic concept of identity.

The story 'Fahrrad auf dem Eis' – as a third city story – continues the reflection
on the issues of national belonging and identity. The emphasis, however, shifts
now that the protagonist has traversed yet another national border. In this story
of Amsterdam, Dutch, German and Turkish identities appear in repeated moments of juxtaposition that punctuate the story's narration. Central in these nar-
rative-structuring juxtapositions are the affective dimensions of historical trauma
in the present of narration. These references to historical encounters with Others
intersect with the protagonist's numerous encounters with inhabitants of Amsterdam. These encounters urge her to reflect on her own position or identity in relation to these – infinitely less absolute – others. The imagination of Amsterdam as
an open-to-the-world port city – despite as well as because of its colonial history –
encourages the protagonist to think about historical as well as actual responsibilities in the maintenance of national as well as transnational community. Again
the protagonist's travelling complicates the coordinates of identity: national origin and national identification continue to shift in her trajectory of identity.

The fact that the story 'Fahrrad auf dem Eis' ends with the enigmatic letter
combination 'Tut sins' (HS 112) is significant in this respect. Although neither a
Dutch expression, nor a German, its meaning can be retrieved with (at least
superficial) knowledge of both languages: Dutch vocabulary and German pho-
netics. Via this detour 'Tut sins' is retraceable to the Dutch expression of goodbye: 'Tot ziens'. In German, the translation of the Dutch phrase 'Tot ziens' is 'Auf
Wiedersehen', or 'See you again', in English. These final words conclude the text
and simultaneously open up the future and hint at a continuation, at a repetition
of the encounter. While in the final scene in the virtual world Özdamar's protago-

nist says 'see you again' to the city of Amsterdam, on the boundary between the virtual and the actual world, the expression also involves the reader in the possibility of a reunion after the goodbye. In the larger text the hybrid expression 'Tut sins' functions as an emblematic expression for the narration's fundamental idea of relation and continuity. Like Özdamar's other stories, it encourages the imagination of transnational connection and community in past, present and future.

IV. Hafid Bouazza

'Long Live Uprooting! Long Live the Imagination!'

'Okay, I am a migrant, but it is twenty-five years later now'
(Bouazza in Heijne 2003).[1]

'In the reading of literature, one might say,
meaning is simultaneously formed and performed'
(Attridge 1999: 27).

Introduction

In 1996 the Dutch cultural press enthusiastically welcomed the literary debut of the young Moroccan-Dutch writer Bouazza: a collection of short prose titled *De voeten van Abdullah* [Abdullah's Feet]. The enthusiasm concerned not only the qualities of the literary work, but hinged at least as much on the writer's non-Dutch origin. Immediately Bouazza vehemently spoke out against ethnicised groupings and marginalising categorisations in the Dutch cultural field. As Tom Kellerhuis describes this process in a retrospective interview with Bouazza: 'Partly thanks to the good care of his mother he hadn't become a fringe group youth, but now to his own irritation he was marked with another stigma: that of national poster child for model immigrants. He was put on a pedestal of compassion' (Kellerhuis 2003).[2] According to Bouazza, Dutch publishers were looking for a Moroccan 'noble savage' and they found the man for the job in him. He, however, did not feel for this position and vehemently rejected the imposed *Moroccan* identity. Moreover, he opposed the idea that 'migrants' literature' necessarily reflected on and contributed to the Dutch multicultural society.

In its year of publication *De voeten van Abdullah* was nominated for several literary prizes and awarded the 'multicultural' E. du Perron Prize 1996.[3] The winning of the Perron Prize, which acknowledges a cultural contribution to a harmonious multiethnic society, posed a problem for Bouazza's self-positioning. In an interview with Wilma Kieskamp in the national newspaper *Trouw* he comments on his ambivalent feelings about the award that in some way also feels like an affront: 'I write because I want to write, not because I have the intention to foster more understanding between the cultures. Please leave off. And I write even less because I see myself as the interpreter of the second-generation 'allochthons'. I am not a social worker' (Bouazza in Kieskamp 1997).[4] Bouazza fiercely criticised both this assumed spokesperson position, and the commercial exoticisation and hypercorrect reception of 'migrants' literature'. In his opinion this combination has fatal consequences for the writers concerned: their non-Dutch ethnic origin overshadows the literary quality of their writing.[5] Bouazza was not alone in taking this position. Several indigenous Dutch (and Flemish) writers and critics had a similar critique of the hyped ethnicisation of Dutch literature. They, however, tended to disqualify the work in response – exactly because of its hyped appearance. They assumed that the public appreciation was solely based on the exotic character of work or writer.[6]

This chapter focuses on several moments of resistance to dominant technologies of reading in Bouazza's writing. After a more elaborate discussion of his explicit protest against the ethnicising literary reception of his work in his Book Week publication *Een beer in bontjas* [*A Bear in a Fur Coat*] (2001), it turns its attention to a more subtle literary intervention in the revised reprint of his debut *De voeten van Abdullah* (2002a). An analysis of the story 'De oversteek' ['The Crossing'], added to the story collection six years after its first appearance, shows how this 'moving' story redirects the dominant way of reading the work. As a depiction of a drama of transnational migration, it forcefully broadens the context of reading the work and urges the reader to also take the Dutch (and not only the Moroccan) dimension of the work into account. The analysis of Bouazza's celebrated novel *Paravion* ([2003] 2004d) appears in the context of his controversially discussed, provocative public interventions in the debate on Dutch multiculturality and Islam. I read Bouazza's novel against the grain and point out several of its narrative ambivalences and structural tensions. These ambivalences and tensions complicate the common but reductive reading of the novel as a referential Islam-critical statement (and a hymn to a Dutch Arcadia). Not culture, but gender, appears as the central determinant factor of human relations in *Paravion*.

Against the Biographical Fallacy of 'Migrants' Literature'

In the context of ethno-marketing and cultural commodification Bouazza (Kellerhuis 2003) kept arguing and pleading for his literary acceptance as a Dutch instead of as a migrant writer. In an interview with Willem Kuipers in the Dutch daily *de Volkskrant* he famously positioned himself as follows: 'I always say: I am a Dutch writer, because I write in the Dutch language and for that reason I have the same rights and obligations as any other Dutch writer whatsoever. (...) I am surely willing to make my contribution to a multicultural society, but only in that what I write has quality' (Bouazza in Kuipers 1998).[7] As proof of the 'Dutchness' of his literature, Bouazza repeatedly refers to the (Dutch) language of his writing as well as to the literary tradition of which he considers himself part. He suggests several literary genealogies – national and international – by positioning his work in the tradition of canonical Dutch writers as Herman Gorter and Geerten Gossaert, and of global literary icons as Vladimir Nabokov and Jorge Luis Borges. In addition to this, he criticises the reductive reception of his work and determinedly refuses a representative role as a 'model Moroccan'. In his opinion the common interpretive practice of searching for biographical traces yields only limited interpretive possibilities. His field of expertise, he stresses, is not the multicultural society, but literature.

The scattered instances of protest against the ethnicising and exoticising readings of his literature come together in the essay that Bouazza wrote for the 2001 National Book Week. The organiser of this annual event, the CPNB, invited Bouazza, partly by 'virtue' of his hyphenated identity, to offer his opinions on that year's theme – 'The Country of Origin. Writing between Two Cultures' – to a very broad audience. On this occasion Bouazza chose to ventilate his irritations about what he calls 'the topographical demarcation of his imagination' (BB 54).[8] He repeated his claim of Dutchness once again, now within the official Book Week framework. In his Book Week 'essay', titled *Een beer in bontjas* (2001), Bouazza confronts the dominant technologies of reading 'migrants' literature' in a forcefully ironic way.[9] The essay opens with the retelling of a fable about the bear in fur coat of the title. The first-person author-narrator explains the symbolic meaning of this fable: 'What the story clarifies in such a beautiful way is that identity is not a question of choice but of dominance. According to the opinion of most critics I am a Moroccan writer. But I do not believe most critics' (BB 9).[10] Here the author-narrator immediately positions himself in opposition to the common opinion that defines his authorship as Moroccan. However, in order to satisfy the exoticist desires of his readership, he nevertheless continues with an elaboration on his biographical background.

In a way this unexpected authorised version of the life story of the writer Bouazza seems an attempt to give a final answer to all questions and then be done with the topic for good. However, in offering a clearly ironic version of the writer's life story, the essay simultaneously questions its own claim of presenting 'the facts', 'verifiable history', and even 'the truth' (BB 22). Memory appears as an 'authority' that cannot be trusted. Bouazza's life story is exactly that and nothing more: *a story*. The dissociating narration effects a mode of estrangement. In looking back to his childhood the author-narrator Bouazza speaks about his younger self in a distancing third-person form. He presents his birth, for instance, as an extraordinary event that he witnessed himself. He writes: 'he is crowned with the name Hafid, Hafid Bouazza, and a writer, this writer, our writer is born' (BB 19).[11]

The ironic, and at times even cynical tone also characterises the argument that follows this life story: Bouazza's 'plea for the imagination' (BB 10) and his opposition against overly strong beliefs in the social referentiality of literature. He argues:

There is, to my taste, too much interest in the cultural, not to say, the touristy, information in foreign literature and, recently, in indigenous literature of writers who have been born abroad. Cultural identification is not necessarily the motivation for writers of this kind. At least not in the best possible situation. An oasis of homesickness is presumed to be behind every palm tree in their work, every carpet is suspected of being a flying vehicle. And when a writer situates his story somewhere else, then this is seen as a spastic deviation of the norm and people will search even more spastically for exotic traces in this new, but for the author familiar, surroundings (Find What The Forty Robbers Have Hidden) – and of course these are found, and in the meantime the spasm has changed into rigidity, a true rigor mortis.

Er is, naar mijn smaak, te veel vraag naar culturele, om niet te zeggen, toeristische, informatie in buitenlandse literatuur en de laatste tijd in inheemse literatuur van buiten het land geboren schrijvers. Culturele identificatie hoeft niet de drijfveer te zijn voor dergelijke schrijvers. In het gunstigste geval niet. Achter elke palmboom in hun werk vermoedt men wel een oase van heimwee, elk tapijt wordt ervan verdacht een vliegend vehikel te zijn. En wanneer een schrijver zijn verhaal elders situeert, dan wordt dat gezien als een krampachtige afwijking van de norm en zal er nog krampachtiger gezocht worden naar exotische sporen in deze nieuwe, maar voor de auteur vertrouwde omgeving (Vind Wat De Veertig Rovers Hebben Verborgen) – en uiteraard worden die gevonden, waarbij de krampachtigheid ondertussen in verstijving is overgegaan, een ware rigor mortis. (BB 32/33)

In this passage Bouazza addresses the tendency to substitute the general for the particular in a way that is predetermined by an ethnicising interpretive frame. Readings within this frame (mis)take any sign in the literary text for a reference to an exotic world of origin. In response to this tendency Bouazza proposes to speak about 'the time of origin' instead of about 'the place of origin' (BB 32), thus allowing and opening up a space for processes of transformation. By referring to a particular period or moment in time rather than to one fixed place, the emphasis shifts from a static to a developmental perception of origin. The 'time of origin' refers to that part of the past that was spent in another country. Moreover, the term draws the attention to the (untrustworthy) memory work that is needed to access this time, in order to describe or reflect on it.

Bouazza's essay ends in a plea for the transcultural power of the imagination that is not geographically located at all. For Bouazza the image of uprootedness becomes a figure for the dissoluteness of the imagination: 'Long live uprooting! Long live homelessness! Long live the lack of ties! Long live the imagination!' (BB 61).[12] He concludes his essay with an invitation to all readers to participate in his celebration. All are invited to enter the 'hall of mirrors of his imagination' (ibid.)

by way of reading his literary works. This last hearty but conditional welcome counts as his reply to the ethnicisation of his literature. His essay urges the reader to forget about his ethnic origin and to *read* his work in 'unconditional love' (BB 12).

Despite Bouazza's passionate plea against the biographical fallacy of 'migrants' literature' only a few literary critics actually leave his biography out of consideration in their discussion of his work. In the exceptional cases where they do not address the possible influence of his ethnic origin on his writing, then they – as I do now – take his strategies of resistance to his migrant marginalisation and to this persistent biographical interest into account. A central strategy of resistance in Bouazza's work concerns the Dutch language. Bouazza strongly criticises the disparagement and neglect of the Dutch language and culture by the average Dutch(wo)man. He claims that contrary to this, he himself loves and cares for this language, his language. In her article 'Schoonheid en betekenis. Hafid Bouazza en de grenzen van taal en verlangen' ['Beauty and Meaning. Hafid Bouazza and the Boundaries of Language and Desire'] (1997) Marita de Sterck offers a pronounced example of this strategy. She cites Bouazza as follows:

I have the impression that the Flemish literary critique appreciates my style better. To me the Flemish in general also seem better readers, they read more carefully. They also treat their language with more respect. Innovation is a good thing as long as it doesn't come at the cost of valuable traditions. The way in which the Dutch language is evolving in the Netherlands, that is something that worries me. I have the impression that the Dutch language is continually becoming impoverished. I count Dutch as my own language.

Ik heb de indruk dat de Vlaamse kritiek mijn stijl meer apprecieert. Vlamingen zijn volgens mij ook betere lezers, ze lezen nauwkeuriger. Ze gaan ook zorgvuldiger met hun taal om. Vernieuwing is goed als het niet ten koste van waardevolle tradities gaat. Hoe het Nederlands in Nederland evolueert, daar maak ik me wel zorgen over. Ik heb de indruk dat het Nederlands voortdurend verarmt. Ik beschouw het Nederlands als mijn eigen taal. (Bouazza in De Sterck 1997: 95/96)

This statement clearly testifies to Bouazza's personal fascination for the archaic dimensions of the Dutch language. The critique on the indifference of the average Dutch language user in combination with his appropriation of the language in the last sentence is extra meaningful. In Bouazza's specific ('migrant') situation, his purist attitude towards language functions as a defensive mode against migrant marginalisation. He parries this marginalisation with a self-confident critique of the alleged Dutch lack of cultural consciousness. Bouazza combines his critique with the explicated intention to counter and compensate for this negligence by literary use of the voluptuous vocabulary that the Dutch language has to offer. His appropriation of the Dutch language coincides with a claim of Dutchness.

Redirecting the Reader

In 1996 *De voeten van Abdullah*, a collection of, at that time, eight interconnected short stories, was received in a positive and welcoming way. The stories were not only praised for their light-heartedness and frivolity, their originality and humour, but also for their abundant style and language of writing. Critics praised Bouazza's rich Dutch language as extraordinary and highly original. They specifically appreciated his 'reinventions' of forgotten Dutch words and expressions.[13] This fascination for Bouazza's alienating and at the same time familiar Dutch language coincides with a fascination for the exotic world that *De voeten van Abdullah* imagines. In their praise for the collection critics make extensive use of obligatory references to the narrative tradition of Scheherazade and her stories of 1001 nights, and adopt several Orientalist tropes. They point out the stories' affirmation of the erotic quality of life in the Orient and mention that the Islamic religion and especially the laughable Islamic clergy in the story-world clearly fail in their efforts to tame the 'natural' voluptuousness of the Oriental space.[14]

Most of the reviews focus on the stories set in this 'Oriental space'.[15] They appreciate the often-absurd scenes of everyday life in the small Moroccan village of Bertollo as Bouazza's tongue-in-cheek, but nevertheless biographically based reminiscences of his Moroccan childhood. The many textual references to dates and names of biographical factuality – a character named Hafid, the writer's birthplace Bertollo, 22 October 1977 as the date of Bouazza's migration – seem to support the suggestion of referentiality and clearly constitute a strong incentive for a biographical reading.[16] Marie-Laure Ryan, however, argues – and I agree – that 'even when fiction uses names that have currency in the real world, it does not refer to real-world objects, but to their counterparts inside its own textual world' (2002: 359). Moreover, in *De voeten van Abdullah* many self-reflective and doubtful interruptions from the side of an extradiegetic narrator also work to undermine a biographical reading.

Several characteristics of *De voeten van Abdullah* effect a narrative confusion that contradicts assumptions of referentiality. First, as in the later *Een beer in bontjas*, memory is represented as selective, partial, and thus not to be trusted.[17] Second, the first-person narration shifts between and throughout the stories; the narrative 'I' is not always easily identifiable. These part-time narrators appear and reappear in various capacities: in minor and major roles, as brothers and sons, (inter)acting and observing, participating and re-telling. Third, the fact that almost all male characters – the father, the brother, the other brother, the greengrocer – in the stories are stereotypically called Abdullah and all female ones – the mother, the sister, the other sister – Fatima, adds up to the narrative confusion. These generic figures ironically resonate the actual tendency to assume a large level of sameness in the category of the ethnic Other, in this case the Moroccan-Muslim Other. Finally, the stories' magic realist elements (feet without a body, a person dissolving into a tree) as well as the many intertextual references to the powerful world of the imagination further complicate the stories' assumed referentiality.[18] However, despite these numerous signs of (narrative) unreliability, reviewers predominantly hold on to a reading of the stories as testimonies about life in Bouazza's country of origin.[19]

Reading the stories in this way, as personal memories of a migrant Other, enables the (indigenous) Dutch readers to dissociate themselves from the content of the stories and read them in a detached way, as amused but uninvolved observers. In this sense *De voeten van Abdullah* presents exotic memories of a very Other world, far away in terms of geography (Morocco), time (childhood), culture (Arab) and religion (Islam). The establishment of Otherness in the stories' reception is based on this multiple faraway-ness. The fact that the two stories located in the Netherlands are neglected by critics appears symptomatic in this respect: no review addresses the work's *Dutch* context. Its relation to or reflection on Dutchness – other than its 'hyper-Dutch' language – is completely ignored. It is this reductive frame of interpretation that Bouazza addresses in *Een beer in Bontjas*: 'What is being forgotten when people read his imaginings that take place in Morocco, is that these stories are not acquired in the country of origin, but in the country of residence' (BB 51/52).[20] Or, as Ernst van Alphen contends in his article 'Imagined Homelands': the 'act of imagining homeland identity is radically framed by the historical dimensions of the place where the imagining act takes place' (2002: 66/67).

The initial ecstatic appreciation for Bouazza's writing did not persist. After the publication of his novella *Momo* (1998b) the overwhelming enthusiasm gave way to a more critical attitude.[21] In her analysis of this novella Henriëtte Louwerse (2000) connects this decline in interest to the fact that in *Momo* Bouazza has left Morocco as theme and literary space behind.[22] In a later interview Bouazza himself comments cynically on *Momo*'s reception: 'they didn't know what to do with it, because there weren't any imams or camels in it' (Bouazza in Heijne 2003).[23] Retrospectively Ton Anbeek recapitulates the growing scepticism among reviewers after the initial hype in one confrontational question: 'What is being praised now, Bouazza's talent, or the fact that he knows more Dutch words than the average native Dutch person?' (1999: 341).[24] Anbeek himself, however, sticks to his positive opinion and distinguishes Bouazza from many other hyped and ethnicised writers: he reconfirms Bouazza's status as a promising literary talent.

The general decline of interest in Bouazza's writing strikingly coincides with a hardening of the public discourse on multiculturality in the Netherlands. The discursive phase of a happy multiculturality develops into the rhetoric of multicultural (dis)illusion. The literary field transforms correspondingly. In what follows, I will discuss two pieces of Bouazza's literary writing as two insightful instances of intervention into this transforming discourse. The following analyses scrutinise if and how these literary works intervene in and, in their particular way, also contribute to the discourse on the multicultural Netherlands.

Critical Crossings

The story 'De oversteek' ['The Crossing'] was first published in 2002 as an addition to the revised edition of Bouazza's debut *De voeten van Abdullah*. This revision not only brings up the question of what has been revised, but it also encourages reflection on possible contextual motivations and literary effects involved in the revision.[25] The work's reception, Bouazza's literary marginalisation, and his resistance to this are all crucial elements in the context of the revision. In his study of the processes of contextual anchoring, David Herman argues that fictions

> can help reshape their own contexts of reception, bringing successive groups of interpreters into closer and closer alignment with the implied reader presupposed by a text that continues to be read and reread. Part of story logic, then, is its power to create new possibilities for projection; narrative itself can work to readjust the contextual parameters in terms of which people produce and understand stories. (Herman 2002: 334)

Although Herman discusses literary works that 'work to reshape' (ibid. 336) their relation to changing contexts of reading but that remain the same themselves, his argument about story logic and the production of new possibilities of interpretation applies to the case of Bouazza's revision in an exceptional way. The actual reshaping of *De voeten van Abdullah* as collection of stories involves not only a shift of meaning caused by the added story, but it also reshapes the context of understanding for the other stories in the collection. In this sense the revision can count as a literary comment, a form of writing back, or, as the following analysis demonstrates, as an impetus to modify the common (exoticising) reading of Bouazza's literary debut.

'De oversteek' can be read as an impressively moving story in several meanings of the term. First, the story is quite literally a story about movement: it addresses the topic of migration, of desperate dislocation in the hope for a more prosperous relocation. Second, 'De oversteek' is emotionally moving in the sense that, as a highly dramatic story, it not only represents intense emotions but also arouses strong feelings of empathy in the reader. Last, in its shape as an addition to a previously otherwise structured collection, 'De oversteek' effects a reconsideration of this collection as well as of its reception. It performs an act of what Herman calls 'boundary work'.

'De oversteek' is situated in the same Moroccan landscape as most of the 1996 stories in the collection. In contrast to these stories, however, 'De oversteek' explicitly takes migration as its central theme.[26] It zooms in on a small group of people: a family consisting of a father, a mother, and their children. Soon it becomes clear that the anonymous family is about to cross the Mediterranean illegally in order to leave Morocco. With the (paid) help of a man called Tarik, a human trafficker, the family is on its way to the (European) North, hoping to enter Fortress Europe. The motivation for the family's migration remains unspoken, but the assumption that it is the hope for an improvement of its economic situation is obvious. Their apparent lack of possessions, their rather shabby appearance, as well as the anxious moment when money changes hands between father and trafficker, makes clear that these people are risking all of their possessions for the promise of a more prosperous future.

The story opens shortly before the actual crossing. The small and exhausted group of tired and hungry people arrives at the seaside, where they settle down to eat and rest before they resume the final part of their journey. This last information is provided by the two sheiks overlooking the scene from under an olive tree on a nearby hill. These sheiks are familiar characters in *De voeten van Abdullah's* Bertollo scenery.[27] They smoke their hashish pipe while lazily commenting – often in a paternalistic tone – on the happenings below. Their conversation informs the reader about the destination of the travellers. When one sheik asks 'Where are they going', the other vaguely points across the water and adds the gloomy and ambiguous reservation '[i]f they survive the miracles of this sea' (VA 146).[28] The use of the positively connotated term 'miracles' along with the doubtful 'if' generates an atmosphere of uncomfortable uncertainty. The regular casual remarks of doubt by the extradiegetic narrator further contribute to this tense atmosphere.

The reader, as it were, spends the evening before departure with these migrant-characters and more or less shares in their last hours ashore their homeland. This situation, however, does not involve any narrative intimacy. Personal details as well as the family's dreams and motives remain in the dark. The characters' anonymity prevents their subjectification as does the fact that none of them ever speaks and that they only appear as objects of focalisation by others – the extradiegetic narrator and the sheiks. A crucial scene in this respect is the moment of financial transaction between the trafficker Tarik – alternately referred to as 'the guide' or 'the leader' – and the father. Tarik summons the father to pay for the services to be performed. The father is shaken by the trafficker's request for payment at a moment when the agreed-upon destination still seems so far away from them: 'He, startled, pointed at the darkness, wanted to speak, grabbed at his breast pocket – but the leader shook his head and comforted: "Don't be afraid. Another man will fetch you. I will bring you to the boat and from there – God bless you"' (VA 147).[29] At the only moment in the text that the migrant father braces himself for a spoken reply, Tarik silences him with a nod of his head. The father remains the stereotypically speechless migrant. This moment of muting, of interrupted speech, illustrates the extreme dependence of the father and the rest of his family on the word(s) of this human trafficker. The forced silence increases both the migrants' objectification and their vulnerability as objects in this story.

Despite the fact that the narrative tone is still, as in the 'original' stories of *De voeten van Abdullah*, of a remarkable light-heartedness, this story on migration introduces a dramatic, disputably even traumatic dimension into the collection. The light-heartedness of the extradiegetic author-narrator who, in four instances, intervenes into his own narration, cannot prevent that a feeling of despair more and more overwhelms the reader. In fact, these interventions even contribute to the dramatic affect prompted by the pre-crossing story. This is the case when, for instance, the author-narrator mixes his rather distanced observations of the family's journey with retrospective remarks on his own former experiences of crossing, on his memories from after migration. He remembers travelling the same route but in the opposite direction, and presents the reader some of his impressions of this bygone experience: 'A familiar image! How often did I see such people in later times – in more comfortable circumstances, on their way to the motherland – at the side of the road resting and eating?' (VA 148).[30] By actualising these memories parallel to the family's experience of crossing, the author-narrator more or less inscribes himself into the story that he is telling.

The author-narrator emphasises the similarity between the two situations of crossing and then elaborates on what he assesses as the (only) flaw in the juxtaposition: the measure of comfort. He presents this assessment in what appears as a rather grotesque comparison: 'More comfortable in the sense that there was no fear, no illegality; the fatigue was the same' (ibid.).[31] His casual invocation of illegality as well as the death-ridden metaphor used in the previous sentence to describe some men lying on their back to repair a car – 'the neck held out like the throat of Scheherazade under the blade of the dawning morning' (ibid.) – are remarkable.[32] As indirect references to the family's situation, they work to increase the story's life-threatening atmosphere, but they hardly disturb the light-heartedness of his remembering narration. The author-narrator continues recalling the moment just before crossing, the actual parallel: the 'tantalising magic' of the now visible 'other side' and the sea as 'a thin carpet of false welcome' (VA 149).[33] The image of a 'false welcome' resonates meaning in several ways here. In the childhood memories of the author-narrator this welcome would refer to the suspicious and sceptical attitude that 'West-European Moroccans' often encountered when returning (for holiday or in terms of remigration) to the 'motherland'. At the same time it recalls the false welcome in the North that their parents encountered after crossing the Mediterranean as 'guest workers'. The most disturbing signification of the 'false welcome' concerns the story of the 'migrating' family, where it functions as a gloomy prediction. Taking the illegality of the family's crossing into account it can very well be that 'the other side' does not portend a welcome at all.

The general effect of the narrative intertwining of the two stories of crossing – at moments it is hard to distinguish between the two – is ambivalent. The image of an 'innocent' reverse crossing in a holiday caravan of former Moroccan-European migrants functions as a kind of contrasting template that initially provides the story with a hopeful perspective: the idea that one day, the family might join this caravan. Besides, the merging of the family's crossing with the daily practice of other, successful, crossings inserts their attempt into a cartography of continual global movement. This suggestion of ongoing movement has a comforting quality.

The positively expectant tone dissipates, however, as the story develops, and references to insecurity, a 'last supper', and the arbitrary power of the sea increasingly prevail.[34] Feelings of anguish rise to a climax when finally the darkness sets and the time has come to commence the actual crossing. At the beach a little rowing boat awaits the travellers. In it is the 'other man' (VA 147) that will bring the family to their final destination. His appearance fails to offer comfort to either family or reader: 'The face of the oarsman was invisible under his hood. He said nothing, just held out his hand for the money' (VA 150).[35] The hooded figure of the ferryman triggers the intertextual association of yet another mythological crossing: the crossing of the river Styx with Charon, the ferryman of the underworld. That the text mentions this ferryman waiting for his 'load' (ibid.) as a designation for his human passengers constitutes another instance of objectification, this time framed by an intertext of death. Whereas dialogic exchange in the text, for example, between the sheiks and Tarik, was already minimal before, now communication falters completely. The figure of the ferryman is enveloped in silence and the family's boarding of the boat – focalised by Tarik – occurs without further comment. The migrants approach their future in silent passivity; they put their fate in the – paid for – hands of others. The narrative imagination of that future – positive and negative, coloured by hope and despair, expectation and resignation – alternates and intermingles as the story shifts inexhaustibly from one affective register to another. This shifting gives the various crossings – between Morocco and Europe, past and future, and life and death – a dramatic indeterminacy.

The Figure of Tarik the Trafficker

The affective impact of 'De oversteek' makes the reader painfully aware of the fact that going through the Mediterranean gate that closes off Fortress Europe from Moroccan northern Africa is a terribly risky enterprise. It involves the crossing of a natural boundary – the sea – that has become highly politicised. The anonymity of the family confers the situation a certain exchangeability. The situation is representative of a whole system of illegal migration, the undercurrents of global capitalism. The text casually hints at this cartography of illegal movement:

> Against the night, the scanty leaves of the tree were visible, and over the soft chattering of the sea a black rock filled the sleeping horizon, towards which so many dreams and effort had been heading. This rock was named after the guide, Tarik, who had brought so many souls to that surly gate.

> Tegen de nacht waren de schrale bladeren van de boom zichtbaar en over het zachte kletsen van de zee vulde een zwarte rots de slapende horizon, waarnaar zo veel dromen en moeite hadden geleid. Deze rots was genoemd naar de gids Tarik, die zovele zielen naar die norse poort had geleid. (VA 147)

Again the vocabulary used for the description is extremely disturbing: it oscillates between the deceptively innocent 'soft chattering' and 'sleeping horizon' on the one hand, and the sinister 'souls' and 'surly gate' on the other. The transition from the anonymous 'crossing collective' to the character identified as Tarik is significant. This Tarik, the taciturn human trafficker who is presented as the namesake of a rock here, is of central importance to the crossing. He is the one who (in exchange for money) makes the crossing possible, and who apparently holds a key to the gate.

At an earlier stage in the story the text informs us that '[i]n his eyes there was the suspicion that his work and origin (the high north) entailed. He had learned to mistrust, not only the people who called upon him, but also the purse-weight in his bony hands – always recount' (VA 146).[36] The importance of his purse as well as his money-counting activity make clear that Tarik is a man of business, a business in which mistrust and suspicion set the terms of transaction. The bracketed mentioning of Tarik's northern origin draws the attention to his identity and prompts the question for the narrative function of this information. The combination of his northern origin with the etymology of his unmistakably Arab name makes Tarik's identity highly ambivalent. The explicit connection of the name Tarik with a Mediterranean rock points back to the eight century, to the historical figure of Tariq ibn Ziyad, the well-known Arab conqueror of the Spanish town of Toledo. Gibraltar is the rock named after this man (and obviously not after this human trafficker), a corruption of 'jabal Tariq', Tariq's mountain.[37] The legend goes that after the successful conquest of Toledo this Tariq found a mirror that reflected the whole world. An obvious interpretation reads the legend as a reference to victories still to come, a promise of a future of global dominance.

The parallels between the historical Tariq and Bouazza's Tarik are obvious. The last repeats, as it were, his homonymic predecessor's border-crossing and gate-opening acts. Whereas the first contributed to the eighth-century expansion of the Muslim-Arab empire on the Christian-European continent, the Tarik of

Bouazza's story organises contemporary 'invasions' on a much smaller scale: he enables illegal migrants to enter Fortress Europe. The etymology of the trafficker's name resonates with a deep-seated Christian-European fear that still features in contemporary public discourses: the fear for (another) takeover by Arab Muslims. However, the text undermines this (one-dimensional) reading of Tarik's character in the same moment that it suggests its possibility. Not only the already-mentioned reference to Tarik's northern origin in combination with his Arab name disturbs any simple opposition between Arab and European identity, several other indications also complicate and modulate Tarik's identity.

Striking, for instance, in the scene of the money-transaction when Tarik half-heartedly reassures the father, is Tarik's invocation of God. Taking the Moroccan context and the expectations attached to Tarik's name into account, the invocation of Allah would have seemed more obvious. Another example is the narrator's self-reflective remark that Tarik's feet are accustomed to rocky grounds: 'if I spread smooth flat ground under his feet, he would lose his balance' (VA 147).[38] Apparently Tarik, despite his northern origin, cannot cope with the green meadows of – for instance – the Netherlands. A particularly significant moment of rupture occurs when the two sheiks, overlooking the scene of departure, hospitably invite Tarik to share in their smoking of the hashish pipe. The text tells us that 'Tarik refused their pipe, preferred his own.' (VA 149).[39] In combination with the mentioning of the sheiks' rather repulsive slurping and sucking the disgusted reader can easily understand that Tarik refuses their offer. Nevertheless, in the context of the story where the two exotic sheiks stereotypically represent North African culture, Tarik's refusal to partake in the bonding smoking ritual is almost offensive. It alienates him from this culture and once again emphasises his indefinable individuality. His distrustful behaviour as well as his taciturn attitude further add to the indeterminate nature of his identity.

To describe Tarik's ambiguous identity, the concept of mimicry as a resisting practice proves useful.[40] Tarik appears as a subject of difference that, in Homi K. Bhabha's often-cited terminology, is 'almost the same but not quite' (Bhabha 1994: 86). Whereas Bhabha discusses the phenomenon of colonial mimicry, in Bouazza's story the power hierarchy involved concerns that between North Africa and North Europe, the space of origin and the space of destination in many contemporary processes of transnational migration. Tarik's figure disrupts both poles of this dichotomy: he is North African, but not quite, just as he is North European, but not quite. The text refuses a final determination of Tarik. Just as there is no textual evidence to interpret the crossing – and the world after – as either positive or negative, Tarik's identity also remains ambivalent. This ambivalence is twofold and is best explained with the distinction that Adelson proposes in respect to the interpretation of Turkish figures in Turkish-German literature of migration. She argues that 'it is important to distinguish between a "Turkish figure" as a character in a fictional text and a rhetorical figure that becomes coded in a given text as some type of Turkish cipher that propels the narrative' (Adelson 2005: 16).

In Bouazza's story Tarik functions both as central character and as rhetorical figure determining the narration. On the one hand, in his role as trafficker Tarik not only enables the desired crossing to take place, but – as a result – also makes it possible to tell its story. Similar to the figure of Jesus, he gathers his 'retinue' (VA 150) with spread arms and directs them – as central characters in the action of the story – towards (the promise of) a more prosperous future. On the other hand, Tarik as an icon of late capitalism appears as the dehumanised exploiter of the desperate, making a profit out of their desire to cross and to escape poverty. The structures of global inequality seem to leave him emotionally unaffected, as does the fate of this family. His particular character blocks communication as well as it rejects any imagination of comforting community in the story of crossing. Not only does he repudiate the sheiks and their invitation to share in their bonding, he also hinders the family's father from speaking and in this way prevents his narrative subjectification. As an ambivalent narrative figure, Tarik both propels the narrative towards the crossing prominently announced in the story's title, and simultaneously prevents the anonymous subjects of this crossing to become speaking subjects in their own story.

In the penultimate scene in which the author-narrator explicitly intervenes in the process of narration, the emotions that are brought about by the crossing-narrative vehemently erupt. Whereas the narrator actually intends to demonstrate his narrative power, the situation turns into its opposite: in the dramatic scene he has to admit his powerlessness:

They are within reach now. My light is getting brighter. See them sailing on the reefs of my lines. It is a vague rock towards which they are rowing. Gibraltar is just a stain in my memory and I can strain myself however I want, no dawn is willing to break in colours. A black cliff, the silhouette of a black cliff I see, and I would so much, with mauve and pink magic, want to erect for them a city of clouds and light: the words of welcome of hospitable places, the bright visions of new countries that sharpen the senses so much and in which everything seems so much out of place: the shadows falling on the wrong side of the streets, the trees growing from paving, it is so silent over there, the windows catching the sun that has set on the wrong side, the body renewing itself, other air filling the lungs, the blood producing other cells, the brains confusing their crosswise functioning, everything spinning, cracking, merging in a crazy kaleidoscope – all this I would want, completed with a wagon for other crossings.

Zij zijn nu binnen bereik. Mijn licht wordt steeds feller. Zie ze varen op de reven van mijn regels. Het is een vage rots waar ze heen roeien. Gibraltar is slechts een vlek in mijn geheugen en ik kan mij inspannen wat ik wil, geen zonsopgang wil in kleuren oplichten. Een zwarte klif, het silhouet van een zwarte klif zie ik en ik zou zo graag met malve en roze magie een stad van wolken en licht voor hen willen oprichten: de welkomstgroet van gastvrije oorden, de felle visioenen van nieuwe landen die de zintuigen zo scherpen en waarin alles zo misplaatst lijkt: de schaduwen vallen aan de verkeerde kant van de straten, de bomen groeien er uit plaveisel, het is er zo stil, de ramen vangen de zon op die aan de verkeerde kant is opgegaan, het lichaam hernieuwt zich, andere lucht vult de longen, het bloed maakt andere cellen aan, de hersenen verwarren hun kruislingse werking, alles tolt, scheurt, vloeit samen in een krankzinnige caleidoscoop – dit alles zou ik willen, compleet met een wagen voor andere oversteken. (VA 151)

In a phantasmatic image the author-narrator describes the 'city of clouds and lights' – both considered common characteristics of the Dutch landscape – which he would want to erect for his migrant characters. A colourful place instead of the black cliff of Gibraltar, a crazy kaleidoscope of images and experiences instead of the vague silhouette of a rock. The hallucinatory descriptions of the wished for transformative crossing – a de-rooting, regenerative sensation – present a positive experience of migration, be it in the subjunctive mood.[41] '[A]ll this I *would* want' (ibid., emphasis LM), if only I could, so the conditional phrasing suggests.[42]

That this is not the case, becomes clear from the lines that follow: 'And then a darkness swoons me, a bed of waves buries me: how long this sea journey takes, the ferryman is rowing imperturbably, patient. There is no light guiding them now' (VA 151/152).[43] The author-narrator has to acknowledge the limits of his imaginative power. His light is not strong enough and not adequate, it seems, to certify this family a safe crossing. The 'magic' needed to secure their destiny and to erect them a new home in a hospitable (European) country fails him. In this passage, the world of the imagination and the world of socio-political actuality come together. On the one hand the author-narrator confirms his position of power: 'see them sailing on the reefs of *my* lines' (VA 151, emphasis LM); without his imagination this crossing would not be represented. On the other hand the dramatic finale of the passage testifies of the limits of his imagination in respect to the harsh reality of illegally passing the Gibraltar gate to Europe. The author-narrator is able to imagine the crossing as story, but his story cannot realise the crossing as actual occurrence. His imagination does not suffice to guarantee these migrants a safe and happy ending.[44] What remains then is darkness, an indeterminate darkness. The family's story ends in the process of crossing and, despite the bad omen, holds back narrative closure.

The narration concludes with an image of dejected indeterminacy: the return of the ferryman with his empty boat in the setting of the morning sun. As there is neither textual evidence that confirms the fate feared for – the dreaded 'dead end'

– nor a reassuring hint of a happy ending, the boundary-crossing journey continues after the story has ended. In its dramatic representation of migration, the story 'De oversteek' appeals to a contemporary collective consciousness: the uncomfortable knowledge that every single night (African) migrants desperately and dangerously try to cross the Mediterranean in order to enter Fortress Europe. Although 'De oversteek' does not explicitly address this context, its story nevertheless makes these shadow sides of globalisation dawn on the reader in a daunting way. The image of Bouazza's anonymous family almost seamlessly blends with the equally anonymous and illegally migrating masses that are incidentally represented – as desperate victims, as criminals, as inanimate bodies – in media accounts of their (failed) attempts. This strong socio-political resonance as well as the story's gloomy atmosphere clearly distinguish 'De oversteek' from the other stories in the collection. It is in this sense that 'De oversteek' intervenes in the exoticising and trivialising context of reading De voeten van Abdullah.

As I have pointed out previously, the common reading of De voeten van Abdullah focused on roots instead of on routes, on the distant Moroccan past instead of on the interconnected Dutch-Moroccan past, present and future. 'De oversteek', however, cannot be read as yet another 'innocent' individual memory, but instead foregrounds this transnational context. Its mere eight pages make painfully clear that the traumatic and ongoing effort of entering Fortress Europe is not just a Moroccan or North African experience and concern. The references to an intertextual field of other experiences of migration work to underline the idea of (a shared) transnational globality. The perilous practice of crossing involves both a point of departure and one of destination, or, in cases of success, arrival. As Saskia Sassen maintains in her study Globalization and Its Discontents: Essays on the New Mobility of People and Money: 'International migrations stand at the intersection of a number of economic and geopolitical processes that link the countries involved; they are not simply the outcome of individuals in search of better opportunities' (1998: 1). The countries involved in the migration described in 'De oversteek' are Morocco in North Africa and – presumably – the Netherlands as the green country in the North.[45] These countries are connected to each other by a shared history of labour and other forms of migration, historical phenomena that occupy only a marginal position within (Dutch and Moroccan) national memory.

It is the detached positioning of the reader in the reception of De voeten van Abdullah – as interested but uninvolved observer of an exotic story-world, as reader without responsibility – that 'De oversteek' questions, and eventually disrupts. By producing a certain discomfort in the act of reading – in fact the act of witnessing a dramatic crossing – it forces its Dutch readers to reconsider their previous readings. Moreover, it prompts them to reflect on their own Dutch complicity in the story-world situations that are represented in this Dutch piece of writing. As such 'De oversteek' functions as an eye-opener, as the catalytic agent in the re-vision, the re-interpretation of De voeten van Abdullah. It successfully subverts the interpretive boundary of exoticising readings of the work, and guides the reader from a particular, culturalist blindness, to a more general, transnational insight. By bringing about this interpretive transference 'De oversteek' intervenes in its own context of reading and performs an important and impressive instance of cultural critique.

How to Acquire Dutch Authorship

In the same year that the revision of *De voeten van Abdullah* subtly intervened into its own context of reading, Bouazza himself stepped into the limelight with out-spoken opinions on socio-political issues.[46] Weary of the tone and themes of the concurrent integration debate, Bouazza changed his strategy and gave up on his self-imposed restriction to the fine arts. He contributed an unvarnished written critique of Dutch multiculturalism – more in particular: of Islamic fundamental-ism and Dutch naïveté – to the opinion page of the well-respected newspaper, NRC *Handelsblad*. In this article titled 'Nederland is blind voor moslim-extremisme' ['The Netherlands Is Blind to Muslim Extremism'] (20 February 2002), Bouazza presents himself as a whistle blower who feels he cannot remain silent any longer. His provocative intervention caused considerable public turbulence, both agreement and protest. In response to this turbulence, Bouazza published a sec-ond article in which he reaffirmed and even intensified his earlier statements: 'Moslims kwetsen Nederland' ['Muslims Hurt the Netherlands'] (2 March 2002).

In both articles Bouazza's critique is twofold. On the one hand he attacks what he sees as the failing equality between men and women in Islam in general, and the suppression of women in the name of Islamic fundamentalism in particular. On the other hand he criticises a lenient political correctness in Dutch politics and society, and warns of the 'outgrowths of the Islam' (Bouazza 2002c) that abuse the achievements of Dutch liberalism. In Bouazza's opinion the 'unprece-dented and glorious freedom of thought and development' (ibid.) that he posits as one of the most valuable characteristics of Dutch culture, is in urgent need of protection.[47] The central issues of interest in both articles concern gender rela-tions and a (supposed) lack of gender emancipation within Islam. As Bouazza expresses his pronounced opinion: 'I do not believe in emancipation with a head-scarf' (Bouazza 2002b).[48]

The novel *Paravion* is the first literary work that Bouazza published after his much-debated newspaper articles. In contrast to Bouazza's previous work – but similar to his debut – the work is praised far and wide and rapidly turns into a bestseller.[49] The novel is nominated for several important national literary prizes, among them the prominent Dutch AKO Prize 2004. In the same year the novel is awarded the prestigious Flemish 'Gouden Uil' 2004. It seems that with *Paravion* Bouazza finally leaves the migrant margin behind and arrives in the dominant Dutch literary field.[50] However, a closer look at the reviews disturbs an all-too rosy image. It makes clear that arguments referring to the literariness or aesthetic complexity of the novel play a minor role in the positive judgement. Instead, most reviewers focus on the relationship between *Paravion* and Bouazza's socio-political interventions and on the parallel import that they believe to distinguish – not completely without ground.[51]

Whereas *De voeten van Abdullah* was predominantly read as a work about an exotic Morocco, the reception of *Paravion* suggests that it is impossible to understand this novel without taking its Dutch socio-political context into account. According to most reviewers work and context are inextricably linked; the novel's insightful social referentiality appears to be its main distinction.[52] In *Paravion* Bouazza eloquently confirms his critique on the failing integration of particularly Moroccan-Dutch migrants, as well as on their backward ideas regarding gender and sexuality. From this assumed and praised concordance between Bouazza's literary and public discourse, the impression arises that it is mainly Bouazza's pronounced *extra*-literary position against Islamic fundamentalism – for the sake of the argument often equated with Islam in general – that lies at the heart of *Paravion's* 'literary' success. *Paravion* marks Bouazza's final breakthrough as a *Dutch* writer, but his newspaper interventions, so it seems, carried out the indispensable preparatory work.

Bouazza's newspaper rhetoric seamlessly fits in with the polarising public discourse of that time, signaled by Fortuyn's pre-election rise to fame. The discursive national category of 'the Dutch' appears as opposed to and threatened by its Islamic Others. The fact that Bouazza himself is of Moroccan migrant background surely adds credibility to his polarising statements. Just like Ayaan Hirsi Ali two years later, he performs from an assumed position of inside knowledge, of experiential 'truth' and authenticity.[53] Bas Heijne positions the Bouazza of that time in the rhetorical tradition of the 'new realism' that I discussed in chapter I.[54] He writes: 'After his tirades against the threat of Islamic fundamentalism on Dutch soil [Bouazza] is condemned as nest fouler, but at the same time idolised by Dutch people who hear from his mouth what they had forbidden themselves to say for such a long time' (Heijne 2003).[55] Bouazza breaks taboos that assumedly, for reasons of an ethnicised form of political correctness, are more easily broken by 'allochthons'. This is the case when he states, for instance: 'Really, I think that Islam is the worst thing that happened to the Netherlands in the last forty years' (Bouazza in Webeling 2004: 18).[56] By means of such provocative statements and positionings, Bouazza emphatically dissociates himself from the appointed image of the (counter-type) Muslim migrant male and positions himself on the Dutch side of secularised and emancipated normative manhood.[57]

In comparison with his previous positioning as 'a Dutch writer' (Kuipers 1998), Bouazza's new public performance is undoubtedly more successful in acquiring the longed for access to the closed category of Dutch authorship. Right from the start Bouazza has presented himself as a defender of Dutch literature and culture, as more Dutch than the Dutch in some ways. Bouazza's earlier warnings, how-ever, that reproached the Dutch themselves as careless keepers of their culture, received hardly as much attention as his warnings that specify the threat to Dutch culture as being of an Islamic nature. It appears that this particular hyper-Dutch presentation is only accepted and positively welcomed insofar as it coincides with the contemporary dominant discourse. In the year 2002, that involves a rejection of the Islamic Other.

A new 'differentiation' is made within the category of the migrant Other. Whereas Bouazza in his role of an emancipated and Islam-critical individual is welcomed as a constitutive part (and proof) of the open Dutch multiethnic so-ciety, the homogenised category of (professing) Muslims now comes to occupy the position of the Dutch Other. Ethnic Otherness is divided into two categories: the integrated, if not – preferably – assimilated ethnic Other who propagates the blessings of Dutch culture, and the non-integrated, absolute Other who poses a threat to Dutch liberal culture. Religion, gender and sexuality function as deter-minative and interrelated factors of differentiation. Bouazza's successful ascen-sion to Dutchness makes this discursive shift particularly clear. Nevertheless, the ethnic minority – and never the (indigenous) 'Dutch' majority – remains the cen-tral frame of reference for the positioning of the writer. Whereas the young Bouazza (of *De voeten van Abdullah*) was considered (and exoticised) as a *representa-tive* of the Moroccan migrant minority, the Bouazza of *Paravion* is now positioned as *exceptional* in respect to this same minority.

Bouazza's repeated claims that he wants to 'step into the breach for the Nether-lands' (Webeling 2004: 18) determine his public performance and seem central in the appraisal of *Paravion*.[58] In her study *Homeless Entertainment. On Hafid Bouazza's Literary Writing* Louwerse convincingly argues that '[i]n *Paravion*, Bouazza achieves a critical dislocation of the discourse he is otherwise defined by' (2007b: 177). However, the question is, who actually notices or pays attention to this skilful narrative performance of discursive dislocation, except for a reader as careful as Louwerse herself. In general, *Paravion's* structural and aesthetic complexity runs the risk of disappearing in the shadows of his public performance as a critic of Islam. In a discussion of Bouazza's oeuvre, Mohammed Benzakour concludes the following: 'Whatever eccentric figure Bouazza may represent in Dutch literature, it is predominantly his essays, his polemics, and his book and film reviews that are of great value' (2004: 316).[59] It is this deficient, one-sided appreciation of Bouazza's literary work that the following analysis of *Paravion* intends to refute. By focusing on the work's binary structure, its parodic narration and the particu-lar interference of a story of migration with an orientalised pastoral, it questions the assumption that the novel reproduces Bouazza's newspaper critique in the one-to-one way that its reception suggests. As counter-analysis it points out sev-eral irresolvable tensions and ambivalences in the novel that complicate the (re-ductive) reading of *Paravion* as a political pamphlet. It does not, however, deny the fact that Bouazza does warn of Islamic fundamentalism. His critical position towards Islamic fundamentalism and towards the Dutch handling of this danger is unabated.[60]

Paravion I: The Threat Posed by Morean Men

Bouazza's novel *Paravion* is generally considered as a parody on Moroccan-Dutch migration. Central in this reading is the migration of a group of 'Morean' men – in their caricaturisation the assumed targets of the parody – to the prosperous city 'Paravion' that is described in the first narrative thread of the novel. Although the novel contains several other substories that intersect in crucial moments, it is mainly this migration story – presented in the first and third part of the novel – that determines the novel's reception. The city Paravion is easily identified as the literary equivalent to the Dutch capital Amsterdam with the river Amstel as most blatant point of congruence. The identification of Morea as Morocco is obvious as well, although the topographical link is not explicated in the text. However, the phonetic resemblance between the two names as well as Bouazza's autobiographical connection to the country support an interpretive parallelisation. The ethnic resonance of especially Morea's second name, the medieval 'Moorlant' (PA II), land of the Moors, is significant as well. It will be discussed in the analysis of the dichotomous constellation of the two narrative spaces.[61] Significantly, the little Morean desert village where the story begins remains nameless. Its anonymity makes it exchangeable for any other Arab village in an assumedly homogenous world that is controlled by Islamic men.[62] Part I of the novel introduces the reader into this patriarchal Morean society. 'Listen' the novel opens, positioning itself in the tradition of oral epic poetry. The narrative request for attention appears over and again throughout the novel, pulling the reader into a rather confusing and enigmatic story. Sometimes it clearly addresses the novel's readers, inviting them into the story. At other times the identities of both speaker and addressee cannot be clearly determined and the address functions as a rhetorical strategy in a narrative game of confusion.[63] Literal repetitions and rewritings of passages with different characters in distinct situations further add to a feeling of disorientation.

What follows after the first 'Listen' is an ironic description of life in the little Morean village that is dominated by rather backwards and oppressive men. Life there is strictly divided according to a traditional gender hierarchy. While the women work in the fields and look after the children, the men hang around idly at the well in the village's centre. In an excited tone of voice the men exchange complaints about the shortcomings of their hard and dissatisfactory life in the village plagued by drought. The novel's extradiegetic narrator describes and comments on this daily routine in a dissociating manner:

Full of self-pity the men mumbled and they crooned the misery of their fate. What could one do about it? Look for a job maybe, someone could have said, migrate to the city or even set out on a journey, but no one said it, because no one thought it. There are people for whom patience or passivity is a kind of labour. A tiring activity even, as could be made up from the many sighs and moans that the men emitted. They had lived through busy times when they, in rainy seasons – but these seemed so far away – in the shade of blossoming almonds, lemons and olives, watched the women who, bent, some with babies in a sling on their back, worked in the field before taking care of the household afterwards.[64]

Vol zelfbeklag mompelden de mannen en ze bezongen de misère van hun lot. Wat kon je ertegen doen? Werk zoeken misschien, had iemand kunnen zeggen, naar de stad trekken of zelf een reis ondernemen, maar niemand zei het, omdat niemand het dacht. Er zijn mensen voor wie geduld of passiviteit een soort arbeid is. Een vermoeiende activiteit zelfs, zoals viel te horen aan de vele zuchten en kreunen die de mannen uitstootten. Zij hadden drukke tijden meegemaakt toen zij, in beregende seizoenen – maar die leken zo ver weg –, in de schaduw van bloeiende amandels, citroenen en olijven, de vrouwen in de gaten hielden die gebogen, sommigen met baby's in een draagzak op de rug, op het land werkten om daarna het huishouden te verzorgen. (PA 29)

Such ironic descriptions set the tone of the migration story. It is clear that it is hard to take these men, despite their self-acclaimed importance, seriously. In fact, their group behaviour – towards their wives as well as more in general – alternately invokes feelings of ridicule or repulsion on the side of the reader. The women suffering from this despicable macho behaviour on the contrary arouse a certain compassion. Their position is clearly far from enviable. In this setting, the announcement of the Morean patriarchs that they will leave the village in order to migrate to Paravion induces a sense of relief. The reader realises that with the departure of the husbands, the life of these women is likely to change: it will free them from their daily oppressors.

After the description of the laziness and the passivity of these men their decision to migrate comes rather as a surprise. It ensues from a spontaneous malignant attempt to thwart a possible escape from the hopeless poverty by the village's only (ethnic) Other man, the outsider Baba Baloek.[65] When the patriarchs find out that Baba Baloek intends to leave for Paravion, their envy culminates and a downright panic breaks out among the usually indolent men: they cannot let this happen. There is no way that Baba Baloek will be allowed to depart alone. The next day the men stupefy Baba Baloek with their spontaneous travelling plans, and even manage to depart for Paravion before he does. Expectantly the herd of Morean men embarks on their flying carpets. Their wives are left behind pregnant. Their sons are in charge now. The moment in which they euphorically take to the sky together as a group and head for Paravion is described in the following ludicrous way:[66]

> Sunlight filled their opened mouths, but could not, bright as it was, brush the yellow and brown to white. The men flew straight into the lily field of daybreak that was an anticipation of the dizzy embrace of Paravion. Paravion called and beckoned and they obeyed. Here we are! Here we are!

> Zonlicht vulde hun geopende monden, maar kon, hel als het was, de gele en bruine tandkantelen niet wit poetsen. De mannen vlogen recht in de lelievelden van de dageraad die een anticipatie was op de duizelingwekkende omarming van Paravion. Paravion riep en wenkte en zij gaven gehoor. Hier zijn wij! Hier zijn wij! (PA 31)

Full of expectations these Morean men leave their homeland behind.

A Disappointing Paravion Reality

After a narrative leap in time, the migration story continues in the third part of the novel. The men, except for Baba Baloek, whose low-quality flying carpet refused to work and has crashed on the way, have arrived and settled down in the city of Paravion. Their initial feelings of triumph have completely disappeared, though. They are disappointed instead. The image of Paravion that appeared so promising at the moment of departure, in no way matches the new world in which they live their lives now. Their positive expectations have fatally collided with disappointing experiences of Paravion 'reality', where there seems no need for, nor interest in, these Morean migrants. The men that left Morea with full confidence and a self-conscious air of victory, now gather in a small teahouse just behind the Paravion gate, where they share their feelings of disappointed frustration. The teahouse is described as a homely Morean enclave that is carefully separated from the alien and disturbing city. Its interior is decorated with Morean images and attributes that encourage the visitors to remember and idealise the homeland they left behind.

The feelings of homeliness and belonging aroused in the teahouse contrast sharply with the feelings of inappropriateness and estrangement experienced in Paravion society. The world of easy and pleasant prosperity that they expected to find there turns out a major disillusion. Instead of the life of glory they dreamt of, the migrants live a marginal life of melancholy and nostalgic longing for the past.[67] Their engagement in the new society is absolutely minimal; it remains restricted to the cashing in of their social allowances. In this situation the men conclude that this new world fails to acknowledge their Morean manhood. They reduce the experienced lack of recognition in Paravion society to a lack of ac-knowledgement of their proud Morean masculinity and of the male role that they are traditionally and 'naturally' supposed to play.

Most of the reviewers of the novel *Paravion* concur in this diagnosis, offered by the migrant men themselves: the Moreans' traditional opinions about gender re-lations on the one hand and the (sexually) licentious life in Paravion on the other are irreconcilable. The next interpretive step quasi-automatically follows in this vein: the novel *Paravion* makes clear that the traditional ideas of *Moroccan* migrants – male supremacy and female subordination – cannot be attuned to tolerant and emancipated *Dutch* liberalism. It is striking to see how Islam is brought into this argument as a determinant factor of meaning. Whereas Bouazza's imagination of the city Paravion is taken to represent a progressive Dutch culture, the novel's migrant characters from Morea come to stand for Muslim migrants, stuck in rigid ideas of male superiority and honour. Several critics argue that with the connec-tion of the two worlds by way of migration, or more specific, by migrating Mor-ean men, two cultures collide.[68] These two cultures, according to the suggestion, are not only divided by a fundamental difference in gender ideologies, but they can also be distinguished from one another on the basis of their religious, respec-tively secular, character.[69] Jeroen Vullings summarises this 'message' of *Paravion* as follows:

> Bouazza paints an easily recognisable urban universe in which the highest minarets pop up like mushrooms, in which the transferred men gaze at their new country both fascinated and full of abhorrence, in which that first genera-tion of immigrants only gets into contact with the scum of the autochthonous population: drunkards and confused people. Moreover it is a threatened uni-verse: 'The gatekeepers of Paravion had dropped off to sleep at the perimeter of the city.'

> Bouazza schetst een maar al te herkenbaar stadsuniversum waarin de hoogste minaretten als paddestoelen verrijzen, waarin de overgevlogen mannen gefas-cineerd en tegelijk vol afkeer naar hun nieuwe land kijken, waarin die eerste generatie landverhuizers slechts contact krijgt met de heffe van het autochtone volk: dronken lorren en verwarden. Het is bovendien een bedreigd westers universum: 'De poortwachters van Paravion waren tegen de singel ingedom-meld.' (Vullings 2003)

In this summarising description *Paravion's* story is read as a repetition of Bouaz-za's essayistic warnings that Dutch society is blind to the dangers threatening it. The dropping off of the Paravion guards comes to stand in for the dereliction of Dutch society. The use of the term 'recognisable' for the represented urban uni-verse directs this quasi-mimetic interpretation that, however, does not limit itself to the Paravion cityscape. The chosen formulation suggests that the mixed feelings of fascination and repulsion have a counterpart in the actual Dutch world as well, just like the very limited intercultural contact and the idea of a threatened western world. The novel, according to Vullings, offers an adequate representation of an actual situation.

Abounding textual evidence makes it impossible to deny Vullings' assessment that the feelings of the Morean men towards Paravion society are extremely contradictory. Several passages in the novel explicate the men's inner controversy in relation to the alien culture. Their observations and experiences in Paravion fling them back and forth between pleasure and desire on the one hand, and the feeling of not being part of this world, of being a mere spectator on the other. The resulting feelings of exclusion and disillusionment bring about the reversal of the initial idealisation of Paravion into its opposite: the demonisation of Paravion culture.

In a similar vein the text supports Vullings' observation that the social interaction between Moreans and Paravionans in the novel remains minimal. The sporadic interaction of some (lucky, enterprising) Moreans with the native inhabitants of the new country is strikingly limited to the female part of the Paravion population. The seldom instances of Morean-Paravionan contact consist of rather loveless sex with 'drunk' or 'confused' women whom Vullings dismisses as 'scum'. The narrator offers the following explanation for the loneliness and psychic inner conflicts that the Moreans experience in their new environment:

> It was the melancholy of an existence in a world that had evolved without them and in which their presence had lost any necessity. Or in other words: life ran its course here in a way over which they had no control. Things took other turns than they would want them to take. They had no authority, there was no recognition of their masculinity, the natural predominance of their male competence got lost here. This could not be right. How should they find alliance? Compromises were necessary for this and especially compromises corroded their being/essence. This was a world without clear distinctions and divisions. Life here ran its course against the natural and cultural hierarchy, their pride crumbled, their honour was being tested, their territory marked out. Nostalgic they were, not for the red earth of Morea, but for their position there.

> Het was de weemoed van een bestaan in een wereld die zonder hen was ontstaan en waarin hun aanwezigheid de noodzakelijkheid had verloren. Of anders gezegd: het leven verliep hier op een manier waarover zij geen zeggenschap hadden. Dingen liepen anders dan zij zouden willen. Zij hadden geen autoriteit, er was geen erkenning voor hun mannelijkheid, het natuurlijke overwicht van hun kunnen ging hier verloren. Dat kon niet goed zijn. Hoe moesten zij aansluiting vinden? Daar waren compromissen voor nodig en juist

compromissen tastten hun wezen aan. Dit was een wereld zonder duidelijke onderscheiding en afscheiding. Het leven ging hier tegen de natuurlijke en culturele hiërarchie in, hun trots brokkelde af, hun eer werd op de proef gesteld, hun territorium afgebakend. Heimwee hadden zij, niet naar de rode aarde van Morea, maar naar hun positie daar. (PA 152)

This passage makes clear that what these men miss is their 'natural' position of patriarchal power. They suffer from the different, 'loosened' gender roles in Paravion and the experienced loss of their honourable status 'as men'. Relegated to the margins of Paravion society the Moroccan men are hardly visible in public life, and when they are, it is not in the way that they would like to be, and were used to being, seen.[70] As the character known as 'the cart man' ponders to himself: '[Life in Paravion] existed outside of him and would continue to exist outside of him' (PA 168).[71] He (fore)sees his own insignificance in both present and future.

The Morean men come to feel that Paravionan women do not esteem 'their male competence' in any suitable way. Nor, the text suggests, do the Paravionan men show appropriate respect for the specific Morean manhood. In general, Paravionan males are strikingly absent from active roles in the story. They only appear as minor characters that contribute to Paravion's *couleur locale*, but whose importance to the narrative is minimal. It is significant that the only instance in which these Paravionan males – some pub regulars – actually speak, consists of a shared mockery of a Morean newcomer in their pub: '"Hey!" it was called in one voice. "There is our little Moor! Come and have a soft drink!"' (PA 187).[72] The derisive meaning of this address is lost on the Morean migrant: he lacks knowledge of the foreign Paravionan language. In incomprehension he helplessly answers the mocking comment with insecure, smiling passivity. The ridiculising attitude, however, fits in with the story's general tone of parodic narration in respect to the Morean men.[73]

The violent conclusion that these men draw from this general lack of recognition is twofold. It functions both as a reconfirmation of their patriarchal masculinity and as a symbolic preference of the Morean above the Paravionan culture. In an attempt to 'solve' their loneliness and to reconfirm their manhood, one of the Moreans, their inofficial leader the carpet salesman, proposes a drastic solution: 'It is necessary to fetch a bouquet of fresh brides, chaste of body and mind from the red mountains of Morea' (PA 183).[74] During a short stay in their home country, where the situation of the women left behind has improved considerably since the departure of the men, this plan is violently executed. The selected brides – in fact the migrants' daughters who were born nine months after their fathers' departure and since have grown up to be young women now – are the first to fall victim to their fathers' aggrieved manhood.

The mode of narration, in particular the ironic-critical focalisation that mainly restricts itself to the group of Morean migrants, strongly directs the identification process of the reader.[75] Its characterisations of the Morean protagonists have little identificatory appeal. The narrative invites the reader to snigger pityingly about the simple and disconcerted Moreans. Out of place in their new surroundings and unable to mentally adjust to the migration, they desperately hold on to what they had and what they were. The text precludes a return to the life of the past – the object of their nostalgia – as a possible way out of this situation: 'No one could survive after return to the native country. Everyone knew this. One was accepted by the soil as corpse only' (PA 143).[76] The story's ironic tone hits hard on the Moreans' marginal teahouse world and prompts the readers to dissociate themselves from these pathetic Morean creatures. In fact, these men are so ridiculous – from their teahouse to their sneezing – that reader identification or even empathy with their fate and position is strongly discouraged.

Both narrator and reader take up an intellectually and morally superior counter-position to the Moreans that – in contrast – distinguishes itself by an enlightened and emancipated (gender) moral. The novel's binary structure reinforces this rhetorical effect of oppositional Otherness. As a result of the extensive use of strongly dichotomised binaries – Morea as opposed to Paravion, men as opposed to women, teahouse as opposed to park – the counter-position overlaps with the narrative position of the men of Paravion. This Paravionan male group that as an exception is not represented by active and personalised characters, assumes an unmarked position, comparable to that which George Mosse denotes as 'normative manhood'.[77] As adversary to the Morean counter-type masculinity this normative manhood only takes shape through the negation of its opposite. Following from this derivation, Paravionan men incorporate everything that Morean men are not: they are not backward (but enlightened), not misogynous (but emancipated) and they do not live lives of failure and disappointment (but are on the contrary self-aware and successful). In general, partly as a result of their absence as individualised characters, they remain clear of the narrator's irony. In contrast to the Morean men they constitute an attractive option for identification.

It seems that the first narrative thread decisively reproduces the stereotypical dichotomies that circulate in contemporary Dutch discourse. The novel's assumed central 'message' – the incompatibility of Morean men and Paravion morals – appears simple and clear.[78] Paravion and Morea are divided by fundamental ideological differences that, according to most of the critics, can be directly retraced to cultural and especially also to religious differences. Read in this way, *Paravion* becomes Bouazza's literary warning against the threat that Arab Muslims – represented by the violent Morean patriarchs – pose to a liberal and emancipated Dutch society.

Bouazza's narrative use of stereotypes is reminiscent of what Katrin Sieg (2002) describes as the strategy of 'ethnic drag'. In her study *Ethnic Drag: Performing Race, Nation and Sexuality in West Germany* she writes: 'By caricaturing the caricatures, the artists deploy Brechtian estrangement techniques for a counteranthropology of sorts' (Sieg 2002: 26/27). This strategy, however, runs the risk of essentialism, the risk of 'authenticating the racial ideologies these figures embody' (ibid.). Bouazza's stereotypical characters in *Paravion* clearly run this risk as well. The reception of *Paravion* that seems to find referential confirmation in Bouazza's stereotypical representations raises doubt about the backfire of this risky strategy.

The motivation for the referential readings, however, cannot be solely retraced to Bouazza's literary text.[79] The assumed impact of Islam, or more precisely, Islamic fundamentalism on the characters' deeds and discourse of violence, for instance, is considerably enlarged in the reception of the novel that blends Bouazza's public persona with the narrative voice of the extradiegetic, anonymous narrator. In this sense *Paravion's* reception fits the contemporary discursive mechanism that Stuart Hall describes as follows:

> The category of 'fundamentalism', revived with new vigour somewhere between the Rushdie affair and the Gulf war, is the latest mechanism whose frontier effect is designed to keep the migrating millions on the other side of the fence. It collapses the extraordinary diversity and proliferation of difference, which is the law of globalisation into the simplifying oppositions of Western rationalism, modernity and liberal tolerance of one side, versus the retreat into the irrationalism of ethnic and religious particularism. (Hall 2005: 185)

The reception of *Paravion* turns the novel into an argument in support of this polarising discourse. Despite the fact that Islam does not play a central role in *Paravion* and that the Muslim identity of the migrants is only a minor (and later) theme in the story, the novel is instrumental to the current Dutch anti-Islamic discourse.[80] This assessment does not do away with the fact that the Morean migrants appear as violent patriarchs that – ultimately – strive for the continuation of their suppressive gender tradition in the new Paravionan environment.

The novel's parallel second narrative thread strongly aggravates the reduction of *Paravion* to a referential political pamphlet. Significantly, most reviewers paid little attention to this second substantial story. The following analysis shows how the ingenious interference of the two narrative threads complicates the offered binary pattern of identification – Moreans as opposed to Paravionans – considerably, and how it shifts the emphasis from cultural to gender difference.

Paravion II: Gendered Imaginations of Paradise

The fascinating complexity of *Paravion* – and with it the key to a more differentiated reading – lies in the parallel and unfathomable world that the novel imagines in its second narrative thread, a pastoral idyll located in the valley Abqar, nearby the Morean village.[81] This enigmatic second story opens nine months after the departure of the Morean men, with the birth of eight babies in the village: one boy and seven girls. The male baby is the son of the pale-skinned Mamoerra and the initiator of the migration, Baba Baloek. The baby boy, whose mother dies in labour, is named after his father (and grandfather): Baba Baloek, Jr.[82] He grows up to be a goatherd and plays the central role in the pastoral Abqar idyll. Every day young Baba Baloek heads for the valley in order to herd his goats there at the side of a small stream. One day this daily rhythm is suddenly disrupted. A mysterious girl – mysterious in origin, appearance and behaviour – intrudes into the herd's private territory and from that moment onwards starts to visit him regularly.[83]

Several remarks allude to the possibility that this girl is not of 'this' world, as for instance the description of her first appearance: 'How to describe her? In parts, similar to the way Baba Baloek took her in when he looked up and saw her. (...) She looked tired, seemed to have covered a long distance. She shook her limbs, smoothened her invisible wrinkles. The leaves rustled' (PA 89/90).[84] Throughout the story the girl's identity remains shrouded in mystery. Sometimes she appears to be a spectral reincarnation of the deceased Mamoerra, Baba Baloek's mother, who has returned from the realm of the dead in order to educate her son. At other times, the girl seems nothing more than another mirage, a delusion caused by the boy's awakening sexuality in combination with the desert heat. A third possibility hints at an interpretation that gains credibility in a later stage in the story: the fantastic idea of the girl as a book, or better, a girl slowly transforming into a book. In this respect the smoothing of wrinkles in the passage cited above is ambivalent, as is the use of the Dutch word *bladeren*, which can signify both the leaves of a tree and the pages of a book.

Despite all the mystification regarding her identity, the central task that the girl has committed herself to is evident. Self-assured and in clear control of the situation, she engages in the erotic education of the young goatherd, teaching him the pleasures and tricks of heterosexual lust and desire. This erotic education consists of a pleasurable praxis part – learning by doing – and a much more serious part, the accompanying instructive rhetoric. In return for the (promise of) sexual satisfaction during praxis, the girl authoritatively demands full concentration from Baba Baloek for that what she has to tell him. Her personal sexual satisfaction is subordinated to the educative process.

From the girl's decisive behaviour the impression arises that there is no time to waste, that somehow time is running out. Her educational involvement with Baba Baloek and her effort to achieve some progress in respect to his attitude and capacities as a lover seem to demand the utmost of her powers. After hours of teaching, the girl is often exhausted, all her energy gone. Her satisfaction with Baba Baloek's progress seems somehow interrelated with the state of a mysterious brew that she is preparing in a bucket filled with water and pieces of rope. The quality of the pulp that originates from this brew appears linked to the educative process. At the same time the pulp quality has an impact on the girl's own preservation that, despite her effort, looks like a rather hopeless project. The brewing ritual cannot prevent the educative involvement taking its toll and the girl's pale skin grows more and more transparent. The mystery of the scene is unfathomable and clues are scattered in various directions, leaving the reader quite lost in interpretation. In comparison to the migration story, with its (relatively) clear-cut focus as well as moral orientation, this second narrative thread remains opaque in its (moral) semantics. This might well be another reason why reviewers of *Paravion* prefer to focus on the first, well-ordered story.

The narrative tone of the valley pastoral is lyrical, the atmosphere of the presented scene erotic. The *locus amoenus* of Theocrit's bucolic romance is transposed into an exotic and mysterious Orient.[85] The depiction of the separate, private space of the valley resembles orientalist depictions of the self-contained harem. What connects the two is both the forbidden, objectifying gaze into a separate and secret eroticised space, and the suggestion of sexual availability of the female figures present in this space. Both the Abqar valley and the harem seem to contain a promise of sexual activity. Karl-Heinz Kohl describes the imagination of the harem (and its male gaze) in nineteenth-century Orientalism as follows:

To the poetic imagination of poets such as Nerval, Gautier or Baudelaire the Orient seemed to be a dream world of exaltation and ecstatic visions, of sensual delight and unheard-of dissipations. But above all it embodied the fantasy of unlimited power of the male over the female body.

Der Orient erschien der dichterischen Imagination eines Nerval, Gautier oder Baudelaire als eine Traumwelt des Rausches und ekstatischer Visionen, des Sinnengenusses und unerhörter Ausschweifungen. Vor allem aber verkörperte sich in ihm die Phantasie der grenzenlosen Macht des Mannes über den weiblichen Körper. (Kohl 1987: 360)

The description also applies to the Abqar valley scene except for the crucial fact that the positions of power are more or less turned around. The girl is far removed from being a passive erotic object, determined by a male gaze and dependent on male initiative. Her behaviour does not match the expectations of awaiting passivity attributed to a harem mistress. On the contrary, in the particular Abqar idyll the secretive male gaze remains, but is now characterised by insecurity and acquiescence. The girl takes her furtive observer by surprise and self-assuredly interrupts his desiring gaze for the sake of his sexual education. In the didactic role that the girl adapts, *she* resolutely determines the sexual course of events and subjects the goatherd to *her* sexual fantasies.[86] Whenever *his* hormones are on the verge of taking charge of their sexual intercourse, she reprimands and corrects his behaviour.

Whereas the girl's conduct breaks with the assumed traditional division of roles in the Oriental harem, it fits wonderfully well into the current debate on sexuality and Islam, more specifically on the idea that Islam constitutes an obstacle to sexual freedom and sexual diversity. This discourse claims (female) sexual liberation to be a typical achievement of the Occident, whereas it ascribes puritanism, male dominance and sexual intolerance to the (Islamic) Orient.[87] Read within this discursive framework, the centrality of the girl's desire in her encounter with the Morean goatherd and the emphasis on the satisfaction of female sexual needs in her educative programme, gains an extra semantic quality. They convey to the girl a certain emancipatory dimension in the Morean story-world that she inhabits. The novel's bucolic idyll offers an image of a hetero-erotic Orient in which a female character appears that – in a very particular meaning of the term – can be considered sexually liberated. In this sense, the valley spectacle comports with the political interest in the liberation of the Muslim woman and with the current Western desire to 'emancipate the Orient'. And although it is very debatable whether the simple reversal of positions of power and sexual gender roles in the novel's valley depiction can count as emancipation, its representation nevertheless tallies with a popular discourse whose representatives make striking use of an emancipated and liberal vocabulary. In the particular depiction of the girl as a self-confident and licentious mistress, she becomes paradigmatic for the strived-for sexual enlightenment in the Islamic world.

In the narration of the valley idyll the reader comes to occupy a voyeuristic position. The extradiegetic narrator's focalisation enables the readers to secretly witness the erotic encounters between goatherd and girl. Following the gaze directed over the goatherd's shoulder, the reader can spy on the girl who combs her mesmerising hair like an Oriental Lorelei.[88] The positive interpretation of the valley as a 'sexually emancipated' Oriental space pales, however, in comparison to the idyllic scene that appears in the girl's hair and becomes clearer with each new stroke: 'Drawing nearer, [Baba Baloek] saw that there were tableaux moving in her tresses like visions, effigies brought to delicate life. What he could discern was bizarre. All of a sudden she turned around and gave him a resounding slap on his cheek' (PA 99).[89] The slap brings Baba Baloek abruptly back from the fantastic spectacle in the girl's hair to the valley's (also already magical) here and now. Her intervention works to underline the power relations in the valley. The punishing gesture confirms the girl's position as a tutor, but simultaneously hints at a kind of motherly role.

The sudden disruption of Baba Baloek's gaze of desire intensifies the narrative tension and (erotic) expectations of the reader. The excitedly expected description of the tableaux and effigies is postponed to a later moment of secret spying. When this moment finally arrives, the image in the girl's hair proves of a paradisiacal quality:

The roosters sang of the advent of the afternoon hour and winged toddlers flew from tree to tree and loosed off golden arrows that had effect right away, as there was lovemaking on view everywhere. How these lovers spent their nights was one of the mysteries of Paravion. Under the brocade duckweed and under the crystal fountains the swimming nymphs offered a miraculous spectacle of elegant (inter)weavings and somersaults; everything started to ripple every time the girl pulled the comb through her tresses, while Baba Baloek's eyes drank up these images.

De hanen bezongen de komst van het middaguur en gevleugelde dreumesen vlogen van boom naar boom en schoten gouden pijlen af, die onmiddelijk resultaat hadden, want overal waren vrijages te bezichtigen. Hoe deze liefdesparen hun nachten doorbrachten was een van de raadselen van Paravion. Onder het brokaten kroos van de vijvers en onder de kristallen bronnen boden de zwemmende nimfen een wonderlijk schouwspel van sierlijke vervlechtingen en buitelingen; alles begon te rimpelen elke keer dat het meisje de kam door haar lokken haalde, terwijl Baba Baloeks ogen deze beelden opdronken. (PA 173/ 174)

In the continuation of the description of the tableau, a remarkable change of perspective occurs that transposes the reader back to the Morean migrants in the first narrative thread: 'In front of the entrance gate the cart man was observing this all and hidden behind shrubs were the other brothers enticing themselves full of repulsion with the vertiginous and diaphanous spectacles' (PA 175).[90]

The story about the migrants in Paravion now intersects in a remarkable way with the pastoral story set in Morea. The wonderful scene that Baba Baloek perceives – or thinks to perceive – in the hair of the mysterious girl of the valley overlaps with the scene that the migrants see from their secret viewpoint behind the fence of the city park in Paravion. The image of a pleasure garden constitutes the point of intersection between the two narrative threads. In the narrative fusion Baba Baloek, Jr. and the Morean migrants simultaneously focalise the same image: a miraculous park inhabited by nymphs, fauns, people and animals, all lovingly enjoying the pleasures of life in harmony.[91] The particular status of the image in the respective story-worlds, however, is distinct. In the Morean pastoral, the image that is set off by the mesmerising working of the girl's hair brushing, is clearly virtual: it is a spectacle image, also on the level of the story. The image is easily interpreted as a projection of Baba Baloek's desire onto the screen of the girl's hair. The scene that the Morean men secretly observe in the Paravion city park is integrated into this story as part of its story-world reality, as a story-world space that one can actually enter. This distinction is important, as it strongly determines the affects that the particular observers attach to this scene.

In the case of the Morean migrants, the experienced affects are much more ambivalent. For them the actual park spectacle represents a fascinating Paravion culture in which they, however, do not partake. The park constitutes a sharp contrast with the melancholic teahouse enclave, where the men normally spend their days. Its world of lust and liberties activates both affects of desire and of exclusion shared among the men. The secrecy that surrounds their viewpoint position underlines this sense of ambivalence. In contrast to Baba Baloek, who mostly has the opportunity to turn the (sexual) impulse of the virtual spectacle into actual sexual activity, the Morean migrants remain passive observers of an actual scene that they do not dare or allow themselves to enter. In order to cope with this disillusioning and frustrating situation, one of the migrants, again the authoritarian figure of the carpet salesman, offers a moral discourse that explains and even justifies their non-participation:

> Obviously, the park was not forbidden for Moreans, but, as the carpet salesman saw it, it was a place for the Paravionans and not proper for them, there were too many temptations and too much sinfulness. Cooling could be found there, but as you know it begins with cooling and it ends in offence.

> Het park was natuurlijk niet verboden voor Moreanen, maar zoals de tapijthandelaar het zag, was het een oord voor de Paravionezen en niet geschikt voor hen, er waren te veel verlokkingen en zondigheden. Wel was daar verkoeling te vinden, maar zoals je weet, het begint met verkoeling en eindigt in misval. (PA 168/169)

The fascinating and tempting park is resignified into a morally abject and thus forbidden cesspool of vice that is not suitable for the 'morally resistant' Moreans. In a situation of dissatisfaction the carpet salesman offers a discourse that establishes a cultural hierarchy hinging on the issue of sexuality. The migrants' patriarchal ideology that had temporarily shifted to the background during the initial excitement of migration, is reactivated here. The Paravion park now appears as a threat to the patriarchal norms and values that they nostalgically connect to a past in which their Morean manhood still guaranteed power and esteem. Anger and disappointment get the upper hand in the perception of their situation after migration. These negative sentiments become the driving forces in the divisive discourse of hate and contempt that the Morean men now assume to compensate for their hurt and disacknowledged Morean manhood.[92]

Complications: The Intersection of Culture and Gender

Again the hostile Morean discourse appears to fit in seamlessly with the gist of Bouazza's essayistic warnings for Islamic fundamentalism, a referential link foregrounded in the novel's reception. *Paravion's* Morean migrants, actual Moroccan-Dutch migrants, and Islamic fundamentalists fuse into one homogenous category that is read as a threat to Dutch society. The Paravion park where men, women, animals and other creatures all share in the (sexual) pleasures that life has to offer, is recognised and accepted without reservations as an 'adequate' synecdoche signifying a liberal and sexually liberated Dutch society under threat. The image of the paradisiacal park is put on a mimetic par with a Dutch Arcadia before the arrival of these dangerous migrant men.

Read as such, the novel *Paravion* confirms the idea of Moroccan-Dutch migration as a story of clashing cultures. This reading, however, overlooks the complex narrative constellation in which the park image appears. Both the park and the girl's hair idyll are, as I have outlined above, solely presented through the eyes of Morean men in affect-driven situations: they are marked by feelings of desire, temptation, frustration, disgust, or hate. The narrative access to the story-world scenes, whether virtual or actual, is completely dependent on Morean focalisation. The strong affective dimension that colours this dependence can hardly account for a 'truthful' mimetic image of Dutch society.

Several other 'non-conforming' passages further complicate the reduction of the novel to a story about a clash of cultures. More than to a clash of cultures, these narrative moments hint at a collision of the sexes. The novel contains two decisive moments that critically address the subordination and oppression of 'women' as a *transcultural* constant. In a depiction of a conversation between the Morean schoolmaster and Mamette, one of the female Paravionan characters, the extradiegetic narrator comments on the problems within their intercultural relationship in the following way: 'Mamette reassured him that there would not be a cultural rift gaping between them, because she understood him and his culture, but the insuperable problem appeared not of a cultural, but of a sexual kind, in the broadest sense of the word. His sexuality came into play' (PA 164).[93] The use of the verb 'appeared' functions as a sort of confirmation here. It adds an affirmative dimension to the extradiegetic narrator's description of the conversation. The narrator agrees that the problem between the schoolmaster and Mamette is neither caused by their cultural differences, nor is it a matter of religion, as several reviewers suggest. The central obstacle consists in the schoolmaster's ideas about gender relations. The combination of his own 'carefully cultivated [masculine] identity' (PA 164) and the supposition that a licentious woman such as Mamette poses a threat to this identity, obstructs a harmonious relationship.[94] Thus colliding gender norms are the primary cause of the collapse of the relationship, not the assumed incompatibility of the cultures of the two partners.

Another decisive moment that resists all-too easy culturalist interpretations occurs by the end of the novel. The girl in the valley addresses Baba Baloek, Jr. who is now about to leave the Morean village behind as well. Whereas throughout the novel the narrating voice of the girl could be more or less clearly identified as hers, in this scene this narrative stability is lost. The girl's voice becomes multiple and also the 'message' of her (rather pathetic) address is confusing and complex. The gist of her address is unequivocally sad, as her interference in the description of the park image in her hair for example indicates. All of a sudden and in a melancholic tone she comments on this image: 'Here, in this enclosed place of pleasure, all good things come together and here I would like to spend my time most of all, if I had the liberty. This place is not destined for me' (PA 171).[95] Striking elements in this text passage are the phrases 'if I had the liberty' and 'not destined for me'. The 'if' in the first remark suggests a want of freedom. The second phrase seems to indicate the existence of some overarching power that decides about the exclusion of the girl.

Such incidental remarks evolve into a sad *grande finale* shortly before the end of the novel. By that time the indications that support the interpretation of the figure of the girl as a personified configuration of a book, of textual discourse, abound. In a dramatic scene the girl is fading away, fantastically transforming into a sheet of written-upon paper, a letter, that is slowly wasting away, dissolving in the ravages of time. She gives up her desperate efforts to conserve herself by attaching new bits and pieces of recycled paper to her disintegrating body. These attempts are, as she concludes in a dejected tone, hopeless: 'There is also no point to this any longer' (PA 216).[96] The use of the denotation 'this' is ambivalent, as it concerns the conservation of her body as well as the broader context of educating Baba Baloek. Apparently the girl also gives up on this last project and dedicates her remaining powers to the address of a dumbfounded Baba Baloek.

In consideration of her earlier crisp attitude and the fact that the novel did not reveal the content of her previous lectures, her dramatic speech comes rather as a surprise:

It is over; I have nothing left to tell you. You can close your ears, the night of my silence has come. And it is a bitter night. (...) Sometimes I cannot control myself, but an imprisoned heart can never control itself. You should only know how we languish here, how I waste away. (...) Everything is moving, everything changes and transforms, except for my condition. The stream has heard my song, the canals repeat my words and echo my song, snow falls like almond blossoms in front of my eyes, the only white in my darkness. (...) A shadow without a body, a voice without a shell – that is what has become of me. My fury was justified. I have done my best, but you will become just like them, I know you will.

Het is voorbij, ik heb je niets meer te vertellen. Je kunt je oren sluiten, de nacht van mijn zwijgen is gevallen. En het is een bittere nacht. (...) Soms heb ik mijzelf niet in de hand, maar een hart in gevangenschap heeft zich nooit in de hand. Je moest eens weten hoe wij hier verkommeren, hoe ik hier verkwijn.

(...) Alles is in beweging, alles verandert en transformeert, behalve mijn toe-stand. De beek heeft mijn lied gehoord, de grachten herhalen mijn woorden en weergalmen mijn lied, sneeuw valt als amandelbloesems voor mijn ogen, het enige wit in mijn duisternis. (...) Een schaduw zonder lichaam, een stem zonder omhulsel – dat is er van mij geworden. Mijn furie was gerechtvaardigd. Ik heb mijn best gedaan, maar jij zult net zoals zij worden, dat weet ik. (PA 217/218)

The girl's whispered address that concludes with the poor comfort that she at least has raised her voice strikingly bears the signature 'Your mother, Mamoerra' (PA 218) thus fusing Baba Baloek's mother and the girl into one voice.[97] In addition to the passed away mother and the licentious girl – Madonna and whore as two cultural icons of the female – several other female voices, Morean and Para-vionan, merge in the final address. This conflation of all female characters in the first-person voice of the girl's lament supplies her words with a general relevance, if not a universal validity. The almost archetypal female voice addresses the continuation of (transcultural) gender inequality within all patriarchal systems.

The heterosexual eroticism as well as the voluptuous rule of lust and desire that initially characterised the relationship between the girl and the herd, have completely disappeared. The patriarchal (power-) division between I/girl and we/women on the one hand, and you/Baba Baloek and they/Men on the other that is brought forward in the girl's address, is of fatal consequence for the female side of the dichotomy. Her address suggests that whereas everything else is changing and transforming, the position of women remains miserable. The dramatic purport of this statement is even aggravated by the advancing dissolution of the girl. The paper girl is crumbling away, falling to pieces.

The idyll of the Abqar valley turns out to be a paradise made of or on paper; the girl herself appears to exist only as a pastoral poem. With the crumbling away of the paper girl crumbles the hope for change as well, and a future paradise for both sexes evaporates. The story ends on a rather negative, pessimistic note. The bitter female voice is doomed to silence. The prediction that Baba Baloek will become 'just like them' (PA 218), despite the effort that the girl has invested into his sexual education, adds to this disappointing prospect. He too, the sole male character in the novel who has had a taste of the only actual paradise in *Paravion's* story-world – the Morean gynocratic society that originates in the village after the departure of the oppressive men – finally chooses to leave this paradise behind. After the birth of his first offspring, traditional family life – effectuated by the young mother – comes to rule the Morean gynocracy. At the moment that a gendered domesticity relegates sexual desire to a secondary position Baba Baloek escapes the drag of daily life by heading for Paravion.[98]

The examples analysed above show some of the complex and ambiguous situations that *Paravion* also represents. *Paravion's* second story, and even more so the interference of both stories, complicates the hierarchised binary of ludicrous Moreans as opposed to unmarked Paravionans that determined the novel's first migration story. In *Paravion* cultural difference intersects with gender difference in a way that does not allow for too easy answers and interpretations. *Paravion's* narrative structure resists simplifying and homogenising assumptions about the novel's referentiality.

Conclusion: Bouazza's Flying Carpet

It seems that the celebrated novel *Paravion* has finally brought about Bouazza's acceptance as a *Dutch* writer. Both this acceptance and the positive judgement of the novel, however, appear more based on socio-political criteria than on literary ones. Bouazza's emancipated and Islam-critical positioning, particularly in respect to issues of gender and sexuality, turns out to be of determinant importance. Whereas the reception of *De voeten van Abdullah* at the time of the 1996 multicultural Book Week mainly focused on the work's Moroccan dimension, the dominant Dutch discourse on the 'multicultural drama' functions as the exclusive frame for interpretation of *Paravion*. Despite the different frames of reading, a striking similarity catches the eye. The central focus in the reception of both works is their imaginations of Otherness. *De voeten van Abdullah* was taken to represent a fascinating and exotic Otherness located in the far-away Morocco. In *Paravion* this situation has changed: the exotic Others have now arrived in the Netherlands. This shift strikingly coincides with the resignification of Otherness in public discourse. Otherness is no longer discussed in terms of cultural enrichment, but has instead come to signify cultural threat. The reception of Bouazza's literary works reflects this discursive shift: its focus moves from an Other that is *interestingly* different in *De voeten van Abdullah* to an Other that is *dangerously* different in *Paravion*.

A particular and prominent Islam-critical strain in Dutch contemporary discourse functions as a new Othering straitjacket of reading. The strongly referential reading of *Paravion* that results from this, comes to function as Bouazza's own quality flying carpet – a recurring orientalist image in the novel itself – and enables his crossing of the migrant-Dutch boundary. With his clear political statements – against the Islamic Other – Bouazza finally gains acknowledgement as a *Dutch* writer. However, as my analysis has pointed out, this success seems rather questionable. *Paravion* predominantly acquires socio-political instead of literary appreciation. Bouazza is praised and accepted as a soapbox orator rather than as a writer.[99]

V. Feridun Zaimoglu

'Here Only the Kanake Has the Say'

'He has the ambition, Zaimoglu says,
to be successful as a German author.
And adds: And that's where the fun ends'
(Gaschke 2003).[1]

'Deterritorialization, hybridization, and multiculturality
should not turn into new structures of power'
(Mosquera 1993: 91).

Introduction

This chapter focuses on a particular part of the literary work by the Turkish-German writer Feridun Zaimoglu, his 'Kanak writing'.[2] This early and, in several respects, provocative work effected Zaimoglu's public breakthrough and settled his reputation as a Kanak rebel, both in literary and non-literary circles. Besides, it (temporarily) conferred to Zaimoglu, in his role as captain of the second and third generation of disenfranchised Turkish-German migrant youth, a more or less heroic (commercial) status as the 'Kanak Che Guevarra' or as the 'Kanak Malcolm X'.[3] The grounds for comparison between Zaimoglu and these popular heroes lies in their shared histories of oppression. The analogy between Che Guevarra, Malcolm X and Feridun Zaimoglu consists in their resistance to structures of domination. In Zaimoglu's Kanak case, this resistance concerns the power structures in German society that divide and order the German population according to ethnic origin. The Kanak writing opposes the discriminatory effects of the long-standing ius sanguinis citizenship law that remained in effect until the year 2000. Additionally, it opposes the discriminatory discourse that – irrespective of issues of citizenship – divides the inhabitants of the German Republic into (visibly) 'real' and 'wanna be' Germans: German Selves and German Others. The continuing prolongation of important aspects of a racist colonial discourse in contemporary German society constitutes another object of vehement attack. As Herbert Uerlings maintains about the German situation: 'In the Federal Germany of today mainly the Turks, the largest German minority, must experience the fact that the colonial discourse has been prolonged towards the interior and beyond the age of decolonisation' (2006: 18).[4] Zaimoglu's *Kanak* literature combats these remaining colonial structures.

The imagination and propagation of *Kanak* identity is Zaimoglu's literary response to the experienced monolithic and exclusionary definition of German national identity. As such, *Kanak* identity can be considered a resistance or national counter-identity that questions and disputably even disrupts the repressive politics of representation of 'Turkish migrants' in German society. In this sense Zaimoglu's literary work shares some important characteristics with the generic category of resistance literature: 'Resistance literature calls attention to itself, and to literature in general, as a political and politicised activity. The literature of resistance sees itself furthermore as immediately and directly involved in a struggle against ascendant or dominant forms of ideological and cultural production' (Harlow 1987: 28/29).[5] In the context of globalisation and transnational mobility, *Kanak* literature contributed to the struggle against (historical and contemporary) structures of cultural imperialism in which ethnicity and national identity play determinant roles. In its local specificity, it responded to the particular German context of a transformed, post-labour migration ethnoscape. The fact that by now Zaimoglu has distanced himself from his *Kanak* writing, its aggressive purport, and his use of the term '*Kanake*' does not undo the socio-cultural impact and relevance of this work at the time of its appearance.[6] Times and the discourse on multiculturality (may) have changed, but it is beyond doubt that Zaimoglu's *Kanak* writing formed an important instigator of this change.

The first sections of this chapter introduce Zaimoglu's *Kanak* project and discuss the appearance as well as possible effects and meanings of his *Kanak* figure in the broader cultural field. They scrutinise the idea and practice of resignification as a strategy of resistance and elaborate on Zaimoglu's *Kanak* politics of position. Following to this I turn to two of Zaimoglu's literary *Kanak* works, his debut *Kanak Sprak. 24 Mißtöne vom Rande der Gesellschaft* [*Kanak Talk: 24 Voices from the Fringe of Society*] (1995) and the *Kanak* novel *Abschaum. Die wahre Geschichte des Ertan Ongun* [*Scum. The True Story of Ertan Ongun*] (1997). First, I focus on Zaimoglu's repeated claim of authenticity and on the mystifying effects that this claim brings about, for instance on the issue of authorship as well as the reception of this claim in public and academic circles is part of this investigation. Subsequently, my analysis compares the imaginations of *Kanak* identity that these two quasi-documentarist, 'authentic', writings offer. Moreover, it questions the distinctive ways in which the *Kanak* characters – the 24 interviewed *Kanaken* in *Kanak Sprak* as well as *Abschaum*'s Ertan Ongun – speak back to author-character Feridun Zaimoglu, who turns out to play an important and powerful role. By studying and comparing the several *Kanak* discourses in these two works, the chapter offers insight into the particular narrative strategies that sustain these *Kanak* identities and simultaneously constitute the reader in an ethnicising way.

Representing the Kanak Margin

The year 1995 marks the beginning of the popular *Kanak* history. In that year a newcomer to the German cultural field, Feridun Zaimoglu, published his best-selling work *Kanak Sprak, 24 Mißtöne vom Rande der Gesellschaft*. This debut, a collection of 24 interview 'protocols' (KS 15), not only made Zaimoglu simultaneously famous and notorious, it also instigated what I call the larger 'Kanak phenomenon'.[7] This *Kanak* phenomenon comprehends a variety of social and cultural effects largely brought about by the extensive media coverage – if not hype – that followed *Kanak Sprak's* first appearance. Central to this phenomenon is the figure of the *Kanake* as it is (re-)imagined and introduced by Zaimoglu's *Kanak Sprak*.

In the original contemporary German context the term *Kanake* is an ethnic slur from the same league of racist epithets as 'Bimbo', 'Fidschi' and 'Kümmel' (the last mentioned by Zaimoglu in *Kanak Sprak's* preface as a synonym to *Kanake*). These terms, despite their well-known injurious value, have common currency in popular discourse. They are used derogatorily to refer to those groups of people that are considered culturally, biologically and/or ethnically inferior, in particular men of Turkish or Arab origin.[8] Whereas scholars agree about the origin of the term in the region of the South Sea, the appearance of *Kanake* as a hate speech term in German discourse causes some difference of opinion. Adelson points out that it is unclear how the term in the German context 'became associated with Turks (meant to be disparaged by the term)' (2005: 193 n. 51). Gerhardt and Link (1991: 147) suspect the term to be an amalgamation of anti-Slavic denotations as 'Kosaken' and 'Polacken' mixed with the racist-colonial myth of 'cannibals'. Pfaff (2005) retraces the appearance of the term in German discourse back to Germany's colonial period. She locates its origin in the colonies in the Bismarck Archipelago where the term 'Kanakas' signified the indigenous population. This last explanation connects the contemporary hate speech meaning of the term to the racist discourse of colonial domination. Annette Seidel-Arpacı (2003) also subscribes to this colonial origin of the term. She reflects on possible explanations for the temporary disappearance of the term after the loss of the colonies and its reappearance as pejorative for ethnic Others after 1945.

Whereas the everyday usage of the epithet discursively activates a variety of negative connotations, Zaimoglu's *Kanak Sprak* more or less successfully appropriates and re-signifies the hate speech term in a way that is reminiscent of resignifications of terms like *gay* and *queer*. Zaimoglu's work makes effective use of what Judith Butler calls the 'possibility for a counter-speech' (1997: 15) that originates in the open temporality of the hate speech act.[9] In her work *Excitable Speech. A Politics of the Performative* she writes: 'The interval between instances of utterance not only makes the repetition and resignification of the utterance possible, but shows how words might, through time, become disjoined from their power to injure and recontextualized in more affirmative modes' (Butler 1997: 15). The term 'affirmative', Butler explains, is linked here to an opening up of the possibility of agency for the subjects made into objects by the hate speech term. Hate speech constitutes these subjects in subordinate positions by the act of interpellation as laid out by Althusser (1971).[10] Central in this interpellative act are the operation of reiteration as well as the citational dimension of the speech act, 'the historicity of convention that exceeds and enables the moment of its enunciation' (Butler 1997: 33). In other words, the injurious impact of the repetition of a certain hate speech term – like, for instance, *Kanake* – exceeds the moment of utterance. The utterance of the term invokes and reconsolidates a larger encoded (traumatic) history.

It is this citational dimension of the hate speech term that not only determines its injurious quality, but that also opens up a space of possibility for its resignification. By using the terms in innovative and unconventional ways in unconventional contexts, a new field of signification is opened up in which new meanings can be produced. This process implies a risk, however, in the sense that a repetition of the hate speech term – and possibly a repetition of its injurious effects – is inevitable. In her essay 'The Question of Social Transformation' (2004) Butler returns to this risk of resignification. Here she asks the question *if*, and if yes, *how* resignification works or might work as a politics in the service of social justice for disenfranchised communities – a question that is particularly relevant for the '*Kanak* case'. Her answer concentrates on the insufficiency – and thus hindrance – of established norms and conventions (as universality, a 'viable life', and politics):[11]

> For the purpose of a radical democratic transformation, we need to know that our fundamental categories can and must be expanded to become more inclusive and more responsive to the full range of cultural populations. (...) It means that the category itself must be subjected to a reworking from myriad directions, that it must emerge anew as a result of the cultural translations it undergoes. (Butler 2004: 223/224)

Zaimoglu's *Kanak Sprak* constituted the literary kick-off for a similar reworking: 'KanakAttack: Rebellion der Minderheiten' ['KanakAttack: Rebellion of Minorities'] (Zaimoglu 2001: 8). It opened up the transformative contest over the power and the patterns of exclusion that work through the hate speech term *Kanake*.

In *Kanak Sprak* the hate speech term *Kanake* is re-adapted as a proud signifier for a Turkish-German group identity. The active and self-assured appropriation of the racist epithet functions as a self-interpellative move. This move is not only followed by the interviewed *Kanaken* in *Kanak Sprak's* story-world, but has also found adaptation by migrant youth in the actual world. The fact that, as Zaimoglu stresses in the preface, in *Kanak Sprak* it is not the indigenous German majority that is using this hate speech to objectify an ethnic Other but the objectified *Ka-*

nake himself, changes the tone, frame and meaning of the devaluative marker. As Jürgen Wertheimer summarises this project: 'Shame turns into demonstration, deficiency into provocation: one is proud of being a stranger' (2002: 132).[12] The appropriating repetition of the epithet by the *Kanake* himself redresses its meaning from a passive one – a specific social minority group being labelled and muted by the term – into an active one – countering the speech violence as well as reshaping the signified. The speech act – effectively repeated in all protocols – impels a semantic shift that opens up a space for self-definition and even identity politics.[13] In name of the *Kanaken* the author-character and preface-narrator Zaimoglu claims a position of discursive power. He states: 'Kanake! This defamatory cussword turns into an identifying password, a connecting link of this "ethnic rabble"' (KS 17).[14] Read in the light of the appropriating procedure this statement gains the quality of a battle cry and functions as prediction, encouragement and speech-act at one and the same time.

With the publication of *Kanak Sprak* Zaimoglu claims to put a lost generation into the German public picture: young males of Turkish origin living in the German Republic. Zaimoglu maintains that these disacknowledged male youngsters, with or without German citizenship, are hardly visible in their position at the fringe of society. In the seldom cases that society perceives of them, they appear as outsiders, outcasts, and as ciphers of the social abject. In her work *Bodies That Matter: On the Discursive Limits of 'Sex'* (1993) Butler defines the abject as 'precisely those "unlivable" and "uninhabitable" zones of social life which are nevertheless densely populated by those who do not enjoy the status of the subject, but whose living under the sign of the "unlivable" is required to circumscribe the domain of the subject' (1993: 3). The *Kanak* abject appears as the constitutive outside of the indigenous German subject. The objectified *Kanaken* appear as the products of particular structures of marginalisation and dominance. As Klaus-Michael Bogdal assesses: 'The "Kanake" approaches the "German" reader as the Doppelgänger of his own prejudices just like Frankenstein. You created me: here I am!' (2000: 229).[15] The reasons for the *Kanake's* social, physical, and rhetorical marginalisation are multiple. A central determinant, however, is the other ethnic origin, mostly in intersection with gender and class.

In *Kanak Sprak*, Zaimoglu's resignification of the hate speech term *Kanake* coincides with a resignification of this abject margin.[16] While the derogatory marker of identity changes its affective semantics, also the margin is resignified from a site of oppression and deprivation into a site of resistance and pride. In her essay 'Choosing the Margin as a Space of Radical Openness' (1990) bell hooks points at the empowering qualities of a reconceptualisation of this margin as a space of resistance. She writes:

> It was this marginality that I was naming as a central location for the production of a counter-hegemonic discourse that is not just found in words but in

habits of being and the way one lives. As such, I was not speaking of a marginality one wishes to lose – to give up or surrender as part of moving into the center – but rather of a site one stays in, clings to even, because it nourishes one's capacity to resist. It offers to one the possibility of radical perspective from which to see and create, to imagine alternatives, new worlds. (hooks 1990: 149/150)

hooks pleads for a reappreciation of marginality as a position that produces a particular critical perspective. Marginality, she insists, enables the imagination of alternative worlds and communities, away from socially imposed norms and standards. *Kanak Sprak* acts up to hooks' appeal. The 'lived experience' of marginality becomes the source of resistance to a defining centre. The *Kanake* and his *Kanak* margin appear as loci of a radical and challenging perspective.

In the literary *Kanak* works that appeared after the successful *Kanak Sprak*, Zaimoglu persisted in this radical perspective as well as in its aggressive tone of voice. Commercially hailed as a kind of 'native informant', the reader's guide to the *Kanak* underworld, he kept up this role in the works that followed. In 1997 he published a quasi-biographical *Kanak* novel titled *Abschaum*, about the true (and sad) story of the small time Turkish-German criminal Ertan Ongun. One year later this work was followed by a second collection of protocols titled *Koppstoff: Kanaka Sprak vom Rande der Gesellschaft* [*Head Stuff. Kanaka Talk from the Fringe of Society*] (1998b). As the counterpart of *Kanak Sprak* this work records interviews with 26 female *Kanakstas*. In 2000 director Lars Becker used the material of *Abschaum* for the film *Kanak Attack!* featuring Luke Piyes in the role of Ertan. Six years after his debut Zaimoglu published the last work to date that he explicitly labelled as *Kanak* writing: *Kopf und Kragen. Kanak-Kultur-Kompendium* [*Head and Neck. Kanak Culture Compendium*] (2001).

The 'Market of Finding Identity' or Catering to the Reader

It is quite amazing how the aggressive and at times even offensive discourse that characterises *Kanak Sprak* has managed to entice a mass German readership that, assumedly, is predominantly of German ethnic origin. *Aleman*-bashing and contemptuous descriptions of the German male and his 'little wife' ['Weiblein'] are part and parcel of the literary *Kanak* performance, but this does not impede a broad public interest – on the contrary.[17] The exact reasons for this success are difficult to determine, as a variety of factors intersect in the *Kanak* phenomenon: the literary work, Zaimoglu's public performances, the *Kanak Attak* network, and *Kanak* manifestations, to name just a few.[18] *Kanak Sprak*, Zaimoglu, and the two of them taken together, position themselves in the cultural field and in the public sphere in a number of ways.

First, the work *Kanak Sprak* caters to a certain interest and curiosity on the side of the German reader in respect to the *Kanak* Other. It ties in with a popular discourse on the shadow sides of multiculturalisation.[19] Central to this discourse are worries, anger and fears about the strong correlation between unemployment, school dropout and criminality on the one hand, and a migrant background on the other. Turkish males in particular appear as iconic subjects of these statistics. While the print media and television discuss the development of an ethnic under-class in alarming terms, to a major part of the German population, this under-class remains virtually invisible in daily life. *Kanak Sprak* promises insight in this hidden and closed-off world at Germany's fringe. It introduces the male young-sters who feature so prominently in these worrying statistics, but who remain mostly anonymous and silent themselves. *Kanak Sprak* offers the German reader an armchair-traveller's introduction to these *Kanaken*: meet the underdog in his authentic and unpolished form. The *Kanak* language functions as a distinctive marker of authenticity and in addition underlines the *Kanaken's* (exotic) difference. This *Kanak* talk is very much an attitudinal language, provocatively signifying pride as well as indifference to dominant society. The represented *Kanaken* talk straight from the shoulder and so does their quasi-creator Zaimoglu, who claims to speak in their name. In this way *Kanak* talk also functions as a way to empha-sise the difference and to hold the reader at bay.[20]

In prose collections such as *Kanaksta. Geschichten von deutschen und anderen Auslän-dern [Stories from German and Other Foreigners]* (Lottmann 1999) and *Morgen Land. Neueste deutsche Literatur [Tomorrow/Morning Land. Newest German Literature]* (Tuschick 2000b) various writers besides Zaimoglu present themselves and their work under the *Kanak* label. With appealing slogans as 'Welcome to Kanakistan', 'You are Kanaksta, when you are on to Germany' and 'When they are too strange, you are too German' they invite the reader to join this *Kanak* collective as well.[21] Both publications open with programmatic introductory texts written by Zaimoglu in 'Kanak language' (Zaimoglu 1999a; Zaimoglu and Tuschick 2000). These pamph-lets combatively announce the *Kanak* advance and its radical innovatory impulse for the German, *Aleman*-dominated cultural field. In the *Kanaksta* collection, Joan Kristin Bleicher (1999: 86-93) presents an overview of the transformation of the German cultural field, brought about by literature of migration. She describes this transformation 'in the culture business' as follows: 'Now new voices can be heard in literature, the voices of the migrants of the second and third generation. They do without the principle of integration and seek their identity in a self-chosen, aggressive segregation: "Kanak Attack"' (Bleicher 1999: 86).[22] In the article's spe-cific context it is clear that Bleicher is not referring to Zaimoglu's literary *Kanak* figures as the new voices that finally speak up. She alludes to the new writers that publish their work in manifesto-like collections like the one to which she is con-tributing: these writers are the new *Kanakstas*. The writer-*Kanakstas* and Zaimoglu's original *Kanak* characters conflate into one species in the identity offensive labelled '*Kanak* attack'.

A Provocative Politics of Position

Whereas in the case of the *Kanak* characters the object under attack is clearly German society and its exclusionary structures, these writers – with Zaimoglu in the frontline – expand their targets of anger. On the one hand they rebuke the German cultural field for its appropriating and instrumentalising practices. On the other hand they reject their literary parents (mostly their fathers, epitomised in the generic figure 'Ali') in provocative terms. In Bleicher's article the literature of this first generation of migrant writers is contemptuously re-labelled as 'victim literature' (Bleicher 1999: 87). Zaimoglu himself initiated this 'father-offensive' trend. Already in the preface to *Kanak Sprak* he explicates his loathing for the writing of the first generation. He speaks of '[a] whimpering, insinuating, publicly supported "guest worker literature"' and pejoratively labels this literature 'dustman prose' ['Müllkutscher-Prosa'] (KS 12).[23]

In the programmatic, polemical piece 'Gastarbeiterliteratur. Ali macht Männchen' ['Guest Worker Literature. Ali Is Grovelling'] (1998) Zaimoglu repeats his provocative repudiations in an even more offensive manner. [24] The text opens with the aggressive speech act announcement that 'this writing is an act of combat' (Zaimoglu 1998a: 85) and concludes with the dismissive statement 'you are through, motherfuckers!' (ibid. 97).[25] The piece functions as a performative act of Oedipal killing. Both the literary fathers and their poetical programme are dismissed in the following hate speech representation:

> he is an emotionally driven Ali poet, a fucking bashed about social sculpture: you put it somewhere, it mustn't move a bit, it is art alibi for 'mültikülti' and a hurdy-gurdy that only whimpers, when you turn the crank, to take a tone that is prescribed to him, of pissing metaphors like forest like tree like pigeon to struggle for a luxury intimacy, that I call the Ali poet's programme.

> er isn alipoet mit emotionsantrieb; eine beschissene ramponierte sozialplastik: die stellt man irgendwo hin, die darf sich nixs bewegen, die is kunstalibi für mültikülti und ne drehorgel, wo die nur winselt, wenn man an der kurbel dreht, ein ton zu geben, die ihm vorgegeben is, aus brunzenden metaphern wie wald wie baum wie taube ne luxus-innigkeit zu erhampeln, das nenn ich programm des alipoeten. (Zaimoglu 1998a: 87)

Distinct from earlier literary manifestos by first generation writers as Schami (1981, 1986), Biondi (1981) and Pazarkaya (1986) Zaimoglu presents his poetical positioning. Central is the rejection of 'guest worker literature's' supposed

NEW GERMANS, NEW DUTCH

authenticity. According to Zaimoglu, authenticity has become both the label and interpretive key for the literature of society's migrant Other. This literature is rarely judged on the basis of its literary merits: its assumed quality depends on the affective dimensions of the descriptions of authentic experiences.[26]

That Zaimoglu's rather one-sided and undifferentiated classification of the literature of first generation migrants has been quite effective can be seen in Wertheimer's 2002 article on 'the new tone of younger authors of migration', in particular Zaimoglu's *Kanak Sprak*. Wertheimer accepts and confirms Zaimoglu's representation of 'guest worker literature' when he writes: 'The new generation of German writers of Turkish origin does not seem to suffer any longer. They have stopped lamenting and shedding tears over the loss of their mother country, their original culture, their native language, etc.' (2002: 130).[27] He almost literally repeats Zaimoglu's description when he dismisses the writing of the first generation as literature 'that produced and supported pseudo-authentic and sentimental emotions, that started from a non-existent solidarity, that revelled in false nostalgia and that sold fake exoticism' (ibid. 131).[28] Wertheimer's representation of the new generation of Turkish-German writers endorses the binary opposition invoked by Zaimoglu without further contextualisation or questioning of this classification.[29]

Wertheimer is not the only one who accepts Zaimoglu's contemptuous polarisation and agrees on the idea of rupture and absolute difference between the works of the successive generations. However, contrary to this assumed black and white depiction, Zaimoglu's political-poetical program and the (ascribed) poetics of 'guest worker literature' actually share a basic assumption. Like Bleicher, Wertheimer asserts that protagonists in 'guest worker literature' are generally represented as 'victims of German culture' (Wertheimer 2002: 131). This same assertion applies to Zaimoglu's *Kanak* work: also Zaimoglu's *Kanaken* appear as victims of German society. The difference between the *Kanaken* and their guest worker fathers is their declared resistance to this victimisation. Under Zaimoglu's command the first lodge a complaint against the social structures that cause their determination as victim.

In general, the 'Turkish Oedipal drama' has a high entertainment value. The reader attends a performative fight that confirms quite some cultural fables about the angry Turk and his merciless violence. Reading Zaimoglu – both his work and his public performances – means attending provocation and witnessing conflict. Zaimoglu's separatist poetics not only implies the patricide discussed above, it also comprehends a fierce dissociation from the contemporary *Popliteratur* scene. On the basis of literary and commercial characteristics, critics and scholars regularly group Zaimoglu in one league with writers as Rainald Goetz, Thomas Meinecke, Benjamin von Stuckrad-Barre and Christian Kracht.[30] In an article in *Die Zeit* Zaimoglu explicitly resists this categorisation and rejects the 'German Popliteratur' as 'Boys' diaper prose' ['Knabenwindelprosa'] and 'reactionary handicraft' ['reaktionäres Kunsthandwerk'] (Zaimoglu 1999b). The article's subtitle – 'A Clearing' ['Eine Abrechnung'] – leaves no doubt about Zaimoglu's stake. He sees a central distinction in respect to both poetical programme and attitude.[31]

In an interview with Johannes Ullmaier, Zaimoglu points out the raw acuteness of his writing: 'I deliver the ruptures, the ugliness, the filthiness, everything that the lukewarm middle-class-neurosis-scribble of German literature – especially *Pop* literature – does not contain' (Zaimoglu in Ullmaier 2001: 133).[32] In opposition to the happy toddlers and carefree schoolboys of *Pop*, Zaimoglu performs an angry hypermasculine pose. He opposes the faded and unmanly *Pop*-writing with his fearful representations of a virile *Kanak* abject and with aggressive claims for social justice.

Strongly gendered virtues such as honour and pride are central features in these literary performances of *Kanak* attitude and masculine power. In this sense both Zaimoglu and his *Kanaken* confirm the thesis by Britta Herrmann and Walter Erhart that 'the model of the Boxer' (2002: 46) reappears on the literary scene of the 1990s: 'At the end of the twentieth century true masculinity steel-plates itself again, rhetorically at least' (ibid. 47).[33] Indirectly the two scholars offer a possible explanation for the popularity of the *Kanak* figure and his hypermasculinity. In their opinion the presentation of particular, socially unaccepted masculinities *as spectacle* allows for their delightful consumption without the fear of social consequences. Such performances accommodate a 'social need' (ibid. 37). Whereas their article concerns performances of specific non-hegemonic masculinities, I think the argument also applies to the performance of *Kanak* hypermasculinity. The *Kanake's* performance of ultra-macho behaviour exposes a contemporary social taboo in a safely consumable form. His emphasised ethnic difference – a result of his 'self-Kanakisation' (Ha 2005: 113-116) – provides an extra guarantee of safety for the non-*Kanak* audience. At the same time this ethnic identity also functions as a justification for this behaviour. In *Kanak Sprak* a *Kanake* postulates: 'We, on the contrary, have nothing but our bollocks to lose' (AB 23).[34]

All in all, many of the popular aspects of *Kanak Sprak* and the subsequent *Kanak* phenomenon seem to satisfy several taboo desires of mainstream culture. They promise access to the world of the social abject in which absolute difference is emphasised as well as celebrated. In the performance of this absolute Otherness, the *Kanak* spectacle provides curiosity and sensationalism, fascination and repulsion, voyeurism and sadomasochism.

Success and Domestication: Rise and Fall of a Kanak Rebel

The exposition above makes clear that resistance – to suppressive social structures, to any pre-given category or classification, to ethnicisation as a mode of Othering, to other players in the literary field – is the most important characteristic of the *Kanak* phenomenon. Arguably this resistance, performed in strongly provocative terms, also accounts for *Kanak Sprak's* commercial success. The *Kanak* revolt and its celebratory mainstream reception, however, seem fundamentally contradictory. To analyse this paradox, Pierre Bourdieu's theory of the cultural field as laid out in the essay collection *The Field of Cultural Production* (1993) proves helpful. Bourdieu argues that – generally – the cultural field is the economic world reversed. The relation between financial success and artistic value is one of negative correlation. The role of the artist – a writer in this case – in this relation is crucial. The writer not only functions as the creator of the cultural object, but also as the creator of this object's value. Bourdieu distinguishes between two roles of the writer, the orator and the fool:

> The writer – or the intellectual – is enjoined to a double status, which is a bit suspect: a possessor of a dominated weak power, he is obliged to situate himself somewhere between the two roles represented, in medieval tradition, by the *orator*, symbolic counterweight of the *bellator*, charged with preaching and praying, with saying the true and the good, with consecrating or condemning by speech, and by the *fool*, a character freed from convention and conformities to whom is accorded transgression without consequences, inspired by the pure pleasure of breaking the rule or of shocking. (Bourdieu 1993: 165)

The writer, according to Bourdieu, is a 'dominated agent' (ibid. 164) who has to position himself on the spectrum between offering a socially relevant, often moral, lecture on the one hand and performing an act of social transgression and disruption on the other.

In the cases of *Kanak Sprak* and *Abschaum*, Zaimoglu convincingly combines both roles: a socio-political accusation in a provocative presentation. However, in Zaimoglu's *public* performances as *Kanak* writer, Bourdieu's role of the fool gains the upper hand. Increasingly, the performance of provocative transgression dominates the message of the orator. Zaimoglu takes central stage as the 'mere' 'demolisher of social illusions' (ibid. 165). It is the dominance of this role of the fool in Zaimoglu's public performances, that Mark Terkessidis critically refers to when he writes: 'Moreover, in articles and performances the author more and more serves an exoticising desire for metropolitan ghetto-romanticism – for a culture that is "excitingly different" (*Spiegel*)' (2000: 89).[35] The shocking quality of the performance of the 'excitingly different' *Kanake* turns into an automatism and becomes an empty gesture. Zaimoglu complies with the demands of mainstream culture by publicly performing its 'constitutive outside', by performing a non-conformist *Kanak* Otherness. He plays the role dominant discourse ascribes to him.[36] It is hard to determine the effects of this performance of *Kanak* Otherness: When is this performance strategically subversive and when is it strategically commercial? And do the two possibilities necessarily exclude each other? Obviously, on an economic level objections to strategic commercialisation lack a rational foundation. Nevertheless, the loss of socio-political impact that commercialisation often entails surely demands critical scrutiny.

Kien Nghi Ha discusses the *Kanak* commercialisation in his work *Hype um Hybridität* [*Hype on Hybridity*] (2005). He points out that the *Kanak* hype – as a particularly German hype – runs the risk of confirming the (ethnic) stereotypes that the initial *Kanak* project aimed to challenge and undermine. The commercial propagation of *Kanak* Otherness turns *Kanak* identity into a popular cultural commodity. Ha writes:

> This instrumentalisation of the Other reduces him to a signifier that has to serve the taste markers 'funky-fresh' or 'exotic-erotic' to stay in the business. The hybridity discourse can aggravate ethnic stereotypes that are connected to the cultural consumption of the imposed authenticity of the Other.

> Diese Instrumentalisierung des Anderen reduziert ihn zu einem Bedeutungsträger, der die Geschmacksnoten 'funky-fresh' oder 'exotisch-erotisch' bedienen muss, um im Geschäft zu bleiben. Der Vermischungsdiskurs kann ethnische Stereotypen verstärken, die an der kulturellen Konsumtion der zugeschriebenen Authentizität des Anderen gebunden sind. (Ha 2005: 80/81)

This critique makes clear that it is only a thin line that distinguishes the effective use of the term *Kanake* as a subversive transgression from an application of the epithet that results in its affirmative repetition. The danger of the last lies in the user's failing awareness or consciousness of the term's injurious history. A mere mentioning of the term without making use of the critical potential opened up by its appropriating resignification persists its hurtful circulation as hate speech.

The problem arises from the fact that appropriating resignification as a strategy of resistance is itself ultimately caught up in the discourse that it attempts to resist. Butler accounts for this problem by referring to the fundamental ambivalence that underpins the performative strategy:

> Thus, performativity has its own social temporality in which it remains enabled precisely by the contexts from which it breaks. This ambivalent structure at the heart of performativity implies that, within political discourse, the very terms of resistance and insurgency are spawned in part by the powers they oppose (which is not to say that the latter are reducible to the former or always already coopted by them in advance). (Butler 1997: 40)

Only a few of the commercial projects that followed in Zaimoglu's footsteps and made use of the (by that time popular) *Kanak* figure warranted and/or realised its critical potential.[37] Most of them prove that performing the *Kanake* is not a subversive practice in itself. Its subversive effectivity is dependent on the time and context of its use. Nevertheless, in the specific case of Zaimoglu's *Kanak* literature the resignificatory project proved a powerful performative move that indisputably resulted in a temporary gain of visibility, both of the group that was (and still is) interpellated as *Kanake*, and of the hate speech dimension of this interpellation. Jamal Tuschick acknowledges this fact when he states: 'The rise of an insult to a category of honour goes back to Zaimoglu. He provided the hate speech term Kanake with a career' (2000a: 108).[38] This statement is also true the other way around: Zaimoglu's career flourished thanks to the epithet.

After his sensational entrance in German literature, Zaimoglu more or less managed to secure a public position, both in the literary and the larger cultural field. He himself transformed from a *Kanak* rebel hero into a respectable migrant intellectual and the tone of his writing changed considerably as well. The opening essay of his last *Kanak* work *Kopf und Kragen. Kanak-Kultur-Kompendium* (2001) concludes with a positive claim of a liveable life in Germany: '[The immigrants] stayed, because it was worth staying in this country' (Zaimoglu 2001: 21).[39] This claim forms the final stage in a transformative movement that travels from complete rejection of German national identity via doubt and insecurity towards acknowledgement and even appreciation of German culture.[40]

Zaimoglu conveys a similar message in his 'guiding article' ['Leitartikel'] to the Easter issue of *Die Zeit* (12 April 2006), titled 'Mein Deutschland. Warum die Einwanderer auf ihre neue Heimat stolz sein können' ['My Germany. Why the Immigrants Can Be Proud of Their New *Heimat*']. In this article he reflects on the future 'mixed-ethnic *Stammtischen*' of the German nation. The tenor of the article is confidently positive when he urges all of his fellow citizens to be 'proud (...) of the German situation' (Zaimoglu 2006d). He adds: 'The presumed cultural model countries like the Netherlands and France have burned down' (ibid.), thus suggesting that now Germany has assumed this role.[41] In the article 'Meine kleine Geschichte der Einwanderung' ['My Small History of Immigration'] in the *Neue Zürcher Zeitung* (26 November 2005) he makes a subject of his own transformation from a *Kanak* rebel into a respected German writer. He concludes this article as follows: 'In the beginning I was a Turkish boy, today I am a German writer. I owe this to my parents and to Germany. I have been very lucky' (Zaimoglu 2005).[42] Apart maybe from the reservation at the end, this final statement displays strong melodramatic (and almost cathartic) qualities. Especially in the light of his previous provocative politics of position as a *Kanak* rebel, the claim of a German identity in combination with the expressed gratitude towards Germany signals an amazing reversal.[43]

The Claim of Authenticity

As I have explained in the previous section, Zaimoglu's debut *Kanak Sprak* constitutes the initiating moment of what I have named the *Kanak* phenomenon. This section focuses on the work's particular format that, as I argue, in important measures caused this *Kanak* fascination. *Kanak Sprak* consists of 24 short texts that are introduced by a rather polemic preface that is subscribed 'Kiel, im Sommer 1995, Feridun Zaimoglu' (KS 18). In this preface, author-*character* Feridun Zaimoglu presents his work to its German readership. He clarifies his motivation for writing this work and explains the particular writing procedure, in order to facilitate a better understanding of the texts to follow. According to this 'Feridun Zaimoglu' the work *Kanak Sprak* is the result of a real-life undertaking. The texts that he names 'protocols' derive from a particular kind of fieldwork that he executed at the fringe of society.[44] They record his interviews with 24 young *Kanak* males of Turkish origin that he went to see 'im Milieu, im Kiez der Männer' (KS 15).[45]

In a detailed manner the preface describes the preparatory research and social investigation that made the writing of *Kanak Sprak* possible. Zaimoglu does not present himself as an inspired creator of a literary work, but instead he stresses the truth value of his work, its rootedness in social realities.[46] About his fieldwork, the process of collecting the data for his book, he writes:

> I dived into the 'Hades of ragamuffins', called on the *Kanake* in his districts and ghetto quarters and dwellings, in his huts and teahouses. It was not easy to fight against the *Kanake's* initial distrust in an 'educated man'. It was necessary to win his confidence in order to convince him that I would not 'sell him to the *Alemanen*'.

> Ich tauchte ab in den 'Lumpen-Hades', suchte den Kanaken auf in seinen Distrikten und Revieren, Ghetto-Quartieren und Stammplätzen, in seinen Verschlägen und Teehäusern. Es war nicht einfach, gegen das anfängliche Mißtrauen anzukämpfen, das der Kanake 'dem Studierten' gegenüber empfindet. Vertrauensbildende Maßnahmen waren vonnöten, um ihn davon zu überzeugen, daß ich ihn nicht 'an die Alemanen verkaufe'. (KS 15)

Here, underworld explorer Zaimoglu stresses his successful immersion in this 'Lumpen-Hades'. The sinister name and his description of the enterprise point out that his exploratory mission into the depths of society was not an easy one. As an educated person, Zaimoglu had to bridge a gap of mistrust and suspicion. That he actually manages to win the *Kanaken's* confidence and make them willing to talk to him about their lives, has much to do with the ethnic origin that he and the *Kanaken* apparently share.[47] Moreover, Zaimoglu claims some familiarity with the life 'im Milieu' as well as some street credibility. Despite his rise from the social underclass to a position of interviewer, of writer, he still strongly sympathises with the *Kanak* case. Nevertheless, he refuses a position as 'Turks' spokesman' ['Türkensprecher'], 'Mouthpiece' ['Sprachrohr'] or any other representative functions. In *Kanak Sprak*, the *Kanaken* offer their personal reflections on their *Kanak* existence. Each *Kanake* individually gives *act de présence* in his own protocol in concordance with the motto: 'Here I stand and use everything I am to make you understand: I show and generate presence' (KS 14).[48] *Kanak Sprak*, as a result, presents the *Kanaken* as much as it represents them.

In the actual world the author-*person* Zaimoglu keeps up the role that he ascribes to his alter ego in the *Kanak Sprak* preface. In an interview Zaimoglu confirms *Kanak Sprak's* real-life calibre and simultaneously emphasises that his methodological approach fundamentally differs from that of social scientists who come to their conclusions – 'exoticising descriptions and objectifications' – from a 'safe' position behind their desks. He claims: 'I am not the explorer of Turkish areas who just rushed over into the overcrowded quarters for a short while, into the Kanaka ghetto to tap the misery of criminals in discotheques and gambling houses, of jacket lifters to say afterwards: Bye – I am leaving now' (Zaimoglu in Ullmaier 2001: 131).[49] Zaimoglu distinguishes himself from researchers who display a solely academic interest in the *Kanak* social sphere, and who he describes as profit-pursuing visitors to the 'zoo of ethnicities' (KS 11). In the preface to *Kanak Sprak*, he mocks these researchers as well as their quasi-neutral, quasi-objective discourse on migrants in Germany. His own description of the *Kanak* customs and language mimics this discourse, albeit in a ridiculing manner. Tom Cheesman denotes this mimicking strategy as 'pseudo-ethnicization' (2004: 84):[50] Zaimoglu 'invents' the *Kanak* ethnicity for the group of young Turkish-German males that is generally 'Turked' in dominant discourse.

The most striking characteristic of this pseudo-ethnic group is its stylised, hybrid language: 'Kanak talk'.[51] Zaimoglu maintains that in *Kanak Sprak*, *Kanaken* speak in their own *Kanak* language, their own *Kanak* sociolect. The protocols, he claims, offer an '"authentic" linguistic image' (KS 18): they retain the original qualities of the *Kanak* talk performances. The importance of this authenticity lies in the particular identity-constitutive quality of this sociolect.[52] He explains:

> For a long time they have developed an underground code and speak their own jargon: the 'Kanak Sprak', a kind of Creole or argot with secret codes and signs. Their speech is related to the free-style sermon in rap, in that as well as in this case one speaks from an attitudinal pose. The language is decisive for one's existence: One gives a completely private performance in words.

> Längst haben sie einen Untergrund-Kodex entwickelt und sprechen einen eigenen Jargon: die 'Kanak Sprak', eine Art Creol oder Rotwelsch mit geheimen Codes und Zeichen. Ihr Reden ist dem Free-Style-Sermon im Rap verwandt, dort wie hier spricht man aus einer Pose heraus. Diese Sprache entscheidet über die Existenz: Man gibt eine ganz und gar private Vorstellung in Worten. (KS 13)

Thus, *Kanak* talk is central to the performance of *Kanak* identity. It comprehends a certain attitude as well as an agitating message: *Kanak* talk is '[t]he linguistic manifestation of our mobilisation' (Zaimoglu 2001).[53] The attitudinal and instigating purport in combination with its raw poetry is strongly reminiscent of the streetwise sound of rap.[54]

The method of 'participatory observation' of the pseudo-ethnic *Kanak* community is supposed to serve a noble cause: author-character Zaimoglu aims to change their 'situation' ['Lage'] and to turn these objects into subjects. *Kanak Sprak* gives a voice to the *Kanak* underdog.[55] In this sense the claim of authenticity not only functions to underline the protocols' credibility, but also to reinforce the socio-political impact of the work. Zaimoglu successfully (mis-)leads the reader in the process of what David Herman in his study *Story Logic. Problems and Possibilities of Narrative* (2002) calls 'contextual anchoring'. Herman argues that 'stories trigger recipients to establish a more or less direct or oblique relationship between the stories they are interpreting and the contexts in which they are interpreting them' (2002: 331). Zaimoglu's *Kanak* work does exactly the same: it prompts its reader to reassess a relation between the story-world of the *Kanak* figures and the actual world in which the term *Kanake* pejoratively refers to an ethnic minority. The reader tends to rely on a certain analogy between these worlds, and the Zaimoglu character in the preface confirms this interpretive tendency as justified. He encourages the reader to read the protocols not only referentially, but even realistically, as text spoken by deprived *Kanaken* living in the actual world. This narrative construction of the protocols as non-mediated and authentic, complicates Zaimoglu's authorship. The subscription underlines the preface's deviant status in respect to the following protocols. Zaimoglu explicitly claims the responsibility for the first, but then draws a dividing line. The protocols, he claims, do not derive from his creative writing. They are the results of his passive recording; in terms of authorship the protocols 'belong' to the interviewed *Kanaken*.[56]

On a public level the discussions about *Kanak Sprak*'s authenticity culminated in a hostile dispute during a broadcasting of the talkshow *Drei nach Neun* (Channel N3, 8 May 1998). Here Zaimoglu got involved in a rather absurd argument with the other talkshow guests Wolf Biermann, Norbert Blüm, Harald Juhnke and Heide Simonis. The argument centred on the (dubious) accuracy of Zaimoglu's *Kanak* identity as representation of 'actual' Turkish-German identity. Zaimoglu was accused of having done an exceptionally bad job. Especially Blüm and Simonis insisted that he had not only failed in the construction of an adequate image of 'the *Kanake*', but that his works *Kanak Sprak* and *Koppstoff* even impede the integration of Turkish-German youth. Zaimoglu's refusal to allow the presenter to address him with the racist epithet *Kanake* during the broadcasting, initiated a vehement discussion about regimes of definition and power relations between the German majority and Turkish-German minority. Simonis took issue with the violent language that Zaimoglu's *Kanaken* and *Kanakstas* use and refused to accept that this language has a real-life equivalent. She argued:

> But a Turk who talks like that...aside from the fact that I don't believe a Turkish woman talks like that. I'd like to see a Turkish woman... I mean, we make every effort in the world to appeal for a little understanding for the Turkish women who live with us, in the third generation, who wear this headscarf, which doesn't look very nice, and which provokes aggression. And now you're showing a sort of Turkish woman that I don't believe you can find a single one of in the whole of Kiel and even in the whole of Berlin, but I don't know them all. Admittedly, that is art...[57]

> Aber ein Türke, der so redet... abgesehen davon, dass ich nicht glaube, dass eine Türkin so redet. Würde ich gerne mal erleben, 'ne Türkin. Aber wir geben uns nun wirklich alle Mühe dieser Welt um zu werben für ein bisschen Verständnis für die Türkinnen, die bei uns leben, in der dritten Generation, die dieses Kopftuch tragen, was nicht sehr kleidsam ist und was auch Aggressionen hervorbringt. Und jetzt zeigen Sie eine Türkin, von der ich behaupte, in ganz Kiel finden Sie keine und in ganz Berlin auch nicht, aber ich kenn' Sie nicht alle. Einverstanden, das ist Kunst... (Ha 2003b: 145)[58]

Simonis' response makes clear that, despite her acknowledgement of *Kanak Sprak* as a piece of literary art, actual and story-worlds fade and fuse in her critique of its violent language. Biermann continues this same referential reasoning, when he reproaches the writer Zaimoglu for his lack of *Kanak* identity: 'I'm afraid you're not a Kanake at all, it's just a pose. Yes, I'd like to know what of you is real (...) What is your real identity?' (ibid. 146).[59] Blüm finally tops the absurd discussion by accusing Zaimoglu and his language of contempt for human life.

The vehement reactions to Zaimoglu's concept of *Kanak* identity are symptomatic for the hegemonic discourse that *Kanak Sprak* questions. Especially Simonis' hostile verbal response to Zaimoglu's claim that his power to resignify a term as *Kanake* is limited, is striking. Her agitation testifies to the threat that the *Kanak* phenomenon contains for the German status quo.[60] Cheesman (2004) comments on Simonis' response as follows: 'But her vehemence, and her own failure to stick to that register, betray her rage at the refusal of what she sees as her caseload of migrants to become what she wants them to be: normal bourgeois citizens, subjects of German *Leitkultur* just like herself' (2004: 98). In *Hype um Hybridität*, Ha judges Zaimoglu's *Kanak* performance as an exceptionally effective moment of strategic subversion. He considers Zaimoglu's provocative 'self-Kanakisation' ['Selbst-Kanakisierung'] in the talkshow as a socially relevant 'speech attack' ['Sprachattakke'] (Ha 2005: 116).

In defence of this sort of accusations of false or non-representativity – partly a result from the work's claim on authenticity – several literary scholars emphasise *Kanak Sprak's* literariness. By underlining the artificial and aesthetic character of the hybrid *Kanak* language, the complete absence of the interviewer in the protocols and the disappearance of any references to the interview situation, they argue against the work's assumed (and claimed) linguistic authenticity and stress Zaimoglu's literary authorship. Nevertheless, and on an academic level, the effectivity of Zaimoglu's narrative mystification is amazing, as the *actuality* of the particular interview format and the 'authentic' *content* of the protocols are hardly questioned at all. Dirk Skiba (2004), for instance, re-inscribes *Kanak Sprak's* myth of origin when he emphasises his doubt about the protocols' adequacy in representing the *original* interviews: 'All attempts at reconstructing the original conversation in the published texts must remain largely speculative. As Zaimoglu erased the tapes, he excluded the possibility to produce transcriptions of the interviews and to compare these with the literary records' (Skiba 2004: 192).[61] Whereas Skiba questions the actual resemblance between interviews and protocols, he persists in the given format. When he writes 'So it is scarcely amazing that [Zaimoglu] met with great scepticism before actualising his interview' (ibid. 189), this observation bespeaks a similar unconditional acceptance of the pretension of real-life interviews.[62]

Sandra Hestermann's analysis of *Kanak Sprak* (2003) testifies to a similar acceptance of Zaimoglu's preface claims. She writes:

> Zaimoglu's *Kanaksprak* contains a series of testimonials which give voice to the beliefs, fears, opinions, desires and, above all, aggressions and frustrations of present-day Turkish migrant society. True to his self-image as chronicler, Zaimoglu goes out into the streets, bars, discos and other public spaces, where he meets the interview partners whose stories he records.[63] (Hestermann 2003: 360)

Before Hestermann goes on to analyse *Kanak Sprak's* discourse of identity, she denotes the protocols as 'testimonials' of the people (not characters) in whose name *Kanak Sprak* lays its claims. By accepting Zaimoglu's 'self-image as chronicler' and affirming his procedure of merely recording the stories of others, she reduces the literary potential of his work to a minimum. The actual writer Zaimoglu and the author-character of the same name in the preface – the interlocutor in the interviews – blend into one and the same person (not figure) whose claims of authenticity – except for those concerning the language – are unquestioningly accepted.

The Zaimoglu scholarship in general gives evidence of the strong temptation and convincing power of *Kanak Sprak's* claimed real-life interview-format. The following analysis of the protocols, however, resists this strongly referential frame of reading, proposed by Zaimoglu's preface and public performance. Instead it focuses on the *Kanak* identity produced by the specific narrative interaction between preface and protocols on the one hand, and the protocols and their readers on the other. This approach does not comprise a final judgement about the work's actual 'authenticity'. This question remains open as a possibility that is, however, of minor importance to my analysis of the text as a work of literature.

Performing Polarisation

'*What's life like as a Kanake in Germany* was the question that I've asked myself and others' (KS 9).[64] The opening sentence of Zaimoglu's *Kanak Sprak* presents the central concern of his work in a nutshell. It immediately localises the literary work in the German here and now where people interpellated as *Kanaken* apparently occupy a deviant position, a position that prompts a question. The author-character Zaimoglu asks this question both to himself and others, thus drawing the attention to the relation between the two, to his position among these (male) *Kanaken*.[65] Whereas the previous section focused on the authenticity effects that follow from this claimed interview format, in the following section I take a closer look at the actual answers, the protocols themselves. What do these *Kanaken* actually say in response to this central interview question? The 24 protocols are constructed as the *Kanaken*'s personal answers to the initial question that is repeated halfway through the preface as 'What is life here like in your skin?' (KS 15).[66] These questions invite the *Kanaken* to narrate, to open up their lives not only to the interviewer Zaimoglu, but also to the German readership. Their answers appear harsh and provocative. The *Kanaken* apparently feel the urge to spit their bottled-up anger at a German society that they hold responsible for their marginal positions. In a language that reflects this anger, the protocols testify to difficult lives in what nowadays is referred to as a 'parallel society', a German shadow world.

With their angry identity performances, these *Kanaken* respond to discursively dominant and homogenising images imposed on Turkish-German migrants. *Kanak Sprak* offers the *Kanaken* the opportunity to present a more accurate and differentiated image of their *Kanak* identity. Now the 'true' *Kanaken* speak out for themselves. In the preface, Zaimoglu explains:

> The *Kanaken* are given the blame for customs and rites. Seen from outside they only appear as a shapeless mass of ragamuffins, that one supposes to know by their external appearance and 'special characteristics'. Even if forced to make a final decision, the *Kanaken* would not look for cultural anchorage. They do not want to make use of the supermarket of identities, nor do they want to be absorbed by an egalitarian herd of *Heimat* expellees. They have their own char-

acteristic features and a clear notion of self-determination. They form the real Generation X that was denied individualisation and ontogenesis.

> Den Kanaken schiebt man Sitten und Riten zu wie einen Schwarzen Peter. Von außen betrachtet kommen sie nur als amorphe Masse von Lumpenproletariern vor, die man an Äußerlichkeiten und 'spezifischen Eigenarten' zu erkennen glaubt. Auch wenn sie zu einer endgültigen Entscheidung gezwungen würden, die Kanaken suchen keine kulturelle Verankerung. Sie möchten sich weder im Supermarkt der Identitäten bedienen, noch in einer egalitären Herde von Heimatvertriebene aufgehen. Sie haben eine eigene innere Prägung und ganz klare Vorstellung von Selbstbestimmung. Sie bilden die eigentliche Generation X, der Individuation und Ontogenese verweigert worden sind. (KS 12/13)

This passage suggests that German society is divided into two social groups: an anonymous, faceless entity referred to with the indefinite pronoun 'man' and the *Kanak* Generation X. The dominant first group appears as a powerful entity that is able to determine, force and hold back certain positions, as the verbs 'to blame', 'to force' and 'to deny' indicate. As such it represents the gaze 'from outside' that anchors the *Kanake* in a certain position. At the same time, according to author-character Zaimoglu's focalisation, this entity is far from infallible and perfect. 'Man' makes mistakes or can be misled, as the use of the verb 'to suppose' in 'suppose to know' suggests: dominant German society assumes that it can identify the *Kanake*, but Zaimoglu contradicts this assumption. *Kanaken*, he knowingly insists, resist any final cultural determination as well as any clear designation of their identity.

Simultaneously – and in apparent contradiction to the first statement – the *Kanaken* themselves know very well who they are and who they want to be. The 24 protocols offer a *self*-image of a neglected and misrepresented generation. Moray McGowan describes the protocols' self-representations as follows:

> Zaimoglu's young Turks reject every externally imposed identity. Instead, like Jean Genet inverting his stigmatisation as a criminal and 'pervert' into a celebration of otherness, they affirm that they are 'Kanakstas' (...) and celebrate with electrifying, angry, linguistically inventive energy this position on the margins of a society for which they affect nothing but scorn. (McGowan 2001: 303/304)

For these *Kanaken*, German society is the source of their marginalised position and thus the object of their anger and scorn. For that reason it is no wonder that these protocols, these self-images, (may well) sound unpleasant to the ears of (dominant) German society. *Kanak Sprak*'s subtitle ironically hints at this effect: 24 *Mißtöne vom Rande der Gesellschaft*. The reader is warned about the discordance right from the beginning. Neither these protocols nor their subjects attempt to fit into the mould prescribed by dominant discourse. They do not try to please their readers; on the contrary, the protocols, as identity statements or poses of *Kanak* identity, intend to disrupt and upset. By means of their repetitive self-*Kanakisation*, these young males appropriate the power of definition and thus of self-determination.

The important question that results from this resignificatory procedure – but is, awkwardly, only seldom asked – concerns the specific construction of their *Kanak* identity. What does this resignified *Kanak* identity look like? How do these *Kanaken* imagine their identity themselves? With which *Kanak* self-image does *Kanak Sprak* (try to) return the verbal violence and replace the hate speech value of the infamous epithet? According to the expert Zaimoglu, true *Kanak* identity predominantly takes shape through the opposition to non-*Kanaken*, through the opposition to those that the text constructs as the *Kanake's* Others.

In the first place, these Others are the dominant and despicable (male) 'Alemanen'.[67] This hate speech term in *Kanak* discourse is in many ways analogous to the term *Kanake* in German popular discourse. It interpellates the majority of indigenous Germans as representatives of a repressive German society. The meanings attached to the epithet *Alemanen* in *Kanak* discourse are twofold, though both originate in the affective realm of hate. On the one hand the *Kanaken* use the term in hateful acknowledgement of the *Aleman* position of (repressive) power. In several instances, interviewed *Kanaken* even refer to the Holocaust in order to underline the *Alemane's* gross misuse of his position of power. These references concern the *Alemane's* historical identity as perpetrator and his proved lethal incapability to deal with (ethnic or religious) Others.[68] On the other hand the *Aleman* male appears as a 'softy' in the *Kanak* hate speech representation, as an effeminate man who had to give up on his male power (and position of superiority) as a result of gender emancipation. In this representation the *Kanak* males emphasise their own masculinist superiority, a position of gendered power still held up within the own pseudo-ethnic *Kanak* group. Irrespective of which of the two stances the interviewed *Kanaken* choose, the bottom line in the divisive *Kanak* discourse remains the same: 'The *alemane* is a piece of misery' (KS 83).[69]

In the second place a rather arbitrary selection of (more or less) marginalised groups is taken to represent the *Kanake's* – other – Other. A very diverse mixture of 'Heimat expellees' ['Heimatvertriebene'], women, and several ethnic minority groups – addressed in the protocols with hate speech signifiers as 'Jamaica nigger, schmaltzy Latino, Yankee nigger' (KS 22) – constitutes the *Kanake's* antagonistic world *within* the margin, aside from the dominant *Aleman* society.[70]

Finally, the first generation of Turkish labour migrants as well as 'sweet little Alis' ['lieb-alileins'], a *Kanak* epithet for 'integrated' or 'successful' Turks or Germans of Turkish descent, also counts to the identities that are rejected. Here again ethnicity intersects with gender in a significant way. The hypermasculine

Kanak self-image opposes the unmanly males of the first generation, disempowered and emasculated by the indignities of the 'guest worker' system.[71] In *Kanak* eyes, the assumed willingness to compromise on the part of the '*lieb-alileins*' is equated with giving up their pride and submitting themselves to the *Alemanen* – and implies a loss of masculinity. Both 'groups' that in dominant discourse surely run the risk of being addressed by the hate speech term *Kanake*, are all the same excluded from *Kanak Sprak*'s 'elitist' *Kanak* selection. The original hate speech term *Kanake* and its resignified *Kanak* discourse version do not refer to the same group of people. The grounds for exclusion of these various groups are manifold. They range from the general rejection of particular identity markers such as the female gender or the older generation, to a more specific contempt for social achievements or a 'privileged' position within the migration legislation (as in the case of the '*Heimat* expellees'). It is this large assembly of non-*Kanaken* or *Kanake*'s Others from whom the 'real' *Kanak* community members dissociate themselves.

The discursive polarisation between the glorious *Kanake* and his despised Others determines almost all protocols and is constitutive for the *Kanak* Self. 'Hakan, 24, motor mechanic apprentice [Kfz-Geselle]' (KS 84-86) positions himself in this hierarchised field of Self and Other in a protocol that is tellingly titled 'I play in the league of the damned' (KS 84).[72] His answer to the question 'What's life like as a *Kanake* in Germany' comes close to a call for rebellion, a declaration of (ethnic) war from a position of ethnic pride. On the one side he presents the '*kanake* like me' (ibid.), who gains status through his absolute difference from the 'bully *alemane* (...) with blond bush on the scalp and nil man-pride talent in his body' (ibid.).[73] In Hakan's proud opinion, the *Kanake* is everything that the *Alemane* is not. The *Alemane* functions as a negative screen for projection. In his protocol, he instigates all other *Kanaken* to build a resisting unity against their absolute *Aleman* Other:

> What the hell is this pomade-shit of german-is-the-number-one-that-exists (...). My appeal to the *kanaken* in *alemania* is: friends, when your roots dry out, you're dead bush in the whirl of the wind. When you shake hands with the uncircumcised, don't forget that he would also send his own mother streetwalking, when it yields him a profit. (...) I cry out to the brothers: build a sturdy unity, and stay far away from the psycho-massacres that rage there in *alemania*. Ruin is the family name of the blond devil.

> Was soll überhaupt dies pomadenschiß von deutsch-ist-nummer-eins-was-gibt (...). Mein ruf an die kanaken in alemania ist: freunde, wenn euch die wurzel trocknet, seid ihr toter busch im wirbel der winde. Wenn ihr die hand gebt dem unbeschnittenen, vergesst nicht, dass er auch seine eigene mutter auf'n strich schicken würde, wenn genug schotter für ihn herausspringt. (...) ich ruf den brüdern zu: bildet ne stramme einheit, und haltet euch fern von

den psychogemetzeln, die da in alemania toben. Verderben ist der stammna-
me des blonden teufels. (KS 86)

As counterpart to his own 'league of the damned' Hakan presents the tribe of the
blond (and uncircumcised) devils, who know neither morals nor pride. By this
opposition his marginalised 'league of the damned' undergoes a semantic shift.
The unwanted exclusion from a dominant centre is resignified as a morally priori-
tised and preferable position in the subcultural space 'Kanakistan'.

The proud self-positioning of 'Abdurrahman, 24, rapper' (KS 19-22) offers another example of this discursive inversion of *Kanak* marginalisation. Abdurrahman dissociates himself from dominant *Aleman* society as follows:

> I have my own basic attitude that goes right through my body from the brain
> to the bottom of my heart; in there my extra-thing, my instinct and my kosher
> will shiver and shake, and this team of three reports all trembling and stretch-
> ing that's going on outside, but that border between me and that outside there
> I carve strictly every day, I pay attention that my skin keeps clean, that no one
> talks me into style and opinion and fashion and trend, because, brother, my
> only possession is my clean morale that houses in this cadaver here through
> and through.

> Ich hab meinen eigenen grundstrang, der geht da mitten durch'n leib vom
> hirn zum herzende, in dem beben und schütteln sich meine extrasache, mein
> instinkt und mein koscherer wille, und diesem dreiergespann teilt sich alles
> zucken und recken mit, was so außen abgeht, aber die zonengrenze zwischen
> mir und dem da draußen meißel ich streng jeden verdammten tag, ich achte,
> daß mir die haut sauber bleibt, daß mir keiner an stil und meinung und mode
> und trend was anhängt, denn, bruder, mein einziges hab und gut is meine
> saubere moral, die hier in diesem kadaver durch und durch steckt. (KS 22)

Despite the rather shocking designation of his own body with the term 'cadaver',
Abdurrahman's personal sphere is clearly superior to the one designated by the
deictic coordinate 'outside there'. The casual use of the Yiddish word 'kosher'
combined with the mentioning of skin that remains clean, functions as an indirect but strong invocation of (memories of) anti-Semitic and racist discourses in
German history.[74] Its combination with aspects of style and opinion, fashion and
trends in the protocols causes an affective rupture with a provocative impact. The
same counts for the sudden transition from attitude and appearance (exterior) to
the clean ethic of this *Kanak* 'cadaver' (interior) in the next sentence.

The occasional use of the unifying, and at the same time excluding, personal
pronoun 'we' in many of the interview protocols also works to underline the division between *Kanak* Selves and non-*Kanak* Others. A few interviewees, however,

refuse the antagonistic rhetoric as well as the forced embrace of the group identity. They – a poet, a sociologist, a transvestite, and an Islamist – dissociate themselves from the prescribed *Kanak* attitudinal discourse and allow themselves to be critical of the group and the norms that are dominant there. In the context of the *Kanak Sprak* story-world these *Kanaken* represent the real discords. Their deviant voices, however, hardly seem to get through, their discords disappeared in the process of reception. The media predominantly presented *Kanak Sprak* as an introduction to the angry *Kanake* and his offensive *Kanak* discourse.

Ethnicising the Reader

The angry mood and inflammatory message of the protocols discussed above are not in any sense exceptional. On the contrary, although the *Kanaken* vary in name, age and profession (although most professions suggest underclass, subculture or petty crime), their protocols – except for the atypical four mentioned – sound more or less the same.[75] The tone is set in the preface: the preface not only defines the *Kanake*, but also his *Kanak* code. Author-character Zaimoglu determines a *Kanak* discourse that only makes a distinction between *Kanak* Self and *Aleman* Other. He functions as a kind of ventriloquist, as the *Kanak* puppeteer who enables the *Kanaken* to speak. However, what they say, the grid of their words, is prescribed by the dominant, all-enveloping preface. Specific mechanisms of address settle the particular, constitutive interaction between protocols and preface. Zaimoglu's silent but determinative presence controls the protocols' compulsory *Kanak* concordance.[76]

The interviewed *Kanaken* repeatedly make use of the second-person singular pronoun '*du*', often in combination with the specific interpellation 'brother'. In the context of an interview this direct form of address is far from extraordinary. In the particular narrative structure of *Kanak Sprak* however, the particular, familiarising mechanism of address has a strategic function. Gathering from the information provided in the preface, the reader is invited to assume that here interviewer Zaimoglu is addressed in a direct speech situation. The explicit forms of address underline this dialogical situation and remind the reader of the presence of an interlocutor. An actual dialogue is not realised, though. In none of the protocols does the addressed '*du*' speak back, nor does he pose another question in his role as interviewer. His presence is marked by silence. It is solely constructed through constitutive interpellations such as 'brother', 'you know', 'man', 'I tell you' used by the interviewed, but in fact soliloquising, *Kanaken*. The semantics of the term 'brother' as an often-recurring form of address hint at a certain familiarity between the interlocutors, a situation of trust between the *Kanaken* and their interviewer, Zaimoglu. The term positions both as equals in a brotherhood that is derived from a shared hyphenated background and involves, as pointed out before, a particular attitude and a common language. Apparently both the interviewer and the interviewees are approved members of the elitist *Kanak* community as presented in the preface. The repeated references to a communal *Kanak* '*wir*' that includes the interviewing '*du*' confirm this supposition: the interviewer holds the status of an insider among the interviewed *Kanaken* and is accepted as one of the (male) gang.

However, the double deictic functions of the personal pronoun '*du*' complicate this apparently well-ordered interview situation.[77] In several protocols the address of the interviewer as '*du*' interferes with two other functions of the '*du*': the address of the reader or interpreter as '*du*' in the specific situation of reading and a self-referential use of '*du*'. In *Story logic*, Herman argues that a conflation of deictic roles of the second-person pronoun '*du*' 'compromises the boundary between the (virtual) fictional protagonist and the (actual) reader' (2002: 361), between text and context, rather than appointing one of the two readings as more or most appropriate.[78] This conflation of these various roles can result in a situation of interpretive indeterminacy.

In the *Kanak Sprak* protocols the '*du*' in the first place refers to the author-character Zaimoglu in his role as interviewer. In the story-world of the protocols this '*du*' is actual: Zaimoglu is the interlocutor to whom the interviewed *Kanaken* relate their *Kanak* experiences. In the actual world in which the narrative is read, this '*du*' would be virtual, as it refers to the literary character Zaimoglu. However, here the preface intervenes and complicates this standardised expectation. The claim to authenticity in the preface contradicts the virtuality of the interview situation as well as that of the characters involved. It resists the interpretation of Zaimoglu and his *Kanaken* as virtual characters.

In the second option, '*du*' (or also '*ihr*'/ 'you plural') functions as an address to the reader and is actualisable in the actual world in which the protocols are read. The interpretation of this '*du*' as an appellation of the reader is independent of whether the protocols' *Kanaken* are virtual or actual. However, taken that they are virtual – which means considering *Kanak Sprak* as a work of the literary imagination and the *Kanaken* as literary characters – then the boundary between story and actual world becomes blended and blurry. The deictic coordinate '*du*' prompts a mingling of story and actual world and the process of contextual anchoring as a means of orientation for the reader becomes increasingly complicated.

The third possible function of the deictic '*du*' causes even further confusion: '*du*' as a form of self-address. In several protocols the interviewed *Kanaken* address themselves, mostly in a generic mode. The protocol of 'Ulku, 28, unemployed' (KS 133-136) offers an example of this self-referential address:

> But, brother, me my 'kummel' motto doesn't give a damn shit about such a
> snot partisan with a socking tick, I do not join in this fucking game, I tell
> myself: *Kanake*, you are and will be an alien, you are and will be a philanthro-
> pist, you are and will be a hater of rich people, you are and will be a winner in

life and a promoter of clarity, and only that makes you into a good old *Kanake* with a brand on your forehead which says: I am and will be a hater of your fucking rules.

Mir meine kümmeldevise aber, bruder, gibt 'n scheißdreck auf so nen popel-partisan mit 'm ballertick, ich mach da man in diesem scheißspiel nicht mit, ich sag mir: kanake, du bist und bleibt 'n anderer, du bist und bleibst 'n men-schenfreund, du bist und bleibst 'n reicheleutehasser, du bist und bleibst 'n lebensgewinnler und klarheitshochrufer, und nur das macht dich zum ollen kanaken mit nem brandstempel auf der stirn, wo der man heißt: ich bin und bleib 'n hasser eurer scheißregeln. (KS 135)[79]

The 'brother' in the first sentence is most probably addressed at the (silent) inter-viewer, Zaimoglu, and thus represents an example of the first type of address. The '*du*' in the phrasing 'I tell myself: *Kanake*, you are and will be an alien' is a form of self-address. Ulku addresses himself as *Kanake*, but uses this *Kanak* address in a generic form: not only 'you, Ulku' are different, but also 'you, *Kanake* in general' are different. In his self-address Ulku features not as an individual but as a repre-sentative member of the homogenous *Kanak* community. The difference that is emphasised here concerns the oppositional difference from 'the old *aleman* peo-ple' ['*das olle alemannenvolk*'] (ibid.) that is evoked a few lines before. Ulku also addresses this despised *Aleman* people in the last sentence of the citation, when he explicates his enduring hate for 'your fucking rules' in the second-person plu-ral form 'your' ['*eurer*']. Zaimoglu is assumedly excluded from this address, as are the other *Kanaken*.[80]

In the narrative combination and arbitrary alternation of virtual, actual and self-referential '*du*', every single '*du*' requires an interpretive act: to whom does this '*du*' refer, who is addressed in this situation? In several narrative situations these ques-tions cannot be decisively answered, leaving the reader-interpreter unsure. The particular blending of functions of the '*du*' results in interpretive indeterminacy. As far as the position of *Kanak Sprak's* reader is concerned, the situation of address is ambivalent right from the start. At first the work in itself, its preface and the interview format, invites the reader to enter into the *Kanak* underworld and to empathise with the *Kanak* fate. Subsequently, however, this affective identification is obstructed. The protocols reproach especially the indigenous German reader with accusations of relentless domination and by means of several hate speech attributions.[81] Addressed as *Alemane*, the reader is held co-responsible for the *Ka-nake's* fate.

This narrative strategy of division and reproach strongly aggravates processes of identification. In this sense *Kanak Sprak* offers an insightful confirmation of Herman's statement about the function of the deictic 'you': 'It is a mode of pro-noun usage that draws attention to and so de-automatizes processes of contextual anchoring' (Herman 2002: 342). Kanak Sprak's shifting and exclusionary modes of address divide its readership into several, hierarchically ordered groups. Readers themselves lose their identificatory agency and, as a result, are forced to passively undergo a process of ethnicisation. Kanak Sprak attributes to its reader a coercive Aleman (or Kanak) identity and in this way turns the ethnicising – or 'Turking' – mechanism of dominant society around.

By means of the language performances of its characters and in their variable divisive use of the deictic 'du', the protocols repeat the dichotomous categories of Kanak Self and non-Kanak (read: inferior, mainly Aleman) Other as established in the preface. In fact, they echo and resonate the authoritarian voice and polarising discourse of the 'puppeteer' Zaimoglu. His guiding voice in the preface disqualifies any possibility of an alternative, more differentiated Kanak identity. Kanak identity appears as a rigid straitjacket discursively dependent on the politics of polarisation: the one and only 'true Kanake' as opposed to all despicable non-Kanak Others.[82] Wertheimer even goes as far as to compare the Kanak counter-identity to that of the German 'skin[head]s':

> The 'Kanaken's' aggressions stand against the aggressions of the 'skins'. 'I am proud of being a foreigner' versus 'I am proud of being a German'. This slogan is seductive (because it is simple) and dangerous (because it is simple). Dangerous, too, because with it one makes use of the opponent's method.

> Die Aggressionen der 'Kanaken' stehen gegen die Aggressionen der 'Skins'. 'Ich bin stolz, ein Fremder zu sein' gegen 'Ich bin stolz, ein Deutscher zu sein'. Die Formel ist verführerisch (weil sie einfach ist) und gefährlich (weil sie einfach ist). Gefährlich auch, weil man sich mit ihr der Methode des Gegners bedient. (Wertheimer 2002: 133)

Wertheimer's warning for the dangers inherent in Kanak discourse seems justified, although his comparison with skinheads problematically overlooks the determinant differences in the causal contexts of the two poses of aggression.

In resistance to his marginalisation, the Kanake repeats the simplifying and homogenising gestures of a violently exclusionary discourse. On the one hand this repetitive characteristic is central to the strategy of appropriating resignification. On the other hand it simultaneously constitutes its main pitfall, as I have discussed before with reference to Butler. In the same sense Ha tempers too-high expectations of Kanak subversity by emphasising its coercive dependency on the discursive context of intervention:

> Adopting and turning around the Kanak discourse actually does not mean a free choice of identity, but dodging an imposed self-awareness. As a fringe

group has no power to stop the 'Kanak-discourse' that is steered from outside, they try to intervene from within the racial discourse.

Bei der Aneignung und Umkehrung des Kanakendiskurses geht es daher gerade nicht um eine freie Identitätswahl, sondern darum, ein aufgezwungenes Selbstbild zu unterlaufen. Da Marginalisierte nicht über die Macht verfügen, den fremdbestimmten 'Kanaken'-diskurs zu beenden, versuchen sie, innerhalb der rassistischen Diskurs zu intervenieren. (Ha 2005: 115)

The effectivity of the resignificatory interventions is dependent on the complex interaction between time and context of the intervention as well as – obviously – on the form it assumes. In the case of *Kanak Sprak* it seems that the subversive potential opened up by the appropriating use of the hate speech term *Kanake* in the preface loses momentum in the uniform and restrictive form of its repetition in the protocols.[83] Whereas *Kanak Sprak* takes effect in terms of its *Kanak* language, its mystifying literary form, its socio-political criticism and in the fundamental idea of *Kanak* self-representation, the work fails in offering a *Kanak* identity that transcends the dichotomous and exclusionary discourse that it aims to undermine.

Kanak Indeterminacy: Abschaum's Ertan

Ertan, the Turkish-German protagonist in Zaimoglu's novel *Abschaum* (1997) seems another specimen of Zaimoglu's *Kanak* community. *Abschaum* functions in a similar narrative mode as *Kanak Sprak*, again claiming – as its subtitle *Die wahre Geschichte von Ertan Ongun* [*The True Story of Ertan Ongun*] indicates – a high degree of *Kanak* 'authenticity'.[84] Whereas the *Kanak Sprak* protocols provided answers to the question 'What's life like as a Kanake in Germany?', Ertan's 35 'stories' can be read as a more elaborate response to the same question. In a first-person narrative, Ertan, a juvenile delinquent of Turkish origin, enlarges on his 'real-life' experiences as a *Kanake* in Germany. Like the *Kanak* protocols, his stories are cast in his own personal *Kanak* jargon and likewise capture a *Kanak couleur locale*. Titles such as 'Die Puff-Aufmisch-Story' ['The Whorehouse Stir Story'] and 'Die Fickst-du-mich-fick-ich-dich-Story' ['The You Fuck Me I Fuck You Story'] are characteristic to the world that originates from his stories.

Similar to the *Kanak Sprak Kanaken*, in his stories Ertan addresses a silent male interlocutor. Forms of address as 'man' and 'you know' point at the presence of a story-world listener. This time, the identity of this addressee initially remains in the dark. However, a reader familiar with Zaimoglu's other *Kanak* work will naturally assume that protagonist Ertan tells his story to the already familiar author-character Zaimoglu. In terms of narrative strategies, however, it is important to assert that up to the book's afterword, the text provides no information that supports this supposition. Only in 'Die letzte Story' ['The Last Story'] does Ertan explicitly refer to the actual situation in which his stories are recorded. In the afterword, the author-character Zaimoglu takes over the narration and explicates *Abschaum's* particular face-to-face interview format. Another important difference concerns the sequence of events in *Abschaum*. Whereas the *Kanak Sprak* protocols mainly consist of here-and-now statements, the *Abschaum* stories move back and forth in time and space.

The previous sections showed how the *Kanak Sprak Kanaken* offer their monologues in strict and obedient adherence to the discursive straitjacket of the preface. Conversely, Ertan's stories chiefly have the character of inner dialogues. Despite the fact that Ertan is addressing an interlocutor, his reflective way of narration suggests that he is also sorting out and more or less critically interpreting his memories for himself. The focalisation in this remembering narration shifts; not between different characters, but between 'different' Ertans: Ertan in various life stages. Some moments in his narration present the vision of a very young, relatively innocent Ertan. Other passages represent an Ertan at the top of his criminal career. Mostly, however, the Ertan of the narrative present focalises the stories. This Ertan has just been released from jail and looks back on the rather sad stories of his life. The differential space between the various focalisers sustains a certain development within the Ertan character. The shift between distinctive Ertans in different stages of his life produces a narrative exchange of opinions and opens up a dialogic space for reflection and contemplation.

With its expression of anticipation the title 'Die Anfang-vom-Ende Story' ['The Beginning of the End Story'] offers a good example of the space for contemplation that is opened up by the shifting focalisation. The title indicates a normative moment of reflection by the older, narrating Ertan in a story that is preponderantly focalised by a younger, much more scrupulous Ertan. Presumably, this young Ertan would not judge his current situation as the 'beginning of the end', as his estimation of his own person and position is another one. Secondary thoughts do not fit the pose that the young Ertan assumes. His *Kanak* attitude does not allow for reflection on possible future effects of his actual behaviour. The title, however, casts doubt on this cool and careless self-understanding and prompts a critical questioning of his *Kanak* attitude. The manifold use of the modal adverb 'maybe' in this same story produces a similar space for contemplation. Apparently, the older Ertan attempts to give meaning to happenings in the past, but he is unsure about how to do this. Referring to his initiation in the world of heroin he comments: 'Man, I smoked that stuff, suddenly became absolutely wide. Perhaps it came in handy, because I was so down and out and could not bear being so lonely and so. Anyway, I took it, that was the first time' (AB 49).[85] Taking Ertan's prior attitude of *Kanak* cool into account, this utterance seems a hesitant attempt to justify an act that the older Ertan retrospectively, overlooking the consequences, judges in a more sceptical way. Ertan's comment sounds like a self-critical apology, an 'I should have known better, but I did it anyway'.

This self-critical mood even increases – in tune with the dramatic developments – in the further course of Ertan's story: 'Then I realised, now you are high, now you are fucked, my boy, now see that you get out of this. Now you are done for, old boy, *yarrağı yedin oğlum, aynaya bakıyodum böyle ve yarrağı yedin oğlum diyodum.* I looked into the mirror and said: Now you are fucked' (AB 51).[86] The rise of this self-critique coincides with a shift in the mode of address. Whereas the 'man' in the first citation is (presumably) a form of address directed at the interlocutor, the deictic '*du*' and 'my boy' in the second citation function as markers of self-address. At certain moments of emotional excitement Ertan seems to forget his *Kanak* attitude as well as the narrative format. The mode of narration changes from a mere factual record into an almost intimate self-reflection on the growth and downfall of a *Kanak* individual. However, these moments of *Kanak* individuation and self-critique are rare. Mostly the use of the self-referential '*du*' functions in a similar way as in *Kanak Sprak*: it refers to the generic *Kanake*.

The self-reflexive dimension in *Abschaum* adds a new element to the narrated *Kanak* identity. The anger and critique no longer only concern the exclusionary ideology of dominant German society, but now also a tentative beginning of self-analysis comes in. 'Die Bruderkrieg-Story' ['The Brother War story'] represents a similar combination: the generic *Kanak* self-address (confirming hegemonic processes of social *Kanak*-isation) and a moment of critical self-reflection:

> My eyes, you know, like Bugs Bunny, 'cash' and dollar signs, but you know, my father, he once said something to me that got somehow stuck in my memory. That was in those days when I went in for sports and did not take drugs, and at night I would loiter about, never went home, always slept somewhere else, did a lot of shit, the time when I was seventeen, eighteen, you grow up, you have an absolutely tough body, you want to have fun, be in robberies, filch cars, you steal car radios, what do I know, everything that occurs. At that time my father already noticed that I was on the wrong track. (...) well, he looked at me and said: Listen, my boy, I know, nothing will ever be made of you. He said it so coolly and therefore it must have got stuck in my mind. (AB 113/114)

> Meine Augen, weißt du, wie Bugs Bunny, 'cash'- und Dollar-Zeichen, aber, weißt du, mein Vater, der hat mir mal was gesagt, das ist irgendwie hängengeblieben bei mir. Das war damals die Zeit, wo ich viel Sport gemacht hab und keine Drogen genommen, und abends viel auf der Piste war, nie nach Haus kam, immer woanders geschlafen hab, so Scheiße gebaut halt, so die Zeit mit siebzehn, achtzehn, du wirst erwachsen, hastn absolut harten Körper, du willst Spaß haben, du machst Raubüberfälle, klaust Autos, du klemmst Autoradios raus, was weiß ich, alles was so anliegt. Da hat mein Vater schon ge-

merkt, ich komm auf die schiefe Bahn. (...) na ja, er hat mich angekuckt und gesagt: Hör zu, mein Junge, ich weiß, aus dir wird nix mehr. Er hat es so cool rübergebracht, und deswegen muß es hängengeblieben sein. (AB 113/114)

As in the previous citation the mode of address shifts in the course of the story. The repeated 'you know' at the beginning of the cited passage confirms the narrative situation without actually signalising dialogue: the '*du*' is casually directed at the interlocutor. The second use of the personal pronoun in Ertan's description of his early days, the beginning of his criminal *Kanak* career, is a generic '*du*'.[87] The 'you grow up' is a statement about young men in general. The referential semantic of the '*du*' then rapidly proceeds in a *Kanak*-specific direction: 'you have an absolutely tough body' and 'you steal car radios'. However, the excusatory and at times celebratory description of the younger Ertan's criminal behaviour as an obvious and substantial part of his *Kanak* identity, is countered by the memory of the father. In those days the father already contested his son's behaviour and this moment of contestation is still prominently present in the older Ertan's mind.[88] In relating this moment this Ertan borrows the condemning phrase that his father used before: 'the wrong track'. The phrase, respectfully repeated by Ertan now, signalises an implicit kind of acknowledgement of the appropriateness of its use in the earlier situation.[89]

The passage clearly shows the moral gap between the two Ertans: the young and cool Ertan who is completely remorseless about his increasing criminality, and the older Ertan who now realises the foresight of his father's warning words. However, the moment of insight that results from the reflective encounter between the two remains without consequences. The older Ertan does not succeed in using its transformative potential. Nevertheless, the reflective dimension provides Ertan's character with the personal profile that the flat *Kanak Sprak Kanaken* lack. In comparison to *Kanaken* like Hakan and Ulku, Ertan's version of *Kanak* identity is dynamic and multidimensional, and often also contradictory. Whereas the young Ertan's use of the self-referential '*du*' generally confirms the *Kanak Sprak* mould of *Kanak* identity, the older Ertan's moments of self-address generally concern situations that are specific for Ertan as a *Kanak* individual (or an individualised *Kanake*). In *Kanak Sprak* the differences *between* the 24 *Kanaken* got lost in the reductive homogenisation of the characters to a single *Kanak* voice; in *Abschaum* Ertan's voice reflects his inner doubts and development, the differences *within*. Ertan's stories testify to an inner polyvocality. His *Kanak* identity is truly in process as a result of the reflective dimension that originates from the difference of opinion between the different Ertans.

This *Kanak* identity in process, however, is by far no cause for celebration. Ertan's stories of inner *Kanak* development resist popular perceptions of hybridity, 'third space' or the 'in between' as a position of (relative) freedom and possibilities outside of the dominant categories of identity. Instead, the older Ertan's retrospective self-reflections carry strong connotations of insecurity, rootlessness and fear. These negative feelings that for a greater part seem to result from an imposed *Kanak* identity, culminate in a huge identity crisis in the last story. In this story, narrative and narrated time finally come together. Ertan announces that today he will either smoke 'H', heroin, or, as an alternative 'tell my last story, to you, old one, and to the fucking machine' (AB 178).[90] This last story – and 'last' is open for various interpretations here – is highly dramatic. Ertan is in an extremely pessimistic state of mind and sees no future perspective for himself in German society. He desperately assesses:

> That's the shit, the shit is: I don't get along with the world out here, I've noticed that again, I simply don't get along with the world out here. Either I don't play the game or I don't want to join in the game. I am fed up with loneliness, is it because of a woman? No, it is not about a woman, I am among thousands of people and feel lonely, I also would like to know why it is so, ne diyim moruk.

> Das is die Scheiße, die Scheiße is: Ich komm nicht klar hier draußen, ich hab das schon wieder gemerkt, ich komm hier draußen einfach nicht klar. Entweder ich kann die Spielregeln nicht beachten, oder ich will auch gar nicht mitspielen. Mir stinkt die Einsamkeit, geht es um ne Frau? Nein, es geht nicht um ne Frau, ich bin zwischen Tausenden von Menschen und fühl mich allein, das wüßt ich auch gerne, warum das so is, ne diyim moruk. (AB 179)

Whether Ertan isn't *able* to participate, or whether he doesn't *want* to, the lonely effect in the end remains the same: Ertan does not manage 'out here'. On the one hand he longs for the time in jail, where the strict rules provided him with an orderly structure to live his life. On the other hand he longs for his former existence as a small-time criminal at the fringe of German society. Opposed to his critical awareness of the negative aspects of his criminal career is the idea that this underworld at least granted him an identity: 'Believe me, old boy, believe me, there are only two things in Germany: on the one hand the dirt, on the other the average society. You know what – to hell with society! There, in the dirt, I at least was somebody, there I was scum, you know, and now I am going down like that' (AB 180).[91]

According to Ertan's analysis German society has only two categories available: the norm and the deviation. As a *Kanake*, as a German person of other ethnic origin, he is socially determined to end up in the latter. Ertan's attempt to find a way out of this dichotomy results in a thorough identity crisis and ends in feelings of loneliness and despair. Not even the identity-constitutive act of telling his stories brings the yearned for relief and (social) recognition. Ertan's expectations in this respect are low: 'for you assholes out there, who read this, it is like a novel, *amına koyum*, you cannot sympathise with me in what I went through there, that's not possible. That's it. Don't feel like it any longer' (AB 182).[92] In this actual address of the reader, Ertan underlines the authenticity of his stories by making a distinction between their value for him and for his readership. What is merely a novel for the one – offensively interpellated as 'you assholes' –, is a true-to-life record of highly emotional impact for the other. The conclusion of this record remains open. Ertan's question 'How do you define something like me?' (AB 181) remains unanswered.[93] His particular, individualised *Kanak* identity turns out socially non-liveable and therefore doomed to failure. Ertan's stories conclude with ambivalent silence. 'That was it. Couldn't be buggered anymore' (AB 182) are the stories' final words.[94]

An afterword breaks this ambivalent finality, this narrative silence at the end of the novel. Here author-character Zaimoglu reveals his share in the whole as Ertan's interlocutor and the ghostwriter of his stories. In this afterword Zaimoglu overrules Ertan's self-chosen silence, not only by taking hold of the last word, but also by subsequently ascribing this last word to Ertan. Whereas Ertan's final contribution precludes narrative closure by leaving his particular identity question open, Zaimoglu, again in his role of native expert, undoes this indeterminacy. He writes: 'At the time of completion of this book, Ertan Ongun is living in Kiel and he is clean. He is 25 years old, was born and grew up in Germany, and it is his story: He has told it to me, the history of *Kanake*, a drug addict, a gangster' (AB 183).[95] Ertan's stories, Zaimoglu claims, are representative of *Kanak* life stories in general. Ertan's concern, he continues, are 'the many migrant children' (ibid.) who live lives similar to that of Ertan and who can be regarded as the future 'Children of Zoo Station' (ibid.).[96] By representing Ertan's character as of iconic quality, Zaimoglu re-instates his *Kanak* straitjacket. Moreover, in his reactivated role as *Kanak* puppeteer he reintroduces the divisive and homogenising *Kanak* discourse of 'we *Kanaken*' vis-à-vis 'you Germans'. In Ertan's name he asserts: 'Ertan's message is: we are the *Kanaken* you Germans have always been warning against. Now here we are, corresponding perfectly to the image and the fears in your heads' (ibid.).[97]

However, this afterword intervention by author-character Zaimoglu comes too late to effect interpretive consequences. Other than in the case of the *Kanak Sprak* protocols, Ertan's stories can resist the coercive straitjacket of Zaimoglu's explanatory 'master voice'. Being the primary reading, they retain their discursive independency, despite, as becomes clear in retrospect, their narratively embedded, secondary status in respect to the afterword. In fact, the stories themselves regularly contradict the message that author-character Zaimoglu attributes to Ertan after the stories, and in this sense this narrative act of power fails. Instead of the image of a tough, proud, and homogenous *Kanak* community as prescribed by the *Kanak Sprak* preface, Ertan's stories imagine an individualised *Kanak* identity. This personal *Kanak* identity is truly dynamic and multiple, but – consequently – also subject to self-doubt and moral reconsideration.

Ertan's own estimation of his stories of *Kanak* existence is negative. He disappointedly comes to the conclusion that in dominant German society there is no space for *Kanak* individuation, no space for an alternative, differential *Kanak* identity. He reads his life story as *necessarily* a story of criminality and downfall. German society has only one category available for him as a young male of Turkish origin. His stories conclude with this sad awareness. The reader who has followed and at times empathised with Ertan's wavering attempt to come to terms with his violent past, is left in disillusion. *Abschaum's* failed imagination of a liveable alternative *Kanak* identity confronts the reader with the destructive ethnicised dichotomies that structure German society. However, the narrative production of this insight deserves appreciation as a literary achievement. As Zafer Şenocak asserts in his article on the pitfalls of 'migrants' literature': 'Not generalisations but breaches in identity break new literary ground' (Şenocak 2006).[98] The comparison of the imaginations of *Kanak* identity in *Kanak Sprak* and *Abschaum* supports this supposition.

Conclusion: Unviable Identities

Zaimoglu's literary appropriation of the hate speech term *Kanake* generally counts as a (more or less successful) example of a resisting resignification. As a sociopolitical intervention this literary resignification not only brought about the visibility of a particular, marginalised (Turkish-German) part of the German population, but it also uncovered and criticised the oppressive social structures that underpin the pejorative term. The appropriating resignification of the term in *Kanak Sprak's* preface in combination with a strong and simultaneously mystifying claim of authenticity opened up a space for the imagination of an alternative *Kanak* identity beyond the hate speech frame.

My analysis of *Kanak Sprak* focused on the inauguration of a specifically polarising *Kanak* discourse, mainly in the 'authored' preface of the work. It pointed out how in *Kanak Sprak's* particular format, the preface by author-character Feridun Zaimoglu sets the stage for a strongly dichotomous discourse that is subsequently performed by 24 'interviewed' *Kanaken*. Despite his claims of diversity and *Kanak* self-representation, Zaimoglu appears as the conductor of the *Kanak* voices in their performance of his composition: 24 variations on one and the same theme. The result is a *Kanak* icon: an angry young Turkish-German male whose generic identity is determined by his offensive opposition to the despicable *Alemane* and some more non-*Kanak* Others. The particular use of the deictic '*du*' in the protocols determines the narrative process of contextual anchoring and ascribes to the reader a position outside of the exclusive *Kanak* community. The 24 *Kanaken* build their own homogenous community that leaves neither space for differentiation, nor for any non-*Kanak* Other, including the reader.

At first sight *Abschaum's* Ertan seems to fit in the same *Kanak* straitjacket. His angry attitude and his criminal career qualify him as a member of the proud *Kanak* community. However, throughout his stories, Ertan's character develops into a multidimensional personality, a development that even author-character Zaimoglu's patronising afterword cannot undo. The narrative oscillation between the younger and the older Ertan, and the use of the self-referential and specific '*du-Ertan*' (instead of the generic '*du-Kanake*') make his identity appear as processual. His stories relate the difficult process of *Kanak* individuation. Unfortunately, Ertan's last story ends in a dramatic denouement: his individualised and differential *Kanak* identity turns out to be socially unviable. German society has no space available for a Turkish-German individual that detonates the existing categories. This last insight – the social and discursive violence of prescribed ethnicised identity categories – is one of the main achievements of Zaimoglu's imagination of the *Kanak* figure. The uncomfortable figure brings a presence in the German ethnoscape to the fore that is often ignored. His aggressive *Kanak* talk and pose return the violence of the dominant dichotomies of public discourse and confront the reader with German society's destructive effects.

VI. Abdelkader Benali

'When the World Goes Mad and Everybody Has Lost Their Words'

'This is my family, thought Lamarat, and things are never going to be okay again' (Benali 1996: 157).[1]

Introduction

The career of the Moroccan-Dutch writer Abdelkader Benali seems more than that of any other Dutch writer of migrant background a story of literary success. Benali's debut novel, *Bruiloft aan zee* [*Wedding by the Sea*] (1996), was awarded with the Geertjan Lubberhuizen Prize 1997 for the best debut; it was also nominated for the renowned Libris Literature Prize in 1997.[2] Although he did not win this last prestigious literary award, the nomination definitely bestowed the author and his novel – that had hardly been noticed and reviewed before its nomination – with a central position in the literary and public media. The young Benali, aged 21 at the moment of publication, was invited to take part in innumerable interviews, contribute to various publications and participate in other public activities. The Dutch media hailed Benali as the embodiment of 'the perfect migrant'. His success story was taken to exemplify what could be achieved in Dutch society, independent of (ethnic) origin. Benali had 'simply' seized the opportunities that Dutch society – assumedly – offers to all its citizens.

Benali represented the positive Moroccan-Dutch role model that Dutch society needed to underline its self-evident and carefree multiculturality. First, Benali's success was taken to illustrate the glorious achievement that a positive attitude and energetic effort could result in. His public presence was supposed to work to stimulate and encourage other 'allochthons', in particular, other Dutch of Moroccan origin, to follow in his 'integrated' footsteps. Second, as an integrated and intelligent migrant who made eloquent use of the Dutch language, Benali also appeared acceptable for that part of the indigenous Dutch majority that was sceptical about Dutch multiculturality. If only all 'allochthons' were like Benali, there would be nothing problematic to Dutch multiculturality... Third, his work – like Zaimoglu's *Kanak* writing – satisfied the reader's curiosity about the exotic Other. *Bruiloft aan zee* presents an inviting story with characters who are 'different', an exotic landscape and a culturally peculiar plot. Together these three rather superficial and mainly extra-literary reasons founded Benali's popularity.

The following chapter explores the ways in which Benali's literature positions itself in a Dutch cultural field that seems determined by an interest in ethnic biographies. It interrogates how Benali's work intervenes in a Dutch popular discourse that seems predominantly obsessed by issues of cultural difference. It considers two cases of positioning and intervention at two different moments in time that, in respect to the dominant discourse, almost represent each other's antipodes. In the period between the publication of these two works, the public attitude towards Dutch multiculturality changed considerably: it shifted from optimistic ideas of a celebratory and happy multiculturality to the sceptical and polarised debates about the 'multicultural drama'. The first section discusses Benali's debut novel Bruiloft aan zee, published at the height of the happy multicultural mood. The analysis of this novel focuses mainly on narrative representations of patriarchal and other violence, and on the narrative strategies that guide the reader along these representations. Besides, the section includes some reflections on the media spectacle that accompanied the debut. It discusses the novel's Dutch reception but also the many interviews and poetic comments by the writer himself as contributions to the specific discourse of that time.

After the extensive analysis of Benali's debut follows a short intermezzo that addresses the six-year period of expectant silence that followed the hyped debut: the waiting for a successor novel. Several dramatic developments, both on a global and a national scale, afflicted this period. The terrorist attacks on the US of 9/11/01 transmitted the global world into a state of shock and effected a global polarisation. The murder of the Dutch populist-right politician Pim Fortuyn one year later caused a national earthquake.[3] The Netherlands ended up in a state of panic and profound (political and multicultural) mistrust. Benali chose to publically respond to these dramatic transformations of the Dutch social climate. He made use of his public position as a writer to vent his worries and to plead for responsibility and social engagement from the side of writers. He finally broke his literary silence with a novel appropriately titled De langverwachte [The Long-Awaited] (2002a).[4] When this novel was again nominated for the Libris Literature Prize 2003 and – contrary to the general expectations – also won the prize, the 1997 media spectacle seemed to repeat itself. The unexpected victory resulted in another surge of media attention for the now clearly more self-assured and media-experienced Benali. This time around he did not let the (often scathing) media uproar silence his literary voice, and, in the same year, in the shadow of De langverwachte, he published the drama Onrein. De vader, de zoon en de hond [Impure. The Father, the Son, and the Dog] (2003). The last section of this chapter focuses on this drama and on its assumed and maintained status as a literary intervention in the by-then seriously hardened Dutch socio-political discourse on issues of multiculturality.

The chapter concludes with a comparison of the literary devices that both works develop and deploy to intervene in the Dutch discourse on the pros and cons of multiculturality. It analyses how Benali's position (as a Dutch writer), his active self-positioning (as a Moroccan-Dutch writer), and the interpretation and appreciation of his literature changed in accordance with the changing discourse. Benali's position developed from the attributed 'Moroccan' role model into a self-chosen role as committed Moroccan-Dutch intermediary. His public persona actively transformed from a 'lucky' Moroccan prodigy into a serious and cautious Moroccan-Dutch intellectual. In this new role, Benali critically strives for mutual understanding in times of multicultural tension. He argues for an acknowledgement of the transformed Dutch ethnoscape as well as for a shared responsibility in the search for new forms of multicultural community. On the one hand he criticises the patriarchal structures and limited traditions of the Moroccan cultural world of his origin. His work makes clear that there is no place for gender discrimination in the multicultural Dutch community. On the other hand he claims an acknowledgement of (the impact of) migratory experiences as well as social inclusion on the basis of (ethnic) equality in the Dutch world. Benali perceives the cultural transformation of the new Netherlands as a common concern. In his literary works he lays bare the difficulties and deficits on both (indigenous and non-indigenous) sides that, despite their true or supposed differences, share a responsibility in the imagination and realisation of an inclusive future community.

Benali's Media Star

As already mentioned, the nomination of the novel Bruiloft aan zee for the national 1997 Libris Literature Prize resulted in Benali's literary breakthrough. After this nomination the interest in Benali's debut took on amazing proportions. Whereas initially, just after its publication, only the literary critic Hans Goedkoop reviewed the novel (in predominantly positive terms) for NRC Handelsblad (25 October 1996), the Libris nomination reshuffled the cards. All of a sudden the young Benali became a literary media star. It is conspicuous that the media mainly focused on Benali as a person, on his other ethnic background and his 'self-made writer' story. The central topic of interest concerned his remarkable career: the astonishing rise from his father's butcher's shop up the social ladder to the exclusive world of literary laureates. The dream ends in the centre of the Dutch cultural field: Benali's literary work competes with prominent Dutch and Belgian writers such as Hugo Claus, A.F.Th. van der Heijden and Margriet de Moor.[5]

Benali's story is a story of accepted challenges and intellectual growth. First of all the Moroccan-Dutch Benali entered university, already an effort in itself as the university represents one of the disputably last indigenous-Dutch bastions of the Netherlands.[6] In 1995 the young Benali triumphed in an essay contest that was organised in honour of the eighty-fourth lustrum of Leiden University. He won the first prize – a year of fee-free studying – with an essay called 'Vernieuwing als traditie' ['Innovation as Tradition']. In the same period he won several other literary prizes.[7] All these successes encouraged the publishing house Vassallucci to invite Benali to write a novel – the dream of every aspiring writer. The literary result of this request is the novel *Bruiloft aan zee* that soon became the object of a literary media hype. The novel was reprinted a considerable number of times, translated into several languages, and awarded with several (international) literary nominations and prizes.[8]

It is often argued that rather than the literary quality of his debut novel, Benali's Moroccan origin constituted a determinative factor in the Libris nomination.[9] The many interviews that were published during that time all praise and comment briefly on his novel, but only as an issue of secondary interest. Much more interesting, it seems, is Benali's already-mentioned stardom story. Benali himself responded to the overwhelming interest in his biography with an attitude that oscillated between irritation and resignation. In an interview with Judith Koelemeijer in *de Volkskrant* he demonstrates a certain pragmatic handling of the interest in his Moroccan background:

> 'They act as if I'm connected to that community as to a political party. (...) But I've said to myself: Abdel, don't clam up, that is not a good tactic. Just let it go and rattle off some clichés.' You have to be aware of your 'market value', is his opinion.[10]

> 'Ze doen alsof ik met die gemeenschap verbonden ben als met een politieke partij. (...) Maar ik heb tegen mezelf gezegd: Abdel, niet dichtklappen, dat is geen goede tactiek. Zet de knop om en ratel wat gemeenplaatsen af.' Je moet wel je 'marktwaarde' kennen, vindt hij. (Benali in Koelemeijer 1997)

A similar biographic tendency characterises the reviews of the novel. In general these reviews praise Benali's originality and enthusiasm, as well as the remarkable (youthful) pace of Benali's story. However, critics often combine their praise with critique of the novel's narrative incoherence – supposedly a side effect of this narrative speed. They find fault with the novel's supposed lack of balance, its imprecise language as well as its nonchalant style.[11] Generally, they consider Benali's work as exceptional, but again this valuation comprehends several reservations. Exceptional comes close to different, and this difference mostly concerns the writer's ethnic origin and age. The reviewers speculate on a temporal nature: the literary signs of immaturity are obvious symptoms of beginner's prose and the signs of a certain unfamiliarity with customary traditions of Dutch writing will disappear with his integration in the Dutch cultural field. In this sense the reception of the novel is ambivalent: whereas reviewers positively characterise Benali's mixing up of literary genres, styles and narrative modes and his creative use of language as original, at the same time they articulate the expectation that these characteristics will (and should) disappear with the professionalisation of his authorship. A more elaborate interpretation of the novel – its plot, its theme, its motives – was not made for years. The first extensive analysis of the novel by Louwerse only appears in 2001.[12] It is not before February 2004 that the entries 'Benali' (by Arno van der Valk) and 'Bruiloft aan zee' (by Ton Brouwers) are included in the two Dutch standard anthologies of Dutch literature, the Kritisch Literatuur Lexicon [Critical Literature Lexicon] and the Lexicon van literaire werken [Lexicon of Literary Works].

In reaction to questions concerning his literary style Benali himself relentlessly refers to Salman Rushdie as his absolute literary forefather and source of inspiration.[13] Not only does Benali recognise himself in Rushdie's theories on the diasporic situation and his reflections on his own position as a diasporic writer, he also greatly appreciates works of literature such as Midnight's Children and especially The Satanic Verses.[14] With these poetical positionings – that, in the light of Rushdie's precarious status, carry definite political connotations – Benali hints at an affinity of his work with that of a writer who is generally considered as an important representative of postcolonial and/or postmodern literature. Critics, however, do not pick up on these references and traces – aside from merely mentioning them. Their frame of reading remains predominantly biographic.[15]

The following analysis of Bruiloft aan zee leaves the question of literary positionings aside and instead focuses on the complexities of migration that the novel represents and brings up for discussion. It considers the novel's description of the wedding by the sea as a critical reconsideration of the desire to hold on to (out-)dated traditions, and to norms and values that, as the novel makes clear, are necessarily and drastically renegotiated in the process of migratory uprooting. The analysis makes clear that gender and generation as determinant factors of difference strongly influence both this desire and the migratory re-negotiation. With reference to Jürgen Link's theories on 'normalism' it critically addresses the technology of reading Bruiloft aan zee and the disruption of dominant patterns of expectation that the novel performs.

The Question of Being at Home

The opening sentence of Bruiloft aan zee introduces two of the novel's main protagonists in an explicitly antagonistic fashion:

> Lamarat Minar didn't live in Iwojen. Unlike Chalid, the man with the brown teeth and reversed rearview mirror, the driver of the white Mercedes cab who knew, by virtue of his profession, every hill, hogback, ridge and gully in the

entire Iwojen region, (...) Chalid, the taxi driver who cruised the roads, never dared to marry and thought lawn chairs were for wimps. (WS 1)[16]

Lamarat Minar was geen bewoner van de landstreek Iwojen. Dit in tegenstelling tot Chalid met de bruine tanden en omgedraaide achteruitkijkspiegel, de bestuurder van de witte Mercedes-taxi die uit hoofde van zijn beroep elke heuvelrug, elke kam en elk dwarsdal in Iwojen kende; (...) Chalid, de taxichauffeur die de wegen afreed, niet durfde te trouwen en tuinstoelen iets voor piemeltjes vond. (BZ 5)

The passage represents the taxi driver Chalid, nicknamed 'Bucket of Bolts Chalid' ['Chalid Blik op de Weg'] as the extremely well-informed native inhabitant of the region Iwojen. Lamarat constitutes his negative opposite: he is the foreign outsider, the uninformed visitor of the North Moroccan region where once his parents were born.[17] Although the active participation of these two men in the dramatic developments around the title event of the novel is rather limited, the two of them together represent the central focalising instances in the novel's narrative structure. As a rather arbitrary team they incorporate the two 'Moroccan' worlds that meet at the occasion of a wedding near the sea: that of the native and that of the emigrant's offspring. The two characters together offer two perspectives on this occasion that oppose and contrast each other as much as they influence and complement each other. The often-humorous tension between these two perspectives is of a productive quality for the novel: it renders the novel's narration a major part of its dynamic speed and fruitful confusion.

Lamarat Minar, the first character, is the rather inconspicuous Moroccan-Dutch young man who visits his (parents') country of origin to be present at his sister's wedding. His sister, Rebekka, is going to marry their father's youngest brother Mosa, their uncle. This Mosa is not much older than his nephew Lamarat and has been living in the region all his life. Now, as a result of the arranged marriage, he gets the opportunity to migrate to the Netherlands as well, just like his older brother. This brother, Lamarat's father, in fact opens the gate to the North and with this, as the text repeatedly suggests, the way to an enviable life of easy prosperity. The father offers his younger brother his daughter in return for his supervision during the construction of a second house in Morocco.[18] Lamarat, the brother of the bride-to-be, would have been nothing more than an obligatory wedding guest, if Uncle Mosa had not panicked and disappeared shortly before the official ceremony, when the wedding guests have already arrived. At the moment that the bridegroom's disappearance is noticed, Lamarat – until then an observing and not particularly involved guest at the wedding – is involuntarily drawn into the centre of the story's action. The perplexed father commands his son to find and bring back his uncle as soon as possible. What is at stake in this assignment is the protection and maintenance of the traditional family honour, which, in the local Moroccan context, has already suffered from a sustainable loss of credibility by the Moroccan-Dutch migration. Although the migration in itself is well seen and valued as an economical achievement, migration is simultaneously thought to incorporate the risk of a loss of cultural norms and values. For that reason, to uphold or even prove the family's good name and reputation, it is crucial that the groom's absence remains unnoticed by the wedding guests. The father puts all his hopes on Lamarat, his son, to avert 'the wind of scandal and shame' (WS 186).

The search for the bridegroom Mosa begins. This search constitutes the core-action in a narrative that ravels in several directions. In her article 'Zwartrijders in de Nederlandse Literatuur' (2001), Henriëtte Louwerse discusses 'the quest' as a recurring motive in 'migrants' literature'. In respect to Benali's *Bruiloft aan zee* she argues that the quest on the one hand determines the structure of the novel, whereas on the other the developing narrative simultaneously deconstructs this motive. The particular narration of *Bruiloft aan zee* disrupts any linear and/or teleological structure based on a movement between beginning and end. Instead it continuously shifts in time, space and sentiments. Interwoven in this shifting narration are poetic and metafictional comments that question the narrative representation of the migratory and quest-related happenings.[19] These – often ironic – metafictional commentaries not only complicate the narrative, but they also bring in several narrative ambivalences and contradictions, or, as Louwerse assesses, 'moments of indeterminacy' (2001: 177). In the novel's reception these moments are often brought forward and (mis-)interpreted as 'mistakes' and 'inconsequences'. In another reading, however, their surplus presence encourages the reader to take nothing at face value. They prompt the reader to consider other possible meanings as well, and as such, they might well be part of a postmodern game of language, or tools in a strategy of disruptive confusion.

A postmodern or disruptive dimension indeed characterises Lamarat's quest. A-typically, the not very committed Lamarat hardly knows what he is looking for. His being on the road is more or less accidental, the act itself initiated by his – still dominant – father and the result of his obedience to the father's will. As the second-generation son of an emigrant, grown up in the Netherlands, his familiarity with Morocco consists of his father's stories and the experience of only one summer vacation in Morocco in the previous year. This very limited experience makes Lamarat rather helpless in respect to his responsible task. He is not familiar with the Moroccan landscape, its people and the customs of his – indirect – country of origin. The text seems to suggest that his 'country of origin' also perceives of him that way. In the eyes of the native Moroccan population, Lamarat is a visitor, a 'foreigner' (WS 46 *et passim*), a boy 'from the north' (WS 48). In fact, Lamarat is nothing more than a stranger in Iwojen.

Lamarat's antagonist complementary counterpart, the taxi driver 'Bucket of Bolts Chalid', is the main and rather disdainful focaliser of the representations of the stranger Lamarat in the Iwojen landscape.[20] As the above-cited fragment already made clear, Chalid is the *legitimate* representative of the region. In contra-distinction to Lamarat, he knows all the roads and settlements of Iwojen. Besides, he is also informed about the inhabitants of the region and, even more impressive and practicable, about the details of their private lives. Chalid knows about their secret pleasures and problems, their inner joys and sorrows.[21] A ride in Chalid's taxi is sort of synonymous with a visit to a psychologist.

As Chalid has been working as a taxi driver all his life, he also knows the personal histories of the members of Lamarat's family, beginning with the story of the father's migration. Thirty years ago taxi driver Chalid delivered the father at the point of departure for his guest labour adventure. In a flashback the novel describes their bygone conversation in detail. This flashback supplies the reader with a not particularly convincing, not particularly powerful image of the father. In the conversation Chalid's low estimation of the father and his undertaking is manifest: 'In the taxi the taxi driver – Bucket of Bolts Chalid, always in the mood to talk and younger then, though his teeth were already in an advanced state of decay – said to the father-to-be: "So you're going to Germany, hmm"' (WS 83).[22] In the manner of a professional psychologist Chalid repeats this rhetorical question – in slight variations – five times during the conversation. Each time it prompts the father to elaborate on his adventurous undertaking. Each time Chalid responds with the doubt raising 'hmm' that adds a rather sceptical, underestimating undertone to his inquiry.

The father, to whom the question is addressed, feels obliged every time anew to defend his decision. He praises the northern country that he is heading for, its beauty as well as the opportunities that are waiting for him and his family there. At the same time, in the same utterances, he explicates his despise for the poverty-ridden region of Iwojen that he is about to leave behind. In an excited spirit he gives way to his dreams:

> It'll be my country, a good country, good money, hard work, success. (...) I'm going to Deutschland, we're going to Deutschland, and one day my children will be going to Deutschland, to see where their father used to work, the steel factories, the slaughterhouses, the high-rise apartments. They'll be proud of me. I'll send them there so they won't forget what I did for them. (WS 83)

> Het wordt mijn land, goed land, hard werken, geld verdienen, zegevieren (...) Ik ga naar Deutschland, wij gaan naar Deutschland en ooit zullen mijn kinderen ook naar Deutschland gaan, kijken naar de plekken waar hun vader werkte, de hoogovens, de slagerijen en de torenflats. Ze zullen trots op mij zijn. Ik zal ze daar naar toe sturen zodat ze niet kunnen vergeten wat ik voor hen heb gedaan. (BZ 75)

The narrative tension that is generated in this short passage and that is increased by Chalid's repeated non-verbalised expressions of doubt, results mainly from the discrepancy in knowledge between the father and the reader. The last possesses a different, more informed state of knowledge about the actual outcomes of such guest workers' dreams. As a result of this discrepancy the passage activates feelings of discomfort and pity at the side of the reader. Moreover, the father's expectant representation also simply contradicts the actual story-world constellation that is presented earlier in the narration: despite the father's intentions the family is still living in the Netherlands and is only visiting the 'homeland' Morocco for a summer holiday.

Although the naïve dream raises feelings of empathy for the well-intending and trustful father, the reader cannot but share the disparaging scepticism as mediated by the repeated question of Chalid. On the one hand the father still claims and possesses a certain iconic position of power as family patriarch: he arranges his daughter's marriage and sends his son away on the search. On the other hand many indications of image decline make clear that his power is eroding. Chalid's cynicism more or less invites the reader to think of the father as silly and credulous. The idea of a short stay and soon return has clearly turned out otherwise. The dream of sending his children to the North to visit the places where their father made his fortune so that they can be proud of him, will always remain a dream. As a matter of fact, the actual situation is the other way around. The father is showing his children his homeland Morocco as their foreign, far-away and exotic country of origin. The dreamt-of life of victory and pride has turned out a double disillusion: both in the Netherlands and in Morocco the father lives a life of rootlessness, of estrangement, and, in the end, of double disappointment.

Chalid's focalisation of the father's departure, especially its derogatory tone, positions the taxi driver himself in an intellectually superior position. Despite the given situation of the father who courageously heads for adventure and Chalid who securely stays behind in the region, the focalisation constitutes the situation in the opposite way. Chalid paradoxically presents himself as a man of the world, an experienced traveller who knows the fitting behaviour in every situation. He shares his worldly knowledge with the less-than-worldly father:[23]

'Next time, in Deutschland or wherever you wind up, always try to have some cash handy, so people won't think you're a poor slob from some backward country.'
The father had nodded, 'Hell of a good tip,' and slammed the door shut. The taxi driver turned the car around for the return trip and leaned out the window to pass on one more bit of advice to the young father.
'If I were you, I'd go to Ollanda,' he said, and stepped on the gas. (WS 84)

'Volgende keer, daarstraks in Deutschland of god weet waar je komen zal, probeer altijd een biljetje bij de hand te hebben, de mensen zouden kunnen denken dat je zo'n arme sloeber uit de een of andere landstreek bent.'
De vader had geknikt, 'Verdomd wat een goede tip,' en de deur dichtgeslagen. De taxichauffeur keerde zijn wagen om richting landstreek maar keek voor vertrek nog een keer uit zijn raam naar de nog jonge vader om hem iets mee te delen.
'Weet je wat, als ik jou was zou ik naar Ollanda gaan,' en snelde weg. (BZ 76)

In this sort of goodbye, it is Chalid who proposes the father to change his intended route of migration. In a seemingly arbitrary way he proposes the father to exchange Germany for the Netherlands as his country of destination. In a similar way, years later, Chalid also determines Lamarat's route in the quest for his uncle Mosa. The hierarchical constellation that arises in this later situation strongly resembles the previous one. The son Lamarat, coming from the North, now takes over the former, passive role of his father. Searching for his uncle, Lamarat is dependent on the directions of the taxi driver Chalid. Chalid again assumes the role of expert, now determining the son's route in a telling repetition of history.

Two Brothers: Father and Fiancé

In spite of the condescending tone and caricature-like characterisation brought in by Chalid's focalisation, the narrative makes clear that the character of the father is more complex than the above-cited passage suggests. Moreover, as the central possessor of (patriarchal) power, the figure of the father is crucial to the development of the story of Bruiloft aan zee. The father's image and reputation strongly depend on the offered perspective. The appreciation for his achievements proves strongly localised and often ambivalent. The inhabitants of the region perceive of the father as a particular kind of victor: as someone who has made his fortune and now brings back money to Iwojen. At the same time his life of success in the North makes him a subject of doubt. In the eyes of the people who have stayed behind, the North also connotates a giving up on traditional norms and values and, as a result, a loss of tradition-based honour. The extradiegetic narrator describes the local appreciation for the emigrants in a predominantly cynical tone, for instance in the following passage:

And yet the people in Al Homey loved the 'foreigners' – after all, they brought in hard cash, held wedding banquets, enabled the young men to go off and seek their fortunes, and the young women to stay at home for the rest of their lives, ordered houses to be built and tore them down again. They put up mosques, put down carpets, hung blackboards, bore children, married them off and remained one hundred percent illiterate until the day they died. And how everybody adored them! Love is so beautiful when it's for sale, just ask Mosa the next time he's had a few too many. (WS 46/47)

En toch hielden de mensen in Nadorp van de 'buitenlanders,' ze brachten pecunia, doekoe, hielden bruiloften, zorgden dat de jongemannen wegkonden en de jonge vrouwen voor de rest van hun leven thuisbleven, lieten huizen bouwen en weer afbreken. Ze bouwden moskeeën, legden er tapijten en hingen er krijtborden op, baarden kinderen, gaven ze weer weg en bleven tot in de dood honderd procent analfabeet. Maar iedereen hield van ze! En wat is de liefde mooi als je die kopen kan, vraag het Mosa als hij weer eens aangeschoten is. (BZ 44)[24]

Read in this context, Chalid's disparaging attitude might as well be prompted by envy: after all the father has managed a life in the North and is prosperous enough to build a second house in his Moroccan home region. That this house is not of the best quality – already crumbling away during its construction – throws only a slight shadow on the attained degree of economical achievement.

Whereas in Iwojen the father can at least perform the role of the successful emigrant who now enables his brother to follow this same successful path, passages set in the Netherlands make clear that there his position is more on the side of the marginalised. It turns out that there, in 'Sesame Seed City' (WS 61), he lives his life in a certain state of despair.[25] More and more the father realises that he is not only losing his job, but also his authority and his bond to his homeland. In the eyes of his children he is the man who imagines the past as future. While doing so on a daily basis, he gets stuck in a rhetoric of return: 'He stayed a year, two years, ten years and finally he'd spent thirty years announcing at every meal that this year would be the last. "I'm going back, for good. Away from this land of pork and rotten bananas"' (WS 26).[26] He repeatedly emphasises his authority and position of power towards his children by referring to his central role in the migration. At the same time he has to acknowledge the fact that his children grow up in another culture. Their bond with Morocco as a 'homeland' is illusionary: from the description of their feelings towards the visit of this faraway country, it becomes clear that they perceive of Morocco in an emotionally detached way. The question whether instead they conceive of the Netherlands as their homeland the novel leaves unanswered. In general the Netherlands remains rather flat in its depiction: all dramatic actions take place in Morocco that, as a result of the backward-directed orientation of the father's gaze, also remains the central space of reference in the family's life in the Netherlands. The image of the Netherlands in the novel mainly takes shape through focalisation by the people of Iwojen. For them France, Belgium, the Netherlands and 'Deutschland' signify more or less the same: places of profit and prosperity in the culturally different North.

In a certain way the migrant father in the novel is representative of a 'lost generation': lost for both communities. No matter how hard this generation of migrants tries to hold on to cultural traditions and 'roots', its (f)actual absence obfuscates its claims of belonging in the homeland in the eyes of those who have stayed there. In the new country that they actually and daily live as their home, often for years in a row, the homeland-directed attitude hampers a new sense of belonging. This attitude not only estranges them from their new environment, but also from their children who lack the homeland-bond that the first-generation migrants cherish. In *Bruiloft aan zee* Lamarat and Rebekka are such children, who grow up with the promise of a return that never comes. At regular occasions the father senses the slipping away of the Moroccan dimension of their life. Besides, he is painfully aware of the erosion of his position of patriarchal power within the family that, as the text suggests, is connected to this other country. His attempts to bring more Moroccan culture as well as more Islam in the house are of little success. His statements of authority meant to reinstate his position of power – 'I'm your father, the, you know, alpha and omega' (WS 26) – sound barely convincing.[27] However, despite his declining status the father succeeds in arranging a marriage between his brother and his daughter. This patriarchal triumph is to be celebrated with a traditional wedding party. In the father's expectation this marriage will not only restrengthen the bonds of the family by connecting two of its members in holy matrimony, but it will also restore the estimation and respect for his person in the left behind homeland. With the wedding arrangement he confirms his enduring authority as the family patriarch and simultaneously illustrates his continuing valuation of the traditions of the homeland. For the father the marriage in this sense represents the hope-charged event that will re-establish his position of honour both in- and outside the family. It will make his world 'in order' again.

The father takes the fact that the reinstatement of his patriarchal power requires an act of patriarchal violence for granted. When he meets his brother to settle the final agreements, he encourages him in a fatherly tone to be patient with his daughter who, as he tells Mosa, cried about her fate for weeks in a row:

> She probably needs to get used to you, little brother, do you know what I mean? She's eighteen now and next year she'll be nineteen, God willing (...) If you only knew how many nights she cried, for weeks on end, but that's all over now. She's not really ready for you, so try to be nice, do you know what I'm saying or don't you? (WS 104/105)

> Ze moet misschien aan je wennen, begrijp je wat ik bedoel broertje, achttien is ze nu en volgend jaar zal ze negentien zijn als-hij-van-boven-het-wil (...). Als je eens wist hoeveel nachten ze heeft gehuild, weken achtereen maar nu is het

NEW GERMANS, NEW DUTCH

over. Ze is nog niet helemaal klaar voor jou, probeer een beetje aardig te zijn, begrijp je me of niet. (BZ 94)

The father represents Rebekka's disquietude as an unavoidable part of the honour-consolidating process. It is up to Mosa now to reassure his future bride and to give her the attentiveness that helps her to come to terms with her fate. During their first encounter, one year before the wedding, Mosa obediently gives his best: 'an ice-cream cone, a kiss and a gold necklace, each of them accompanied by a hug, until she had no choice but to say, 'Yes, but I want to be independent. Yes, but you have to treat me with respect. Yes, but how do I know you aren't lying?' (WS 105).[28] Under the pressure of her father and mislead – as the reader realises – by Mosa's calculated declarations of affection, Rebekka gives in to the long-decided family agreement. The reader witnesses how she puts away her doubts, dries her tears and reconciles herself to a dream of romantic love. The fact that several of these scenes are focalised by her well-intending brother Lamarat lends them a reassuring character. Lamarat's focalisation does not question the father's authority aside from some moments of accidental irony. Lamarat approaches his father with respect and, as the immediate acceptance of the search command testifies, in juvenile obedience to his father's patriarchal power.

The novel's extradiegetic narrator regularly undermines both Rebekka's (more or less enforced) dream of romantic love as well as the father's positive perception of the preservation of the family honour with the help of Mosa. Several times the narrator cynically explicates his doubts about the event by referring to the father's (as well as Rebekka's) ignorance about the bridegroom's secret life of sexual pleasures in the red light district of Iwojen's border city Melilliar. He comments:

What if the father had known about Mosa's trips to Melilliar? (...) Would he have dared to marry off his daughter, as she looked on from her crib, would he have dared to put her and her unsullied reputation in Mosa's hands? We don't know. But the father talked about his brother and tickled his son until he collapsed into giggles. (WS 19)

Wat als de vader weet zou hebben gehad van Mosa's gang naar Melilliaar? (...) Zou hij het hebben aangedurfd om zijn dochter die vanuit het ledikant toekeek, aan hem uit te huwelijken, haar te geef en te grabbel te gooien? We weten het niet. Maar de vader sprak over zijn broer en kietelde zijn zoon de lucht in. (BZ 21)

The absence of daughter Rebekka, the bride-to-be, from the father's attention is striking. Despite the fact that her agreement on the arrangements is of central enabling importance for the ritual reassurance of the family honour, her existence is deemed irrelevant in the father's male-focused perception. In his patriarchal ideology Rebekka merely functions as symbolic chattel à la Lévi-Strauss in a male-to-male transaction. The terms of the wedding agreement appoint Mosa to take care of the father's Moroccan house and the father to supply his brother with the attractive access to the North.[29] Rebekka enables this transaction without being a partner in the deal. The narrator's casual suggestion that the father might know of Mosa's illicit behaviour does not influence the respectability of the transaction. His sexual escapades in Melilliar's red light district contain neither a threat to the family honour nor to dominant notions of honourable masculinity. In respect to Rebekka the situation is fundamentally different: honour has two discrepantly gendered levels of meaning here. Her virginity stands in a synecdochal relation to the family honour, so that pre-matrimonial sexual activity is out of the question. It would destroy both Rebekka's respectable womanhood and the family's impeccable reputation.

The textual indications of doubt about Mosa's honorability are contrasted and complemented (again a double-sided perspective) by the bridegroom's own doubts about the wedding. It becomes clear that his decision to accept his brother's wedding arrangements is neither an eager nor a completely voluntary one. It results from external social pressure to exchange his life of poor laziness in the region for a life of diligent prosperity up North, more than from his own willingness to marry and the conviction that going North is the right thing to do. The regional perception of his brother as a successful emigrant increases the pressure considerably. The family bond functions as an easy invitation, incorporated by Rebekka, to the land of 'golden streets' (BZ 22). Despite his heartfelt doubts Mosa gives in to the social pressure:

> But how can you avoid so much attention when everybody is always asking, 'when will you be heading north?' After all, he had a brother there, someone who could help him with money, a job, the trip over. And not just to any old country in Europe – not Spain where those dirty Franco dogs spit on you, not France, not Deutschland, but the best country in the whole wide world: Ollanda! Only a fool would pass up a chance like that. (...) Is that true, Mosa wondered to himself, or am I starting to think like them? 'Well, honey, let me tell you, the money's up there where your brother is, no matter how you look at it, no matter what kind of work he has to do to earn it.' Every time he ran into someone, it was always the same story, and you'd have to be crazy not to admit that they were right, even if the streets up north weren't really paved with gold. (WS 19/20)

> Maar hoe kun je je aan zoveel aandacht onttrekken wanneer iedereen zegt: 'En wanneer ga jij nou eens naar het noorden?' Hij had toch een broer daar, iemand die hem aan geld kon helpen, aan werk, aan een oversteek naar Europa

– en wat voor een Europa, niet dat Spanje waar die Franco-honden op je spuugden, niet Frankrijk, niet Deutschland, maar het allerbeste van de hele wereld: Ollanda! Dus hij was een stommeling als hij het zou laten.
(...) Is het waar wat ze zeggen, of laat ik me te veel imponeren, overwoog Mosa bij zichzelf. 'Nee, lieve schat, het geld is boven bij je broer, hoe dan ook en wat voor werk het ook is wat hij daar doet,' En zo ging het altijd als hij iemand tegenkwam en je zou wel gek zijn als je ze niet een klein beetje gelijk gaf, hoe abstract de gouden straten daarboven ook werden voorgesteld.' (BZ 21/22)

And thus, reluctantly, Mosa agrees to the marriage with his niece Rebekka. He himself does not seem to be bothered very much about either his dishonourable reputation, or about his dishonesty towards his brother and future bride. Mosa is troubled about his own future.

What worries Mosa is the prospect of marrying a woman from the North, stereotypically known as dominant and demanding. Besides, the marriage entails the obligatory goodbye to his favourite prostitute, Chatischa. Mosa's fear and second thoughts rise to a climax on the day of the wedding, when Chalid the taxi driver rebukes Mosa for his decision:

'I hear you've decided to head out for Europe after all, you crazy guy. At any rate, the girl you're marrying will be your ticket to Ollanda. This country might be hek-o-hek, so-so, but you couldn't persuade me to go to a country where the women boss you around and walk over you (...).'
Words like that hit hard. They made you wonder about the motives of your friends. (...) First you wish me luck and kiss me on cheek and the forehead, but once you're through slobbering, your true mentality comes to the fore: you're nothing but a bunch of hypocrites luring innocent people into a trap. And it was true – no one envied him. (WZ 30/31)

'Je wilt dus toch naar dat Europa, jij goeie gek. Goed: je trouwt met een meisje dat je naar 'Ollanda zal brengen en deze streek mag dan wel hek-o-hek, zozo zijn maar voor geen geld zou ik naar een streek gaan waar de vrouw de baas over je is en met haar voeten op je trapt (...).'
Zulke woorden komen hard aan. Dan ga je toch anders denken over de drijfveren van je vrienden. (...) Eerst mij gelukwensen en op wang en voorhoofd kussen maar eenmaal uitgekust kwijlt jullie ware mentaliteit pas op: huichelaars die onschuldige mensen in de val lokken. En het was waar: er was niemand die hem nog benijdde. (BZ 31/32)

As the passage makes clear Mosa feels trapped and betrayed. Full of self-pity he flees to Chatischa and forgets about his fearful fate in the comfort of her presence (and doped by excessive alcohol consumption). Lamarat finally finds his uncle in this fuddled state of consciousness. It is in this state that he brings Mosa back to his waiting bride.

An (Ab-)Normal Journey Towards a Wedding

At first sight, the narration offers this outcome – the return of the groom to the bride – as the positive conclusion of the search. Mosa's return enables a happy end. Lamarat's quest has been successful and the reader, who more or less identifies with Lamarat as part-time focaliser, is sort of relieved that now the wedding can take place as planned. This relief comes up despite the fact that the reader also experiences a certain discomfort at the scene of the crying Rebekka, or as a result of Chalid's and the extradiegetic narrator's cynicism. However, Rebekka has arranged herself with the wedding prospect and the cynical focalisation also arouses feelings of pity and compassion for the targeted object: the disempowered and slightly dopey father. Besides, after all, now the threatened family honour seems saved and the bride is spared a disappointment. Mosa's flight into sex and alcohol does not trouble the relief on the side of the father. The dénouement is offered as a 'fine' solution to a temporal problem, and it seems that the reader can look forward in satisfaction to the promised wedding by the sea. At second sight, however, this pattern of reader expectation appears problematical. Jürgen Link's theories on 'normalism' and his elaborations on '(ab-)normal journeys' in works of literature provide a tool to question the offered 'experience of relief' as well as the narrative structure that invites (or prescribes) this experience.

In the introduction to his fascinating study *Versuch über den Normalismus. Wie Normalität produziert wird* [*Exertion on Normalism. How Normality Is Produced*] (1999) Link decisively distinguishes between the categories 'normality' and 'normativity', two categories that in his opinion are often mistaken for one and the same. Normality, Link insists, is in no case the same as 'the application of norms' ['Normgeltung'] (1999: 16), and normal is not identical with 'according to the norm'. Link considers normality as a gradual 'culture and subject-constitutive category' ['kultur- und subjektkonstitutive Kategorie'] (ibid. 49) that is dependent on precarious 'boundaries of behaviour' ['Verhaltens-Grenzen'] (ibid. 21). These 'boundaries of behaviour' constitute a particular continuum that separates the normal from the a-normal or the deviant. The negotiation of these boundaries – and thus the determination of normality – moves between attitudes of tolerance and the (experienced) necessity to intervene. Link defines the resulting web of rules and (fluid) boundaries as 'normalism' ['Normalismus']. About the relation between normalism and literature Link maintains that: '[i]n normalism the main function of art and literature can be understood as [the] preparation of application models for denormalisations (e.g. 'marginalisations')' (ibid. 58).[30] Aesthetically challenging literature, he argues, does not simply affirm the status quo of normality, but instead plays with or even crosses given boundaries. This does not automatically mean, as Link contends, that literature can bring about 'actual' de-normalisations on a social level. Literature performs denormalisations by means of the imagination, and offers these imagined performances to its readers as possible patterns of identification. Link names the basic type of such staged denormalisations in transgressive narratives '(ab-)normal journeys' ['(nicht) normale Fahrten'] (ibid.).

An application of Link's theories on normality and (ab-)normal journeys to the novel Bruiloft aan zee offers an interesting and alternative perspective on the final dénouement of the novel's story. In the story-world discourse of Bruiloft aan zee, normality is a category that is strongly linked to honour. As I have pointed out before, this honour in its turn – the family honour – is strongly gendered. The quest that determines the novel's central story can be considered an (ab-)normal journey, aimed at maintaining a certain state of normality that is threatened by a denormalisation: the disappearance of the groom. The father's fear for denormalisation, for the loss of the family honour, forms the accelerating spirit of the story. The novel's narrative speed, the feeling of time running out, is connected to this fear. The reader of the novel is invited to identify with the main story's thrilling, breathless search, alternately focalised by the two members of the 'search team' Chalid and Lamarat.

Despite certain feelings of ambivalence and doubt about the father's patriarchal project, in the fervour of the story the reader easily 'forgets' about Dutch moral objections to arranged marriages and uncle-niece liaisons. The reader identifies with Lamarat's assignment of returning the runaway groom. 'Dutch normativity' is overshadowed by the acceptance of and even longing for what is narratively represented as 'Moroccan normality'. The intended wedding is presented as the novel's final instalment of this 'Moroccan normality'. It will not only confirm the father's adherence to Moroccan traditions and values, but also turn Uncle Mosa's up till then rather 'ab-normal' biography into a 'normal' one. His life of unemployed laziness combined with sexual excess will move, so the story suggests, within the boundaries of normality by means of his marriage to his niece Rebekka. A reading according to 'Western norms', resisting a similar arranged uncle-niece marriage, would contrarily approve of a denormalisation. It would make the whole quest superfluous, its story irrelevant. In general, instead of objecting to a successful conclusion of Lamarat's quest, the reader follows the offered pattern of identification and – alongside the father – longs for a reversion to the (narrative) state of story normality.

The reversion to this normality seems extremely close, when, almost at the end of the novel, Lamarat indeed returns with the retrieved uncle at his side. However, in this moment the narrative disrupts its own pattern of expectation and undermines the pattern of identification that it has previously installed itself. It is Rebekka, the bride-to-be, who now takes over the direction. She resists the 'happy ending of Moroccan normality' that the narrative is heading for and to which, one has to add, she has initially agreed herself. In the crucial (and supposedly relieving) moment of return, Rebekka approaches her brother and uncle. In a renewed instance of denormalisation she angrily re-routes their journey home that aims for a concluding, normalising wedding. Her comment:

> Rebekka turned to Lamarat. 'If you only knew, sweet, innocent Ratty, how I watched you run up and down the street when I was a little girl and dreamed of a wedding by the sea: a roaring fire, a huge bowl of punch, guitar music everywhere and a husband who'd wait on me hand and foot. (...) Humph, in this godforsaken village you can't get lighters, punch or glasses, but there's plenty of sea, more than enough sea... Come on,' sister shouted, 'we're going to the sea. And remember: we're taking that scuzzbag with us.' (WS 169/170)

> Rebekka wendde zich tot Lamarat: 'Je zou eens moeten weten, toen ik nog klein was, lieve, onnozele Ratje, toen jij buiten voor de deur je rot rende, droomde ik al van een bruiloft aan zee. Groot kampvuur, een groot glas bowl, overal gitaarmuziek en een man die zich de hele dag voor me zou kapotrennen om het me maar naar de zin te maken. (...) Welnu, er is hier in dit godvergeten dorp dan wel geen bowl, aansteker of glas te krijgen maar zee is er genoeg, meer dan genoeg... Kom op,' kraaide zus, 'we gaan naar zee. En niet vergeten: we nemen die slampamper mee.' (BZ 145)

It is, as if a terrible furiosity takes possession of Rebekka who until this determinative moment has played a rather passive role in the narrative. All of a sudden she takes over the course of the story and resists the offered 'normal' conclusion.

As the above-cited passage makes clear, Rebekka realises that the fulfilment of her naïve fantasy of a romantic future wedding is out of the question. Not only the required conditions fail, but also the fuddled state of mind and body of her future husband leaves much to be desired. The last sentence of the cited passage, in its reminiscence of a famous Dutch children's song about a joyful day out at the sea, introduces a melodic lightness in the scene that strangely collides with the threatening content of Rebekka's words.[31] The awaited end – a return to the assumed 'normality' – all of a sudden becomes insecure. Why not return to the waiting family and wedding guests to get the ceremony over and done with? What is the enraged bride going to do with this 'scuzzbag'?

These questions not only come to the reader's mind, but also occupy the minds of the members of Rebekka's family, who by that time have been alarmed by the raised sound of her voice. Very much like in a comic book, father, mother and grandparents set off in pursuit of the threesome, thus heading for the sea as well. The chaotic pace of the chase is reflected in the playful, almost dancing language of its description:

NEW GERMANS, NEW DUTCH

Too stunned to say another word, the mother, the grandfather and the grand-mother – where *does* she get the energy – bounded down the hillside, going down down down, terrace by terrace, step by step, weaving one by one, in single file, close on each other's heels and tangled in a bumpy conga, around the cactuses, over the rocks and down the terraces, until between their feet and the sea there was only a young man [boy, LM], a young woman and a victim. (WS 177) [32]

Verbouwereerd, met stomheid geslagen sprongen de moeder, de opa en de oma – waar haalt zij de energie vandaan – de een na de ander naar beneden, steeds lager, terras na terras, trap na trap slalomden zij een voor een, achter elkaar, op elkaar, door elkaar in een schokkerige een-twee-hupsakee-pas om de cactusplanten, de rotsen en terrasjes heen totdat er tussen hun voeten en de zee slechts een jongen, een vrouw en een slachtoffer was. (BZ 151/152)

The used formulation of 'boy, woman and victim' for the threesome at the sea is striking. It contains a remarkable division that anticipates on the 'maturation ri-tual' to come. Lamarat and Rebekka, brother and sister, are distinctively repre-sented as boy and woman, child and adult. Lamarat remains the boy-child, who still falls under the paternal guidance of the father patriarch, and who, by contri-buting his bit to the restoration of the novel's narrative normality, becomes com-plicit in its patriarchal ideology of family honour. Rebekka, who initially also obeyed to the father's will and agreed to the arranged marriage, crosses the threshold to adulthood in the moment that she independently chooses to change the course of events against her father's explicit will.

A Gender-Roles-Reversing Ritual

In terms of the novel's discourse, Rebekka's act of female independence constitu-tes another denormalisation, this time, as will soon become clear, of an irreversi-ble quality. Rebekka's intervention not only threatens the family honour, but also reshuffles the traditionally gendered power relations. Rebekka's anger at the run-away Mosa appears rather grotesque. It is as if condensed rage about her status as chattel, as object of exchange in the male-to-male-transaction, now hits Mosa in his symbolic role, as representative of a patriarchal system. Rebekka disrupts the transaction as well as the traditional gender roles by violently altering the wed-ding ritual. The altered ritual implies a subversion of the gender roles: Mosa is 'sacrificed' and – arguably – acquires the status of a victim.

The alternative wedding performance constitutes the ab-normal apotheosis fol-lowing on the normalising quest and chase. The bride takes centre stage with a symbolically charged act of violence in revenge for Mosa's sexual deceit and dis-loyalty. She dryly comments on her violent act as follows:

Sometimes you just have to act. So to save Mosa from a life of fornifuckation with other women, I'm going to cut his hose.'

It got blurry... and Rebekka (...) cut.

And the object of her undivided attention? He winced and yawned again.

She tucked a piece of flesh – the top of a Merquez sausage – in her cleavage and said, 'And now, my dear man and husband, it's off to the water with you, or what's left of you, so you can wash away your drunkenness along with the blood of the sacrifice.' (WS 180/181)[33]

Soms moeten dingen gewoon gedaan worden. En om Mosa voor de rest van zijn leven te redden van alle ongewenste inmenging van andere vrouwen, snijd ik nu zijn slangetje door.'

Dus het werd wazig... Rebekka (...) knipte.

En het lijdend voorwerp zelf? Dat bleef maar gapen, trilde alleen een stuk heviger.

Ze moffelde een stukje vlees – het puntje van een merquez-worstje zonder darm – in haar decolleté en zei: 'En nu, lieve man en echtgenoot, naar het water met jou, je ziel en zaligheid, om je dronkenschap en het bloed van je opoffering netjes weg te spoelen.' (BZ 154/155)

Rebekka's act of vengeance turns the traditional ritual of the defloration of the bride around. It is the bride who self-righteous and decidedly directs the alternative ceremony.

Rebekka becomes a woman through her active and independent intervention in the story of an (ab-)normal journey. The blood of Mosa's emasculation symbolically substitutes the blood that for the wedding guests should have proved Rebekka's pre-matrimonial virginity. The blood that in the end counts as proof of Rebekka's initiation into womanhood is not hers but his, and it has no connection whatsoever with matters of virginity. In this sense Rebekka's intervention – an irreversible denormalisation – radically resignifies the blood ritual of a traditional wedding:

Rebekka turned and tugged at her bridegroom, who had lost not only his blood, but also his honour, his strength, his everything that makes a man a man:

The wedding by the sea, the wedding by the sea.

And they only came out of the water when the wedding night had been celebrated to her satisfaction. (WS 181/182)

Rebekka draaide en rukte aan haar Mosa die samen met zijn bloed zijn eer, zijn kracht, zijn alles wat een man een man maakt verloor,

aan de bruiloft aan zee, de bruiloft aan zee.

En ze kwamen pas het water uit toen de huwelijksnacht voldoende naar haar zin voltrokken was. (BZ 155/156)

In this violent moment *Bruiloft aan zee*'s readers who have been following the compelling, quest-like stream of narration heading for the normalising wedding are all of a sudden forced to reconsider their own moral position. The unexpected violence confronts them with the awareness that the longed for wedding in fact collides with the normative Dutch disapproval of arranged intra-family marriages. The previous identification with the quest contrarily implied consent with the arranged marriage and a certain degree of acceptance of the novel's narrative discourse of honour.

Both (forced) marriage arrangements and cultural customs of honour are heavily debated at the moment. The current Dutch discourse on multiculturality strongly focuses on issues in which culture, gender and honour intersect in problematic ways.[34] At the time of *Bruiloft aan zee*'s first appearance however, in 1996, the Dutch discourse on multiculturality was of a substantially more positive and optimistic composition. Central issues at that time were interest and respect for other cultures as well as tolerance and understanding for cultural specificities. In the meantime this attitude has been fiercely criticised as naïve and culturalist, the Dutch 'multicultural paradise' resignified as a Dutch 'multicultural drama'.[35] Especially since 9/11 the Dutch boundaries of tolerance have shifted considerably.

The novel *Bruiloft aan zee* addresses the initial attitude of cultural relativism in a compelling way. The narrative itself, through the rupture caused by Rebekka's intervention, prompts a change of perspective and a more critical consciousness on the side of the reader. The denormalisation that Rebekka performs forces the reader to question both the narrative normality that the novel in first instance propagates, and the reader's acceptance of this 'normality'. It appears that the boundaries of tolerance, determining the range of normality, are applied in culturally specific ways. *Bruiloft aan zee*'s normality concerns a 'Moroccan normality', thus suggesting a cultural distance between the novel's story-world and the actual world of the Dutch reader. This cultural distance – or cultural difference – assumedly satisfies a certain exoticising interest in the (promised) wedding performance of the cultural Other. The reader's Dutch norm (rejecting the forcefully arranged wedding event) is overruled by the narrative desire and culturalist curiosity for what is in fact, from a critical gender perspective, a highly problematic normality.

Read in this way Rebekka's act of violence becomes an act of resistance both on a narrative and a discursive level. On the level of the story Rebekka symbolically breaks with a patriarchal tradition by literally cutting off a piece of her bridegroom's penis. By this violent act she prevents the 'normal' conclusion of the story. The traditional blood ritual cannot be consummated. Also the normalisation of Mosa's ab-normal biography fatally fails: as the epilogue of the novel makes clear he seeks refuge in Dutch anonymity and dies alone and insane, in an extreme case of ab-normality. It is salient that it is particularly Mosa who is sacrificed as representative of the patriarchal system. His brother – the actual family patriarch who so much insisted on the preservation of his honour and actually initiated the wedding agreements – remains safeguarded from his daughter's fury. Moreover, retrospectively it seems that the dramatic dénouement also confirms Mosa's fear of women of the North. The fear that made him run away for his wedding obligations turns out fatally justified: a woman from the North, Rebekka, subjects him to her violent will and finally causes his downfall.

Rebekka's own fate, despite her 'heroic' intervention, is of doubtful outcome as well. She resists patriarchal normalisation in Morocco, but then afterwards chooses for silence back home in the Netherlands. Her active act of denormalisation does not effect a fundamental change in her 'normal', traditional female fate of muteness. Her victory turns out of a paradoxical quality. She prevents the restoration of story-world normality but – disappointingly – does not profit from a turn to ab-normality. Another form of normality takes over in the end.

Nevertheless, despite these tragic biographical destinies, the general conclusion of the novel cannot be solely read in terms of disappointment and defeat. It is the crucial scene of Rebekka's resistance in Bruiloft aan zee that dominantly determines the reading experience. This scene prompts or even forces a critical reconsideration at the side of the reader of cultural norms and normalities, as well as of the cultural specificity of discursive boundaries of tolerance.

Defending Dutch Multiculturality

In the time after the publication (and Libris Prize nomination) of Bruiloft aan zee the media and Benali's readership were waiting impatiently for its successor, the second novel that would live up to the literary promises made by the first. The pressure on Benali was enormous, especially since most of the negative critique on Bruiloft aan zee concerned stylistic shortcomings that were ascribed to his youth and immaturity. These beginner's symptoms would disappear with the second try, if, according to the expectations, Benali was really a talented writer. Thus, the six years of (relative) silence were filled with speculations about a writer's block, a nine days' wonder and Benali's suffering from the great-expectations syndrome.[36] It was up to Benali to prove that, as a Dutch writer of Moroccan origin, he was up to the 'serious' demands of the Dutch literary field.

Simultaneously, all sorts of media invited Benali to give his opinion on various issues of public interest as a representative of the Moroccan-Dutch part of the population. Benali was supposed to provide 'the Moroccan perspective'. His responses to this automatism were rather ambivalent, oscillating between acceptance and refusal. In an interview with Sietse Meijer in the newspaper Het Parool he pleads for a general dismissal of the Dutch label 'allochthonous' for Dutch of 'other' ethnic origins:[37]

It is a word of little substance. But when it's applied to you, it gains an impact, you don't like it anyway. (...) you should just call everyone Dutch, then you solve the problem. In a few years it won't exist anymore. And the Netherlands will surely remain the Netherlands, you don't have to worry about that. Because of its location, tradition, history. It can stand rough handling. The barbarian hordes will not take over here. (...) The country changes colour, but won't lose its identity.

Het is een inhoudsloos woord. Maar als het op jou wordt betrokken, krijgt het een lading, vind je het toch niet leuk. (...) Je moet gewoon iedereen Nederlander noemen, dan ben je van het probleem af. Over een paar jaar bestaat het niet meer. En Nederland blijft wel Nederland, daar hoef je je geen zorgen over te maken. Door zijn ligging, traditie, geschiedenis. Het kan wel tegen een stotje. De barbaarse horden gaan het hier niet overnemen. (...) Het land verspringt van kleur, maar zal niet zijn identiteit kwijtraken. (Benali in Meijer 2003)

His application of the term 'barbarians' for Dutch of non-Dutch origin is reminiscent of Zaimoglu's strategy of self-*Kanakisation*. With the appropriation of the pejorative epithet 'barbarian' Benali responds to the extremely polarised discourse of that time in which Dutch Selves and barbarian Others appear as opposed, mutually exclusive categories. In his statement Benali decisively disconnects 'colour' and national identity, rejecting the idea of the Dutch nation as an ethnically homogenous community.[38] Benali addresses the cultural fear of losing 'Dutch identity' among the indigenous Dutch part of the population in post-mortem contradiction to Fortuyn. He states that the change of 'colour' of the country – as metonymy for the Dutch population – will not inflect 'Dutch identity'.

Other than, for instance, Bouazza, who right from the start refused to answer questions as a Moroccan representative, Benali accepts a certain socio-political responsibility as a member of an (ethnic) minority group. Although he puts his literature in the first place and wishes to be treated as a writer of *Dutch* literature, he is nevertheless of the opinion that he has a certain responsible position of influence. As a writer he has a visibility as well as audibility that minority members in general do not have and that he cannot take for granted. As a writer he accepts his responsibility in his *literary* work. He offers comments and reflections on socio-political issues in a specifically literary form.

In several interviews Benali elaborates on his politicised poetics. Especially the dramatic events of 9/11 recur as decisive for his determination to make a socio-politically relevant difference by way of his literature. He explains how 9/11 intruded in the process of his writing and how its (direct and indirect) consequences of social and political polarisation, both on a global and a national scale, confirmed his particular self-perception as a writer:[39]

On September 11, I was very busy with my novel. I was confused for two days. On September 13, I went back behind my computer, looked where I had got stuck and continued. You can always continue, also in times of cholera. You have to. It is a duty. No one else can do it for you. Also when the world goes mad and everybody has lost their words.

Op 11 september was ik volop bezig met mijn roman. Twee dagen was ik van slag. Op 13 september kroop ik achter mijn computer, keek waar ik was gebleven, en ging door. Je kunt altijd verder, ook in tijden van cholera. Dat moet. Het is een plicht. Niemand anders kan het voor je doen. Ook als de wereld gek wordt en iedereen zijn woorden kwijt is. (Benali in Peters 2004)

Benali suggests that the shock made him realise the urgency and necessity of his writing, his literature even more. He considers his writing as an obligation, as his personal task. This positioning testifies of a strong belief in literature's socio-political impact. In a time in which Dutch multiculturalism is heavily debated and ethnic minority groups among the Dutch population are fiercely criticised, Benali keeps believing in the transformative power of the imagination. His literature constitutes his personal and positive contribution to a polarising discourse.

However, at a certain point Benali feels that he cannot stand in for this position outside of public discourse anymore. His literary interventions appear too marginal. Whereas Bouazza claimed that his decision for public intervention resulted from the fact that he could no longer accept 'Dutch blindness' to Islamic fundamentalism, Benali argues that he can no longer bear the Dutch indifference about the increasing polarisation in Dutch society. He seriously worries about the curious popular phenomenon around Pim Fortuyn who adroitly makes use of and aggravates the tensions between several parts of the Dutch population after 9/11. For Benali, Fortuyn's public proposal to abolish the first article of the Dutch Constitution constitutes the proverbial last straw.[40] He gives up on the idea of solely literary contributions and now chooses to intervene more directly. Under the title 'Voor de Zonnekoning is artikel 1 maar lastig' ['For the Sun King, Article 1 is Merely a Nuisance'] he writes a cynical contribution to the opinion page of the daily NRC Handelsblad (11 February 2002) in response to Fortuyn's demagogy. In this contribution he strongly criticises the polarising and discriminating media circus that seems directed by Fortuyn's capricious and narcissistic character. Additionally, he targets Fortuyn's claim to finally speak the truth.

Benali continues his socio-political commitment after the murder of Fortuyn. In September 2002 he publishes an article in Vrij Nederland titled 'Waarom zwijgen de Nederlandse schrijvers?' ['Why Do Dutch Writers Keep Silent?'] (14 September 2002). In this article Benali reformulates his personal poetics into a general demand for all Dutch writers and propagates the assumption of a responsible position as an obligation for any writer. He assesses an 'identity crisis' in the Netherlands that is brought about by the terrorist attacks of 9/11 and by the 'phenomenon Fortuyn'. Benali wonders about the fact that Dutch writers do not take this identity crisis as an opportunity to reimagine Dutch national identity. He proposes a reimagination of Dutch identity in a way that includes the growing part of the Dutch population that is of non-Dutch ethnic origin. He blames Dutch writers for their indifference towards the question of 'who are we?' and criticises their lack of engagement in such an important matter as rethinking this Dutch 'we' and reimagining Dutch national identity. In its accusatory tone, the article is strongly reminiscent of an earlier appeal to Dutch writers by the Surinamese-Dutch writer-critic Anil Ramdas in NRC Handelsblad (14 March 1997). In his intervention titled 'Niemand heeft oog voor het vreemde. Moedwil en kwade trouw bij blanke schrijvers' ['Nobody Has an Eye for the Other. Malice and False-Heartedness of White Writers'] Ramdas ventilates his anger and lack of understanding for the fact that Dutch writers only imagine homogenously white (Dutch) worlds.

In the case of Benali's accusation the writers Louis Ferron, Robert Anker and Karel Glastra van Loon accept the challenge and contribute essays in Vrij Nederland in response. They formulate a variety of often vehement (counter-)arguments that discuss matters of 'responsibility', 'intention' and 'authorship'. Ferron (21 September 2002) and Anker (28 September 2002) determinedly reject Benali's demand – with more and less sophisticated arguments – as reductive and intentionalist. They especially object to the idea to prescribe a socio-political dimension to the 'free', unbound field of literature. In the article 'Abdelkader en de kaaskoppen' ['Abdelkader and the Cheese Heads'] (7 December 2002) Glastra van Loon, as final contributor to the polemic, allies himself with Benali. He carefully analyses the argumentative discourse of the two other contributors and convincingly shows how the specific phrasing of their rejections in fact confirm Benali's fundamental assessment that Dutchness remains a closed construct. He concludes his differentiating essay with a confirmation of the 'urgent need for original new answers to the question what it means to be Dutch': 'Benali's call still stands up straight' (Glastra van Loon 2002: 85).[41]

Next to all this public and socio-political turbulence Benali also persists in his plea for a serious treatment of his literary work. Just like Bouazza he resists exoticising readings that he rejects as 'stranglehold' (Benali 2004c: 26) for all writers of non-Dutch ethnic origin.[42] More than any other hyphenated writer – and probably in some relation to his explicit socio-political commitment – Benali has to defend himself against insinuations of political correctness as determinant criterion in the positive reception of his work. This discussion reached a climax after the unexpected award of the 2003 Libris Literature Prize for his long-awaited novel De langverwachte (2002a).[43] The jury, under the direction of the labour-democrats politician Jeltje van Nieuwenhoven, praised De langverwachte for its playful, rich and daring style and its 'grand view of the whole coloured contemporary society' (Van der Valk 2004: 6).[44]

The literary press was much more reserved about the novel's literary qualities. Several critics publicly wondered about the jury's motives for the selection of Benali's work.[45] They suggested that his selection had been a socio-political decision, an instance of political correctness in a multicultural society under debate.[46] The voices in defence of Benali's selection did not always support Benali's literary case. In de Volkskrant the successful and respected Persian-Dutch writer Kader Abdolah enthusiastically claimed the prize as an award for all 'allochthons'. He argued that Benali's selection implied a general acknowledgement of their presence in Dutch culture. Benali himself responded annoyed to this claim and vehemently resisted its import. Abdolah's statement seemed to confirm the idea that, more than the literary quality of his novel Benali's other ethnic origin had determined his selection. In an interview with Arjan Peters, Benali rejected Abdolah's assumption by stating that: 'A jury awards the best book, not the book of a commendable allochthon. If that circumstance has been a deliberation, then I'm still ready to immediately return the prize, the money inclusive' (Benali in Peters 2004).[47]

In general it seems that, after this second Libris Prize fuss, Benali did not let great expectations and media pressure deter him. Already in the year following De langverwachte, Benali published a drama with the conspicuous title Onrein. De vader, de zoon en de hond [Impure. The Father, the Son, and the Dog] (2003).[48] In an interview he comments on the work – again taking up the issue of responsibility – in the following way:

> In your work you can't get away from social commentary. (...) I don't want to spend too much time on the social debate. My preference goes to a novel or a drama as Onrein, in which by means of a tragic-comedy, or comical tragedy, I want to say something about the past three years. I prefer to say on paper, or have said on the stage, that man and woman are equal. Shouting such a thing in a mosque doesn't work, there is no discourse there. They do not want to listen, or have already gone it alone. In my opinion it will take two more generations before things really change. In the meantime I process the conflicts that I detect now.

> In je werk kom je niet uit onder sociaal commentaar. (...) Ik wil niet te veel tijd besteden aan het maatschappelijk debat. Mijn voorkeur heeft een roman of een toneelstuk als Onrein, waarin ik aan de hand van een multiculturele tragikomedie, of komische tragedie, iets wil zeggen over de afgelopen drie jaar. Ik zeg liever op papier, of laat op het toneel zeggen, dat man en vrouw gelijk zijn. Zoiets roepen in een moskee werkt niet, daar is geen discours. Ze willen niet luisteren, of hebben hun boontjes al gedopt. Volgens mij duurt het nog twee generaties voordat er echt iets verandert. In de tussentijd verwerk ik de conflicten die ik nu bespeur. (Benali in Peters 2004)

In this statement the drama *Onrein* appears as an example of Benali's literary digestion of the socio-political tensions that characterise the Dutch society of the early millennium. The following analysis investigates the ways in which *Onrein*, as a literary project of both marginal and explicitly political status, responds to and disputably also intervenes in the dominant public discourse of its time.

In comparison with *Bruiloft aan zee* and its successor novel *De langverwachte* the publication of *Onrein* (as well as its theatrical performance) was hardly discussed.[49] Whereas the contemporaneous award-winning novel *De langverwachte* clearly ends on a positive, hopeful note, fitting to Benali's repeated political poetics of positivism and reconciliation, *Onrein* is of a much more negative purport. The following analysis discusses these distinctions and relates them to Benali's (active and passive) positioning in the socio-political discourse on the Dutch multicultural future.[50] It particularly focuses on the significance of the identity-constitutive factors gender and generation that Benali himself explicitly addresses in his above-cited comment on the drama.

Onrein: a 'Different' Multicultural Drama

The first performance of the drama *Onrein* as well as the publication of its text took place in the winter of 2003/2004, after a period of heightened sensitivity and multicultural excitement. The rhetoric of a clash of (religious) cultures and the polarisation between the Islam Other and the Western world caused growing feelings of insecurity and threat, both on a global and on a national level. Benali used this situation of suspicion as material for his drama. In the publicity campaign for the performance of *Onrein*, the theatre company 'De Toneelschuur' announced the drama as a piece that comments on the political actuality: 'In the process of writing *Onrein* Abdelkader Benali was inspired by recent political and social developments: the emotion of politics, the politics of emotions and the desire to put security instead of adventure in the centre of life' (Press release Toneelschuurproducties, November 2003).[51] The reception of the actual performance of the drama was minimal as well as rather diverse. Whereas Hans Oranje in *de Volkskrant* (11 December 2003) praised the mild irony with which Benali depicts his characters in *Onrein*, Jowi Schmitz in *NRC Handelsblad* (8 December 2003) criticised the lack of a plot. Servaes Nelissen, one of the three actors in the play, confirmed this ambivalent reception in respect to the actual performances. In an interview with Hans Kottmann of the *Noordhollands Dagblad* (19 February 2004) he expressed his amazement about the fact that whereas the one performance was awarded with a standing ovation, the other met with an audience that remained completely silent.

The title of the drama, *Onrein* [Impure], highlights one term of an opposition that activates weighty connotations, both in a historical and socio-political sense. In the drama's contemporary context of debated ethnic diversity and multiculturalism, it even works as a provocative term that invokes a highly contested dichotomy. In the first place the term 'impure' is reminiscent of late-nineteenth century theories of race.[52] It calls to mind the historical 'natural science' discourses on the (essentialist and taxonomic) determination of pure and impure races, discourses that the German national socialists used in lethal ways. In the second place the concept connotates a more contemporary association: its current re-establishment within a radical(ised) religious discourse. In this sense, the dichotomy functions to justify and even propagate and sanction violence by the self-defined 'pure' against the assumed 'impure'. Islamist terrorists make use of the divisive rhetoric of (im)purity in their fight against Christians, Jews and atheists alike.

Whereas the title immediately positions the drama in a discursive field of hierarchised binaries, *Onrein's* rather simplistic subtitle 'de vader, de zoon en de hond' [the father, the son, and the dog] introduces the three characters in the drama in their symbolic family roles. The combination of title and subtitle invites speculations about the assignment of this impurity to one of the three characters. The assumption that the dog – an animal opposite two humans – incorporates the factor of impurity seems most obvious. The dog represents the exceptional factor in the family constellation that is indicated by the elements father and son. Similar to the situation in the novel *Bruiloft aan zee*, an intergenerational father-son relationship takes up a central position in *Onrein*. However, the serious heaviness already invoked by the drama's title, replaces the non-committal tone of uncomplicated lightness that characterised *Bruiloft aan zee*.

The drama, consisting of four acts and a coda, opens with a time indication in the form of a stage direction: '*It is Friday*' (OR 5, italics in original).[53] The nameless son enters the stage, dressed in a childish scout's uniform. He carries a shopping bag and pushes a box into the room, while speaking, monologising to himself. From his nervous behaviour and incoherent, confused comments it becomes clear that the son is hiding something from his father – denoted by the unspecified 'stuff' (OR 6) – with whom he shares a small apartment. The son appears tied up in a drug deal with certain men he refers to as 'the bastards' or 'the guys' (OR 5 *et passim*). Although the fact of the matter remains unclear, the son's nervous monologue indicates that he and these 'guys' are having a disagreement. He tries to hide the 'stuff' from them and, as he is sure that they will come to fetch it, his immediate concern is to find some means of protection. The fact that his father, once a 'guest worker', does not know about his affairs, turns the situation into one of split secrecy. The father and the 'guys' do not know about each other's existence and the son desperately tries to keep the situation this way.

The son anxiously searches for a solution to get himself out of the awkward situation of this external threat without informing his father about his illegal affairs. However, there is little space for secrets in the small apartment that the two characters share. Moreover, the father's life strongly revolves around his only son, especially since the mother has passed away. He is full of great expectations concerning his son's future and he perceives of the son's future success – defined in his own particular terms of honour and respect – as his personal responsibility. The ambivalent feelings and pressure that this paternal discourse of family honour exerts on the son, becomes evident in the son's spoken self-reflections. In the opening monologue the deliberations of the son, who grew up in Dutch society, and is much more active in this society than his father, continuously shift. On the one hand he tends to accept his father's position of respect and power, and to give in to his father's will. On the other hand the son's freely flowing thoughts show he doubts his father's sense of reality and contradict his (internal) fantasies of glory. These thoughts assure the son that he wants to live in 'the world', to study mathematics – his strongest subject in school – and to take part in Dutch society. Above all he wants to design his future in 'my own way' (OR 10). On the first page of the drama he argues with himself:

SON
If I follow my father, then I will end at the edge of the ravine (…)
Being heir to the throne is magnificent. You are chosen. In this house at least we still believe in God. I dream of this day and night. About God, about the heir to the throne. (…) The world ogles me, with her eyelashes she casts her cool shade on me, she says: Please come my way, I can exploit your talents, I will cherish your talents. But I can't, I have to say: I'm sorry, I have to wake up my father. I must not give in to her glow!

ZOON
Als ik mijn vader volg dan eindig ik aan de rand van het ravijn (…)
Troonopvolger zijn is schitterend. Je bent uitverkoren. In dit huis geloven we tenminste nog in God. Ik droom er dag en nacht van. Over God, over de troonopvolger. (…) De wereld lonkt naar me, met haar wimpers werpt ze me haar koele schaduw toe, ze zegt: Kom alsjeblieft mijn kant op, ik kan je talenten uitbuiten, ik zal je talenten koesteren. Maar ik kan niet, ik moet zeggen: het spijt me, ik moet mijn vader wakker maken. Ik mag niet toegeven aan haar roes! (OR 5-7)

The son is torn between the father's promise of succession to 'the throne' and 'the world's' promise of the realisation and appreciation of his talents. To the reader, however, both promises appear rather vague. Both the 'throne' and the (gendered as well as sexualised) 'world' seem signifiers of desire without solid objects of references in *Onrein's* actual world – be it in- or outside the apartment.

The father resolutely counts on the continuation of family traditions and accepts no deviations, or alternative routes, that would alter this personal and strongly gendered dream of family succession. In this dream the son is destined to become the father's 'heir to the throne' by way of receiving and accepting his 'instructions'. What exactly this 'throne' or these 'instructions' are, only the father seems to know. Like the reader, the son, whose interest shifts between positive curiosity and downright rejection, gropes in the dark here.

The family honour in any case takes up a central position in the father's discourse of expectations and disappointment. In an authoritarian way he instructs his son on the particular demands and characteristics of a heroic future ('Follow the instructions'):

FATHER

I am right! Do you know what your problem is and do you know what the old one is going to bring to an end? You cannot speak, you do not have your own tongue yet. Our house is called Mansoer. Mansoer means 'victor'. Your tongue is a pillar of the family (of) Victors. If I still had your strength and youth, I would by long have finished the study of mathematics, I would have installed the protection system, and in this house of war I would have caused a considerable stir. My tongue would be looking forward to it.

VADER

Ik héb gelijk! Weet je wat jouw probleem is en weet je waar de oude een eind aan gaat maken? Je kan niet praten, je hebt nog geen tong van jezelf. Ons huis heet Mansoer. Mansoer betekent 'overwinnaar'. Je tong is een zuil van de familie Overwinnaars. Als ik jouw kracht en jeugd nog had, zou ik al lang de wiskundestudie hebben afgemaakt, ik zou zeven talen spreken, ik zou het beveiligingssysteem hebben geïnstalleerd en in dit huis van oorlog voor flink wat opschudding hebben gezorgd. Mijn tong zou er zin in hebben. (OR 14)

The son feels emotionally and intellectually split between two contrasting worlds: his father's world of Mansoer and the outside world of Dutch society that his father pejoratively denotes as 'the house of war'.[54] The son's thoughts circle around the concepts that his father forces and projects on him: 'respect', 'disappointment', 'being a man' and 'the instructions'.

In a certain way the son – quite realistically – sees his father as an old and lonely man who has come to the Netherlands in high spirits and now, after a hardworking life full of disappointments, is obsessed by the idea of his son's succession. The father's boisterous and self-assured discourse covers up the impression that there is in fact little to inherit – the house of Victory is a chimaera rooted in a glorified and bygone past. The rather violent discourse strongly builds on feelings of (moral) superiority and disgust towards Dutch society. Conversely, the son perceives of Dutch society as a land of possibilities: possibilities to develop his talents, for instance his talent for mathematics. It is because of his precarious situation in the outside world that the son at times also agrees with his father and his bragging about the family Mansoer as 'family Victory'. In these moments he affirms the father's slogans and shows respect for and curiosity about the wisdom and strength to be transmitted. The idea of being a heir to the throne appeals to the son as much as it repulses him. On the one hand it seems an empty promise, on the other a future possibility – he is not sure. His own indecisiveness strongly confuses him. Respecting the will of his (migrant) father seems to necessarily coincide with denying the actual state of affairs in society, if not with estranging himself from Dutch society in general.

In the often-vehement exchange of arguments between father and son, the deceased mother – a mother who is not mentioned in the subtitle – takes up a central, symbolic role. Both male characters use the reference to her and her remembered perfection to exercise pressure on each other: each measures the other's behaviour against her supposed standards. The mother symbolically represents the time when the world, including the family, was still in order. Her loveable presence guaranteed an atmosphere of sweet harmony and mutual understanding. She represents the stereotypical, idealised woman as the centre of the family, holding the gendered constellation in balance by her caring, 'female' qualities.

In former times the mother used to function as the negotiating, communicative link between father and son, a link that is now lost and dearly missed. The situation has even dramatically reversed itself. Meanwhile, the cherished memory of the mother drives a wedge between father and son. Whereas the father blames the son for hurting the mother with his disobedient behaviour, the son even goes as far as accusing his father of being responsible for the mother's death:

FATHER
The old one didn't hear it. Your mother has a lot of sorrow because of you.
(...) She was worried. She would give everything to keep us together, to always see us the way we were. Her absence keeps us together.
SON
She didn't fall off the balcony for us, she fell off the balcony because you had done something to her.

VADER
De oude heeft het niet gehoord. Je moeder heeft veel verdriet om jou.
(...) Ze maakte zich zorgen. Ze zou er alles voor overhebben om ons bij elkaar te houden, ons voor altijd te zien zoals wij waren. Haar afwezigheid houdt ons bij elkaar.
ZOON
Ze viel niet van het balkon voor ons, ze viel van het balkon omdat jij haar iets had aangedaan. (OR 35)

The son's last remark hints at the existence of a hidden drama: the mother's violent death. It casts the father as the dominant aggressor in this drama. The accusation remains singular and rather implicit; it leaves out the full facts. Nevertheless, its disruptive impact runs through the rest of the story. The impression that the death of the mother is shrouded in mystery and that the father is not innocent, determines the tone of the remainder of the play. As an effect the absent mother – once the glue holding the family together – now constitutes an influential factor in the development and final explosion of the generational conflict.

The 'Fun-and-Amusement Dog' of Dutch Society

At a certain point a dog intrudes in the small family world of ambivalence, mistrust and conflict. It is the son who introduces the dog. Without informing his father he acquires the animal as a means of protection against 'the guys' who threaten him. The dog – in fact not a watchdog but a 'fun-and-amusement dog' ['pret-en-vermaak-hond'] (OR 22) as the speaking animal describes itself – (fantastically) performs as the third (male) character in the piece. It represents a third, quasi-independent voice in the generational discussion. For both father and son, the dog becomes the addressee with whom opinions about the familial tensions can be exchanged. The nature of this exchange changes considerably in the course of the drama, especially at the side of the father. His initial attitude towards the dog is one of absolute and rigid dismissal. A dog is 'impure' (OR 20), as he states. As such the animal typically symbolises Dutch society in all its despicability.[55] The father experiences the presence of the dog as an intrusion of Dutch society into his indoor empire of Mansoer, into the House of Victory.

In the eyes of the father the son's introduction of the dog signals a lack of respect. Its unasked-for presence undermines the father's position of patriarchal power and is an instance of inviting the enemy into the house. He angrily reproaches his son: 'Because of this animal we entirely lose the bit of respect that we had. The instructions are clear: the father has to be respected!' (OR 23).[56] The father ignores the dog's eloquent and often venomous objections to his rejecting behaviour and refuses to speak to the animal. However, the rather arrogant, self-satisfied dog – that indeed seems to incorporate a whole range of 'Occidental' vices – doesn't let itself be intimidated or scared off by the father's reproaching attitude. And, as the mutual understanding between father and son diminishes, the father's estimation of the familial status-quo-provoking dog grows. He starts comparing the behaviour of his son to that of the dog and decides that he appreciates the dog's behaviour better. In this transposition the son gains the label 'impure' in the sense that he is disqualified as a suitable successor to the house of Mansoer.

The dog's actual position in the father-son conflict is hard to determine. The dog easily changes roles as well as sides, stimulating the discussion in a seemingly opportunistic but at the same time evasive vein. In its discussions with the son, the dog ridicules the father. In its exchange of ideas with the father, it criticises the son. The standpoint from which the dog argues is as shifting and ambivalent as its attitude is. At times it behaves as the representative of a superior Dutch society, looking down in a condescending way on the out-of-date discourse of the shut off, old-fashioned father, and scoffing at the small-time criminal activities of the lost and confused son. In this mode the dog lists several current stereotypes about Muslim migrants, often in the quasi-harmless form of well-intended good advice on how to behave in Dutch society. In a statement that is strongly reminiscent of and links to contemporary discussions in Dutch society – regarding Islamic and Islamist (mis)behaviour – the dog argues as follows:

DOG
Plasters! Airplanes in high-rise flats I do not call plasters. We all have wounds, right, but that doesn't mean that for every trifle you prepare for the highest state of standby to begin a holy war? (...)
So that is the first point: we call jihad not jihad but 'putting a plaster on a wound'. We can always still discuss the size of the wound. Point two is that you can do with less beards. I know that in your eyes it looks very hip, but let's say that following the fashion is also a form of jihad. (...) Point three is maybe a difficult point: stop badgering people who hold different ideas, if I'm allowed to say something about that in name of the Society of Dogs who Fancy Dogs. (...) Point four: take a dog into your home.

HOND
Pleisters. Vliegtuigen in torenflats noem ik geen pleisters. We hebben allemaal wonden, toch, maar dat betekent niet dat je voor elk wissewasje meteen in de hoogste staat van paraatheid schiet om een heilige oorlog te beginnen? (...)
Dat is dus het eerste punt: we noemen jihad geen jihad maar 'het plakken van een pleister op een wond'. We kunnen altijd nog discussiëren over de grootte van die wond. Punt twee is dat jullie met minder baarden toe kunnen. Ik weet dat het heel hip staat in jullie ogen, maar met de mode meegaan is ook een vorm van jihad zullen we maar zeggen. (...) Punt drie is misschien een moeilijk punt: kappen met mensen die er andere ideeën op na houden te pesten, als ik daar namens de Bond Van Honden Die Op Honden Vallen iets over mag zeggen. (...) Punt vier: neem een hond in huis. (OR 28/29)

The dog's advice connects to discussions and incidents in Dutch society after 9/11 that centred on the (in)compatibility of (a conservative interpretation of) Islam, 'Muslim morals' and the Dutch liberal democracy. The dog's four hints address issues as diverse as the highly problematic perpetrator-victim discourse, the public presence and media representation of Muslims and the Dutch 'El Moumni-affair' on Islam and homosexuality.[57] The last hint – adopt a dog – underlines the arbitrary absurdity of the combination of arguments as well as the problematic intersection of very distinct levels of argumentation. Simultaneously, it clearly indicates the dog's implication in its own argument. Despite its exalted rhetoric of help and support, it is clear that the dog takes an opportunist stance from which it has something to gain as well.

At other times, aware of its doggish dependence, the dog begs for the son's and especially the father's care and acceptance. As an animal, it is located at the lowest levels of society. The dog tries to convince the dog-sceptical father to have compassion and accept 'him' as an equal, by pointing out their shared marginal position in Dutch society: 'Man, we are surely more alike than you think. After all you have also been treated like a dog by this society' (OR 47).[58] By comparing the father's experiences in Dutch society to its own life as an animal, the dog apparently hits the nail of the father's social disappointment on the head. At other times the dog ties in with and appropriates the father's discourse of respect. It tries to extend the father's range of respect by arguing for mutuality: 'If you respect me, I will respect you as well. Respect for the father, the son and the dog!' (OR 23).[59]

Another strategy that the dog deploys in his attempts to convince the father is the suggestion of agreement on issues concerning the unruly son. The dog pretends to be (or is – this remains unclear) of the same opinion in respect to the son's 'disobedience'. It regularly takes on the father's side in his effort to direct the son in what he considers the right direction. In accordance with the father the dog emphasises the importance for the son, for the heir to the throne, to become a man, a 'real' man. However, this supportive stance appears rather ironic as the dog simultaneously performs the stereotype of the effeminate homosexual. Its confirmation of the father's authoritarian voice at the same time works to subvert.

To both father and son, the dog maintains that the family Mansoer should improve the way it presents itself to the outside world. It contends that there lies the major source for their problems: 'It is a matter of presentation. This is important for your son, he has to carry on your name. The problem of family Mansoer is that you don't have a performance' (OR 27).[60] In its advice to the father the dog, as representative of Dutch society, emphasises the importance of (re-)presentation. In concordance with the earlier hints on the representation of Muslims in Dutch society, here the dog recommends an adaptation of the family's outer appearance to the demands of Dutch mainstream culture. The dog claims that everything revolves around appearances in Dutch society.

In the end, during a confidential mode of exchange between father and dog, the figure of the mother reappears. In a sphere of growing mutuality the dog evokes the serene and calm presence of the mother. It begins to reflect on the mother's significance for the father-son relationship that, without her presence, has transformed into a fragile constellation of barely tolerant co-existence. In a conversation with the father, the dog remarks:

Our life is over, old man. (...) I look at you now with other eyes. Not only because my eyes are clean, but also because I have to think of your wife. (...) That is because of her picture. I make contact with her. She has a good influence on me. I only need to look at it and I calm down. Your son makes me crazy; sometimes I would like to tear him apart with all his violence and aggression. You get on my nerves, you can only say: impure, impure, impure... But your wife radiates rest. She kept you together.

Ons leven is voorbij, oude baas. (...) Ik kijk nu naar je met andere ogen. Niet alleen omdat mijn ogen schoon zijn, maar ook omdat ik aan je vrouw moet denken. (...) Dat komt door haar foto. Ik maak contact met haar. Ze heeft een goede uitwerking op me. Ik hoef er maar naar te kijken en ik kom tot rust. Je zoon maakt me gek, die zou ik soms willen verscheuren met al zijn geweld en agressie. Jij werkt me ook op de zenuwen, jij kunt alleen maar zeggen: onrein, onrein, onrein... Maar je vrouw straalt rust uit. Zij hield jullie bij elkaar. (OR 48/49)

By means of the emotional reference to the mother, the dog finally succeeds in overcoming the father's distanced refusal and manages to break through his strong façade of male superiority, honour and pride.

The dog then actually assumes the role of the dead mother and in this state of transfiguration the dog-mother and the father enter in a conversation about (the future of) their son. In this moment the boundaries of identity between dog and mother disappear: the dog speaks with her mild voice and it is the mother to whom the father replies. 'She' tries to persuade him to let go of their son, to allow him the freedom to make his own decisions and to find out for himself which way to go. The father vehemently refuses this idea and the conversation rapidly turns into a dispute, in which he starts threatening 'her'. At the moment that 'she' gives in and wants to make up again with a kiss, the dog-mother transfiguration is all of a sudden undone – to the father's shock:[61]

FATHER
(surrenders, then is scared) What are you doing? Stop it! Go away from me! Impure animal!
DOG
That was not I; that was she. She was it.
FATHER
Where is she?

DOG
Off to the balcony.

VADER
(*geeft zich over, schrikt dan*) Wat doe je!? Hou op! Ga weg van mij! Onrein beest!!
HOND
Dat was ik niet, dat was zij. Zij was het.
VADER
Waar is ze?
HOND
Naar het balkon. (OR 50)

With the reference to the balcony, the location that the son connects to the mother's death, the dog now also seems to insinuate a past crime. It is suggested that the balcony holds a secret that would undermine the father's patriarchal position of respect as well as his discourse of family honour.

In the address that follows, the dog now sides with the son. It warns the father that he is going to lose his only son and that his obsession with the 'honourable' continuation of the House of Mansoer will result in a honourless and, above all, lonely end: 'You will stay behind alone, just as alone as when you arrived here; this house will become your asylum; your soul will climb up the windows like my soul climbed up the bars. I'm just warning you because I like you' (OR 50).[62] The dog, however, does not succeed in convincing the father of an alternative policy, and also the son cannot change his father's mind. Although the father secretly longs for reconciliation within the remaining family as well, he can only accept a solution on his terms. 'His terms' involve a return to the patriarchal order. He demands absolute respect for the father's will and a tacit and obedient acceptance of the traditional instructions. Only in this way can the son become heir to the family throne. The father permits no space for retort or for an exchange of opinions. He accepts no change of the traditional status quo or of the hierarchic power relations.

A Sad Coda: From Polyphony to Silence

At the end of the drama there is a short moment in which all seems to end well, despite the father's rigidity: a shared family future in harmony and in understanding. In this scene the son more or less gives in to his adamant father and proposes to make up again, to unite their powers in order to come along in the world, in Dutch society. He hesitatively asks his father to confirm the basic idea that they, father and son, despite all tensions, understand each other. The father answers affirmatively, referring to their common heritage: 'We understand each other very well. After all, we are Victors' (OR 56).[63] However, the son's initial relief following this affirmation soon turns out to be premature. The moment of assumed understanding appears to be another instance of miscommunication. Whereas the son interprets his father's words as a sign of agreement and reassurance, the father's preceding behaviour speaks the opposite message. Without spending many more words on his son, the father leaves for the mosque with a final goodbye: 'when I come back, I never want to see you here again' (OR 57).[64] According to his rigid patriarchal ideology, a constellation of the House of Mansoer with two victors simultaneously in charge is impossible.

The drama ends with a coda: a dialogue between the dog and the son at the end of the enervating Friday. The biblical connotations are blatant: the son feels deserted by the almighty father. He blames the dog for the loss of the father. The dog defends himself and, during this defence, again assumes the role of the mother who offers comfort in the son's situation of desolate loneliness. In 'her' presence the son forgets his fears again – his fears for the separation from his father, for 'the guys', and for the future. But the imaginary moment of comfort and security is interrupted when the mother leaves to collect the laundry on the death-ridden balcony. The scene ends with an image of the waiting son: waiting for his mother, waiting for his father and waiting for 'the guys' who seem to incorporate the shame brought onto the House of Mansoer. The son waits passively and listlessly. Obviously he has given up on his dreams of future change. In a tone of defeat and surrender he presents his prediction for the future in a final, exhausted monologue:

> I can't look [the guys] in the face, for I don't have a face anymore.
> I will stay at home, become dumb, put a thumb in my mouth, until the day arrives that my father returns and hates me, because I'm stuck to that couch, because I've become just like him. Then together we will think back to this evening.
> He will die, I will bury him and only then there will be space for planning. When this house doesn't exist anymore. When dogs without teeth are being delivered.

> Ik kan [de jongens] niet aankijken, want ik heb geen gezicht meer.
> Ik zal thuisblijven, stom worden, een duim in mijn mond steken, tot de dag komt dat mijn vader terugkeert en me haat omdat ik aan die bank zit vastgeplakt, omdat ik zoals hij geworden ben. Dan zullen we samen herinneringen ophalen aan deze avond.
> Hij zal sterven, ik zal hem begraven en dan pas zal er ruimte zijn om plannen te maken. Als dit huis niet meer bestaat. Als er honden zonder tanden worden afgeleverd. (OR 61/62)

Disappointment and disillusion determine the drama's final scene.

The dog has disappeared. It has done its 'work' as an intrusive catalyst, accelerating the process of father-son estrangement: the communicative exchange between father and son has ended here. The promising future of the heroic House of Mansoer is ruined: the dream of the throne as well as the dream of a career as a mathematician in Dutch society has abruptly come to an end. Father and son Mansoer are both losers in an emotional clash without a victor. Both have failed to determine their own futures and to realise their own ideals. Both have failed in their efforts to change the other. With the disappearance of the dog, Dutch society has also withdrawn itself from the scene. The drama shows a family drama in the social margin. It has no acute significance and, as a result, is easily overlooked.

As a piece of Dutch literature *Onrein* clearly connects to a more general mood of disappointment and disillusion in Dutch society. The three different voices represented in the piece – the father as representative of the traditional first generation of labour migrants, the son as representative of the second, more integrated and secularised generation, and the homosexual atheist dog as the symbolic representative of a liberal Dutch society – do not manage to really communicate with each other. They speak alongside each other, in a disharmonious confusion of voices. They monologise to themselves without really listening to the other, demanding respect without offering it themselves. The scene in which they all simultaneously sing their own songs symbolises this dissonant multivocality: the dog sings an English pop song, the father an Arab sura and the son a Dutch children's song. This representation of sonic dissonance functions as a literary commentary on the current misunderstandings between the different – ethnic, generational and religious – groups in Dutch society.

By way of its ironic tone the drama criticises a particular negative and destructive dimension of the contemporary Dutch multicultural society: the mutual stereotypes, the arrogant attitudes of superiority, and the short-sighted and disinterested opinions about the Other on all sides of the various ethnic, generational and religious divides. All three dramatic characters are actively involved in these negative practices of representation, just as all three characters suffer from them. In matters of sympathy the drama privileges none of the three. Agreement and rejection on the side of the reader are determined by the dramatic narration that shifts from character to character. The dramatic text offers neither answers nor solutions. At the end there is only the insight that after this multivocal misunderstanding there is loneliness and disappointment awaiting. The obtrusive biblical intertext of a *Good* Friday is not enough to change this impression. After the dissonant polyphony all characters end up in a sad, silent state of mind and being. The termination of communication seems final.

Benali's drama *Onrein* stages a painful collision between different, nonnegotiable expectations. Simultaneously, below this dramatic surface, it pleads for an effort at mutual understanding by way of careful communication, of listening instead of rash moral judgement. The more or less unmediated presentation of the three different (male) standpoints does not imply that the piece leaves the father's patriarchal violence and the dog's offensive discourse unquestioned. *Onrein* applies the relatively mild tools of humour and irony in order to express criticism. In instances of discursive abuse the text overturns its irony into absurdity. The spatial separation of the closed apartment from the surrounding Dutch society can be read as a critical comment on the often-isolated world after migration. The fact that the characters remain nameless and are only denoted by their function in the apartment's social constellation makes the constellation into a general one: *Onrein* depicts any suchlike situation. The absence of women in this constellation (stereotypically) suggests that the failing communicating is mainly a male-made problem. The positive (but temporary) influence of the ghostly mother figure on the process of communication – as well as the mildness of her memory – corroborates this idea of the problem's genderedness.

In the course of the play the apartment turns into a trap: it incorporates the dead end of social marginalisation. The son who tries to get out and enter into the outside world, stereotypically only manages this through his involvement in criminal acts. His dreams of a way out and of a successful future by means of education never exceed this dream level. In respect to the son, the dog's ambiguous role can be considered as a point of critique towards a Dutch society that simultaneously invites and rejects, welcomes and dismisses. In respect to the father, its opportunist attitude characterises a society that expects assimilation from others, but is not willing to adapt to and invest in any new sort of community itself. It is neither interested in what inspires, nor in what bothers, the other. At the end of the play it is clear that all parties are caught in a downward spiral. *Onrein* does not imagine a way of escape. Instead it is up to the reader to make sense of a senselessly sad ending determined by loneliness and cultural isolation.

Conclusion: Benali's Writing for Reconciliation

Benali's literary works *Bruiloft aan zee* and *Onrein* constitute two distinct moments of literary intervention in public discourse. *Bruiloft aan zee* addresses the pitfalls of cultural relativism in an engaging story of an (ab-)normal journey. This story of a situation after migration very much resembles a roller coaster: it first sweeps its reader up in its speedy story, and then, all of a sudden, pulls the emergency brake. The disruptive moment functions as an eye-opener and confronts its readers with their assumptions of culturally distinctive 'normality'. The literary negotiation of generational tensions as well as gendered traditions and expectations recurs in Benali's drama *Onrein*. Much more than *Bruiloft aan zee*, however, *Onrein* responds to socio-political tensions or, the other way around, seems embedded in – by means of direct textual references – (Dutch) actuality. The tone of the narration of *Bruiloft aan zee* is clearly more positive and optimistic than that of *Onrein*.

Whereas the second-generation Rebekka resists the familial expectations and (more or less) redirects her fate by actively intervening into a problematic tradition, the second-generation son in *Onrein* is less decisive. He does not manage to free himself from the normative binds laid down by his father that obstruct his personal development. His attempts come to nothing, while in the meantime – and here is where a fierce critique of Dutch society comes in – the outside world (the dog as representative of Dutch society) mediates shifting, often contrary, messages and positions.

In both works of literature the father figures are quite stereotypical in their representation. Both have gone through a process of migration that they judge in retrospect, from their position in the narrative present, as disappointing, as failure, as loss. A patriarchal discourse of (family) honour, infiltrated and invigorated by feelings of nostalgia, takes up a central position in their perception. According to this discourse liberal Dutch society hampers the maintenance of the family honour that was guaranteed in the country and culture of origin. The second-generation children have become estranged from their (fathers') cultural roots and increasingly identify with Dutch ways of thinking. Both in *Bruiloft aan zee* and *Onrein* this situation results in generational collisions. The children of migration generally try to be loyal and respectful towards the fathers, but at the same time this next generation has to acknowledge that these fathers live in outdated, incompatible worlds of memory and patriarchal projection that are fatally resistant to a changing future.

Both works of literature put the complexities of situations after migration at the centre of the narration. Traditional ideas about family and honour collide with the new situation that these fathers and families find themselves in. Change is proposed by the children, but the realisation of this proposed change – adaptation, participation, integration – depends on many factors, as especially *Onrein* makes clear. Whereas *Bruiloft aan zee* represents a radical intervention in a culturally specific and narratively undisputed state of 'normality', *Onrein* on the contrary is of a more warning character. The drama sketches a polyvocal dissonance and offers little perspective for a future of multicultural understanding. It imagines what can happen when also the 'promising' second generation fails to connect to the new situation. It reflects on the situation in which this generation, like the one of the fathers, also loses contact and gets stuck in a hopeless in-between.

Benali has repeatedly contended that he wants to contribute to a process of intercultural rapprochement and mutual understanding by means of his literature.[65] In his opinion literature provides a privileged space for reflections on and experiments with 'Dutch multiculturality':

> In literature I want to present the discourse in which I give many voices and ways of thinking an opportunity by playing them off against one another. In an essay one has to choose sides; you fix yourself in a polarisation. I prefer to go a

bit further, by reaching above this and to catch the metaphors that do not immediately appeal to the newspaper reader; by investigating possible results in the literary laboratory.

In literatuur wil ik het discours houden waarbij ik velerlei stemmen en denkwijzen een kans geef door ze tegen elkaar uit te spelen. In een essay moet je partij kiezen, je zet je vast in een polarisatie. Ik ga liever iets verder, door erboven te reiken en te grijpen naar metaforen die de krantenlezer niet meteen iets zeggen; door in het literaire laboratorium te onderzoeken wat dat oplevert. (Benali in Peters 2004)

Until now Dutch readers have been enthusiastically interested in especially the positively pitched experiments evolving from Benali's literary laboratory. His light-hearted and confident literary messages of a shared responsibility for the positive outcome of Dutch multiculturality, as can be found in *Bruiloft aan zee* and *De langverwachte*, reverberate in wide circles of Dutch society. This is much less the case for his rather pessimistic warning for multicultural failure and default as represented in *Onrein*; for the time being, this uncomfortable text falls on deaf ears.

Conclusion

Literary Negotiations of Germanness and Dutchness

'In the analysis of identity shift through migration
it can be argued that creative literature contains
some of the most effective explorations of identity issues'
(White 1995: 2).

'[O]ur understanding of multiculturalism and hybridity must also involve
an examination of the circumstances under which such interactions play out
institutionalized, and historically and nationally sanctioned relationships of power'
(Hassan and Didi 2001: 13).

Introduction

Contemporary discourses on multiculturality and migration often revolve around
two opposite positions in respect to the contested issue of national identity. On
the one side you find the opponents of the concept who plead for a view on the
contemporary, globalised world as trans- or even postnational. They argue that as
a result of transnational migration the importance of the national as a structuring
principle has been substituted by an emphasis on either the local or the global.
Transnationalists often perceive of the nation state as an obsolete, out-of-date
concept and of national identity as a construct that is losing ground in a world
increasingly determined by processes of a transnational character. They often
propagate the blessings of the globalising movement as a chance to overcome
national hierarchies and power divides, and propose (sometimes rather romanti-
cised) definitions of cosmopolitanism and/or nomadic subjectivity as alternatives
instead. On the other side of the contestation you find the staunch defenders of
the nation(-state) and of a conception of national identity as rooted in a shared
history and tradition. This group generally sees globalisation, as well as the advancing European unification, as a threat to national stability, and as a danger for
(the imagined homogeneity of) a specific national character. They generally plead
for a re-valuation of the national and, especially since 9/11, for a reinforcement of
its 'protective' borders in order to keep the 'invading Other' out. Their definition

of this Other – in striking contrast to their rather rigid definition of national identity – is versatile and dynamic. It oscillates between ethnic, cultural, and religious terms, depending on its particular function in discourse.

Although I strongly sympathise with the idealist dimension of the first 'transnational project', the proclamation of the end of the nation(-state) and of a postnational identity is in my opinion simply premature. Despite the fact that the studied works of literature actually result from transnational migration, the imaginations of identity that these works propose confirm this supposition of prematurity. The imaginations of identity in the story-worlds of globalisation testify of the *ongoing* importance and influence of the national as a (divisive) discursive construct. In her study *Limits of Citizenship. Migrants and Postnational Membership in Europe* Yasemin Soysal insists that 'we can no longer frame our debates on membership and identities within the dichotomy of national and transnational, and the expected linear transition from one to the other' (2000: 13). Instead the current situation demands a scalar understanding of discursive constellations in process, and of the constructions and imaginations determined by these. The study *New Germans, New Dutch* addresses this demand and brings alternative imaginations of national identity, ranging from trans- to hyper-national, to the fore. These imaginations do not exclude one another, but are concurrent responses to a world in flux. Together and in interaction they offer a fascinating literary 'identity-scape' of German and Dutch national worlds subject to (actual and discursive) transformation.

The following conclusion offers a short overview of the results of the four literary case studies central in this study. Their juxtaposition makes it possible to draw attention to some important parallels between the German cases on the one hand and the Dutch cases on the other. The German-Dutch distinctions will be framed by the specificity of the German and Dutch discourses on national identity, as discussed in the first chapter of *New Germans, New Dutch*. The studied works of literature share an interest in four particular fields of meaning that can be connected to the idea of a world and identity-scape in transition: inclusive forms of cultural memory, the negotiation of tradition in a situation after migration, (social) marginalisation, and the search for alternative forms of community. The (narrative and performative) strategies used to address these fields of heightened socio-cultural interest and to imagine transformative story-worlds of migration turn out as diverse as the pieces of literary writing themselves. When focusing on these critical strategies, literature of migration appears as a alternative mode of critical thought, as counter-discursive cultural text and/or as active instigator of change in respect to dominant (and often reductive) technologies of reading. Again I link these various strategies to the German and Dutch contexts of writing and to the specificity of the discourses into which the literary works intervene. Again the German-Dutch comparison proves extraordinarily insightful.

Whereas the *centrality* of national identity in public discourses on migration and multiculturality is similar in both Germany and the Netherlands, its historical status, its legal dimension, and its discursive semantics differ considerably. These differences have important consequences on a cultural level. The imaginations of national identity in German and Dutch literature of migration respond to the particularities of the German and Dutch contexts of writing in various ways. In the last section of this conclusion I explicate and elaborate on the intricate connection between national citizenship (the juridical-political level), national self-images (the discursive construction of national identity in past and present), and the literary imaginations that this study brings to the fore.

Özdamar's Imaginations of 'Transnational Identity'

The detailed analyses of three short stories by the Turkish-German writer Emine Sevgi Özdamar – 'Mein Istanbul', 'Mein Berlin', and 'Fahrrad auf dem Eis' (all 2001) – focused on the identity-constitutive practice of travelling and boundary crossing. As literary travelogues the stories on the one hand map personal memories and on the other question and negotiate 'official' cartographies of cultural memory (and thus of national identity) on the other.

In 'Mein Istanbul' and 'Mein Berlin' Özdamar's protagonist 'Sevgi' connects the two title cities in reflective memories. Historical parallels between the two cities, such as, for instance, their geographical and political division and the student revolts in the 1960s, link the cities as much as the protagonist's travelling between Berlin and Istanbul does. The stories constitute acts of re-territorialisation: they redraw the official map of hegemonic history. Central in this practice of re-drawing is the protagonist's disruptive travelling. As an East-West commuter in the time of German-German separation, she has the opportunity to observe and compare East *and* West Berlin. Simultaneously, however, she remains an outsider on both sides of the Berlin Wall, here *and* there. 'Sevgi' refrains from making any political judgements or from taking position in the German-German field of tensions. Instead she assumes a mode of observation that is strategically naïve and that enables her to address issues of contestation in a seemingly depoliticised manner. A subtle critique, however, is nevertheless inherent in exactly this particular performance of naïveté.

The imaginations of identity that evolve from the unusual travelogues can be characterised as nomadic, trans- or even postnational. It is from a transnational outsider position that 'Sevgi' wonders (in confronting and often insightful ways) about assumed national specificities. By her nomadic crossing of divisive (national) boundaries she interrogates these boundaries, and in many cases reveals them as artificial. Özdamar's stories do not leave out the negative, complicating side of this (often-romanticised) nomadism. On the one hand the 'nomadic subject' 'Sevgi' enjoys and celebrates the freedom of her self-designed position 'in between' (Turkish and German, East and West, home and abroad). On the other, however, she struggles with feelings of loneliness and with a lack of emotional belonging. The death of her grandmother for instance (and in 'Fahrrad auf dem Eis', the death of her mother) confronts her with a hurtful dimension of her up-rootedness: the distance from and the failing comfort of (the construct called) 'home'. Özdamar's protagonist experiences that, as Martha Nussbaum states: 'Becoming a citizen of the world is often a lonely business' (1996: 15). It involves giving up on traditional structures of comfort and security in favour of webs of relation that demand an active engagement in their establishment and mainte-nance. Özdamar's writing explores the possibilities for similar new forms of con-nection and community.

This undertaking becomes particularly clear in the story 'Fahrrad auf dem Eis'. In this story the protagonist's wandering through Amsterdam and her numerous encounters with the inhabitants of this ethnically diverse metropolis prompt a process of self-reflection. The narrative juxtaposition of German and Dutch na-tional traumas – the Holocaust and colonialism – and of their affective impact in the present, works as instigation for a responsible re-orientation of the Self in relation to these national traumas. In this sense 'Fahrrad auf dem Eis' makes clear that transnationality is not a free-floating identity. It requires certain points of attachment too, as much as it involves certain (historical) responsibilities. Özda-mar's stories explore paths and directions for the imagination of alternative forms of transnational community based on the concept of Relation.

In contrast to Özdamar the other three writers whose work I have studied all grew up in Germany and the Netherlands. They are hardly migrants in the com-mon meaning of the term and all three, in accordance with Leslie Adelson's 'Against between'-manifesto (2001), decisively resist a position 'in between'. As a first-generation labour migrant – albeit one of an exceptional kind – Özdamar made a conscious and more or less independent decision to migrate and thus to 'become transnational'. The other writers generally have to deal with situations of imposed 'in betweenness' which often comes down to imposed Alterity. The in-terventions in exclusionary constructions of national identity that their literature performs, indicate (possibly as a reaction to these attributions) a strong desire to ground their identities and to secure their belonging: nationally, or, if that aim appears impossible, then locally. The second case study of German literature of Turkish migration concerns an instance of such a 'local grounding'.

Zaimoglu's Imaginations of a 'Kanak Counter-Identity'

Just like Özdamar's literature, the early, provocative literary work of Feridun Zai-moglu, links its imaginations of identity to an outsider position. Despite the con-siderable differences – in style, in tone, in 'message' of their literature – the ap-plied strategies resemble each other in that both Özdamar's and Zaimoglu's literature present characters that choose to be or to remain marginal, outside of the dominant German identity. The protagonists in the work of both writers reject national frames of identification. Whereas Özdamar's 'Sevgi' dismisses identification with a German national identity in favour of a transnational nomadism, Zaimoglu gives voice to a strongly localised *Kanak* underdog in works of literature that claim a high degree of 'authenticity'. With this claim Zaimoglu on the one hand fits within a dominant pattern of reading 'migrants' literature'. On the other hand he strategically satisfies the desire of German readers who are particularly interested in 'true stories' about a fascinating, exotic Other. The *Kanak* characters in his collection of 'authentic protocols' *Kanak Sprak* (1995) refuse to be German, displaying instead a strong attitude of contempt. As a consistent consequence of their social marginalisation and discursive exclusion they reject the German norm (ality) and opt for a *Kanak* counter-culture. The interviewed members of this *Kanak* community in the margin, perform their identity in strict concordance with the *Kanak* code that is prescribed by the author-character Zaimoglu in the *Kanak Sprak* preface.

In extremely provocative language combined with an aggressive masculinist pose the *Kanaken* spit on the *Alemane* – the *Kanake's* despicable antipode – who does not acknowledge their existence. By means of their *Kanak* language performances, they claim a German counter-identity that they, in imitation of the author-character Zaimoglu, label with the pejorative *Kanake*. The appropriating repetition of this epithet as a proud form of self-description, brings about a resisting resignification: the term *Kanake* gains an iconic quality in the process of self-*Kanakisation*. Their counter-national *Kanak* identity becomes a source for feelings of moral superiority. Their verbally violent 'counter-attacks' ['*Gegenattacke*'] and their poses of a *Kanak* hypermasculinity not only respond to, but also mirror the hierarchising discourse of dominant culture. Now the roles are turned around, and the *Kanaken* themselves engage in hate speech acts towards the *Alemane* as well as towards others who do not meet the demands of the *Kanak* code. The particular narrative structure of *Kanak Sprak* also implicates its readership in this reversed process of ethnicisation. By the strategically shifting use of the deictic '*du*', the protocols exclude the readers from the closed and homogenous *Kanak* community and interpellate them as belonging to the group of despised Others.

The *Kanak* novel *Abschaum* (1997) complicates the one-sided celebration of *Kanak* identity and the *Kanake's* hateful, polarising discourse. The 'real-life' story of protagonist Ertan Ongun makes clear that *Kanak* identity, as it is prescribed by the *Kanak Sprak* preface and propagated by the interviewed *Kanaken*, leaves little space for self-reflection, doubt or difference. The straitjacket of group identity does not allow for individual development. Moreover, the discursive strategy of the 'counter-attack' entails an indiscriminate repetition of the hated and criticised dichotomies. As such this counter-identity exists in fatal dependence on the dominant discourse that it resists, but to which it in fact simultaneously holds on. As Ertan's story of social and emotional downfall makes clear, an individualised *Kanak* identity is at present practically non-viable in the larger society. Ertan ends up in the lonely emptiness behind the masculinist speech performance, between the static *Kanak* straitjacket and an exclusionary German society. In this sense Ertan's sad story actually underscores what Butler describes as 'the limits and risks of resignification as a strategy of opposition' (1997: 38). The *Kanak* performance of an aggressive counter-identity neither protects Ertan from the pain of social exclusion, nor from the destructive dimensions of a mimicked dichotomous discourse.

Bouazza's Imaginations of a 'Hyper-Dutch Identity'

The Moroccan-Dutch writer Hafid Bouazza entered the Dutch cultural field with the collection of short prose entitled *De voeten van Abdullah* (1996). This debut was enthusiastically welcomed and highly acclaimed. The dominant mode of its reception, however, was strongly exoticist. Most critics reduced the stories to the writer's (aestheticised – but this aspect was left out of consideration) memories of his childhood in Morocco: his stories offered insight in an exotic and faraway Otherness. The literary works that Bouazza published after his debut can be seen as (more or less explicitly) resisting reactions to this Othering and reductive mode of reading. Bouazza's 2002 revision of *De voeten van Abdullah* performs a similar act of literary resistance. It redirects its readers by narrative means. The added story 'De oversteek' works to reshape the context of reading the collection of stories. It disables an interpretation of the *Dutch* work of literature that does not account for its *Dutch* dimension. The addition of the dramatically moving story has an eye-opening effect and prompts its readers to read responsibly. In the particular case of 'De oversteek' this means an acknowledgement and contemplation of Dutch complicity in histories of migration. In respect to the collection of stories in general, it implies a critical interrogation of too-easily applied, divisive markers of Dutch Self and migrant Other, and of the exclusion of this Other from the realm of Dutch cultural memory.

The subtle critique of processes of (ethnic) Othering in Bouazza's literature pales in comparison with his rather sudden public performance as a critic of Islam and as society's whistleblower in the same year as the literary revision discussed above. In an alarming and provocative tone Bouazza warns against Dutch blindness for Islamist dangers and calls on 'the Dutch' – whom he accuses of negligence of their cultural heritage – to defend Dutch liberalism. In the context of this performance it is hardly surprising that his subsequent novel *Paravion* (2003), a bucolic parody on Moroccan-Dutch migration, was predominantly read in the same warning mode: as a political pamphlet. The novel's stereotypical representation of Morean migrants and their growing frustration in a licentious host country certainly invites a critical stance towards the migrant males that this representation ridicules. However, there is (much) more to *Paravion* than this one narrative layer and its caricatural image of the migrant Other. Using a complex narrative structure, the novel interweaves several worlds and stories in which gender – more than culture or ethnicity – features as the central determinant in problematic male-female relations. Additionally, the story-world status of the various versions of paradisiacal spaces varies in semantically significant ways. Nevertheless, the combination of Bouazza's public performance and – assumedly – narrative performance of what I call a 'hyper-Dutch' identity – including a negative marking of the Muslim Other – gained him access to Dutch national identity. *Paravion*'s caricature of the migrant Other in combination with its assumed imagination of the Netherlands as a Dutch Arcadia threatened by the migrant Other effected Bouazza's final acceptance as a Dutch instead of as a migrant writer.

Benali's Imaginations of a 'Multi-Ethnic Dutchness'

Like Bouazza, the writer Abdelkader Benali also self-assuredly postulates his Dutch identity. Other than Bouazza, however, Benali does not completely reject the significance of his ethnic identity. In his opinion his Moroccan roots and his public status as writer give him a certain responsibility as Moroccan-Dutch representative and role model. The emphasis on the Moroccan part of his identity does not, as far as Benali is concerned, in any way obstruct his Dutchness. Benali's literary work makes a subject out of the (emotionally) complex collisions between the first and the following generations of migrants, especially in respect to gendered customs and traditions. It zooms in on the difficult negotiation between often-contrary demands of family, tradition and Dutch society. His work's imaginations of identity have regard for the enormous transformative pressure of migratory movements. Benali's first novel *Bruiloft aan zee* (1996) was published during the Dutch 'happy multiculturality' phase, before 9/11. In its speedy and humoristic narration of a quest for a bridegroom who has disappeared shortly before his wedding, the novel not only criticises Moroccan patriarchy, it also repudiates Dutch cultural relativism. By means of a particularly directive narration and a sudden moment of narrative rupture, it confronts its readers with the slackening of norms in an assumedly tolerant, culturalist acceptance of the story-world's 'Moroccan normality'.

In the drama *Onrein. De vader, de zoon en de hond* (2003), written after 9/11, similar generational and patriarchal problems as in *Bruiloft aan zee* take centre stage, but this time the tenor of the story has turned more sceptical. In the drama, a migrant father, his son and Dutch society are stuck in a fatal three-way constellation of great expectations and mutual misunderstandings. Whereas Benali's literature generally propagates and disseminates a kind of positive trust in the possibility of intercultural reconciliation, *Onrein* – which Benali himself labelled a literary reaction to the polarisations in Dutch discourse – is clearly of a more pessimistic purport. Nonetheless, this literary work also offers a space for reflection on the sometimes-painful complexities and personal dramas that are involved in the current (ethnic) transformation of Dutch society. It raises awareness of the dangers of social exclusion and warns of the desperate radicalisation that this exclusion can ensue. Benali's imaginations of national identity encourage both 'allochthonous' and 'autochthonous' Dutch to take up responsibility for a successful outcome of Dutch multiculturality and for an inclusive definition of multicultural Dutchness. His work pleads for a dynamic and open conception of Dutch national identity that acknowledges its own multiplicity and demands a positive effort of all who do or would like to identify themselves as Dutch. Self-reflection, self-critique and commitment to the newly developing national community are central virtues in Benali's 'literary recipes'.

Literary Imaginations of Germanness vis-à-vis Dutchness

None of the discussed protagonists in the German works of literature shows any interest in obtaining a German national identity, nor – and this is striking – in opening up and transforming the dominant concept of German national identity. Zaimoglu's literary work represents German identity as exclusionary and unattractive, not worth the effort of any further investment. It imagines *Kanak* identity as its hostile and preferable antagonist: a national counter-identity. Özdamar's imaginations of identity (desire to) transcend national boundaries altogether and reject any form of national identification. Instead her literary work explores new forms of community based on webs of (other kinds of) Relation. In general this German literature of migration does not offer any alternative or re-imaginations of German national identity, but imagines a transnational and a counter-German identity as two forms of pertinent outsider-identities. The fact that both writers adopt an *accented* language that resists and undermines the norm of standard German, works to underline this preferred outsider-position on another level. Özdamar writes in a poetically alienated German and intersperses her writing with Turkish idiom and Turkish sayings in literal translation. Zaimoglu's literary performance of *Kanak* identity makes use of a hybridised German vernacular that counts as constitutive of this identity. In their consciously Other German language these writers offer imaginations of identity that seem to result from a search for alternative forms of community *beyond* the national frame of an exclusionary Germanness.

In contrast to the German works, the Dutch literature of migration actually does negotiate traditional national boundaries in order to imagine and claim new and inclusive versions of Dutch national identity. Bouazza's work addresses and questions dominant conceptions of the Other as well as dominant structures of Othering that both function to define the Dutch Self. His literature intervenes in the process of Dutch self-definition and critically contributes to the ongoing ne-

gotiation of Dutch national identity. His literary interventions as well as their reception are strongly implicated in an increasingly polarised public discourse on
Dutch multiculturality. Both testify of the shift from a (culturalist) celebration of a
'happy multiculturality' to the 'multicultural drama' and the supposed clash of
cultures after 9/11. This same discursive shift can be assessed in respect to Benali's writing and its reception. More than Bouazza, Benali's imaginations of Dutchness – pre- and post-9/11 – try to get rid of 'the Dutch Self vis-à-vis the migrant
Other' dichotomy. His imaginations appeal to self-criticism and to a responsible
attitude by all parties involved in the current transformation of Dutch society. In
Benali's 'responsible writings' the future of Dutch identity is the outcome of a
shared undertaking.

Whatever the particular co-ordinates of their literature, both Bouazza and Benali actively engage in the critical (re-)imagination of Dutch identity. Their imaginations give proof of their indisputable membership of the Dutch national community. This membership includes critique of and participation in the ongoing
discursive construction of Dutchness by the aesthetic means of their literature
and by their public performances as Dutch writers. In contrast to their German
colleagues who write in an accented German that seems to underline their outsider status, these Dutch writers creatively and self-confidently make use of their
Dutch language. They process and produce Dutch cultural material and self-con-
sciously position themselves in a Dutch tradition of writing.

Both Bouazza's and Benali's debuts – published before 9/11 – were predominantly read in ethnicising terms. About ten years later the public interest has
shifted from their ethnic Otherness to their 'representative Dutchness'. The participation of these writers in the cultural sphere is taken as a demonstration of
Dutch multiculturality; their acceptance is considered indicative of the (self-)as-
sumed and celebrated Dutch tolerance. The acknowledgement of the Dutchness
of these writers coincides with an emphasis on their emancipated gender sensitivity as well as on their critical stance towards Islamic traditions and customs. Perceived as 'well-integrated' Dutch citizens of non-Dutch ethnic origin, Bouazza
and Benali count as exemplary. In Dutch public discourse they appear in opposition to the 'non-integrated allochthonous' Others who are increasingly defined in
religious terms.

Discursive Constructions of German and Dutch National Identity

This section tentatively reads the striking discrepancy between the strategies and
position of the German and Dutch literature of migration in the light of the discursive construction of Germanness and Dutchness as discussed in the first chapter of this study. The assessment of indifference to or even repudiation of the
German national identity in German literature of migration, can be connected to
two interlinked levels of meaning of Germanness that seriously hinder 'becoming

national' in the sense of 'becoming German'. First the juridical level: for a long time the official determination of Germanness in the sense of German citizenship has left little space for ethnic diversity. Until the year 2000 a very restrictive, *ius sanguinis*-based citizenship legislation made it extremely difficult for 'foreigners' of other ethnic origin (in contrast to foreigners of German ethnicity) to obtain German citizenship. The historical self-understanding constitutes a second level of restriction. On the one hand there is the initial but still effective imagination of the German nation state as a unity of one *Volk*: originary, ethnically homogenous, continuous. On the other hand there is the contemporary, negative and burdened German self-image that comprehends the responsibility for the Holocaust. These two levels of meaning interact with and sustain the contemporary discourse on migration and multiculturality in Germany in various ways.

The discursive construction of Germanness and its imagination in literature of migration appear mutually constitutive. On the one hand the various intersecting discourses – as contexts of writing – 'co-produce' the literary imaginations. The outdated but still influential 'ideal of ethnic homogeneity', together with the minor appeal of a stained national identity, affect the imaginations of *non*-national identity: the complete rejection or disregard of German national identity.[1] On the other hand these imaginations simultaneously intervene in the discourses that co-produce them, and that they in their turn and in their specific capacity as works of literature respond to. As aesthetic interventions they contribute to the ongoing production of German national identity and participate in the accompanying process of negotiating national boundaries.

To refine and substantiate this thesis the German-Dutch comparison proves of value. In comparison to the German situation the combined *ius soli* and *ius sanguinis* citizenship legislation in the Netherlands has made it 'easier' for people of non-Dutch descent (especially for those who were born in the Netherlands) to obtain the Dutch nationality. The relatively early political acknowledgement of the permanent character of the multiculturalisation of Dutch society in 1983 resulted in an official national policy on the integration of the distinctive minority groups. In line with the Dutch tradition of 'pillarisation' this policy regulated and furthered a cultural pluralist approach in respect to the transforming Dutch society. It is only since the 2000 multicultural drama debate that this official policy has come under intense attack as actually obstructing integration, and as furthering ethnic segregation instead. Nevertheless, despite the polarisations that followed in the wake of this debate and that were augmented after the socio-politically influential murders of Fortuyn and Van Gogh, the celebrated idea of tolerance as well as openness to (ethnic) Others remain central markers of the Dutch national self-understanding.

Clearly, this Dutch self-image is strongly idealised and in current times it is hardly recognised in daily practice. Nevertheless, as a discursive construct it is still influential and appears to have a positive effect. It both suggests accessibility and implies that ethnic Others are welcome to identify themselves as Dutch. The fact that the Dutch self-image still disregards the Dutch role in atrocities committed during colonialism cannot be left unmentioned here: Dutch national memory simply blots out this national stain. However, other than Dutch postcolonial writers, the migrant writers whose work I have discussed in this study hardly reflect on this aspect of Dutchness. Colonial trauma plays no role in their re-imaginations of Dutch identity.

In general the (more or less) inclusive construction of Dutchness seems to effect (more or less) inclusive imaginations of Dutch national identity in Bouazza's and Benali's literature of migration. Their writing self-assuredly participates in the larger discursive production of Dutch national identity and simultaneously works to confirm both writers' indisputable Dutchness.

Conclusion: Literary Variety and National Specificity

The analyses of several works of contemporary German and Dutch literature of Turkish and Moroccan migration collected in this study have made clear that the imaginations of German and Dutch national identity in these works vary substantially, in character as well as in the strategies that these writings employ. Imagined identities range from trans- and counter-national in the German case to hyper-national and multiethnic in Dutch literature. They result from literary strategies as diverse as staged naïveté, performative aggression, parody, and strongly directive structures of narration – to name just a few. Despite clear parallels between the two neighbouring countries in respect to histories of labour migration, the evolving discourses on migration and multiculturality, and the marginality of literature of migration in the dominant cultural fields, the specificity of the German and Dutch national contexts – the distinctive juridical and discursive constructions of national identity and citizenship – proves to be of overriding importance. As literary interventions into public discourse the literary imaginations of identity address and question these particular constructions. In both national contexts national identity takes shape through the marking out of difference with Others. However, the studied works of literature negotiate the various (symbolic) boundaries that divide German and Dutch Selves from their Others in *nationally specific* ways.

Whereas the almost parallel debates about a 'German *Leitkultur*' and a Dutch 'multicultural drama' at the beginning of the new millennium pointed at a shared heightened discursivity of issues of national identity, migration and multiculturality, German and Dutch national specificities still set the terms for the imaginations of national identity in literature of migration. The alternative identities that the literary works by Özdamar, Zaimoglu, Bouazza and Benali imagine appear contextually anchored in national ways. In spite of the current polarisations in Dutch politics and society, the Dutch writers of migrant background appear to feel freer and to have more opportunities – albeit conditional ones – to *re*-imagine Dutchness, to create new meanings of what it means to be Dutch. Whereas the reflections on national identity in the work of Özdamar and Zaimoglu either plead for transnationality or reject Germanness altogether, the writing by Bouazza and Benali sets out to appropriate Dutchness and to transform its traditional semantics. The German literature of migration searches for alternative forms of community *outside* of the national framework; the Dutch literature of migration endeavours to negotiate difference and diversity *within* the national framework.

There is, however, no reason for an idealisation of the Dutch situation. As I have emphasised before, the *terms* of this national 're-rooting' are highly disputable, and the acceptance of the writers' Dutchness is strongly conditional. Whereas the hardened social climate and the increasingly restrictive citizenship policy in the Netherlands might well affect future imaginations of national belonging in Dutch literature of migration in negative ways, the opposite could be true for the German situation. The 2000 citizenship reform and the hesitative but growing acknowledgement that Germany is a multiethnic country of migration might well open up a new creative space for transformative imaginations of Germanness: imaginations that reflect on and aim for a lived multicultural future without forgetting about the monocultural discourse of the past.

Notes

Introduction

1. I use inverted commas here in order to underscore that the term 'Muslim' is a diffuse identity marker that is often ascribed in a homogenising manner. Dominant discourse in the West does not differentiate between people who actually identify as Muslim, those who have turned their back on Islam and all the variations in between. Besides, it often conflates 'Muslim' as a marker of religion with 'Arab-looking' as a determination of outer appearance.

2. Jonathan Culler makes a useful distinction between the notions of context and frame in his study *Framing the Sign. Criticism and its Institutions* (1988). Culler warns that 'context is not fundamentally different from what it contextualizes; context is not given but produced; what belongs to a context is determined by interpretive strategies' (1988: ix). The notion of framing has several advantages over that of context including the emphasis on the active involvement of the interpreters: 'framing is something we do' (ibid.). See also Bal (2002: 133-138) on the relation between framing and context. Leslie Adelson warns that '[t]he question of context is a minefield' (Adelson 2005: 11). She pleads for 'a scalar understanding of interactive contexts' (ibid.) in which literature intervenes. My understanding of 'discourse' is Foucauldian (cf. Foucault [1969] 2003 and [1971] 1976).

3. I capitalise the terms 'Self' and 'Other' (as well as the derived 'Othering') in order to underscore the symbolic and normative dimensions that are at work in and through this binary opposition. Arjun Appadurai uses the suffix '-scapes' in his exploration of the various dimensions of global cultural flows. He explains: 'The suffix *-scape* allows us to point to the fluid, irregular shapes of these landscapes (...). These terms with the common suffix *-scape* also indicate that these are not objectively given relations that look the same from every angle of vision but, rather, that they are deeply perspectival constructs, inflected by the historical, linguistic, and political situatedness of different sorts of actors: nation-states, multinationals, diasporic communities' (Appadurai 1997: 33). In his article 'The power of the imagination' he defines 'ethnoscape' as 'the landscape of persons who make up the shifting world in which we live' (Appadurai 2005: 50).

4. In this study I use Adelson's term 'literature of migration' rather than the more common term 'migrants' literature' (Grüttemeier 2001: 22 n. 1). I prefer the first term as, other than the second, it disconnects the literary corpus that it appoints from the criterion of the writer's biography. It seems rather absurd to continue to apply the term 'migrant' to (the literary work of) writers of the second or even third generation who, as Moray McGowan describes, often live in a cultural environment that is 'shaped to some degree by migrant experience' (2001: 293), but have not had an active

part in the actual process themselves. The term 'literature of migration' refers to literary performances of cultural transformation resulting from migration. This implies that 'literature of migration' is not necessarily authored by writers of migrant background. The term 'migratory literature' could function as a new alternative for the particular kind of literature of migration that involves a certain transformative dimension. However, yet another label might add extra confusion to an already disorderly field of contested terms and categorisations.

5. In the particular frame of this study I refer to the selected writers by using the hyphenations 'Turkish-German' and 'Moroccan-Dutch'. However, with this notation I do not intend to suggest that these cultures come together as two seamless wholes into a new combined identity. On the contrary: the seemingly bi-cultural epithet should be considered as a dynamic process of cultural métissage in itself. Most of the writers whose work I have studied reject the idea of identity-hyphenation altogether.

I. National Identity

1. Ernest Gellner (1983) and Ernest Renan ([1882] 1996) wrote classical studies on the nation and nationalism. Eric Hobsbawn (1990), and Hobsbawn and Terence Ranger (1983) offer important contributions to the discussion on the nation and its 'invented traditions'. Numerous scholars point out that the process of (re-)appropriating and (re-)defining national identity is strongly gendered (Anthias and Yuval-Davis 1989, 1992; Blom et al. 2000; Brinker-Gabler and Smith 1997; Herminghouse and Mueller 1997; Kosta and Kraft 2003; McClintock 1993; Wenk 2000; Yuval-Davis 1997). In her influential study *Gender and Nation* Nira Yuval Davis states that 'constructions of nationhood usually involve specific notions of both "manhood" and "womanhood"' (1997: 1) and that 'it is women – and not (just?) the bureaucracy and the intelligentsia – who reproduce nations, biologically, culturally and symbolically' (ibid. 2). The range of this study does not allow for a detailed study of the gendered dimensions of this process.

2. In various writings Hall (1990, 1993, 1996a, 1996b, 1997) conceptualises 'identity' as a process that is never accomplished. Rather than to a situation of being, an essential Self, identity refers to a never-ending production of becoming. From this it follows that identities are social, political and cultural constructs determined by (chronotopical) boundaries that are never natural or stable, but always a matter of negotiation. In his introduction to the edited volume *Questions of Cultural Identity* (1996), Hall writes: 'Identities are thus points of temporary attachment to the subject positions which discursive practices construct for us' (1996a: 5/6). According to Hall representation is key to all productions of identity. Identity as a concept has been the topic of numerous critical interrogations that oscillate between various forms of identity politics on the one hand and a radical dismissal of the concept on the other. See Alcoff and Mendieta (2003), Brah (1996), Chambers (1994), Gilroy (1991), Hall and Du Gay (1996), LaCapra (2004), Mohanty (1993), Moya and Hames-García (2000), Rajchmann (1995), Rutherford (1990), and Schobert and Jäger (2004).

3. In *Imagined Communities* Anderson perceives of the nation as a specific articulation of modernity, preconditioned by the demise of Latin as a universal language, the emergence of a new sense of time and the rise of print capitalism. The winter volume of

Diacritics (1999) edited by Pheng Cheah offers critical discussions of the meaning and impact of Anderson's work. In his study *National Identity* (1993), Anthony D. Smith lists five fundamental features of 'national identity': the sharing of a historic territory or homeland, common myths and historical memories, a mass public culture, a common economy, and common legal rights and duties for all members. This list testifies of both the complexity and the abstract nature of the concept that he considers as fundamentally multidimensional. National identity does not 'just' refer to an ideology or a form of politics, but instead comprehends several distinctive, intersecting dimensions that Smith denotes as 'ethnic, cultural, territorial, economic and legal-political' (1993: 15).

4. Berlant and Freeman cite from Berlant (1991): 'Its traditional icons, its metaphors, its heroes, its rituals, and its narratives, provide an alphabet for a collective consciousness or national subjectivity; through the National Symbolic the historical nation aspires to achieve the inevitability of the status of natural law, a birthright' (Berlant and Freeman 1993: 197).

5. In the Dutch case the 'Belgian' struggle for independence between 1830 and 1839 as well as the German occupation of Dutch territory during the Second World War constitute historical moments of heightened discussion. In the German case the Napoleonic Wars as well as the First and the Second World War are moments of violent nation building, whereas the occasions of the *Wende* and the German reunification are of a more peaceful, but equally drastic nature. For both countries counts that also 'smaller', inner border tensions as for instance economic crises, the student revolts of the 1960s or the current politics of fear constitute important factors in processes of national re-orientation.

6. For discussions and new conceptualisations of boundaries see Boer (1996, 2006), Kosta and Kraft (2003), Sassen (1998), and Stolcke (1995).

7. In present times the legal-political dimension – in the sense of registered citizenship or nationality – disputably makes out the most decisive and radical dimension for people's experiences of the everyday. This is the regulating dimension of national identity that decides about the legitimacy and illegitimacy of people's national membership, about legitimate and illegitimate inhabitants of (for instance) the German and the Dutch national space.

8. For reflections on and imaginations of postnational worlds see Beck (2000, 2004), Cheah and Robbins (1998), Göktürk et al. (2007: 471-494), Habermas (1998), Hedetoft and Hjort (2002), Kristeva (1993), Nussbaum (1996), Römhild (2005), Soysal (1994, 2000), and Vertovec (2001).

9. 'In dem Maße, in dem eine Mehrheit von Individuen an diesem Bild der einheitlichen Nation mitwirkt, sich und andere darüber definiert (sich einschließt, andere ausschließt), in dem Maße existiert die einheitliche Nation.'

10. Aleida Assmann (1998) and Andreas Huyssen (2003) discuss more positive qualities of national identity.

11. I am aware of the fact that this positive-toned interpretation of the possibilities of the national is rather unusual, if not taboo, in the progressive scholarship on issues of migration and multiculturality to which this study contributes. I use the term 'multi-

culturality' to refer to the actual (multicultural) makeup of society. Multiculturalism pertains to a particular (political) ideology.

12. Brennan writes: 'Cosmopolitanism is *local* while denying its local character. This denial is an intrinsic feature of cosmopolitanism and inherent to its appeal' (2001: 660). In his opinion transnationalism is nothing more than a 'substantively altered competition among national states' (ibid. 673). Steven Vertovec (2000) also criticises that cosmopolitanism is mainly a *rhetorical* concern.

13. Some of the literary works that I discuss in the following sections provide similar insights: they work to legitimate the desire to become national in a society that hesitates or even refuses to recognise one as such.

14. As a result of the focus on the organised labour migration in the 1960s and 1970s, this overview is restricted to the situation in the former Federal Republic of Germany (FRG) and in the unified Germany. The situation in the German Democratic Republic (GDR) was fundamentally different and so were the discourses on migration (and multiculturality).

15. In 2007 the collaboration between eminent experts on migration from Germany and the Netherlands – Klaus J. Bade, Pieter C. Emmer, Leo Lucassen, and Jochen Oltmer – resulted in the *Enzyklopädie Migration in Europa. Vom 17. Jahrhundert bis zur Gegenwart*. Jan Lucassen and Rinus Penninx (1985, 1994) offer extensive overviews and analyses of the Dutch experience with migration, including labour migration. Ruben S. Gowricharn (1993) collects several essays on aspects of Dutch multiculturality. Anita Böcker and Kees Groenendijk (2004) discuss migration and integration in the postwar Netherlands. Klaus J. Bade (1983, 1992, 2005 with Jochen Oltmer) published several studies on German histories of migration. Ulrich Herbert (1986, 2001), Karl-Heinz Meier-Braun (1995, 2002) and Karin Hunn (2005) focus on the particular phenomenon of organised labour migration. Mark Terkessidis (2000) offers a short critical introduction into the theme in his work *Migranten*. Kien Nghi Ha (2003a) analyses the colonial patterns of (German) labour migration. The volume *Projekt Migration* (Frangenberg 2005) that appeared in connection to the comprehensive exhibition project of the same name in Cologne collects a rich variety of critical contributions, art works and historical documentation on migration. The reference book *Germany in Transit. Nation and Migration 1955-2005* (Göktürk et al. 2007) offers a rich archive of texts that chart Germany's history of (labour) migration and multiculturalisation.

16. See Herbert (2001: 208) and Terkessidis (2000: 17/18). Germany made foreign recruitment agreements with Italy (1955), Spain and Greece (both 1960), Morocco (1963), Portugal (1964), Tunisia (1965) and Yugoslavia (1968). Bilateral agreements with the Republic of Turkey date from 1961 and 1964. The fact that Turkey was a member of the NATO surely contributed to its 'election' as first non-European recruitment country. The European or non-European status of Turkey remains a topic of controversial discussion, as the ongoing debate on Turkey's EU membership makes clear.

17. Compare Fennell (1997: 20).

18. Germany intentionally recruited more skilled labourers than the Netherlands. Skilled labourers themselves also had a preference for Germany because of the higher wages (Böcker and Thränhardt 2003b: 37). Before the bilateral agreements on governmental

level, Dutch industrial concerns already made use of foreign labour on a smaller, self-organised scale (Lucassen and Penninx 1985: 50/51).

19. This element distinguishes 'guest labourers' from for instance the German labour migrants in the Netherlands in the 1920s and early 1930s, and the Polish labourers in the German Ruhr area in the early twentieth century.

20. The obscuring labels 'guest labour' and 'guest workers' have been a topic of discussion for a long time. In 1972 the radio broadcast company WDR organised a contest to find an alternative to the term. Despite 32,000 entries no proposal was accepted as appropriate. According to Ruth Mandel the term 'reduces the migrants to their function. This marginalisation and objectification of the migrants leave little conceptual, social or linguistic space for meaningful incorporation into the society' (1989: 29).

21. Several reasons made staying in Germany and the Netherlands into an attractive option. These reasons varied from political instability and economic insecurity in the home country (as for instance in the cases of Turkey and Morocco) to the better future perspectives for family and children (e.g. education) in the host countries. The awareness that a return to the country of origin could not be made undone, was another important factor of influence. There is a striking discrepancy between the numbers of returned migrants from economically ascending (EU) countries like Italy, Spain and Greece on the one side, and Turkey and the North-African countries on the other.

22. Scholars disagree about the actual effects of the return-promoting policy (Böcker and Thränhardt 2003b; Koopmans 2003b). Despite the recruitment ban, processes of family reunion initially caused an increase in the migration rates. Contrary to the popular image of the guest worker as male, a considerable percentage of the labour migrants was in fact female (over 25 per cent). Mostly, however, these women were single and returned 'home' after the ban. A smaller number – but still more than their male counterparts – married Germans.

23. The decision on this law coincided with the change of government from SPD to CDU/CSU. During the pre-election phase the presence of migrants was strongly politicised and turned into political capital. See the section on the German discourse on multiculturality.

24. Koopmans explains the typically Dutch phenomenon of 'pillarisation' [verzuiling] as follows: 'The Dutch system of pillarisation was developed in the early twentieth century as a means to pacify conflicts between indigenous religious and political groups, and has been quite successful at that. However, it was never meant to serve as an instrument for the integration of immigrants, and has proven to be very inadequate for that purpose' (2003a: 168). It is especially this idea of minority culture(s) as another pillar in the polder that has come under vehement attack in the multicultural drama debate. By now many critics retrospectively perceive of the system as an important obstacle for integration. See also the edited volume on Dutch multiculturalism by C.H.M. Geuijen (1998) and Koopmans et al. (2005).

25. There is a clear intersection of decolonisation effects and labour migration in the Dutch situation. Labour migrants in the Netherlands profited from legal claims made by (radical) activists from the former Dutch colonies. The minorities policy bears on both groups.

26. Duyvené de Wit and Koopmans (2001) show that the migrant population in Germany mostly made either claims that concerned specifically ethnic or cultural issues (as for instance the fight against racism and xenophobia), or claims that were decided by the politics of the country of origin. The claims that ethnic minorities in the Netherlands made mostly had to do with their (legitimate) position in Dutch society. Compare Koopmans (2003b), Koopmans and Statham (2001), and Koopmans et al. (2005).

27. The national terminologies – 'foreigners' and 'allochthons' – are telling here. In Germany in the 1980s the term 'foreigner' replaced the term 'guest worker' as dominant denotation for the marginalized group. According to Jeffrey Peck the colloquial use of the term 'foreigner' in German discourse is problematic as the term 'collapses distinctions among the many kinds of non-Germans and distracts attention from the racial underpinnings of xenophobia, while simultaneously reifying the notion of the German' (1996: 482). Böcker and Groenendijk (2004: 306-307) discuss the terminology for non-indigenous Dutch in the Dutch discourse on migration where several terms have been proposed and rejected again (for reasons of stigmatisation). At this moment the term most commonly used is 'allochthons' as opposed to 'autochthons' (from the Greek roots allos/other, authos/same, and chton/land). This term, however, is also subject of discussion for its static and ideological impact. A 'politically correct' alternative is the assemblage 'zmv' for 'black [zwart], migrant and refugee [vluchteling]' that aims to capture the diversity among minorities.

28. For discussions of the citizenship and naturalisation legislation in Germany and the Netherlands see Bade (2001), Bade et al. (2007), Böcker and Groenendijk (2004), Brubaker (1992), Dietrich (2005), Entzinger (2006), Gosewinkel (1998), Heijs (1995), Joppke, (1999), Joppke and Morawska (2003), Kurthen (1995) and Spijkerboer (1993).

29. This is especially true for immigrants of Turkish and Moroccan origin. Citizenship legislation in their countries of origin makes it practically impossible to give up their original citizenship.

30. The required measure of integration for naturalisation is an ongoing topic of debate in both Germany and the Netherlands. In Germany the federal states determine the particular requirements as well as the kind of assessment of this condition. The tests that both countries introduced in order to assess the measure of integration are discussed controversially.

31. In the 1990s the Netherlands had the highest naturalisation rates of all European countries, partly as a result of this provisional permission. In the time between 1985 and 1999 the naturalisation rates in the Netherlands were on average seven times higher than in Germany (Duyvené de Wit and Koopmans 2001: 30). Although there have been some changes since 2000, the Dutch naturalisation percentages remain considerably higher. See Böcker and Thränhardt (2003a: 119).

32. In 1993 the naturalisation law was slightly moderated in a liberal direction: the time set for the acquisition of German citizenship for foreigners was reduced from fifteen to ten years. The fact that the ethnic principle of descent was only removed from the German law in the year 2000, is as remarkable as it is inappropriate, especially in the light of the National Socialist atrocities that were so strongly linked to the idea of an ethnically homogenous community. For that reason and other than in the Nether-

lands, citizenship legislation is a central issue in German discussions on multiculturality.

33. This better position of migrants on the German labour market is relative: they are still lagging behind in respect to indigenous Germans. Experts disagree about the exact reasons for the discrepancy between Germany and the Netherlands. See Böcker and Thränhardt (2003b), Koopmans (2002, 2003b), and Van Tubergen and Maas (2006).

34. In a special edition of the Dutch journal *Migrantenstudies* (2002) Baukje Prins and Boris Slijper position the German and the Dutch debates on the multicultural society in a broader European and international context. They present articles on strikingly similar public discourses in seven different countries: Belgium, France, Germany, the Nether-lands, Norway, Australia and Canada. Prins and Slijper assess that despite national differences as colonial histories or historical traditions of governance, these debates are increasingly determined by international developments as for instance the Rushdie affair, the explosive increase of migration movements and asylum requests, and 9/11.

35. 'Wij kunnen het vreemde niet weren en willen het niet weren.' This motto is a much-cited statement from Johan Huizinga's classical study *Nederland's geestesmerk* [The Nether-lands' national spirit]. Conservative and progressive speakers alike invoke the statement as early proof of the famous Dutch tolerance.

36. See (for instance) Bolkestein (2003, 2004) and Couwenberg (1992, 1996, 2001). Van Ginkel (1999) en Hoving (2005) offer broader discussions of senses of Dutchness.

37. I borrow the term 'culture-nationalists' from Peter van der Veer (2000). Culture-na-tionalists are strong opponents of culture relativism. Other, more pejorative terms that circulate in (the polarised) public discourse for this group of speakers are 'cul-ture-' or also 'Enlightenment-fundamentalists'. See also Brady (2004), Buruma (2006), Chervel and Seeliger (2007), and Stolcke (1995). Bhabha's term of 'nationalist nostal-gia' also applies here (1994).

38. 'Natie leidt tot nationalisme en daar doen Nederlanders niet aan. Althans dat zeggen ze zelf.'

39. The standard term 'Golden Age' is highly problematic. The 'Dutch' prosperity of that time was a direct result of colonial expansion and imperialist violence conducted around the world in the name of discovery, trade and progress.

40. 'Wat blijft er over van de Nederlandse identiteit als in de grote steden, de cultuurdra-gers van een land, autochtone Nederlanders een minderheid vormen?' In the article in question Bolkestein makes several problematic statements that he does not substanti-ate, for instance: 'Many [Muslims] reject the Dutch identity and still live in the Nether-lands. (...) The second and third generations often possess no identity at all. They live in between two worlds' ['Velen [islamieten] wijzen de Nederlandse identiteit af en wonen toch in Nederland. (...) De tweede en derde generaties hebben vaak helemaal geen identiteit. Zij leven tussen twee werelden'] (2003: 493).

41. Bolkestein's rhetorical question clearly does not take into account that many Dutch who are now considered 'autochthonous' have once come from elsewhere as well.

42. In 2003 Stefan Sanders and Xandra Schutte published an overview article about the origins of the (in)famous multicultural drama debate in *Vrij Nederland*. In this article nine Dutch intellectuals (central figures as Vuijsje, Bolkestein and Scheffer, but also new allochthonous voices as Bouazza and Hirsi Ali) give their retrospective opinion on

the discourse in which they participated themselves. Seven of the nine maintain that the multicultural drama debate had a positive effect on Dutch discourse. In their shared opinion it did away with several (ethnic) taboos and an evasive mode of discourse.

43. Like Vuijsje before him, Scheffer links the present situation to the Second World War. He assesses a parallel of 'naive blindness' in both situations and warns for repetition: 'And in this way a whole nation lost sight of reality' ['En zo verloor een hele natie het zicht op de werkelijkheid'] (Scheffer 2000).

44. The gender specificity of the problems was left out of consideration. The ethnic generalisation in public discourse conceals that criminality and school dropout almost exclusively concern young males. Also the enormous differences among Dutch minorities got lost in the dichotomising structure of the debate. Diversity in ethnic, historical and linguistic terms was reduced to the simplifying opposition of 'real Dutch' and their Others.

45. The first edition of Prins' work, titled *Voorbij de onschuld. Het debat over de multiculturele samenleving* [*Beyond Innocence. The Debate on the Multicultural Society*] appeared in the year 2000. I use the 2004 revised edition that includes a discussion of the 'populist phenomenon' Pim Fortuyn. Prins borrows the term 'new realists' from Vuijsje (1986: 59-68). See also Lutz (2002).

46. 'Nederlander zijn staat gelijk aan open, recht door zee en realistisch zijn.' In its resonance of the traditional assumption of Dutch openness this claim seems to refer more to a recovered, reclaimed identity than to something completely new.

47. David Ingleby's oration *Psychologie en de multiculturele samenleving: Een gemiste aansluiting* [*Psychology and the Multicultural Society. A Missed Connection*] (2000) and the volume *Caleidoscopische visies. De zwarte, migranten- en vluchtelingenvrouwenbeweging in Nederland* [*Kaleidoscopic Visions. The Black, Migrant and Refugee Women's Movement in the Netherlands*] (2001) edited by Maayke Botman, Nancy Jouwe and Gloria Wekker, can also be read as resisting response to the dominant discourse. J.E. Overdijk-Francis and H.M.A.G. Smeets (2000) aim to counter the 'drama' debate with a collection of positive reflections on the Dutch multicultural society.

48. 'Dit soort conservatieve ideologen zijn over het algemeen beter in het beschrijven van wat de Nederlandse eigenheid bedreigt dan wat de Nederlandse eigenheid is.'

49. 'De discussie over de Nederlandse cultuur is in feite een negatieve. Het gaat om de afwijzing van de culturen (en eigenlijk alleen de islam) die door migranten in Nederland gebracht worden en niet om het definiëren van de Nederlandse cultuur.' Van der Veer even goes as far as to dismiss the relevance of 'Dutch culture' at all. His justified critique seems to overreach itself when he radically reduces Dutchness to a regional identity and the Dutch language to an outdated dialect. Whereas his analysis of the discourse of his opponents is sharp and convincing, his general critique of Dutch culture leans on a static definition of (Dutch) culture.

50. Especially the location and the ceremonial presentation of the monument – an artwork by Erwin de Vries – were topics of vehement critique. The Amsterdam Oosterpark lies quite a distance away from the city's (tourist) centre. The initiators of the monument as well as the 'common' Dutch people from the former colonies were excluded from the inaugural ceremony. Both this topographical marginalisation and the exclusion

from a moment of important symbolic impact constitute hurtful re-enactments of a historical trauma. See also Oostindie (2001a), Paasman (2002), and Smith (2005) for a discussion of the commemoration of slavery in the Netherlands.

51. Böcker and Groenendijk (2004), Entzinger (2006), Pels (2003), and Prins (2004) critically discuss 'the phenomenon Pim Fortuyn'.

52. 'de inzet om deze met hand en tand te verdedigen tegen uitholling c.q. aanvallen van binnenuit en van buitenaf' (Fortuyn 2001: 11). Fortuyn's appeal for more national consciousness also entailed a strong emphasis on the preservation and protection of national sovereignty against the growing influence of 'Europe'.

53. It is both against the progressive political elite and the 'inner enemy' that Fortuyn wants to deploy 'the word as weapon', as the military added second subtitle of the reprint indicates. The performative qualities of (hurtful) language acquire a central meaning in the developing discourse, especially in respect to the tensions between an unlimited freedom of speech on the one hand and the right to insult on the other. See Chervel and Seeliger (2007). Ian Buruma interestingly argues that Fortuyn's loathing of the Islam is connected to the (painful) liberation from Calvinist Christianity: 'And here were these newcomers injecting society with religion once again' (2006: 69).

54. Pim Fortuyn started his political career as a candidate for the party 'Leefbaar Nederland' ['Liveable Netherlands']. Only shortly before the elections he was suspended from this party for publicly stating that the Islam is a backwards religion. Hereafter he started his own party 'Pim Fortuyn's List' [Lijst Pim Fortuyn].

55. Berkeljon and Wansink (2006), Ghorashi (2004), and De Leeuw and van Wichelen (2005) offer insightful analyses of the 'phenomenon Hirsi Ali'. See also Chorus and Olgun (2005) on 'the year of Theo van Gogh'.

56. The German debate – on the shared Dutch and German 'problem' of subnational parallel societies – very much echoed the critique by Scheffer and Schnabel.

57. Buruma argues that the emotive, moralising stance that entered Dutch discourse is a legacy of the rapid secularisation. Central to his argument is the thesis that '[t]he Netherlands, like the rest of western Europe, may have become a largely secular society in recent decades, but the habits of faith die hard. Preaching still comes naturally to the Dutch, as does the venting of moralising emotion' (Buruma 2006: 230).

58. 'The right to insult' is the title of a speech that Ayaan Hirsi Ali held in Berlin on 9 February 2006. See Hirsi Ali in Chervel and Seeliger (2007: 23-29).

59. Halleh Ghorashi makes a similar claim in her oration 'Paradoxen van culturele erkenning. Management van Diversiteit in Nieuw Nederland' ['Paradoxes of Cultural Recognition. Management of Diversity in the New Netherlands'] (2006). She published a polemic article on the basis of the oration in de Volkskrant (14 October 2006). In the essay 'Verdwijnt de Nederlandse identiteit?' ['Is Dutch Identity Vanishing?'] (1996) E. H. Kossmann argues that the (continuous) discussions about national identity – its existence, its disappearance, its protection, its deterioration – have a unifying character in themselves. He maintains that these are national identity's sole certainty. At the same time Kossmann puts too-definite claims of the blessings of Dutch identity into perspective. In response to the idea that Dutch national identity stands for tolerance, consensus policy and egalitarianism Kossmann writes: 'That is romanticism. There are many reasons to appreciate the codes mentioned. But there is no reason to con-

sider them as characteristics of a particular nation and as core of a national identity' ['Dat is romantiek. Er is alle reden de genoemde codes positief te waarderen. Er is geen reden ze als eigenschappen van een bepaalde natie en kern van een nationale identiteit te beschouwen'] (1996: 65).

60. The German Empire arose from a confederation of several smaller and often formerly hostile states, of which Prussia and Bavaria were the most powerful ones. The national format was seen as a key to success. The cases of France, Spain, England and the Netherlands counted as proof of this assumption.

61. 'Modern' is used here in distinction to the traditional, territorial model, rooted in the feudal legal system. In earlier times the unspecified concept of 'the German people' determined membership within the German Confederation. The anticipated constitution of 1848 had aimed to standardise the membership to the different states and to regulate the massive inter-state migration of an impoverished rural population. The 1871 nationality code of the German Empire largely based on the (restrictive) Prussian citizenship law and determined descent from a German citizen as the main criterion for German citizenship. Naturalization became dependent on socio-economic integration into the local community and on proof of respectability. Territorial aspects did not play a role in this definition of citizenship. See also Bielefeld and Engel (1998), Brubaker (1992), El-Tayeb (2001), Göktürk et al. (2007: 149-192), and Gosewinkel (1998).

62. Central in the concept of a Kulturnation is the idea of the exceptionality of German culture in relation to Western civilisation. The term Volksnation refers to the myth of a homogenous ethnic community that shares a common origin: a Volk. The Netherlands, on the contrary, counts as a Staatsnation, a self-determining political nation with a strong civic ideology.

63. The retainment of the ethnic principle seems incredible in the light of its deadly consequences under National Socialism. However, Article 116 was maintained in consideration of the postwar refugees from the former territories in the East. In postwar Germany, Article 116 effected an awkward discrepancy in the possibilities to attain German citizenship between, for instance, the children of labour migrants, often born and raised in Germany, and the xth generation of ethnic Germans whose antecedents had emigrated to territories in the East several centuries ago.

64. 'die Mehrheitsdeutschen nicht unbefangen ihrer Traditionen bedienen können und die meisten von ihnen Probleme mit ihrem Deutsch-Sein haben. Die Nation als Medium von Integration und Stabilität hat sich verkehrt in eine Quelle von Verunsicherung. Die Heimat ist unheimlich geworden.'

65. The inscription of the (responsibility for the) Holocaust and Auschwitz into the German national consciousness only commenced with the anti-authoritarian struggles for a more democratic Germany in the late 1960s. Since that time the demand to account for the fascist past has been a constitutive element of German national identity. During the Historians' Debate (1985-1987) a revisionist representation of the Holocaust was vehemently discussed. See for instance Huyssen (1980) and LaCapra (1997).

66. See Brumlik and Leggewie (1992) and McFalls (1997).

67. For instance Ludwig Erhardt, Helmut Schmidt, and Alfred Dregger, but also, in more recent times, Edmund Stoiber and – at least initially – Gerhard Schröder.

68. El-Tayeb (2001: 80 n. 3) rightly points out that the terms 'anti-foreign' and 'xenophobic' are in fact misleading, as in several instances the targets of violence were German citizens of Turkish origin who had been living in Germany for many years. The importance of religious Otherness – whether apparent or assumed – can hardly be underestimated. The tokening of Turkish foreign workers ('Turking') seems to be a matter not only of number, but also of religion.

69. Brady (2004), von Dirke (1994), Schneider (2001), and Thränhardt (2002) critically interrogate the recurrent metaphorical use of the terms 'flood' and 'deluge' in public discourse to represent a fearful image of an overburdened society. A major reason for the growth of the Turkish minority at that time is the process of family reunion that started after the foreign recruitment ban. This ban made many Turkish labourers decide to stay in Germany for a longer time.

70. There are two versions of the manifest that make use of different rhetorical strategies: the public and the signatories' version. The last rhetorically much more upsetting version leaked to the press before the public version was published. Some of the signatories turned out to have been actively involved in National Socialism. See the extensive analysis of the manifesto in von Dirke (1994).

71. Like in the Netherlands, the US-based concept of multiculturalism entered the intellectual and public discourse in Germany in the early 1980s. See Bade (1996), Göktürk et al. (2007), Jordan (2006), and Thränhardt (2002).

72. Günter Wallraff's undercover reportage *Ganz Unten* (1985) represents a public counterpoise to the Heidelberg Manifesto. His best-selling work presents a shameful picture of the exploitation of Turkish workers in the German industry. Irrespective of whether this picture is exaggerated and objectifying or not, it effected a moment of great public shock and indignation. For a critical analysis of the politics of representation in *Ganz Unten*, see Şölçün (1992: 125-142) and Teraoka (1989).

73. See Bade (1996) and Von Dirke (1994). Von Dirke maintains that in the end these debates on multiculturalism ideologically charged the public discourse more than that they clarified the terms of the German multicultural society.

74. Both Bade (1994: 57) and Terkessidis (2000: 33) argue that the issues of asylum and foreign labour overlap in such a way that especially former foreign workers of Turkish and Kurdish origin – and their children – were subjected to processes of ethnicisation and Othering, irrespective of their long-time residency.

75. Uerlings considers this last absence – the absence of 'foreigners' as active participants in public discourse – as characteristic for the German situation. In his study on (post-) colonialism and gender in various works of German literature he writes: 'Compared to countries like Portugal and Spain, France and Great Britain the colonial discourse in Germany seems to be characterized by a distinct absence of voices of the so-called "Others". (...) Not the presence, but the absence of "the others" and their voices characterizes the situation in Germany' ['Im Vergleich mit Ländern wie Portugal und Spanien, Frankreich und Großbritannien scheint der koloniale Diskurs in Deutschland durch ein besonders ausgeprägte Abwesenheit der Stimmen der sogenannten "Anderen" gekennzeichnet zu sein. (...) Nicht die Präsenz, sondern die Absenz der "Anderen" und ihrer Stimmen kennzeichnet die Situation in Deutschland'] (Uerlings 2006:

22). This counts for Germans of Turkish origin as much as it counts for Afro-Germans or other ethnic minority groups.

76. The political reversal of 1989/1990 is referred to as *die Wende*. Especially the fall of the Berlin Wall counts as a heroic moment in history that invites a positive national identification. In the 2005 *Du bist Deutschland* social-marketing campaign – a further elaboration on this campaign follows – this moment appears as encouraging basis for a positive national group identity: 'Already once before we have torn down a wall' ['Doch einmal schon haben wir eine Mauer niedergerissen']. Scholars often argue that the idea of one ethnically homogenous *Volk* was reinvigorated in the process of German reunification. The famous slogans 'We are the people' ['Wir sind das Volk'] at the Leipzig 'Monday protests' and 'We are one people' ['Wir sind ein Volk'] shortly after the fall of the Berlin Wall appear as significant in this respect. The neighbouring European countries initially examined German reunification rather sceptically. In the Netherlands an irrational fear for an 'oversized' Germany and a repetition of history featured as topics in public discourse (Couwenberg 1992; von der Dunk 1994; Linthout 2006).

77. Räthzel speaks in this respect of a 'double contradiction' and maintains: 'Along with this emphasis on difference goes a general, rather indefinable belief in unity' ['Die Hervorhebung des Unterschieds ist begleitet von einem allgemeinen, nicht weiter definierbaren Bekenntnis zur Einheit'] (1997: 164).

78. In his article 'Diaspora and Nation: Migration into Other Pasts' Huyssen states that '[i]n 1989/90 Turks in Berlin were double outsiders, both in the present and in relation to the past' (2003: 156). See also Beitter (2000), Göktürk et al. (2007), Huyssen (1995a, 1995b), Joppke (1999), and Taberner and Finlay (2002) for reflections on the effects of the *Wende* on the situation of 'foreigners'. Peck (1996), Räthzel (1997), and Schneider (2001) discuss the relation between the presence of ethnic Others and perceptions of Germanness and the German nation. All studies make clear that it is easier to define the non-German (ethnicised) Other than to define the (renewed) German Self. The issue of German self-hatred (on the basis of the historical burdens of fascism and totalitarian communism) and its impact on relations with ethnic Others remains largely underexposed and deserves further scrutiny.

79. These numbers further increased after the breakdown of the communist block. In general, Germany's economic prosperity made the country into an attractive destination for asylum seekers. Besides, Article 16 in the 1948 Basic Law, a direct result of the Holocaust, guaranteed politically persecuted persons the right to asylum. Adding to this Article 116 of the Basic Law allowed 'ethnic Germans' ['Volksdeutsche'] legal immigration into Germany as well as German citizenship. This lead to the remarkable situation in which long-term resident Turkish foreign workers as well as their children had great difficulties obtaining German citizenship and newly arrived ethnic Germans (especially from the East) could acquire German citizenship right away. Rommelspacher describes this situation and the abiding political attitude as one of 'double negation': 'One group were no real immigrants, as they were Germans, the other group were no real immigrants as they were only guests and would leave again. Thus Germany could keep cultivating the image of itself as an ethnically homogenous state. By reasoning this way Germany could contra-factually maintain not to be a country of

immigration' ['Die einen waren keine richtige Einwanderinnen, weil sie ja Deutsche waren, und die anderen waren keine, weil sie ja nur Gäste waren und wieder gehen würden. Deutschland konnte so von sich das Bild eines ethnisch homogenen Staates weiter pflegen und aus dieser Logik heraus über Jahrzehnte kontrafaktisch behaupten, Deutschland sei kein Einwanderungsland'] (Rommelspacher 2002: 152/153). See also Fennel (1997: 33).

80. 'In keinem Land gibt es so wenig Lust, und so viel Leiden an der eigenen Identität. "Deutschsein" erschwert "Deutschwerden" erheblich'.

81. Both Gemünden (1999) and Huyssen (1995a) plead for a critical reoccupation of the discursive terrain of the nation. They warn for the tendency among leftist intellectuals to dismiss of the important theme and thus to leave it to the conservative right.

82. See Boehncke and Wittich (1991), Geier et al. (1991), Göktürk et al. (2007), and Leggewie (1990).

83. According to Habermas' influential concept of 'postnational identity', citizenship is not conceptually tied to the idea of the nation, but to a practice of citizens who actively exercise their civil rights. Habermas only accepts a constitutional patriotism. For a discussion of Tibi's ambivalent role in the German *Leitkultur* debate see Dürr (2000). Tibi's plea for a European *Leitkultur* (and not a German *Leitkultur*) cannot be disconnected from the discussion about the significance of the Holocaust-legacy for German national identity.

84. Merz responded to the *Leitkultur* debate that developed in the wake of his speech with the publication of the article 'Einwanderung und Identität' ['Immigration and identity'] in the daily newspaper *Die Welt* (25 October 2000).

85. 'ihre verloren gegangene Hegemonie auf dem politischen Feld der Migration zurückzugewinnen'.

86. Pautz offers an elaborate discussion of the New Right and its neo-racist discourse. For a discussion of cultural racism in the context of the nation(-state) see also Balibar (1996, 1998), Balibar and Wallerstein (1991), Göktürk et al. (2007: 105-148), Lutz et al. (1995), and Steyerl and Gutiérrez Rodríguez (2003).

87. In the volume Lammert collects forty-two positions in respect to the contested theme. Contributors to the volume vary from Chancellor Angela Merkel to the Turkish-German lawyer Seyran Ates to the film director Wim Wenders.

88. In autumn 2005 the ethnic riots in the Paris suburbs brought about a similar response in German discourse. The apparent 'failure' of the neighbour was not only interpreted as a putting into perspective of French multiculturality, but also as an affirmation of the own approach.

89. The Islamic headscarf counts as central symbol of the assumed collision of (religious) cultures. For critical interrogations of the symbolic function of the headscarf in public discourse see Auslander (2000), Lutz (1996), and Mandel (1989).

90. Thränhardt (2002) asserts that in contrast to the Netherlands, where the terrorism of 9/11 brought about several violent counter-attacks on mosques and Islamic institutions, in Germany the Islamist terrorism did not effect an increase in Islamophobia.

91. The dispute and ultimate compromise on the namegiving of this new law – the less definite 'Migration law' [*Zuwanderungsgesetz*] instead of the (f)actual 'immigration law'

[*Einwanderungsgesetz*] – offer a marvellous example of the power of language. See also Göktürk et al. (2007: 149-192) and Pautz (2005: 40, 47) on the migration law debate.

92. An example of the persistent interest in questions concerning Islam and (European) multiculturalism is the 2006/07 debate on the webpages of *perlentaucher.de* and *signandsight.com*. Responding to Hirsi Ali's plea for the right to insult, intellectuals as Timothy Garton Ash, Ian Buruma, Pascal Bruckner, Paul Cliteur and Necla Kelek engaged in a fierce polemic on Enlightenment vis-à-vis Islamic fundamentalism. Thierry Chervel and Anja Seeliger collected the various contributions to this debate in the collection *Islam in Europa* (2007).

93. The *Du bist Deutschland* campaign determined several public media (a.o. a prime time television commercial) for four months in a row. Its aim was to encourage German citizens to be more self-confident and to initiate a movement of self-initiative. Many German celebrities – including a few token-'foreigners' as Xavier Naidoo and Gerald Assamoa – participated in the campaign. The campaign released a vehement discussion. Especially its new-nationalist tone and its manipulative and one-sided idolisation of Germany were criticised.

94. For instance in the two collections of essays *Atlas des tropischen Deutschland* (1992) and *Zungenentfernung. Bericht aus der Quarantänestation* (2001). Şenocak also writes poetry and prose, but the recognition for his literary work in Germany is meagre (in contrary to the appreciation for his writing in France, Great Britain and the US). See Adelson (2000a).

95. Şenocak brings this terminology forward in his novel *Gefährliche Verwandtschaft* (1998) that offers an interesting literary reflection on the triangulation between German, Jewish and Turkish identity. This novel contains the often-cited observation: 'But when the question of who is a German and who is not is asked today, one looks at the Turks. They provide the test cases for the limits of Germanness. Jews trying to come to terms with their Germanness discover the Turks in the mirror' ['Wenn aber heute die Frage gestellt wird, wer ein Deutscher ist und wer nicht, schaut man auf die Türken. An ihnen werden die Grenzen des Deutschseins getestet. Juden, die sich über ihr Deutschsein klar werden wollen, entdecken im Spiegel die Türken'] (Şenocak 1998: 90). See also Huyssen (2003), Koopmans (2001) and Yeşilada (2000) for reflections on the triangular relation between Germans, Jews and migrants.

96. In 2005 the display of an 'African Village' in the Augsburg Zoo caused a major commotion. Critics objected to the continuation of the racist tradition of the colonial 'people's exhibitions' [*Völkerschau*] and saw the 'African Village' as a traumatic re-enactment of racist colonial structures.

97. The tendency to (ritually) allocate racist and xenophobic opinions to a position that is denoted as 'extreme (Right)' works to cover up the spread of a racist and/or xenophobic ideology in the centre and throughout the whole political spectrum.

98. In February 2008 the European Council published an alarming report on the increase of (racist) intolerance and Islamophobia in Dutch society. See also Entzinger (2006), Koopmans et al. (2005) and Van Tubergen and Maas (2006) on this topic. In Germany the Centre for Conflict and Violence Studies at the University Bielefeld every year presents a report titled *Deutsche Zustände* [*German Conditions*] on the state of 'group-related

hostility against persons' ['gruppenbezogene Menschenfeindlichkeit']. See Heitmeyer (2005, 2006, 2007).

II. Literature of Migration

1. Leslie Adelson (2005), Isabel Hoving (2005) and Azade Seyhan (2001) refer to and/or critically interrogate Appadurai's claim. Another study (in the social sciences) that often features in similar ways as Appadurai's study, is Dilip Gaonkar's 'Towards New Imaginaries: An Introduction' (2002).
2. The responsibility of reading in a differentiated manner is important here. Derek Attridge defines a text as 'a field of potential meaning awaiting realization without wholly determining it in advance' (1999: 25). It is up to the reader to retrieve a meaning that does justice to literature's aesthetic difference.
3. In his study *History in Transit: Experience, Identity, Critical Theory* (2004) LaCapra argues that experiential processes are central to identity and to processes of identity formation. He understands identity as 'a problematic constellation or more or less changing configuration of subject positions' (LaCapra 2004: 5) that are neither fixed nor complacent. These subject positions – their coordination, integration and prioritisation – are crucial for the understanding of both identity and experience. Drawing on his work on Holocaust memory and trauma, LaCapra adds an observation that applies to the history and memory of labour migration as well, be it – obviously – in a fundamentally different way: 'But it is to say that in certain respects people are implicated in a past (...) and at some level are subject to experiences that require an attempt to situate themselves historically and work with and through that situatedness' (ibid.). The selected writers' personal experiences with labour migration urge them to negotiate this experience in respect to their identity. Literature is one (performative) process by which this can be done.
4. Several factors of difference intersect in these discursive processes of Othering. Intersectional theory emphasises the dynamic interaction of factors of differentiation as diverse as gender, ethnicity, race, class, age, and sexuality. See for instance Aerts and Saharso (1994), Anthias and Yuval-Davis (1992), Botman et al. (2001), Crenshaw (1995), Daum et al. (2005), Gelbin et al. (1999), Grewal and Kaplan (1994), hooks (1981, 1990), Lorde (1993), Sterk (2004), and Wekker (2002). With the use of the terms 'cultural field' and 'literary field' I follow Bourdieu (1993).
5. Özdamar first came to West Germany (West Berlin) in 1965 on a foreign labour contract for two years. See also Abel (2006) and Cheesman (2006) on the question of generation.
6. I leave minority groups from the former Dutch colonies – Indonesia, the Moluccas, Surinam and the Netherlands Antilles – out of consideration here.
7. The significant differences between the two countries of origin – e.g. the fact that Turkey is a secular republic and Morocco an Islamic monarchy – hardly play a role in the homogenising representation of these migrants as Islamic. See also McGowan (2000b) on discursive constructions of Turkey and/in 'Europe'.
8. Scholars and reviewers predominantly position and interpret 'migrants' literature' in either the thematic frame of migration or the national frame set by the country and

culture of origin. The focus on the (possibility of a) national German and Dutch semantic dimension in the interpretation of literature of migration is exceptional. The
reductive interpretation of literature within a politics of identity is not the same as
paying attention to the 'oppositional consciousness' or the 'deterritorialisation coeffi-
cient' that literature of migration might – or might not – represent. Compare Gilles
Deleuze and Felix Guattari's concept of 'minor literature' (1976: 24-39). See also Adelson (1997a), Fachinger (2001), Louwerse (2007b) and Seyhan (2001).

9. In his introduction to the edited volume *Nation and Narration* Bhabha writes: 'In this
sense, then, the ambivalent antagonistic perspective of nation as narration will establish the cultural boundaries of the nation so that they may be acknowledged as "con-
taining" thresholds of meaning that must be crossed, erased, and translated in the
process of cultural production' (1990: 4).

10. Tom Cheesman (2007) also reads Turkish German literature as an effect of globalisation within the German borders that works to extend the concept of Germanness.
However, whereas he presents 'cosmopolitanism' as an alternative mode of identity
beyond the national paradigm, in this study I hold on to the idea of a national identity
in process. The concepts of both Germanness and Dutchness are subjected to processes
of critical interrogation and of radical redefinition.

11. See Jordan (2006) for a critical discussion of the (development of the) 'two worlds
paradigm' in the context of the debates on multiculturalism.

12. 'The Anxieties of Comparison' is the title of Bernheimer's introduction to the 1995
ACLA collection (1995: 1-17). The subsequent 2006 ACLA collection, edited by Haun
Saussy and titled *Comparative Literature in an Age of Globalization*, both echoes its predecessor and testifies of the shift to and current interest in comparative *world* literature.
On the issue of comparison see also Melas (1995) and Cheah (1999). In their respective
introductions to comparative literature and literary theory, Bassnett (1993) and Culler
(1997) address many of the topics under debate.

13. While comparing two *Western* literatures in relatively *minor* languages, *New Germans,
New Dutch* manages to escape most of the ideology critique on the (English) cultural
hegemony in comparative (world) literature. Pascale Casanova (2005), David Damrosch (2003), and Franco Moretti (2000) have attempted to come up with new meth-
odologies for a contemporary (comparative) study of (world) literature.

14. Cheah also acknowledges, however, that in the past 'the grounds of comparison were
undeniably Eurocentric' (1999: 3).

15. Clearly, the actual meaning of these 'traits' differs considerably between the two countries, especially in respect to the legacies of colonialism and of the Holocaust. The
general positions of power, however, are similar.

16. Again differentiation is necessary here. In the Dutch discourse the effects of decolonisation – for instance the presence of minority groups from the former colonies – play
a considerable role in the discourse on multiculturality. In Germany the presence of
'other Others' as for instance Jews, Russian-Germans and refugees from various countries in the former East Block only plays a minor role in a discourse that strongly
concentrates on the Turkish minority.

17. Like Adelson, Seyhan (2001) attributes an archival status to works of literature. She
reads literature as a form of cultural memory: 'As important social documents of the

culture(s) of dislocation and exile, literary and critical texts of diasporas serve as condensed archives of national, ethnic, and linguistic memories' (Seyhan 2001: 13). Mieke Bal argues in her introduction to *Acts of Memory. Cultural Recall in the Present* that '[c]ultural memory can be located in literary texts because the latter are continuous with the communal fictionalising, idealising, monumentalising impulses thriving in a conflicted culture' (1999: xiii).

18. Especially Herman's chapter on processes and strategies of what he calls 'contextual anchoring' (2002: 331-371) provides insight in the ways in which literary texts 'trigger recipients to establish a more or less direct or oblique relationship between the stories they are interpreting and the contexts in which they are interpreting them' (ibid. 331).

19. For critical reflections on the performative dimensions of language and literature see Austin (1975), Butler (1990), Culler (1998), Johnson (1992), Miller (2001), and Pratt (1977).

20. Gert Oostindie brings up social conditions and a closed-up cultural field as grounds for the relatively late appearance of 'immigrants' on the Dutch literary scene: 'Most immigrants have other things to worry about than writing; and whoever is after all born for writing has to see how to obtain an audience' ['De meeste immigranten hebben wel wat anders aan hun hoofd dan schrijven, en wie daarvoor toch in de wieg gelegd is, moet maar zien ergens een gehoor te vinden'] (2001b, no pagination). Henriëtte Louwerse argues that '[h]ard physical labour, long working hours, the dream of returning to Morocco or Turkey and in many cases a lack of education sentenced [first generation labour migrants] to silence' (1997: 69). However, these arguments count for the German situation in similar ways and cannot account for the assessed discrepancy. Except maybe for the issue of education, as Germany acquired more educated foreign workers than the Netherlands (Böcker and Thränhardt 2003: 37).

21. The fact that in 1983 the Dutch government acknowledged the enduring presence of the former guest workers and their families in Dutch society and decided upon a policy that provided and (financially) supported the possibility to participate politically as minority group, constituted the Dutch framework that allowed for the retainment and the cultivation of the 'original' cultural identity. The German government on the contrary persisted in the refusal to accept its changing identity as immigration country and did not provide for any arrangements of that kind. This distinction resulted in a state-financed multicultural network of representative 'ethnic' self-organisations in the Netherlands vis-à-vis a very low degree of independent and privately funded cultural self-organisation and institutionalisation in Germany. See the previous chapter for a more elaborate discussion of German and Dutch migration policy.

22. US-based German Studies scholars have made early and important contributions to the academic discussion on German literature by authors of non-German background. On the particularities of German Studies see Teraoka (1997). In this section I focus on literature of *labour* migration, and thus do not address the work and reception of 'other kind' of 'migrant writers' such as, for instance, Zsuzsanne Gahse, Libuše Moníková or Yoko Tawada.

23. Suhr adds a fourth section of writing under the heading '*Ausländerinnenliteratur*' ['Literature by female foreigners'] (1989: 92-96). The female writers grouped in this category participated and published in anthologies produced by all mentioned groups.

24. Ackermann and Weinrich organised a yearly writing contest for non-native German writers. Selected contributions were published in various anthologies (a.o. Ackermann 1982, 1983). Compare Ackermann and Weinrich (1986). Since 1984 the Robert Bosch Stiftung annually awards the Adelbert von Chamisso Prize to writers for whom German is not their native language. The prize is named after the French migrant and later German poet Adelbert von Chamisso (1781-1838). Both Teraoka and Suhr criticise that there are few correspondences between the situation of the elitist von Chamisso and that of labour migrants in the 1980s. Aras Ören was the first winner of the Adelbert von Chamisso Prize (and Rafik Schami the first recipient of the Encouragement Prize). Both Emine Sevgi Özdamar and Feridun Zaimoglu received the award as well: Özdamar in 1999 and Zaimoglu in 2005. Karl Esselborn (2004) discusses the pros and cons of the prize.

25. Compare Adelson (1990), Fischer and McGowan (1995, 1996), Suhr (1989), Teraoka (1987). Teraoka judges the academic engagement in terms of a colonial situation: 'The implicit attitude of the German academics toward the foreigners seems in fact to approach the colonialist stereotype of the lazy, indolent natives whose labor potential can be realized only under the external coercion of the advanced, culturally and technologically superior Europeans' (1987: 93/94). However, taking the discrepancy between the Dutch and the German situation in respect to first generation migrant writing into account, this almost unanimously negative judgment requires some adjustment. It seems that the absence of a counterpart to the Munich institute in the Netherlands has resulted in an *absolute* invisibility of first generation migrant writing from the Dutch literary scene. The striking pattern of a division in 'two evils' – stereotyped visibility or complete invisibility – deserves further scrutiny.

26. In the Netherlands, however, the discussion in the cultural field about adequate terminology coincided with a broader public discussion on the most appropriate term for ethnic minorities in general. This discussion resulted in a genealogy of successive politically correct designations. In German public discourse the efforts (mainly on the left) to replace the problematic and in many cases factually incorrect term 'foreigner' have still not been successful.

27. See the chapter on Feridun Zaimoglu's '*Kanak* writing'.

28. Abel (2006), Adelson (1990), Amirsedghi and Bleicher (1997), Amodeo (1996), Arens (2000), Blioumi (2000), Cheesman (2007: 33-52), Chiellino (2000), Fischer and McGowan (1995, 1996), Gerstenberger (2004), Gökberk (1991), Grünefeld (1995), Howard (1997), Keiner (1999), Kersting (2007), Kreuzer (1984), Şölçün (1992), and Weigel (1992) all offer overviews of the search for the most suitable term and conceptualisation of the literature by writers of migrant background. In most cases these scholars also take position themselves and plead for one 'best' option. In his introduction to the text collection *Döner in Walhalla. Texte aus der anderen deutschen Literatur* Ilija Trojanow maintains that '[t]he failure of the search for a name is a result of the richness and heterogeneity of this literature' ['[d]as Scheitern der Namensfindung ist Folge des Reichtums und der Vielfalt dieser Literatur'] (2000: 14). In 2006 two collections on literature of migration appeared – a special edition of *Text+Kritik* (2006) titled 'Literatur und Migration' and the autumn issue of *German Life and Letters* (2006) – that symptomatically refrain from using the term 'migrant' as identity marker. Whereas the first col-

lection focuses on 'migration' as theme, the second makes use of the concept 'diasporic literature'. In his contribution to the first volume Tom Cheesman proposes an
alternative categorisation of Turkish-German writing based on the strategies used. He
distinguishes the following four basic strategies that writers use to juggle 'the burdens
of representation' and to explore their position within German culture: '1. Axialism; 2.
Refusal; 3. Parodic ethnicisation; 4. Glocalism' (2006: 477). With his proposal for a
typology of strategies he aims to counter the tendency to categorise Turkish-German
literature in terms of a generational teleology. One year later Cheesman introduces the
term 'literature of settlement' (2007) for a literature that is not so much concerned
about coming to Germany, but much more so with being and settling there.

29. See for instance Gökberk (1997a, 1997b), Krusche (1985), Mecklenburg (1990), Uerlings (1997), Wierlacher (1985), Wierlacher and Bogner (2003), and Zimmermann
(1989).

30. Joan Scott argues that any category is a formation of 'illusory sameness' (2001: 285)
that needs to be historicised. She insists on the critical interrogation of 'categories' *as*
historical formations that function in a discursive matrix of power and interests. See
also Scott (1995).

31. The statement makes a claim on Germanness – whether of the writers or of their work
– and uses the reference to the 'accented' German writer Franz Kafka to support this
claim. The interviewed writers (Terézia Mora, Imran Ayata, Wladimir Kaminer, and
Navid Kermani) critically question the grounds for their grouping. Angelika Bammer
(1997) discusses (the work of) several 'accented' German writers who complicate the
notions of Germanness and German literature.

32. I do not address the situation for Flemish writers of migrant background in the Belgium cultural field which is different again. Bekers (2008) discusses the relatively late
appearance of Flemish literature of migration in the light of (post-)colonial structures
and the Belgian language situation.

33. Herbert van Uffelen (2004a) comes to opposite conclusions in his article on the reception of Dutch 'migrants' literature' in the German cultural field. He argues that German critics pay more attention to the literary aspects of 'migrants' literature' and seem
less interested in the migrant background of its writers.

34. 'in Nederland de migrantenliteratuur naar het centrum van de positie-bepalende de-
batten in het literaire veld is doorgedrongen, terwijl ze in Duitsland eerder nog een
soort subveld vormt dat naar erkenning streeft'.

35. This E. du Perron prize was installed in 1986 on initiative of the municipality of Tilburg in co-operation with the Arts Faculty of Tilburg University. The prize is named
after the Dutch writer E. du Perron (1899-1940) who spent the first twenty years of his
life in the former Dutch Indies, now Indonesia. His (colonial) experiences there figure
prominently in his literary work.

36. In the Dutch situation it is important to emphasise the distinction between 'migrant's
literature' as a cultural effect of labour migration and (post-)colonial literature.
Although in many cases postcolonial writers have gone through processes of migration as well, the huge differences in background and history necessitate careful differentiation. Literature in Dutch from the former colonies as well as Dutch literature by
writers of Surinamese, Antillean or Indonesian background has been an object of re-

search for a longer time. The Dutch language – as a colonial language – obviously has another significance in this literature.

37. 'Het is vooral in de kunsten dat een bevolking iets kan uitdrukken wat haar eigen is; wanneer het buitenland dat eigene herkent, waardeert en navolgt, toont zij haar nationaliteit, is zij, met andere woorden, een natie.'

38. Ton Anbeek (1999) and Lisa Kuitert (1999) address the commercial aspects of 'migrants' literature'. Kuitert discusses the policy of Dutch publishers in respect to literature by ethnic Others. She assesses that literary quality appears to be of secondary importance after the commercial interest of 'exotic-sounding names' ['exotisch klinkende namen'] (Kuitert 1999: 364).

39. Huggan's study focuses on postcolonial literature. His argument, however, also applies to the emergence of 'migrants' literature' in the Dutch situation, and to the marketing hype that followed after the publication of Zaimoglu's debut *Kanak Sprak* (see chapter V).

40. '[b]ehalve hun verhuizing hebben migrantenschrijvers niet zo veel gemeen, de individuele verbeeldingskracht wint het met afstand van de gedeelde ervaring.'

41. 'Ze lichten de maatschappij door op een wijze die buiten het bereik van de 'autochtone' schrijver ligt.' Van Kempen assumes that literature by the ethnic Other offers a particular outsider perspective on dominant society. He argues that the marginalisation of these writers provides them with 'privileged knowledge': knowledge that is exclusively connected to a subjugated position. Compare 'standpoint feminism' (Harding 1987), black feminism (a.o. Collins 1990 and hooks 1984) or also Donna Haraway's theory of 'situated knowledges' (Haraway 1991).

42. 'Nederland verandert. (...) De Nederlandse literatuur verandert. (...) De contouren van één Nederlandse literaire traditie vervagen en tegelijkertijd wordt de canon omvangrijker en veelkleuriger, omdat allochtone auteurs hun eigen plaats verwerven.'

43. 'dat hun roots in een ander land met een andere cultuur liggen, dat ze in meer of mindere mate bi-cultureel zijn'. My main objection to Paasman's terminology is that it ignores the fact that indigenous Dutchness constitutes an ethnic category as well. In his use the term 'ethnic' is problematically connected to Otherness. The structural invisibility of whiteness as an ethnic category is critically discussed within the field of inquiry within academia known as whiteness studies. Ruth Frankenberg's *White Women, Race Matters. The Social Construction of Whiteness* (1993) is a signposting example in whiteness studies.

44. Three years later Anbeek published an updated version of the same article in the collection *Europa Buitengaats. Koloniale en postkoloniale literaturen in Europese talen* (2002) edited by Theo D'Haen. Tellingly, he changed its title from 'Fatal success' into 'Cuddling to death' ['Doodknuffelen']. The introduction of a verb of action causes a slight shift in meaning.

45. Anbeek adds a remark of doubt to this categorisation: 'in how far does it really make sense to speak of Moroccan-Dutch authors as if it concerns a separate group?' ['in hoeverre is het werkelijk zinvol van Marokkaans-Nederlandse auteurs te praten alsof het om een afzonderlijke groep gaat?'] (1999: 290). Later in the article he answers that the thematic commonality between their work is one reason to group these writers. He concludes the article with the assessment: 'When the scenery of the emigrant life fails,

obviously also the ground for the label "Moroccan-Dutch" falls away' ['Wanneer de decorstukken van het emigrantenleven ontbreken, valt uiteraard de basis weg voor het etiket "Marokkaans-Nederlands"'] (ibid. 342). However, Anbeek worries that 'migration' might be their most 'fruitful theme'.

46. The yearly National Book Week event, organised by the Foundation Collective Propaganda for the Dutch Book [*Stichting Collectieve Propaganda van het Nederlandse Boek*], is comparable to the German 'Buchmesse' or the French 'Le Salon du Livre' in terms of media attention. The 2001 title is again a reference to the Dutch author E. du Perron (see footnote 35). *Het land van herkomst* [*The Country of Origin*] is the title of his canonised work from 1935. Every year the CPNB foundation invites two Dutch writers to write the Book Week gift and the Book Week essay, respectively. The Book Week gift of 2001, *Woede*, was an exception in that it was written by a foreign migrant: Salman Rushdie. This choice caused a minor uproar, as it seemed to indicate a lack of confidence in the quality of the work of Dutch migrant writers.

47. 'het dilemma van het terugvoeren van literaire werken op identiteit enerzijds en het ontkennen van verschil en differentiatie door sociale afkomst anderzijds.'

48. In fact the 2001 Book Week fell in a relatively quiet period, in between the multicultural drama debate in the spring and summer of 2000 on the one hand, and the terrorist attacks of 9/11 and subsequent rise of Pim Fortuyn on the other. Louwerse argues that a 'national identity search' followed on the time of high multicultural expectations: 'a kind of slightly melancholic and nostalgic search for authenticity and the own identity' ['een soort licht-melancholisch en nostalgisch onderzoek naar authenticiteit en eigen identiteit'] (2007a: 3). In her excellent monograph on Bouazza's literary work, *Homeless Entertainment* (2007b), she expands this argument on the 'Dutch discontent' at the beginning of the twenty-first century.

49. In his preface, Oostindie (2001b) underlines the significant difference between the subtitle of *Tussenfiguren* – 'writing between the cultures' – and the Book Week theme – 'writing between two [sic] cultures'. He claims that only the first takes the transformative processuality of several involved cultures into account.

50. The volumes *Kunsten in beweging, 1900-1980* (2003) and *Kunsten in beweging, 1980-2000* (2004) from the series *Cultuur en migratie in Nederland*, both edited by Rosemarie Buikema and Maaike Meijer, make an important contribution to the study of these processes of cultural transformation. However, only two contributions in the second volume (the contributions by Benzakour on Bouazza and by Breure and Brouwer on the debate on 'migrants' literature') focus on literature of (labour) migration.

51. I speak of long-term residence and not of long-term citizenship here. The discrepancy between the two can be considerable, especially in the German case. Despite her long-term residence in Germany, Özdamar, for instance, 'only just' became a German citizen in 1996.

III. Emine Sevgi Özdamar
'Ich wußte gar nicht, daß dein Paß auch dein Tagebuch ist' (Özdamar 2001: 120).

1. 'Mir gefällt es nicht sich zu einer Nation gehörig zu fühlen.'

2. In his analysis of transnational cinema Hamid Naficy (2001) points out that 'accent' is simultaneously a marker of belonging and of displacement. The writers Feridun Zaimoglu and Hafid Bouazza have both (though in distinctive ways) responded fiercely to the alleged ex- or inclusion of their literary work as 'accented' literature. Özdamar, by contrast, has generally refrained from outspoken (extra-)literary positionings of either claiming (Bouazza) or countering (Zaimoglu) the national identity of the 'new' (literary) homeland.

3. See Ahmed (1992), Göckede and Karentzos (2006), Lewis (1996), Nochlin (1989), and Yeğenoğlu (1998) for a critical investigation of the trope of the Oriental woman.

4. 'Entfaltung von Gegendiskursen in den Zwischenräumen einer kolonisierten oder auch eurozentristischen Topographie'.

5. Frölich (1997, 2003), Horrocks (1996), Johnson (2001), and Seyhan (2001) focus on the multiple traces of and reflections on Turkish history. Dayıoğlu-Yücel (2005), Krause (2000), Littler (2002), and Wierschke (1996, 1997) interrogate the intercultural dimensions of Özdamar's writing.

6. 'Mein Berlin' was originally published in Der Tagesspiegel (13 June 1999) and 'Mein Istanbul' in Die Weltwoche (6 August 1998). Most of the stories in Der Hof im Spiegel are reprints from earlier publications. They have been written for several occasions and were published in a variety of written media in the period between 1993 ('Schwarzauge in Deutschland' in Die Zeit) and 2000 ('Ulis Weinen' in Vorwärts). The length of the stories ranges from three to thirty-five pages. The last text in the volume is the speech of thanks, as read at the celebratory ceremony for the award of the Adelbert von Chamisso Prize in 1999. The only new piece of material that this volume contains is the short story 'Fahrrad auf dem Eis', which I discuss in the second half of this chapter. For citations from Der Hof im Spiegel I use the abbreviation HS.

7. In the subsequent text I use the following abbreviations of the mentioned titles: Das Leben, Die Brücke and Seltsame Sterne.

8. Compare Adelson (2005), Bird (2003), Boa (2006), Breger (1999), Konuk (1999), Minnaard (2006), Şölçün (2002), and Wierschke (1996).

9. Adelson (2005: 131) points out the 'gender functions' of Özdamar's assumed naïveté. See also Müller (1997) and Şölçün (2002).

10. 'partielle Anschmiegung des erzählenden Ich an die Form des autobiographischen Romans'.

11. I use Michael Bakhtin's concept of the chronotope as 'the intrinsic connectedness of temporal and spatial relationships that are artistically expressed in literature' (Holquist 1981: 84).

12. Compare conceptualisations of the 'nomad' and 'nomadism' by Boer (1996), Braidotti (1993, 1994), Breger (2003), Deleuze and Guattari (2004), and Minnaard (2006). In acknowledgement of the criticism on intellectual idealisations of the concept of nomadism that overlook its coercive dimensions, I want to emphasise the self-chosen character of the nomadism of Özdamar's protagonist.

13. In the story 'Fahrrad auf dem Eis' the protagonist speaks about her 'personal city map' ['persönlichen Stadplan'] (HS 85): a map of Amsterdam that is based on routes of personal experience. This map appears part of a larger project: Özdamar's literary remapping of all-too rigidly divided national identities: Turkish, German and Other.

14. As Seyhan argues in her introduction to *Writing Outside the Nation*: 'Literature tends to record what history and public memory often forget. Furthermore, it can narrate both obliquely and allegorically, thereby preserving what can be censured and encouraging interpretation and commentary in the public sphere. Through the lens of personal recollection and interpretation, the specificity of class, ethnic, and gender experiences gains a stature that is often erased, forgotten, or ignored in the larger management of public memory' (2001: 12).

15. Trains, train journeys and railway stations are recurring tropes in Özdamar's literary work. The novel *Das Leben* opens with a remarkable train journey during which the first-person narrator, still unborn, addresses the reader from her mother's belly. A central site in the story of *Die Brücke* is the Anhalter railway station nicknamed 'divided railway station' ['geteilter Bahnhof'] by the protagonist.

16. See Moray McGowan's article '"The Bridge of the Golden Horn": Istanbul, Europe and the "Fractured Gaze from the West" in Turkish Writing in Germany' for a discussion of 'Istanbul's and Turkey's metaphoric identity as the bridge between two worlds' (2000: 66) and Özdamar's ambiguous re-literalisation of this metaphor.

17. '1976 kehrte ich nach neun Jahren nach Berlin zurück.'

18. At various occasions Özdamar has emphasised the connection between the worrisome political situation in Turkey in the early 1970s and her choice for German as her literary language. In her 'Kleist-Rede 2004' Özdamar explains: 'I became unhappy in the Turkish language' ['Ich wurde unglücklich in der türkischen Sprache'] (2004: 16). She maintains that she has recovered her happiness in the German language: 'I turned my tongue in German, and all of a sudden I was happy' ['Ich drehte meine Zunge ins Deutsche, und plötzlich war ich glücklich'] (ibid. 17). Özdamar's protagonist makes a similar claim in the debut novel *Mutterzunge*. For reflections on Özdamar's creative use of the Turkish language in her German writing see Aytaç (1997), Beil (2005), Bird (2003), Boa (1997), Brandt (2004), Konuk (1997, 1999), Littler (2002), Neubert (1997), and Seyhan (1996).

19. With the term 'Berlin writings' I refer to Özdamar's writing that is narratively situated in the German capital and im- or explicitly makes the city's exceptional state of division into a theme. This last criterion applies to *Seltsame Sterne* and the stories 'Mein Berlin' and 'Ulis Weinen' in *Der Hof im Spiegel*, but 'disqualifies' the Berlin-based stories in *Mutterzunge*.

20. Adelson applies Brockmann's definition of *Wende* literature as representing 'a privileged sphere for reflection' (2002: 327) to the cultural effects of national unification.

21. Jonathan Crewe writes about South African literature of the transitional post-apartheid phase: 'Emergent genres of testimonial fiction and postcolonial writing e.g. are recognized as important bearers and construction sites of cultural memory. In many instances, the cultural memories inscribed in these genres are at odds with official history' (1999: 76). Özdamar's literature can in my opinion be seen as a particular Turkish-German form of similar testimonial fiction or even – in a particularly broad use of the term – postcolonial writing. Compare Radhakrishnan (2003) for a critical investigation of the (inflationary use of the) term 'postcolonial'.

22. 'Alles Vergessene schreit im Traum um Hilfe...', 'Wir brauchen kein Tränengas, wir haben genug Grund zum Heulen...', 'DDR: Deutscher DReck...', 'Attention! You are

entering the Axel Springer sector...', 'Brennholz – Kartoffelschalen' and 'Särge in allen Preislagen'.

23. As I discuss in the section on the German discourse on multiculturality, Huyssen (1995a: 81/82; 1995b: 80/81) claims that after the *Wende* the conceptions of German national identity and its Other were reshuffled, and national scepticism and even hostility were redirected: away from the 'other' indigenous Germans toward *ethnic* Others.

24. 'Heiner sagte: 'Sie wissen, daß das Stück verboten wird, wenn sie zuviel lachen. Deshalb lachen sie nicht, sie verständigen sich über das Nicht-Lachen'.

25. See Opitz (2003) and Hartung (2003).

26. Compare Konuk (2000), Krause (2000), Littler (2002), and Wierschke (1996) on Özdamar's explorations of identity.

27. The censorship situation and the importance of German intellectuals for the Turkish student opposition sustain similar transnational connections between the German states and the Turkish one.

28. '[t]ote Bahnschienen, zwischen denen Gras wuchs'.

29. 'So lebte ich tagsüber in Ost-Berlin am Theater, und in der Nacht kehrte ich nach West-Berlin zu Kati und Theo zurück. Jedesmal, wenn ich aus der U-Bahn herauskam, staunte ich: 'Ah, hier im Westen hat es auch geschneit. Ah, hier hat es auch geregnet'.'

30. 'Und der Mond war immer da über Europa und Asien.'

31. Following Arnold van Gennep's theories on the transitional phase in 'rites de passage' Ortwin de Graef and Henriëtte Louwerse (2000, 2001) conceptualise liminality, the liminal or liminoid, as a phase of transition, a period and/or area of ambiguity, a social limbo. In a phase of liminality, the consolidated order is challenged. In Van Gennep's words: 'people "play" with the elements of the familiar and defamiliarize them' (cited in De Graef and Louwerse 2000: 38).

32. 'Die Brücke wurde wie eine Bühne: Juden, Türken, Griechen, Araber, Albaner, Armenier, Europäer, Perser, Tscherkessen, Frauen, Männer, Pferde, Esel, Kühe, Hühner, Kamele, alle liefen über diese Brücke.'

33. In an interview with David Horrocks and Eva Kolinsky, Özdamar maintains: 'Since unification [most Germans] seem to have been preoccupied with questions of identity. (...) The wall that divided Germans wasn't one of stone, but of time' (1996: 53). She adds that crossing the East-West border was like moving between different time zones.

34. The two moments in which Özdamar imagines life in rupture as a performative crossing of boundaries, constitute a striking contrast to the petrified photographic images – signifying separation and division – that I have discussed previously.

35. Throughout Özdamar's oeuvre 'the dead' take up an important position in the life and thinking of the protagonist. In his speech given at the awards ceremony for the Kleist Prize 2004, Günter Blamberger even maintains that it is exactly this fascination with death that effects the lively intensity of Özdamar's quasi-autobiographical stories (2005: 4). The last story in *Der Hof im Spiegel* is titled 'Die neuen Friedhöfe in Deutschland' ['The New Cemeteries in Germany'].

36. 'Fichte starb an Thyphus, Hegel an Cholera.'

37. 'In der nähe von Bulgarien.'

38. 'Und [Can Yücel] sagte, die Identitätssuche in einem anderen Land ist etwas anders als wenn man in einem fremden Land seine Identität sucht.'

39. The following sections on 'Fahrrad auf dem Eis' profited greatly from Leslie Adelson's generous and intellectually stimulating comments on an earlier version.

40. The 'Foundation for Cultural Exchange between the Netherlands and Germany' actually exists; located in Laren, it aims to foster Dutch-German cultural relations by enabling German writers and other 'workers in the cultural field' to spend time in Amsterdam. Özdamar's story-world and the actual world – once again – overlap here.

41. Of course one can argue that either Germany (East and/or West) or Turkey formally represents an 'abroad' for the protagonist as well. My argument in the previous section focused on the celebration of a certain kind of homelessness in combination with shifting chronotopical identifications that mediate places that the protagonist temporarily calls home.

42. In several ways 'Fahrrad auf dem Eis' seems a companion piece to the city stories discussed in the previous section. In this respect 'Mein Amsterdam' would be an appropriate alternative title, indicating the stories' correlation.

43. De Graef and Louwerse (2000, 2001) offer an alternative interpretation of the verb 'to entertain' as the cultural practice of making liminality. See also footnote 31.

44. Özdamar uses a lot of propositional constructions in her writing, often signalling both possibility and doubt. They are characteristic of what I have called the wondering attitude of the protagonist and underscore the idea of interpretive openness and possibility.

45. Adelson (2005: 123-127 *et passim*) points out the distinction between Saskia Sassen's 'emblematic' and Yasemin Soysal's 'symbolic' subjects of migration and globalisation. Whereas Sassen (1998) considers migrant workers as emblematic subjects of migration because of their central participation in the structural transformations brought about by globalisation, Soysal (1994) argues that labour migrants function as 'symbolic foreigners', stuck in an 'ethnocultural paradigm' that 'cannot index the changing sociality of migration' (Adelson 2005: 126). Adelson elaborates on this last idea.

46. In 'Fahrrad auf dem Eis' canals and bridges constitute 'boundary spaces'. Bridges appear as tropes of liminality throughout Özdamar's oeuvre. As mentioned before, 'migrants' literature' is often associated with (the building of) bridges between cultures. For critical discussions of this metaphor see Adelson (2001) and McGowan (2000).

47. '[d]as Fahrrad fuhr und erzählte'.

48. The interpretive confusion here cannot be resolved unless the reader checks the mentioned sources.

49. 'Man muß sich in einer fremden Stadt an irgendeinem Punkt festhalten.' She recalls applying a similar strategy of orientation in New York, a city that she mentions several times in a comparative strand. In New York her city explorations circled around a black man: 'Dieser Mann war für mich der Mittelpunkt meines persönlichen Stadtplans' (HS 86). Özdamar's narration juxtaposes New York, an iconic city of migration and well known as multicultural melting pot, with Amsterdam.

50. 'Wenn ich vor diesen Stühlen stehe, kann ich mich in der Stadt verlieren, aber wenn ich diese Stühle wiederfinde, bin ich eben bei diesen Stühlen.' The phrase 'bei diesen

Stühlen' brings up the association with the German proverb 'zwischen zwei Stühlen sitzen' and with the conception of the migrant situation as 'in between'. Adelson (2001, 2005) criticises the last as a rhetorical conceit and an anachronistic cultural fable. Özdamar could well be considered a female version of 'the flaneur'. Franz Hessel has famously described 'strolling' ['Flanieren'] as 'a kind of interpretation of the street' ['eine Art Lektüre der Straße'] ([1929] 1968: 131). Özdamar's reflective dwelling through Amsterdam (as well as her dwelling through Berlin in 'Mein Berlin') is strongly reminiscent of the idea of 'Flanerie' as collecting 'thought impressions' ['Denkbilder'].

51. Like the bicycle, the chairs become structuring entities in the protagonist's story. They are of determinate influence on the trajectory that she chooses to take: 'Rudi, will you join me to these chairs? Before I go home, I must go to the two chairs' ['Rudi, begleitest du mich zu meinen Stühlen? Ich muß, bevor ich nach Hause gehe, zu den beiden Stühlen']. At the end of the story the protagonist ascertains that the chairs as her new point of orientation have also disappeared from their customary location: 'Last night the chairs were not in the street anymore' ['Die Stühle standen heute nacht nicht mehr auf der Straße'] (HS 103). Their disappearance symbolically coincides with the protagonist's departure from Amsterdam, thus underscoring their relatedness.

52. 'Vielleicht könnte man, wenn Van Gogh es gemalt hätte, die Geschichte dieses Fahrrads erfahren.' The bibliography at the end of the collection lists the volumes I and VI of the German translation of Van Gogh's collected letters (*Sämtliche Briefe* 1985) as the source for the citations in 'Fahrrad auf dem Eis'.

53. Berger is well known for his work on 'looking' and 'seeing' and on the relationship between the two. He speaks of an 'always-present gap' (1972: 7) between *words* and seeing. Özdamar lists two German translations of his works on this theme – *The Sense of Sight* (1985) and *About Looking* (1980) – as sources in the bibliography. In the dedication of *Der Hof im Spiegel* Berger's name appears in the company of Özdamar's father Mustafa Bey and the Turkish poet Can Yücel.

54. '[Van Gogh] trug die enzelnen Teile für das Endprodukt zusammen: Beine, Querhölzer, Lehne, Sitz. Oder: Sohle, Oberleder, Absätze – so als wollte er sie auch zusammenfügen und als ob sie durch dieses Zusammengefügtwerden wirklich würden.' Quotations in the text that derive from the sources listed in the bibliography of *Der Hof im Spiegel* are printed in italics.

55. Özdamar's work collects images, impressions and observations in a literary language that often – and especially in her earlier work – seems fabricated as assemblage itself. The protagonist's narrative 'self-description', '*Wörtersammlerin*' [a female collector of words] (Özdamar 1998: 48), coined in the early story 'Großvaterzunge' in Özdamar's debut *Mutterzunge*, represents a meaningful word and concept in Özdamar's poetics.

56. Compare Adelson (2005), especially her analysis of 'Der Hof im Spiegel' (41-77).

57. 'Ich saß vor einem [von Van Goghs] Selbstporträts und schaute nicht das Bild an, sondern den Museumswächter. Ein Mann. Er war der Wächter des Wartens. (...) Ich weinte um ihn und glaubte, dass Van Gogh ihn jeden Tag aus einem Bild ansieht.'

58. 'Das ist ein Beruf, der mich traurig macht. Sie sind wie ein unscharfes Bild. So viele Menschen sind hier und keiner schaut ihn an.'

59. Compare the several (metaphorical) dimensions of 'invisibility' in respect to intersubjectivity as discussed by Axel Honneth (2003). Charles Taylor (1992) uses an intersub-

jective conception of identity in his influential essay 'Multiculturalism and "The Politics of Recognition"'. Seyla Benhabib (2002), however, criticises Taylor's conflation of the individual and the collective level. In reference to Nancy Fraser she pleads for a distinction between a 'politics of recognition and identity politics of group affirmation' (Benhabib 2002: 70) in order to 'allow democratic dissent, debate, contestation, and challenge to be at the center of practices through which cultures are appropriated' (ibid. 71).

60. Silverman proposes an 'ethics of the look' that would take 'the dependence of the social subject upon the Other for his or her own meaning' into account. The gaze in her theory represents an 'inevitable feature of all social existence' (Silverman 1996: 134).

61. The protagonist first sees the image of the woman living with the man in this mirror. The image of the man is framed only by the two windowsills. Mirrors as media of seeing in a metaphorical sense are present everywhere in the city in the form of the typically Dutch canals that mirror Amsterdam's houses. In one of his letters Van Gogh also describes the city through its reflection in the water.

62. See Adelson (2005: 54-68) for an analysis of this scene and other narrative moments of affective relationality in 'Der Hof im Spiegel'.

63. 'Er stand nackt am Fenster und schaute mich an. Er sah, daß ich weinte. Er stand unbeweglich.'

64. '[Museumswächter] sind wie ein unscharfes Bild.'

65. In the protagonist's last night in Amsterdam the man, like the chairs, disappears: 'Der Mann, der immer tippte, war heute nacht nicht da' (HS 103).

66. 'Er schoß sich eine Revolverkugel in den Bauch, und wenige Stunden später starb er im Bett, seine Pfeife rauchend, bei völliger geistiger Klarheit, voll Liebe für die Kunst, ohne Haß für die anderen.'

67. The responses by 'Herr van de Wakker' (HS 81) and 'Fräulein Braat' (HS 83) offer two examples testifying of Van Gogh's social extraordinariness.

68. There is a parallel here with the working of Özdamar's literary art. Françoise Lionnet writes in her study of postcolonial literature by women writers that their works 'insist on the relational nature of identity and difference, on the productive tensions between the two, and on the intricate and interdependent ways in which human agents function' (1995: 5/6). Their work, she argues, is 'engaged in the deconstruction of hierarchies, not in their reversal' (ibid. 6).

69. '100. Brief, Amsterdam, 4. Juni 1877' (HS 78).

70. 'Ich kann Dir nicht sagen, wie schön es da war in der Dämmerung.'

71. 'von allerlei Dingen zu sprechen'.

72. In the story 'Fahrrad auf dem Eis' the protagonist expands the narrative world outside her window and sets out to explore the city and to meet various people. This distinguishes it from the story 'Der Hof im Spiegel' where the affective web-weaving predominantly centres around the title's courtyard.

73. 'Ich ging in viele Läden. Die Verkäufer fragten: "Where are you from?"'.

74. 'In New York ist jeder fremd.'

75. 'Hafenstädte. Immer sind von den Treppen der Schiffe neue fremde Menschen heruntergestiegen. Kann eine Stadt süchtig werden nach den Fremden?' In the 1996 inter-

view with Annette Wierschke Özdamar maintains: 'Well, I think it wouldn't be bad for Germany, when still more *Überfremdung* – this word is used everywhere in Germany – comes about. (...) And with this I do not just refer to just the Russians and the Poles, but to all who have immigrated. The whole city should be filled with them, not just the ghettos and the train station, but the whole city' ['Also ich finde es nicht schlecht für Deutschland, wenn noch mehr Überfremdung – dieses Wort wird ja überall in Deutschland benutzt – passiert. (...) Und damit meine ich jetzt nicht nur die Russen und die Polen, sondern alle die so eingewandert sind. Aber die ganze Stadt müßte damit voll sein, nicht nur Ghettos und der Bahnhof, sondern die ganze Stadt'] (Özdamar in Wierschke 1996: 263).

76. Both the historical store houses and the toys and attributes that the protagonist mentions, are historical traces of the Dutch 'Golden Age' that is so violently entwined with the colonial past. This aspect of Amsterdam's history as a prosperous port city is foregrounded when the protagonist metaphorically imagines its city plan as a spider-web. Again it is a Dutch character, Christany's father, who alters the image by stating that half of the web was 'knitted' ['gestrickt'] (HS 86) over the heads of foreign countries during the colonial dominion.

77. The term 'zmv-vrouwenbeweging' is a self-identificatory term that in literal translation means 'black, migrant and refugee women's movement'. The term has been developed by zmv-emancipation project AISA and tries to take the diversity of the histories behind the presence of these women in the Netherlands into account. See Botman et al. (2001), Sterk (2004) and Wekker (2002).

78. It is necessary here to distinguish between the protagonist, who as a tourist is asked where she is from – a common question – and non-native Dutch citizens, for whom the question often entails an exclusionary gesture (based on vision). Sterk and Ghorashi (2001: 153-185) propose to substitute the 'where are you from?' question, which in their opinion sifts and categorises people according to a fixed origin, with the more future-oriented and ethnically neutral question, 'where are you going?', a variation of Paul Gilroy's 'where are you at?' (Gilroy 1991). See also Yue (2000).

79. '"Goedemorgen. Spreekt u Duits?" Ich werde hinter ihm herrennen. "Ja"'.

80. See also the chapter on national identity. This assessment is particularly interesting in respect to the field of literature, in which language is the central means of cultural production. Compare the special issue of the Dutch journal *Literatuur* (1994) on the Dutchness of Dutch literature.

81. 'ich fragte sie: "Welche Sprache sprechen Sie?" "Was Sie wollen, Englisch, Deutsch, Holländisch, Französisch, Spanisch".'

82. 'Er konnte Deutsch, wir sprachen aber Französisch. Der berühmte Fußballer Cruyff war auch da. "Entschuldigung, ich kann kein Holländisch." Cruyff sagte: "Reden wir doch Deutsch".'

83. 'sprichst du nur Deutsch, kannst du nicht Französisch?' and 'Ich will nicht Deutsch reden. Kannst du nicht Holländisch?'

84. Zafer Şenocak offers several interesting reflections on this topic in, among other places, the essay 'Deutschland – Heimat für Türken?' in his collection of essays entitled, *Atlas des tropischen Deutschland* (1992) and in the newspaper article 'Dunkle deutsche Seele' (2005). See also Huyssen (2003).

85. 'Das Land hat ein Drama.'
86. This counts, for instance, for the very first person that the protagonist meets: Isis. Isis responds to the question whether she likes her city: 'The city is pretty, but our history is not pretty. And young people don't know anything about our colonial time. Young people believe that our prosperity has always been there' ['Die Stadt ist schön, aber unsere Geschichte ist nicht schön. Und die Jugend weiß nichts von unserer kolonia-listischen Zeit. Die Jugend glaubt, dass unser Reichtum immer da war'] (HS 84).
87. 'Christany, weißt du, du bist heute schon der dritte Mensch in Amsterdam, der mir von der Kolonialzeit erzählt. Manchmal passiert das in Deutschland auch. Ich höre dort auch manchmal dreimal an einem Tag von meinen Freunden "Scheiß Nazis".'
88. Adelson (2005: 20-23) proposes the concept of 'touching tales' for similar (in her ex-ample Turkish-German) contact narratives with strong affective dimensions that are seldomly thought in relation to one another.
89. Huyssen poses the question of the memory of the Holocaust in respect to the Turkish-German population. He argues that 'the public memory discourse in Germany re-mains fundamentally and persistently national, focused on German perpetrators and Jewish victims. (...) Turkish immigrants and their German descendants remain largely absent from Germany's memorial culture' (Huyssen 2003: 164). See my discussion of Huyssen's concept of triangulation in the section on German identity.
90. 'Wenn man an unsere Vorfahren denkt, sind sie es nicht. Holländische Männer haben im 17. Jahrhundert in den Kolonien alles ausgesaugt. Ich hoffe, daß sich jetzt alles in Holland vermischen wird.' He continues to say that sport, as the last field in which the public entertainment of national sentiments is allowed, offers a positive example: 'In sports people have mixed better (...) We Dutch lose ourselves in football' ['Im Sport haben sich die Menschen besser vermischt. (...) Wir Holländer verlieren uns im Fuß-ball'] (HS 87). This is also significant while in both countries football is considered the field par excellence where nationalist sentiments are tolerated and even celebrated. It is generally argued that the world championship 2006 energised a new German self-understanding. See also Hoving (1998) on football and multiculturality.
91. Whereas the German term 'Ausländer' is a common (albeit also criticised) designation for people of non-German ethnic origin – irrespective of whether these people hold German citizenship or not – the equivalent term 'buitenlander' in the Dutch language holds strongly pejorative connotations. In the Dutch language context the term cannot be used in the relatively neutral meaning in which it is used in the citation. For that reason I continue to use the term in quotation marks when referring to the Dutch situation. The Dutch equivalent for the term – although under attack as well – is 'allochthon'.
92. In this second possibility his answer resonates the word that many first-generation guest workers associated with Germany – also in its double semantics of meteorologi-cal and interpersonal climate. Several studies address the topic of the (tense) Dutch-German relation (Von der Dunk 1994; Linthout 2006).
93. This last attitude reached a peak in 1993 when a racist attack on 'foreigners' (in fact German citizens) in the small town of Solingen shocked Germany as well as its neigh-bours. A Dutch broadcast company responded with a (successful) campaign in which it encouraged its listeners to send a postcard to the German government with the

simple text: 'I am angry'. For a long time the German *communis opinio* seemed to foster the idea of a Dutch superiority in respect to issues of multiculturality. It is only since the Islamist-fundamentalist murder of the Dutch film director Theo van Gogh and the outcries of violence following his death, that this assumed Dutch superiority has come to be seen in another light. Compare De Leeuw and Van Wichelen (2005) and Minnaard (2005). See the chapter on national identity for a more elaborate discussion of the discourses involved.

94. Multiple dimensions of the acquisition of a foreign language appear in Özdamar's early writings, for instance in her debut *Mutterzunge*.

95. In Özdamar's story-world Amsterdam is as open to homosexuality as it is to ethnic diversity. 'Fahrrad auf dem Eis' confirms Amsterdam's acclaimed symbolic status as the gay capital of Europe. Although by now several other European cities such as Berlin, London and Madrid lay claim to this status as well, the fact that Amsterdam accommodates an official 'homo monument' that commemorates the homosexual victims of the Nazi regime lends the city some surplus symbolic value.

96. This passage echoes the line of reasoning – linking 'successful' colonialism to 'successful' multiculturality – that Özdamar developed earlier in an interview with Horrocks and Kolinsky: 'It is true that the older colonial powers have managed the business of immigration more successfully. The Germans came by their colonies relatively late in the day, and they have ended up creating new colonies on their home territory' (1996: 52/53). Simultaneously the passage echoes the myth of German colonial innocence that Susanne Zantop discusses in her study *Colonial Fantasies. Conquest, Family and Nation in Precolonial Germany, 1770-1870* (1997).

97. Only recently, Germany's colonial history has become a topic of research in various disciplines.

98. The distinction between the protagonist's and the text's perspective is important, as the one modifies the other. The protagonist's narration seems to foreground a positive valuation of the idea that the Dutch managed to acquire more colonies than the Germans did. It suggests that either the Dutch had no guest workers or, if they had, that these – other than the guest workers who appear as the new colonised within German society – have been fully integrated into Dutch society. The rhetoric of the larger text, however, undermines these assumptions.

IV. Hafid Bouazza
'Leve de ontworteling! (...) Leve de verbeelding!' (Bouazza 2001: 61).

1. 'Goed, ik ben een migrant, maar het is nu vijfentwintig jaar later.'

2. 'Mede dankzij de goede zorgen van zijn moeder was hij geen randgroepjongere geworden, maar nu kreeg hij tot zijn eigen ergernis een ander stigma opgeplakt: dat van nationale troetelallochtoon. Hij werd op het voetstuk van barmhartigheid tentoongesteld.'

3. *De voeten van Abdullah* was nominated for the NPS Culture Prize, the ECI Prize 'voor schrijvers van Nu', and the Groene Watermanprijs.

4. 'Ik schrijf omdat ik wil schrijven, niet omdat ik de bedoeling heb om meer begrip tussen de culturen te kweken. Hou toch op. En ik schrijf al helemaal niet omdat ik me

de tolk voel van de tweede generatie allochtonen. Ik ben geen maatschappelijk werker.'

5. In this respect it is interesting as well as telling that whereas the cover text of the first print of *De voeten van Abdullah* presented the work of 'the Dutch author Hafid Bouazza' ['de Nederlandse auteur Hafid Bouazza'] (Francken 1999: 7), this national designation had disappeared on the second print. The alteration is symptomatic of a discourse that is more interested in the ethnic Other than in ethnic variations of the Dutch Self.

6. The literary authority Jeroen Brouwers formulated this critique in his provocative collection of pamphlet- and persiflage-like texts *Feuilletons* (1996). He explicitly attacks Hans Sahar as a 'youthful Hague-Moroccan pilferer and giggling gigolo' ['jeugdige Haags-Marokkaanse kruimelaar en giegelende gigolo'] and describes the publication of his work as an illustrative example of the commodification of literature. The real target of Brouwers' anger, however, are the publishing houses that he accuses of merely thinking in terms of profit: '"Allochthonous literature": that could well become a lucrative Trend (...)!' ['"Allochtone literatuur": dat zou wel eens een lucratieve Trend! kunnen worden (...)!'] (Brouwers 1996: 64).

7. 'Ik zeg altijd: ik ben een Nederlandse schrijver, want ik schrijf in de Nederlandse taal en daarom heb ik dezelfde rechten en plichten als welke andere Nederlandse schrijver ook. (...) Ik wil best mijn bijdrage leveren aan een multiculturele samenleving, maar alleen doordat wat ik schrijf niveau heeft.'

8. 'de topografische afbakening van zijn verbeelding'.

9. I use the abbreviation BB for quotations from the 2001 edition of *Een beer in bontjas*. In 2004 the publishing house Prometheus published a revised and extended edition of the essay. The new cover shows a picture of the writer Hafid Bouazza as a toddler, and the essay has doubled in length (120 instead of 64 pages). The adaptations and additions in the revised reprint of the essay are of special interest. Not only can this revision count as another moment of intervention, but it also reflects the change in Bouazza's public positioning. I elaborate on this shift in the section on the novel *Paravion*. *Paravion* and the reprint of *Een beer in Bontjas* were published in the same year.

10. 'Wat het verhaal zo mooi duidelijk maakt, is dat identiteit geen kwestie van keuze is maar van overheersing. Als ik de meeste critici mag geloven, dan ben ik een Marokkaanse schrijver. Maar ik geloof de meeste critici niet.' In *Een beer in bontjas* Bouazza proposes the abbreviation 'D.W.M.O.D.N. (Dutch Writer of Moroccan Origin with Dutch Nationality)' ['N.S.M.A.N.N. (Nederlandse Schrijver van Marokkaanse Afkomst met Nederlandse Nationaliteit)'] (BB 9) as the only factually correct term for his authorship. He comments on his own proposal in a playfully critical way: 'It sounds like a rare illness. The D.W.M.O.D.N. syndrome' ['Het klinkt als een zeldzame ziekte. Het N.S.M.A.N.N.-syndroom'] (BB 9/10). In Bouazza's opinion the term Moroccan-Dutch writer is not a better option, as it involves walking on mule and clog at the same time: 'that is a damned hard way to walk' ['dat loopt verdomd moeilijk'] (BB 9).

11. 'Hij wordt gekroond met de naam Hafid, Hafid Bouazza, en een schrijver, *deze* schrijver, *onze* schrijver is geboren.'

12. 'Leve de ontworteling! Leve de thuisloosheid! Leve de ongebondenheid! Leve de verbeelding!' Louwerse (2007b) describes Bouazza's poetic position as one of permanent homelessness and continuous movement. Hybridity or in-betweenness counts as a

positive, creative force in Bouazza's writing, a force that enables him to break free from and interrogate all categorisations that attempt to fix people to one place or within one stable and homogenous culture. Louwerse asserts some interesting parallels between Bouazza's appeal for artistic freedom and that of the poets of the 'Eighties-movement' (1880s), in particular, its spokesman the poet Willem Kloos.

13. See, for instance, Anbeek (1996: 339-40; 2002: 295-7) and Goedegebuure (1996). 'Re-invention' in this context refers to the recycling of forgotten words both in their original, but also in contextually adapted meanings. Bouazza's language reminds several critics of canonical Dutch writers such as Lodewijck van Deyssel, Herman Gorter and Geerten Gossaert, literary predecessors with whom Bouazza himself eagerly identifies. Bouazza's use of a forgotten Dutch vocabulary is particularly interesting in comparison with the common strategy in the work of writers of migrant background to make use of their native language. In both cases the 'unknown' language brings about estrangement or even excludes the reader. However, whereas in the second case the use of the foreign language functions to 'other' the reader, Bouazza's use of an archaic Dutch confronts his readers with their insufficient knowledge of the own cultural heritage. In 2004 Rosemarie Buikema and Maaike Meijer retrospectively claimed: 'By means of Bouazza's work the Dutch regain their language in transformed form' ['Door Bouazza's werk krijgen Nederlanders hun eigen taal in getransformeerde gedaante terug'] (Buikema and Meijer 2004: 13).

14. At the time of the first publication of *De voeten van Abdullah*, the issues that Bouazza addresses in his pieces of short prose do not yet have the counterparts in public discourse (in the way) that they currently have. The stories' provocative staging of the intersection of sexuality and (Islamic) religion would surely have met another reception, if they had been published ten years later. See Louwerse (2007b: 79-124) for an insightful analysis of the way in which *De voeten van Abdullah* actually explores and ultimately explodes all-too simple cultural oppositions and stereotypes of Orient and Occident.

15. The two stories in the collection that are (mainly) set in the contemporary Netherlands, were generally left out of consideration or read as another kind of account of exotic alterity, an alterity-after-migration. See De Graef and Louwerse (2000) for an analysis of the Netherlands-based story 'Apollien' that comments on and resists this mechanism.

16. Bouazza lists all these 'biographical facts' himself in his Book Week essay *Een beer in bontjas*.

17. In one story the narrator states: 'But remembrance is biased, my own memory prudish, my rear-view mirror clouded' ['Maar het geheugen is partijdig, mijn geheugen is preuts, zijn achteruitkijkspiegel besmeurd'] (VA 23). For citations from the revised 2002 edition of *De voeten van Abdullah* I use the abbreviation VA, for citations from the novel *Paravion* the abbreviation PA.

18. More or less obvious and easily retraceable intertexts include the Koran and the Bible, as well as several canonical works and folk tales of world literature. The intertextual opulence in Bouazza's work is an object of study in itself. Adding the mentioned characteristics – all addressing and questioning the relation between (narrative) representation and reality, between fiction and fact – it seems appropriate to read Bouazza's

stories within a postmodernist framework rather than within that of (auto-)biography. The stories not only strongly manipulate their textual reality and weave a semantic web of images and intertextual allusions, the author interventions also self-reflexively draw attention to the stories' origin in the imagination. See Louwerse (2007b: 79-124) for readings that – as an exception – take the narrative complexity and interpretive indeterminacy of the stories into account.

19. The publishing house's commercial presentation of the prose collection supports this reading to a certain extent. By emphasising the stories' grounding in the writer's memories it strategically ties in with the public interest in 'migrants' stories' of that time. Both the cover texts of the Dutch and English editions mention the author's childhood memories. The text on the dustjacket of the English edition (2000) reads 'Based on the writer's memories of a lively village with its own idiot and mosque in Morocco' and thus immediately sets a biographical frame for the reading of the stories. Interesting in this same short piece of text is the opposition that is established between the writer's childhood in this small Moroccan village and 'his cosmopolitan adulthood in Amsterdam'. As a result of this opposition the Moroccan village comes to stand for a naïve, simple, underdeveloped and instinct-driven world.

20. 'Wat vergeten wordt, wanneer men zijn fantasieën leest die zich in Marokko afspelen, is dat de verhalen niet zijn opgedaan in het land van herkomst, maar in het land van vestiging.'

21. Compare Goedegebure (1998), Goedkoop (1998), and Van Kempen (1998). A similarly critical reception occurred with Bouazza's novel *Salomon* (2001) and his drama *De slachting in Parijs* [*Slaughter in Paris*] (2001).

22. The novella is geographically set in a small, imaginary, 'typically Dutch' village named 'Herfsthoven'. The complete absence of any references to ethnic Otherness in the novella thwarted dominant reader expectations. Louwerse (2000) maintains that this absence might well have played a determinative role in the disappointed reviews written about *Momo*. See also Louwerse (2007b: 125-144).

23. 'daar kon men niets mee, omdat er geen imams en kamelen in voor kwamen.'

24. 'Wat wordt er nu geprezen, Bouazza's talent of het feit dat hij meer Nederlandse woorden kent dan de gemiddelde autochtoon?'

25. In the afterword Bouazza comments on the process of rewriting himself. He poetically positions himself in between the two Russian composers Rimsky-Korsakof and Shostakovitsch. Whereas the first kept reworking his compositions endlessly, the second pragmatically argued that this energy was better invested in the composition of new work. Bouazza assesses that he has resisted the temptation to rework his debut for two reasons: the book 'leaves him rather indifferent in a creative respect' ['laat hem in creatief opzicht enigszins onverschillig'] and – more importantly in his opinion – it has developed a certain autonomy by now (VA 156). The question why he nevertheless and contradictorily added a new story, thus affecting the structure and reading of the collection despite his decision not to do so, remains unanswered. Louwerse maintains that the thematic and narrative difference of 'De oversteek' already points towards the 'distinctive cultural poetics' (2007b: 123) as presented in the later *Paravion*.

26. 'De oversteek' functions as a spring hinge between the six stories set in Morocco and the two stories set in the Netherlands. Despite its later origin it is embedded in the

collection by means of cross-references and the appearance of characters that are already familiar to the reader.

27. In the story 'De visser en de zee' ['The Fisherman and the Sea'] the sheiks already appear as rather simple and narrow-minded observers of the extraordinary life at the seaside.

28. '[a]ls zij de wonderen van deze zee overleven.'

29. 'Deze, verschrikt, wees naar de duisternis, wilde spreken, greep naar zijn borstzak – maar de leider schudde het hoofd en troostte: "Wees niet bang. Een andere man zal jullie ophalen. Ik zal jullie naar de boot brengen en vandaar – God zij met jullie."'

30. 'Een bekend gezicht! Hoe vaak zag ik zulke mensen niet in latere tijden, in comfortabelere omstandigheden, op weg naar het moederland, aan de weg rusten en eten?'

31. 'Comfortabeler in de zin dat er geen angst was, geen onwettigheid; de vermoeienissen waren eender.'

32. 'de nek uitgestoken als de hals van Shahrazaad onder het lemmet van de dagende ochtend'.

33. This mentioning of the 'strange motherland' enables the reader to identify the author-narrator as presumably belonging to the generation of Moroccan migrant children. These children grew up in the countries of Western Europe that had invited their fathers to fill in the labour shortage.

34. The story's last supper scene has strong biblical connotations. The depicted situation is of a deceptively happy homeliness.

35. 'Het gezicht van de roeier was onzichtbaar onder zijn kovel. Hij zei niets, stak alleen zijn hand uit voor het geld.'

36. '[i]n zijn ogen was er de achterdocht die zijn werk en afkomst (het hoge noorden) met zich meebrachten. Hij had geleerd te wantrouwen, niet alleen de mensen die een beroep op hem deden, maar ook het buidelgewicht in zijn handen: altijd natellen.'

37. Tariq ibn Ziyad is one of the most prominent heroes in Arab culture. He is known as the conqueror of Labtayt Toledo in 711. According to the legend attached to his historical person Tariq set fire to his own fleet after his army had disembarked the ships at the Spanish shore. Strongly determined to conquer 'al-Andalus', the Arab name for the Iberian peninsula, he spoke the famous words: 'Now there is no return for us. Here we will conquer or die fighting.'

38. 'als ik zachte vlakke grond onder zijn voeten zou spreiden zou hij het evenwicht verliezen'.

39. 'Tarik weigerde hun pijp, gaf de voorkeur aan zijn eigen.'

40. In his work *The Location of Culture* Bhabha defines colonial mimicry as 'the desire for a reformed, recognizable Other, *as a subject of difference that is almost the same, but not quite*' (1994: 86). He describes mimicry as 'at once resemblance and menace' (ibid.), a subversive characteristic that applies to Tarik's 'North South' mimicry as well. On mimicry as a strategy of resistance see Breger (1999) and Silverman (1996).

41. In the revised edition of *Een beer in bontjas* Bouazza writes 'Life is metamorphosis' ['Leven is metamorfose'] (BB 110). The experience of migration accelerates this process of metamorphosis in a particular way. The conceptualisation of migration as a particular favourable but also coercive condition of metamorphosis recurs as a trope in *Paravion*.

42. 'Dit alles zou ik willen'.

43. 'En dan bezwijmt mij een duisternis, begraaft mij een golvenbed: wat duurt die zeetocht lang, de veerman roeit onverstoorbaar, geduldig. Geen licht leidt hen nu.'

44. Here the intertext of Scheherazade with its particular connection of storytelling and survival again thrusts itself on the reader.

45. 'De oversteek' does not explicitly denominate the countries of origin and destination as Morocco and the Netherlands. This identification derives from various clues in the text and from the Moroccan-Dutch context supplied by the other stories in the collection.

46. Taking into account the distinctive durations of the processes of writing and publishing a literary story or a newspaper article, the assumption that the (work on the) story preceded the article seems justified.

47. 'ongekende en glorieuze vrijheid van denken en ontwikkeling'.

48. 'Ik geloof niet in emancipatie met een hoofddoek.' In an interview with Emma Brunt, Bouazza claims a fundamental right on looks, on appearance. In his opinion a headscarf, in his eyes a symbol of patriarchal suppression, is not included in this right. He claims: 'Emancipation is a liberation from patriarchal structures, but a headscarf neatly toes the patriarchal line' ['Emancipatie is een bevrijding uit patriarchale structuren, maar een hoofddoekje loopt keurig in het patriarchale gareel'] (Bouazza in Brunt 2003). Several studies critically interrogate both the symbolic and discursive meaning of the headscarf. See (for instance) Ahmed (1992), Lutz (1996) and Mandel (1989).

49. *Vrij Nederland* critic Jeroen Vullings calls *Paravion* Bouazza's 'most accurate literary achievement so far' ['zijn trefzekerste literaire prestatie tot nu toe'] (Vullings 2003).

50. The award of the Amsterdam Prize for the Arts 2003 for his oeuvre is an earlier indication of Bouazza's acceptance and public prominence as a Dutch author and intellectual. The same counts for the 2003 invitation to compile an edition of the VPRO's popular Sunday night television programme 'Zomergasten' ['Summer Guests'], a yearly summer talk show for an intellectual audience. In 2004 the programme featured Ayaan Hirsi Ali who showed, among other things, her and Van Gogh's film *Submission* (2004). By now both Bouazza and Hirsi Ali count as prominent Islam-critical voices in the Netherlands. They share sides in the fight against (what they perceive as) Islamic fundamentalism.

51. This concerns the reviews by Pam (2003), Preter (2004), Vanegeren (2003b), Vullings (2003) and to a lesser extent also the one by Fortuin (2003). Despite the fact that Arjen Fortuin actually addresses the literary qualities of *Paravion* in his elaborate book review, he too links a 'grim realism' to Bouazza's statements about the approach of 'the enemy'. He maintains: 'A hymn to love and the imagination coincides with a grim realism about emigration and the conservatism of culture and religion' ['Een lofzang op liefde en verbeelding gaat samen met grimmig realisme over emigratie en de behoudzucht van cultuur en geloof'] (Fortuin 2003).

52. For an elaborate discussion of *Paravion's* reception see Minnaard (2006a). In his article 'Over schrijverschap en politiek' ['On Authorship and Politics'] Nico Dros argues that there is presently only one concern for a politically committed writer: 'the relation between Islam and Western society' ['de verhouding van de islam tot de westerse samenleving'] (2003: 48). He continues his article praising Bouazza's critique of Islam, and encourages all to follow Bouazza's example.

53. Marc de Leeuw and Sonja van Wichelen (2005) argue that Hirsi Ali's testimonial film *Submission* performs a problematical role in an increasingly popular, anti-Islamic discourse. In respect to the 'phenomenon Hirsi Ali' they maintain that 'the authoritative voice of the mediated self as "other" tends to close off dialogue and turn the viewer into a passive spectator. In speaking on behalf of Muslim women through her self as "other" (especially as victim "other") she creates a *moral closure* for critical opponents' (De Leeuw and Van Wichelen 2005: 331).

54. For an elaboration on the rhetoric of 'new realism' and Fortuyn's 'hyperrealism' see the section on Dutch public discourse. In contrast to Benali, Bouazza did not dissociate himself from Fortuyn's hyperrealism. In an interview with Martin Hendriksma, Bouazza states: 'But not everything Fortuyn said, was nonsense.' ['Maar niet alles wat Pim Fortuyn zei, was onzin'] (Bouazza in Hendriksma 2004).

55. 'Na zijn filippica's tegen de dreiging van islamitisch fundamentalisme op Hollandse bodem wordt [Bouazza] veroordeeld als een nest-bevuiler, maar tegelijk op handen gedragen door Nederlanders die uit zijn mond horen wat ze van zichzelf zo lang niet mochten zeggen.'

56. 'Echt, ik vind de islam het slechtste wat Nederland in de laatste veertig jaar is overkomen.'

57. In his study *The Image of Man: The Creation of Modern Masculinity* (1996), George Mosse makes the distinction between normative and counter-type manhood. He argues that normative manhood as a construct is directly related to the preservation of dominant norms and values in a society that needs to be protected against influences from outside. Whereas Mosse discusses the concept of normative manhood in the context of an advancing modernisation of the twentieth-century Western society, in the present Dutch situation the advancing multiculturalisation appears to necessitate a 'protection' of Dutch cultural norms and Enlightenment values. More and more, Muslim males are discursively determined as what Mosse calls the 'counter-type' male, the threatening as well as constitutive counterpart of the normative male. See also Minnaard (2006a: 51-54).

58. 'opkomen voor Nederland'.

59. 'Wat voor eigenzinnige verschijning Bouazza in de Nederlandse literatuur ook moge zijn, het zijn vooral zijn essays, zijn polemieken, en zijn boek- en filmkritieken die van grote waarde zijn.'

60. In reviews, interviews, and written comments Bouazza continues to share his opinions on socio-political issues with the public (e.g. Dresselhuys 2004; Piryns 2003; Visser 2003). A provocative example of his writing on the topic gender and Islam is his newspaper article 'Angstige mannen, afvallige vrouwen en het voorbeeld van de profeet – een gevaarlijke combinatie' ['Anxious men, unfaithful women and the example of the prophet – a dangerous combination'] published in *NRC Handelsblad* (13 November 2004). See also Bouazza (2002d, 2003, 2004c). Also the reprint of *Een beer in bontjas* contains various additions that concern Muslim masculinity and the position of Muslim women (BB 18, 33/34, 110).

61. The historical term 'Moors' refers to the medieval Muslim inhabitants of the Maghreb and Al-Andalus. Bouazza himself endorses the Morea-Morocco conflation in several interviews. At the same time he warns for all too referential readings. In an interview

with Arjan Peters he explains: 'I give the country that old name to indicate that my book is a fairytale, not a realist narration' ['Ik geef het land die oude naam om aan te geven dat mijn boek een sprookje is, geen realistische vertelling'] (Bouazza in Peters 2003).

62. By using the adjective 'Islamic' I paraphrase the common strand of interpretation that I criticise later on in this chapter. In an interview with Stefanie de Jonge (2004) in the Belgian magazine *Humo*, Bouazza points out that Islam does not play a major role in the Morean village in his novel, but only gains symbolic value for the migrants in the alien world of Paravion.

63. Like in *De voeten van Abdullah*, the conflation of characters and perspectives functions as a narrative strategy of confusion.

64. All translations from the novel *Paravion* are my own.

65. This Baba Baloek, Sr., the father of the novel's main protagonist Baba Balock, Jr., and his wife Mamoerra are considered the village's outsiders. Mamoerra made her appearance in the village community as a foundling and was raised by witchlike Siamese twins. The reason for Baba Baloek's exclusion by the villagers is initially unclear. Only much later in the story the appellation of Baba Baloek as 'nigger' ['neger'] (PA 202) suggests that his exclusion might well result from racial discrimination. The *love* couple – an exception in the village – tries to hide Baba Baloek's travelling plans, but in the small village community where gossiping birds fly from windowsill to windowsill, the news spreads swiftly.

66. The migratory crossing of the 'Narvelsea' invokes the mythological intertext of Icarus' flight. Icarus pays for his hubris with his life. Several versions of the tragic myth end with an image of the feathers of his wings floating on the surface of the sea after his fall from the sky. In the novel *Paravion* the image of these feathers on the sea surface reappears, but now the story continues. The feathers gather again and refigure into owls. These owls, symbolising the migrants' souls, return to the homeland.

67. Assumedly, nostalgia features as a central trope in 'guest worker literature'. The often-exclusive focus on this trope in technologies of reading literature of migration overshadows other issues of possible interest. See also Vromen (1993).

68. See De Preter (2004), Schouten (2003), Vanegeren (2003b), and Vullings (2003). Compare also the analysis of these reviews in Minnaard (2006a).

69. In this distinction the term secular is appropriated by the entity that used to – or still does – identify itself as Christian. In dominant discourse 'secular' and 'Christian' do not appear as contradictory terms; Christianity is not marked as a religious category. Also see Auslander (2000).

70. In the eyes of the Morean migrants the exuberant visibility of women in Paravion public life opposes their own social invisibility. This causes an exceptional thorn in the migrants' side and seems to confront them most harshly with their outsider status. The public appearance of two women of Morean origin (reincarnations of the Siamese twins Cheira and Heira who have raised Mamoerra) particularly horrifies the Morean migrants.

71. 'Het [leven in Paravion] bestond buiten hem om en zou voortbestaan zonder hem.'

72. '"Hé!" werd er in koor geroepen. "Daar hebben we onze Morekijn! Kom en neem een limonade!"'. The term 'Morekijn', a diminutive form of Moor, resonates an ethnicising, in this particular case even racist discourse.

73. In this scene the parodic mode exceptionally affects the Paravonian speakers pub regulars who address the Morean migrant as 'Morekijn'. In their drunken state they too appears as objects of parodic focalisation.

74. 'Een boeket van verse bruiden, zedig van lichaam en geest, moest uit de rode bergen van Morea worden geplukt.'

75. As a result of the predominantly male focalisation and the novel's binary structure, identification with the female characters goes against the grain of narration. In the city of Paravion female characters mostly appear as objects rather than as subjects of focalisation.

76. 'Niemand kon overleven na terugkeer in het geboorteland. Dat wist iedereen. Alleen als lijk werd men daar door de grond aanvaard.'

77. The female characters in the novel – the Paravonian Marijke and her daughter Mamette, the Morean Mamoerra, some Morean 'daughters' and the girl in the valley that I will discuss in the following section – also play a minor role. Nevertheless, especially in comparison to the Paravonian men, they gain a certain individuality by means of their names, their spoken contributions to the novel's discourse and their (exceptional) moments of focalisation.

78. The stereotypical representation of the Morean fathers as violent family patriarchs resonates with contemporary cultural clichés in Dutch (and German) public discourse about forced marriage and honour killings in Muslim circles. These violent practices are taken as representative of Islamic customs and as proof of Islamic backwardness.

79. In a comment made during an interview on the story-world that the novel imagines, Bouazza puts *Paravion's* supposed referentiality into perspective. He maintains: 'I have situated all sorts of bucolic elements in a Moroccan village. It is more a Western projection than reality' ['Allerlei bucolische elementen heb ik in een Marokkaans dorpje gesitueerd. Het is meer een westerse projectie dan werkelijkheid'] (Bouazza in Peters 2003). The reference to 'a Western projection' in this statement resonates Said's famous thesis that the Orient is in fact a product of the Western imagination (Said 1995). Bouazza takes up and recycles this Orientalism into another product of the imagination: Paravion. See Louwerse (2007b: 177-218) and Minnaard (2005) for readings that give priority to the interpretation of the aesthetic difference of *Paravion*.

80. In an interview with Stefanie de Jonge (2004), Bouazza himself remarked that Islam only acquires significance for these male characters after the disappointing experiences in Paravion. In the novel the Morean migrants discuss the (actual or imagined) changing Paravion cityscape in which minarets slowly take over the position of church towers as the characteristic markers of the skyline. The carpet salesman predicts that this transformation is only a question of time (PA 139).

81. Louwerse (2004b, 2007b: 180-188) offers a fascinating analysis of *Paravion's* application of the pastoral tradition in a story about migration. She shows how both the pastoral and migration can be considered as modes of displacement. The one concerns imaginary displacement driven by desire and the other is a matter of bodily movement mainly driven by need. Bouazza, she maintains, makes use of this analogy

in order to complicate any simple assumption about the migrant condition, as well as to rewrite what Louwerse calls pastoral ideology. Thus, the novel results in a critical redefinition of migration 'from the physical movement of some to a general movement of desire for the other open to everyone' (Louwerse 2004b: 112).

82. The fact that the men of three following generations are all named Baba Baloek engenders an extra amount of confusion. In an interview with Arjan Peters (2003), Bouazza explained the naming as an ironic comment on Marianne Fredriksson's bestselling family saga with the Dutch title *Anna, Hanna en Johanna* (translated into English as *Hanna's daughters*). Bouazza applies a same strategy of (parodic) identity confusion in several stories of *De voeten van Abdullah* where a major part of the male and female characters in the Moroccan village is named Abdullah and Fatima.

83. The appearance of mysterious, delusive and alluring female characters that resonate famous fatal females as Melusine and the Lorelei is a recurring motif in Bouazza's oeuvre. *Paravion's* mysterious girl resembles the 'Apollien'-character in the story of that name in *De voeten van Abdullah* and the drama *Apollien* (1998a).

84. 'Hoe haar te beschrijven? In gedeelten, zoals Baba Baloek haar opnam toen hij opkeek en haar zag. (...) Ze zag er vermoeid uit, leek een lange afstand te hebben afgelegd. Ze schudde haar ledematen, streek haar onzichtbare kreukels weg. De bladeren ritselden.'

85. The exotic Orient appears as a strongly gendered, eroticised space or, as Kohl describes: 'The exotic comes to be a metonymy for the erotic, the *Other* a paragon for desire' ['Das Exotische wird zum Metonym des Erotischen, die *Fremde* zum Inbegriff des Begehrens'] (Kohl 1987: 356). For a critical discussion of Western perceptions of the harem see Ahmed (1982, 1992), Förschler (2005), and Yeğenoğlu (1998).

86. The depicted situation mirrors a similar situation of sexual education in Bouazza's story 'Apollien'. In this story the character Apollien takes up the role of sexual educator. In contradistinction to Baba Baloek, her lover Humayd, however, has huge difficulties with his submission to the female-determined educational regime.

87. In this discourse, the new realists build an unexpected coalition with a particular brand of feminism. Multiculturalism and feminism appear as competing, or even mutually exclusive ideologies. Compare Adelson (1997b), Cohen et al. (1999), and Saharso (2000).

88. The intertext of the Lorelei, evoked by the girl's tempting hair, charges the scene with an ominous tension.

89. 'Maar naderbij gekomen zag [Baba Baloek] dat het taferelen waren die visioensgewijs in haar lokken bewogen, beeltenissen tot zacht leven gewekt. Wat hij kon onderscheiden was bizar. Plotseling draaide ze zich om en gaf de herder een ketsende klap tegen zijn wang.'

90. 'Voor de toegangspoort stond de karrenman dit alles gade te slaan en verscholen achter struwelen zaten andere broeders zich vol walging te verlekkeren aan de duizelingwekkende en diafane schouwspelen.'

91. The elaborate description of the abundant park spectacle in the migration story contains several references that encourage the reader to identify the park as Paravion's equivalent to the Amsterdam Vondelpark, the green heart and central site of leisure and pleasure in the Dutch capital in the real world. The presence of a 'statue of a

writer, enveloped in sculptured pleats, decorated with excrement, searching for the forgotten word that could further unwind his story' ['standbeeld van een verteller, gehuld in gesculptuurde plooien, gedecoreerd met uitwerpselen, op zoek naar het vergeten woord dat zijn vertelling verder kon doen rollen'] (PA 172) is an obvious reference to the namesake of the park, the seventeenth-century Dutch playwright, Joost van den Vondel.

92. In his article 'Multiple Masculinities in Turkish-German Men's Writing', Moray McGowan describes a social situation of first generation Turkish-German migrants that he considers of constitutive (though not per se referential) importance for Turkish-German male writing: 'Nonetheless, many men retained and sometimes even intensified a simplistic and derogatory attitude towards German women, and towards German society in general, as being culturally and ethically inferior. Their authority and patriarchal identity unsettled by general social marginalisation and the indignities of their workplace, they might turn back to these half-atrophied Islamic roots to reassert their threatened masculinity' (2001: 293).

93. 'Mamette stelde hem gerust dat er geen culturele kloof tussen hen zou gapen, omdat zij hem en zijn cultuur *begreep*, maar het onoverkomelijke probleem bleek niet cultureel van aard, maar seksueel, in de ruimste zin van het woord. Zijn seksuele identiteit kwam in het geding.'

94. 'zorgvuldig gecultiveerde [mannelijke] identiteit'.

95. 'Hier, in dit omheinde oord van genot, komt al het goede bij elkaar en hier zou ik mijn tijd het liefst doorbrengen, als ik de vrijheid had. Deze plaats is niet voor mij bestemd.' At an earlier occasion the girl sighs to Baba Baloek: 'Oh, my dear goatherd. Being a woman is not so easy' ['Ach, mijn lieve herder. Het valt niet mee om een vrouw te zijn'] (PA 125).

96. 'Dit heeft ook geen zin meer.'

97. Louwerse (2007b: 188-196, 201-208) reads the girl as a spectral reincarnation of Mamoerra whose intervention in her son Baba Baloek's life has created the erotic Abqar idyll. She rejects an allegorical interpretation that diametrically opposes the previous situation of patriarchal suppression to the new state of quasi-feminist gynocratic harmony. According to Louwerse, *Paravion* investigates the tension between difference and sameness. The novel propagates the transgression of boundaries as an important prerequisite for individual freedom in general, without, however, disacknowledging the human – male and female – need for belonging and settlement. *Paravion* offers no clear-cut messages, but explores the multiple dimensions of desire as an elusive force of change.

98. Family life and sexual desire appear in opposition to each other. In *Paravion* the birth of the first child signifies the death of desire and the end of Baba Baloek's 'carefree singing' (PA 205). Louwerse, however, argues that '[i]f migration is associated with the movement of desire (...), the sedentary arrangement of the home spells the end of desire. At least for men mentally managing women into domestic acquisitions that quite literally leave nothing to be desired' (2004b: 116).

99. In the first interview after his notorious newspaper articles, Bouazza explains his rejection of all earlier invitations to comment on socio-political issues with the statement: 'I am a writer, not a soapbox orator' ['Ik ben een schrijver, geen zeepkistorator']

(Bouazza in Kouters 2002). My analysis of *Paravion's* reception throws doubt on the motivations underlying Bouazza's acceptance.

V. Feridun Zaimoglu
'Hier hat allein der Kanake das Wort' (Zaimoglu 1995: 18).

1. 'Er habe den Ehrgeiz, sagt Zaimoglu, es als deutscher Autor weit zu bringen. Und da hört der Spaß auf.'

2. With the term 'Kanak writing' I refer to the titles *Kanak Sprak* (1995), *Abschaum* (1997), *Koppstoff* (1998b), *Kopf und Kragen* (2001), as well as to several other short pieces of writing on the 'Kanak issue'. In the following section of this chapter I expand on the (use of the) derogatory term *Kanak(e)* as a form of hate speech. In order to dissociate my use of the term from this hate speech dimension, I write the term in italics. In order to prevent a repetition of the term's injurious impact, my use of the term restricts itself to the critical resignification that was initiated by Zaimoglu's (literary) appropriation of the term. Judith Butler warns for the possibility of hurtful repetition: 'The critical and legal discourse on hate speech is itself a restaging of the performance of hate speech' (1997: 14).

3. See for instance Teipel (2001). The popular invocation of these names invoke Afro-American and Latin American histories of resistance. Their appearance as 'touching tales' (Adelson 2000b, 2005: 20-23) requires further scrutiny.

4. 'Daß der koloniale Diskurs hier seine Verlängerung nach innen und auch über das Zeitalter der Dekolonisierung hinaus erfahren hat, das müssen in der bundes-deutschen Gegenwart bekanntlich vor allem die Türken, die größte deutsche Minder-heit, erfahren.'

5. Harlow discusses the concept of resistance literature or – broader – 'cultural resis-tance' in her study of the same name, *Resistance Literature* (1987). She provisionally de-fines resistance literature as 'a particular category of literature that emerged signifi-cantly as part of the organized national liberation struggles and resistance movements in Africa, Latin America and the Middle East' (Harlow 1987: xvii). Her investigation brings forward several aspects that resistance literature shares, independent of its of-ten very diverse geographic and socio-political contexts. Zaimoglu's *Kanak* literature displays many of these representative aspects, despite its very different and in any case less 'existence-threatening' situationality than the literatures that Harlow dis-cusses. As Rosemary Marangoly George (1996) points out, Harlow names a literary genre by political and ideological contents rather than by formal attributes. She herself follows this example by proposing the term 'immigrant genre' for contemporary writ-ing in which 'the politics and experience of location (or rather 'dislocation') are the central narratives' (George 1996: 171). In the German literary tradition resistance lit-erature in the sense of protest literature mostly refers to the writing that appeared in the wake of the student protests of 1968.

6. In an interview with Sebastian Hammelehle (2006) Zaimoglu maintains about his de-but *Kanak Sprak* that 'the book is out of date' ['Das Buch hat sich überholt'] and the term Kanak(e) 'is through' ['ist durch'] – to his explicit contentment.

7. In *Kanak Sprak's* preface author-character Zaimoglu himself denotes his 24 texts as 'protocols'. For citations taken from *Kanak Sprak* and *Abschaum* I use the abbreviations KS and AB.

8. Various scholars offer explanations for the origin of the term. Cheesman (2004: 86 n.10) lists the descriptions to the lemma '*Kanake*' in four reference works ranging from 1936 to 1983 in order to underline the term's historical shifts in meaning. Whereas according to the 1936 *Knaurs Konversations-Lexikon* the term '*Kanake*' derives from the Polynesian word for human being or for a native of Hawaii, the 2000 version of the *Wahrig deutsches Wörterbuch* mentions the signification 'native inhabitant of the Pacific islands' and the pejorative use as 'uneducated person' and 'foreigner'. *Kluge Etymologisches Wörterbuch der deutschen Sprache* (1999) denominates *Kanake* as vulgar and also mentions its denigratory usage to denote 'foreigners'. Pfaff (2005: 201) points out that according to *The Australian Encyclopaedia* the term was used for the indentured labourers that came form the South Sea Islands to work in Australia, especially in Queensland. She mentions that people from the other Australian colonies nicknamed the colony of Queensland 'Kanakaland'.

9. Butler's research is strongly indebted to Austin's work on the speech act ([1962] 1975), Althusser's work on interpellation (1971) and Derrida's theories of iterability ([1967] 1997).

10. 'The utterances of hate speech are part of the continuous and uninterrupted process to which we are subjected, an on-going subjection (*assujetissement*) that is the very operation of interpellation, that continually repeated action of discourse by which subjects are formed in subjugation' (Butler 1997: 27).

11. Butler elaborates on her as well as the general use of the highly contested – among reactionary and progressive groups – terms 'viable' and 'life' (as well as 'human') in this and several other essays in her collection *Undoing Gender* (2004).

12. 'Aus Scham wird Demonstration, Defizite werden zu Provokationen: man ist stolz, Fremder zu sein.'

13. Zaimoglu would surely (make his *Kanaken*) object to the interpretation of his *Kanak* project as a politics of identity. I, too, object to a reading that reduces the literary work to a socio-political positioning.

14. 'Kanake! Dieses verunglimpfende Hetzwort wird zum identitätsstiftenden Kennwort, zur verbindenden Klammer dieser "Lumpenethnier".'

15. 'Der "Kanake" tritt dem "deutschen" Leser als Doppelgänger seiner eigenen Vorurteile entgegen wie Frankenstein. Du hast mich geschaffen: Hier bin ich!'

16. In the second chapter of *The Location of Culture*, 'Interrogating Identity. Frantz Fanon and the postcolonial prerogative' (1994: 40-65), Bhabha argues that invisibility involves a loss of identity.

17. *Kanak Sprak* achieved an enormous commercial success with sales numbers that are without precedent in the history of 'migrants' literature'. The literary work by an acknowledged writer as Emine Sevgi Özdamar, or also the popular detective novels by Akif Pirinçi never received as much public acclaim as Zaimoglu with his *Kanak* performance. Zaimoglu himself coins the phrase 'market of identity' ['Markt der Identitätsfindung'] in an interview with Olaf Neumann in the journal *Jungle World* (3 March 2004).

18. In 1997/1998 a group of activists established a loose anti-racist network under the name *Kanak Attak*. In their 1999 manifest they write: 'Kanak Attak is anti-nationalist, anti-racist and rejects any form of identity politics, as they are enforced by ethnological ascriptions' ['Kanak Attak ist anti-nationalistisch, anti-rassistisch und lehnt jegliche Form von Identitätspolitiken ab, wie sie sich etwas aus ethnologischen Zuschreibungen speisen'] (*Kanak Attak* 1999). The network is not organised around (ethnic) identity markers, but is open to all who share its cause. One of the central goals of its activism is the acquisition of equal formal-juridical rights for all persons living in Germany. Ha describes the political project *Kanak Attak* as a 'hybridised identity politics of self-Kanakisation' ['hybridisierten Identitätspolitik der Selbst-Kanakisierung'] (2005: 112/113). He locates the resistance movement within the history of colonisation and globalisation: 'Kanak identity politics as a perspective of resistance tries to withdraw itself from the power of colonial language, in that the colonized define themselves through speech-acts and thus discursively step outside of their status as objects' ['Kanakische Identitätspolitik als Widerstandsperspektive versucht, sich der Macht der Kolonialsprache zu entziehen, indem sich die Kolonisierten in Sprechakten selbst definieren und damit diskursiv aus ihrem Objektstatus heraustreten'] (ibid. 113). Although Zaimoglu initially participated in the network as well, his (literary) 'project' and the network's political aims are not to be confused. At a certain point the *Kanak Attak* network and Zaimoglu moved in different directions.

19. Adding to this, Zaimoglu's work also satisfies a more positively cast, socio-cultural yearning for difference, a greediness for the exotic Other. The writer Imran Ayata comments this desire for difference as follows: 'I call this "boutique of difference": the German mainstream has an enormous greed for difference in the cultural sector (...). [This difference] must not question the consensus substantially, it should always be enriching in some way – exotic, just different, but also smart somehow' ['Ich nenne das Differenz-Boutique: Es gibt im kulturellen Bereich eine unbeschreibliche Gier des deutschen Mainstream nach Differenz (...). [Die Differenz] darf den Konsens nicht substanziell in Frage stellen, sie muss immer ein bisschen bereichernd sein – exotisch, eben anders, aber auch irgendwie klug'] (*Literaturen* 2005: 29).

20. In an interview with Patricia Persch, Zaimoglu retrospectively puts his authenticity claim into perspective and emphasises that entertainment was his primary objective: 'And on stage I indeed wanted to entertain, and entertainment involves that you actually offer yourself as an unambiguous figure' ['Und ich wollte auf der Bühne tatsächlich unterhalten und zur Unterhaltung gehört, dass man sich auch als eine eindeutige Figur anbietet'] (Zaimoglu in Persch 2004: 88). The following sections discuss both Zaimoglu's authenticity-claim and the one-dimensionality of his *Kanak* figure.

21. 'Willkommen in Kanakistan', 'Kanaksta bist du, wenn du Deutschland durchschaut hast' and 'Sind sie zu fremd, bist du zu deutsch'. These slogans appear on the dust jackets of the mentioned prose collections. For a discussion of anthologies of migration literature see Abel (2006).

22. 'Jetzt werden in der Literatur neue Stimmen hörbar, die Stimmen der Migranten in der zweiten und der dritten Generation. Sie verzichten auf das Prinzip der Integration und suchen ihre Identität in der selbstgewählten aggressiven Abgrenzung: "Kanak Attack".'

23. '[e]ine weinerliche, sich anbiedernde und öffentlich geförderte "Gastarbeiterliteratur".' Female writers hardly feature in this match of males. Zaimoglu mentions one female first name in his list of literary 'waiters': Renan (assumedly Demirkan) (Zaimoglu 1998a: 86). His reference to 'Mother tongue' ['Mutterzunge'] in Kanak Sprak's preface is a clear reference to Özdamar's prose collection of the same name.

24. In his repetitive use of the generic 'Ali', a particular form of hate speech as well, Zaimoglu does not deploy possibilities for an appropriating resignification of this term. Instead he uses 'Ali' in a way that repeats and confirms its pejorative meaning. It seems that the appropriation of the term 'Kanake' occurs for a considerable part on the costs of the migrant fathers who once again get fixed in the 'Ali'-stereotype. Arguably, the Kanak use of the 'Ali' epithet even reinforces its 'common' hate speech impact. For a discussion of the representation of 'Ali' as the epitome of migrant victimhood see Cheesman (2007: 145-182).

25. 'diese schrift ist eine kampfhandlung' and 'ihr seid erledigt, motherfuckers!' In defiance of the grammatical rules of the German language, Zaimoglu writes substantives without capitals in the Kanak language. Compare the opening of Peter Handke's provocative work Publikumsbeschimpfung: 'This piece is an introductory speech' ['Dieses Stück ist eine Vorrede'] (Handke 1972: 19).

26. This migrant Other – 'Ali' – is stereotyped as a complacent, 'poor but kind-hearted' (KS 12) character whose work enables its readers to identify as the 'better German' (ibid.) in several ways. On the one hand the described social difficulties that Ali has to go through, affect the empathic readers. On the other hand these readers can simultaneously dissociate themselves from the fundamentally different migrant Other. On the cultural figure of 'Ali' see also Cheesman (2007), Mani (2002), Silverman (1992), Teraoka (1989), and Wise (1995). Adelson (2005: 130/131) points out that by now the masculinist icon of the aggressive young Turk has replaced the cultural stereotype of the deprived, kind-hearted guest worker 'Ali'.

27. 'Die neue Generation deutscher Schriftsteller türkischer Herkunft scheint nicht mehr zu leiden. Sie hat aufgehört zu jammern und Tränen über den Verlust ihres Heimatlandes, ihrer Ursprungskultur, ihrer Muttersprache etc. zu vergießen.'

28. 'die pseudoauthentische und sentimentale Gefühle produzierte und bediente, die von einer nicht existenten Solidarität ausging, in falscher Nostalgie schwelgte und unechte Exotik verkaufte.'

29. As an example of this contemptible 'guest worker literature' Wertheimer explicitly mentions Aras Ören's novella Bitte nix Polizei (1981). Adelson (2005: 139-149) demonstrates that this novella offers more, if not something different than Wertheimer's indiscriminate rejection of the work suggests (for instance none of the characteristics that Wertheimer mentions apply to Ören's novella). In order to discern the work's multiple dimensions Adelson proposes to read Ören's protagonist Ali Itir not as a victim of social circumstances and racist structures, but as a narrative 'phantom figure'. More than a truthful representation of a guest worker in the 1970s, Ali Itir functions as a narrative tool that makes it possible to tell other stories about postwar German society. Also Cheesman (2006) criticises the tendency in literary criticism of work by 'migrant writers' to use a teleological model of generational progress.

30. These critics argue that all these writers share an awareness of commercial possibilities, a focus on issues of lifestyle and (capitalist) consumption, a strategic application of the various media, as well as a particular scepticism about politics and other institutionalised forms of organisation. For discussions of Zaimoglu's work in the context of *Popliteratur* see Cheesman (2002, 2004) and Ernst (2005).

31. A year later Maxim Biller topped Zaimoglu's term 'Knabenwindelprosa' by categorising *Popliteratur* as 'flaccid dick literature' ['Schlappschwanz-Literatur'] (Biller 2000). Both writers stay in the same masculinist-corporeal register. By dismissing Von Stuckrad-Barre's work as lamenting 'school boys' reports' ['Schulbubenreporte'] Zaimoglu implicitly claims a more mature and worldly character for his own writing. Whereas the *Pop* writers are just playing around and having fun, Zaimoglu claims a more serious writer attitude for himself, including socio-political commitment. Cheesman (2004) nevertheless contends that *Popliteratur* (and the media spectacle that comes with this brand of writing) offers a fitting frame for the interpretation of Zaimoglu's literature, including the *Kanak* phenomenon.

32. 'Ich bringe die Brüche, die Häßlichkeiten, die Beschmutztheit, all das, was in der lauen Mittelstandsneurosenschreibe der deutschen Literatur – zumal der Popliteraten nicht enthalten ist.'

33. 'Am Ende des 20. Jahrhunderts taucht also die wahre Männlichkeit zumindest rhetorisch wieder ins Stahlbad ein.' Inge Stephan maintains that '"masculinity as performance", respectively, doing masculinity is a "style-forming activity" of ambivalent character' ['"Männlichkeit als Performanz" bzw. doing masculinity eine "stilbildende Aktivität" ist, die einen ambivalenten Charakter hat'] (2003: 22). The ambivalence in doing *Kanak* hypermasculinity lies in the simultaneous confirmation and subversion of the cultural stereotype of the potent and criminal Turkish-German male.

34. 'Wir dagegen haben nix außer unsere Eier zu verlieren.'

35. 'Zudem bedient der Autor in Artikeln und Auftritten mehr und mehr ein exotisierendes Bedürfnis nach metropolitaner Ghettoromantik – eben nach einer Kultur, die "erregend anders" (*Spiegel*) ist.'

36. See also Çağlar (1998), El-Tayeb et al. (2005), Ha (1999: 149-168), and Römhild (2005). Masquerade, mimicry, transvestism and drag have become key fields of interest for scholars interested in performative practices of resistance to and subversion of coercive identities. Katrin Sieg's study of 'ethnic drag' offers interesting insights in the particular performance of race or ethnicity as masquerade. She argues about the above-mentioned forms of subversion: 'These poststructuralist strategies all hinge on the severing of signifier and signified, act and essence, performer and mask, in order to contest the truth claims undergirding mimesis, identity, and the structuring of social orders around innate, supposedly "natural" differences' (Sieg 2002: 15).

37. Followers of Zaimoglu's figure of the *Kanake* are the comedian Kaya Yanar, the ethno-comedy Erkan & Stefan, and the *Sprakkurse Kanakisch* [*Kanak talk language courses*] by Michael Freidank (2001a, 2001b).

38. 'Der Aufstieg einer Beleidigung zur Ordenskategorie geht auf Zaimoglu zurück. Er verschaffte dem Schimpfwort Kanake eine Karriere.'

39. '[Die Immigranten] sind geblieben, weil es sich lohnte zu bleiben in diesem Land.' The marketing discourse on the work's dust jacket tries to keep up the initial, success-

ful format. It claims that *Kanak Sprak* has brought about a change in the German literature and that Feridun Zaimoglu, 'rebel among belletrists' ['Rebell unter den Literaten'], now guarantees for a new dose of angry protest. However, although the essence of the essay still comprises a fierce critique of suppressive social structures, the critique is no longer wrapped in aggression. A resolute but conciliatory spirit has replaced the outright anger that characterised the early *Kanak* work.

40. Since *Kopf und Kragen* Zaimoglu has published several novels on neither *Kanak*, nor particular migrant themes. In response to the reserved reception of this 'general' writing Zaimoglu maintains: 'I can't get rid of the suspicion that for some people I am a galleon figure of new migrant literature, and this galleon figure is not allowed to change course too much in the direction of migrant-unspecific stories' ['Ich werde den Verdacht nicht los, daß ich für bestimmte Leute eine Gallionsfigur der neueren Migrantenliteratur bin, und diese Gallionsfigur darf jetzt nicht zu sehr umschwenken auf migranten-unspezifische Geschichten'] (Zaimoglu in Meyer 2001). This remark concurs with Hafid Bouazza's objections to the ethnicisation of his work.

41. 'Die vermeintlichen kulturellen Musterländer wie Holland und Frankreich sind abgebrannt.'

42. 'Im Anfang war ich der Türkenjunge, heute bin ich ein deutscher Schriftsteller. Das habe ich meinen Eltern und Deutschland zu verdanken. Ich habe viel Glück gehabt.'

43. Zaimoglu continues his public praise of Germany, for instance in contributions with titles as 'Der Liebe zu Deutschland nicht schämen' ['To not be ashamed of love for Germany'] (2006a) and 'Für all das liebe ich Deutschland' ['For all that I love Germany'] (2006b). The acknowledgement of Zaimoglu as a German writer seems to coincide with the depoliticisation of his literary work, or, maybe more appropriate, its adaptation to dominant discourse. Arguably Zaimoglu's highly acclaimed novel *Leyla* (2006c), a coming of age narrative of a Turkish girl, offers an insightful example of this discursive assimilation. Its story seamlessly fits in with the current discourse on Islamic culture and its popular interest in 'authentic' stories about female victims of Muslim patriarchy. It ties in with the discursive shift from the emasculated guest worker 'Ali', via the masculinist *Kanak* youngster, to the suppressed Muslim woman as the iconic figure for the German Other. See also Mecklenburg (2006) and Şenocak (2006) on the cultural stir that branded Zaimoglu's *Leyla* after accusations of plagiarism. The central concern of the literary press in this alleged case of plagiarism was – once again – the question of authenticity. Authenticity appears as the main marker of distinction and the dominant criterion in the appreciation of 'migrants' literature'. Şenocak speaks of a 'generalisability of Turkish migrant adventures' ['Verallgemeinerbarkeit türkischer Migrantenschicksale'] in the literary press.

44. Zaimoglu himself puts the word 'protocols' (KS 15) in inverted commas, thus opening up a space for doubt about the semantic suitability of the term.

45. By using the format of the interview with the outsider Zaimoglu inscribes himself in a particular (semi-) literary tradition. Literary predecessors as Erika Runge's *Bottroper Protokolle* (1968), Sarah Kirsch's *Die Pantherfrau. Fünf unfrisierte Erzählungen aus dem Kassetten-Recorder* (1973), Maxie Wander's women's portraits in *Guten Morgen, du Schöne* (1977) and also Hans Eppendorfer's *Der Ledermann spricht mit Hubert Fichte* (1977) present a similar, documentarist starting situation. The bilingual work *Deutsches Heim – Glück*

allein: Wie Türken Deutsche sehen. Alaman Ocağı: Türkler Almanları anlatıyor (1982) by Dursun Akçam is an example of a precursor that concerns the similar group of males of Turkish origin in German society. See Cheesman (2002). All examples offer a series of (more or less) unedited interviews that are supposed to offer the reader insight in a subcultural or marginal world that normally does not disclose itself to the reader's eye. They all cater to the reader's basic curiosity for the 'authentic' voice of the outsider.

46. In his study *The Postcolonial Exotic* (2001) Graham Huggan devotes a chapter on the theme of ethnic autobiography and the cult of authenticity connected to it. Although Huggan focuses on (hyped) postcolonial literature, his arguments apply to migrant writing in Germany as well. Huggan argues that literary work by writers of minority background is generally (or best) marketed as autobiographical. In the case of minority writing, authenticity functions as a quality label, a promise of access to exotic other worlds. Independent of a work's specific content, migrant writing is ethnicised and commodified as such. Zaimoglu's interviews with 'authentic' *Kanaken* perfectly fit in with this trend.

47. In an interview with Marit Hofman, Zaimoglu insists: 'I was *Kanake* before my books and I will also be so afterwards' ['Vor meinen Bücher war ich Kanake und werde es auch danach sein'] (Zaimoglu in Hofman 1999: 189). Nevertheless it is important to underline the author-character Zaimoglu's social mobility: in contrast to his *Kanak* interviewees, for Zaimoglu his 'equal' participation in the 'Lumpen-Hades' is just a temporary project. Despite his *Kanak* familiarity or even identity, he also designates himself as 'stranger' ['Fremde'] in the *Kanak* underworld (KS 15).

48. 'Hier stehe ich und gebe mit allem, was ich bin, zu verstehen: Ich zeige und erzeuge Präsenz.'

49. 'Ich bin nicht der Türkenfeldforscher, der mal kurz rübergemacht hat in die Ballungsviertel, ins Kanakenghetto, um da das Elend der Diskothekenverbrecher, der Spielotheken-Machmods, der Jacken-Abzocker anzuzapfen und nachher zu sagen: Tschüs – ich geh dann.'

50. Manuela Günter (1999) considers ethnicisation as a strategy that reconstructs the dichotomy of Self and Other in an affirmative way. She writes: 'the strategy of ethnicisation by the use of the label 'Turkish' must be repeated again and again to make the Other actually visible as such' ['stets muß nämlich die Strategie der Ethnisierung durch die Markierung als 'türkisch' wiederholt werden, damit der/die Andere als solche(r) überhaupt sichtbar werden kann'] (Günter 1999: 15/16). Zaimoglu's strategy of (pseudo-)ethnicisation stands in striking contrast to the position that the Moroccan-Dutch Hafid Bouazza almost synchronically claims in the Dutch cultural field. Whereas he, as laid out in the previous chapter, vehemently resists all ethnicising tendencies in the reception of his literary debut, Zaimoglu takes up the public interest in the (ethnic) Other and caters to this fascination.

51. Undoubtedly, *Kanak* talk is the aspect of Zaimoglu's debut that has attracted most attention in the public sphere. This popularity of the *Kanak* language can also be assessed in the academic research on Zaimoglu's work. See, for instance, Abel (2005), Mein (2004), Skiba (2004), and Yildiz (2004). Many studies focus on the assumed authenticity or poetic artificiality of the work's language.

52. The importance of language as aspect of identity is another aspect that *Kanak* literature and resistance literature have in common: 'The very choice of the language in which to compose is itself a political statement on the part of the writer' (Harlow 1987: xviii). Zaimoglu's recurrence to the claim of authenticity reeffectuates a persistent and much-criticised criterion in the assessment and appreciation of migrant writing. Günter (1999) argues that: 'obviously, by legitimating his texts as interviews Zaimoglu answers to a norm which has served as a standard of the so-called 'guest worker literature' from the beginning: authenticity (in the sense of genuineness and affliction) as a means to construct the Other as the exotic' ['In der Legitimierung der Texte als Interviews antwortet Zaimoglu allerdings auf eine Norm, die die sogenannte 'Gastarbeiterliteratur' von Anfang an begleitet hat: diejenige der Authentizität (im Sinne von Echtheit und Betroffenheit), mit deren Hilfe das Andere als das Exotische konstruiert wird'] (1999: 17). Yasemin Yildiz argues that '[t]his use of the vernacular locates the text in a specific German region, rather than in the nation at large. Within the monologues the local region is frequently evoked as a point of reference (...). Such a local affiliation is not unusual for ethnic minorities globally and seems to offer a site of belonging alternative to the nation' (2004: 326).

53. '[d]ie sprachliche Manifestation unserer Mobilmachung'.

54. Both rap and *Kanak* talk are criticised for their violent character as performative languages. The *Kanak* protocols exceed the boundaries of the politically correct and balance on the edge of the social permissible. Günter argues that with their aggressive language, the *Kanaken* respond to their marginalisation and to the discursive violence that 'their social constitution as "Turks"' ['ihrer gesellschaftlichen Konstitution als "Türken"'] (1999: 23) involves. Pfaff argues that 'Zaimoglu's attention-getting poetic language and language mixture in the *Kanak Sprak* books is itself a significant part of the message in a genre which might be called "poetic polemic"' (2005: 222). The agitating and at times violent content of both rap and the performative *Kanak* talk also raises critique. According to the *Kanak Sprak* preface, however, Russell Potter's defence of rap's violent speech applies to the *Kanak* situation as well. Potter argues that 'those who attack hip-hop for "violence" have not yet accounted for the interpretive or cultural contexts in which they already *consume* violence' (1995: 86). Ayşe Çağlar points out the centrality of hegemonic German discourse in the violent language of Turkish-German rap: 'All this once again illustrates the assumption of many mainstream categories of hegemonic discourse about German-Turks by German-Turkish rappers. German-Turkish rap stylises itself by way of the categories of the centre' ['All das illustriert ein weiteres Mal die Übernahme vieler Mainstream-Kategorien des hegemonialen Diskurses über Deutsch-Türken durch deutsch-türkische Rapper. Deutsch-türkischer Rap stilisierte sich über die Kategorien des Zentrums'] (1998: 48).

55. This procedure can be seen as Zaimoglu's attempt to enable the *Kanak* subaltern to speak by providing the *Kanaken* both the means and the discourse (compare Spivak 1993). Adelson points out that '[i]n this sense, *Kanak Sprak* challenges the cultural icon of the Turkish migrant whose powers of speech fail him in Germany' (2005: 97).

56. This division is especially interesting in the light of the protocols' violent language: who is responsible for their hurtful impact? Günter assumes that this mystification,

the indefiniteness in terms of authorship, has contributed decisively to *Kanak Sprak's* broad public resonance (1999: 17).

57. Translation: Cheesman (2004: 94/95).

58. Ha presents a literal transcription of the broadcasting in his article 'Sprechakte – Sprachattakken' (2003: 143-149). An earlier, less accurate transcription was published anonymously under the title 'Erbe und Auftrag – Bemerkungen zu einem rassistischen Auftritt' in the journal *Karoshi* (1999).

59. 'Ich habe die Befürchtung, dass Sie überhaupt kein Kanake sind, dass das nur eine Pose ist. Ja, ich möchte wissen, was an Ihnen echt ist. (...) Was sind Sie wirklich?'

60. Compare Potter's statement about the role of ethnicity or race in the social reception of the outsider: 'When the outlaw is white, it seems, he is a counterculture hero; when he is black, he is reduced to yet another avatar of the stereotypical violent black male' (Potter 1995: 88).

61. 'Alle Versuche, anhand der publizierten Texten die ursprünglichen Gespräche zu rekonstruieren, müssen weitgehend spekulativ bleiben. Da Zaimoglu die Bänder löschte, schloß er die Möglichkeit aus, Transkriptionen der Interviews anzufertigen und diese mit den literarisierten Protokollen zu vergleichen.'

62. 'Daher verwundert es kaum, daß [Zaimoglu] vor Durchführung der Interviews große Skepsis entgegenschlug.'

63. Hestermann (2003) writes the title of Zaimoglu's debut as one word: *Kanaksprak*.

64. '*Wie lebt es sich als Kanake in Deutschland*, war die Frage, die ich mir und anderen gestellt habe' (KS 9). Italics in original.

65. On the one hand author-character Zaimoglu hints at a *Kanak* identity that he shares with his interviewees. He too is able to tell what life as a *Kanake* in Germany is like. On the other hand the phrase asking oneself a question also refers to the idea of investigating a particular issue; Looking for answers to a question that occupies one's mind. As Zaimoglu's own personal answer to the question in the form of a protocol is missing, the second possibility lies most at hand. Nevertheless, the identificatory bonding between him and the interviewed *Kanaken* (as discussed in the previous section) already commences in *Kanak Sprak's* opening sentence. Zaimoglu only asks his question to male *Kanaken*. In the preface he 'justifies' this absence of female voices with a resigned, stereotype-confirming explanation: 'She is placed under house arrest, cut off from the outside world and out of every stranger's reach – and so also of mine' ['Sie steht unter Hausarrest, von der außenwelt abgeschnitten und für jeden Fremden, somit auch für mich unerreichbar'] (KS 15). The later work *Koppstoff* tries to make up for this absence of female voices.

66. 'Wie lebt es sich hier in deiner Haut?'

67. The term '*Alemanen*', used as an epithet comparable to *Kanaken* in *Kanak* colloquial, is one of the few word creations in *Kanak* talk that is of Turkish lingual origin. Also see Adelson (2005), Cheesman (2002), Pfaff (2005), and Yildiz (2004). As with the term '*Kanake*' I use the pejorative '*Alemane*' in italics to dissociate my usage from its hate speech application.

68. Adelson (2000b, 2005) takes an alternative approach to Zaimoglu's *Kanak Sprak*. She investigates the question: 'How does [*Kanak Sprak*] weave a genocidal legacy and ongoing cultural taboos surrounding the Holocaust into a story of Turkish migration?'

(Adelson 2005: 96). Adelson maintains that the *Kanaken's* 'defiant rhetoric of abjection bespeaks something unsettled within German culture' that 'exceeds German prejudices vis-à-vis young Turkish men on the edge' (ibid. 100).

69. 'Der alemanne is 'n elend.' This pointed remark appears in the protocol of 'Fikret, 25, unemployed' (KS 78-83), but fits the discourse in most of the other protocols as well. Ha explains the macho behaviour or the pose of extremely potent masculinity on the side of the *Kanak* male as a form of compensation for their actual lack of power (1999: 45-63).

70. 'jamaicanigger, schmalzlatino, yankee-nigger'. Most *Kanaken* make use of the hate speech terminology of dominant discourse. The *Kanake* Abdurrahman comments on what he calls the 'multikultiliste', a racist hierarchy of favoured ethnic minorities. According to his opinion the *Kanake* is positioned at the very bottom of this list (KS 22). See also Minnaard (2004).

71. Compare Bogdal (2000) and McGowan (2001).

72. 'Ich spiel in der liga der verdammten.'

73. 'ochsige alemanne (...) mit blondem busch auf'm schädel und nullmannesstolz talent im leib'.

74. A straightforward racist vocabulary, sexist language and highly problematic essentialisms (for instance in respect to 'skin') are characteristic for most of the protocols.

75. The protocol of 'Memet, 29, poet' (KS 108-114) represents a striking exception in the general communifying *Kanak* discourse. He relates about 'the *Kanake*' in a rather distanced mode and in a cultivated standard German. When he states 'They are the real riff-raff' ['Sie sind das wahre lumpenproletariat'] (KS 109), he clearly dissociates himself from the group that he is referring to. Nevertheless, his position is ambivalent, as he does identify with the *Kanak*-ised position of Turkish-German males in society as the repeated use of the first-person plural in this matter indicates. His profound reflections, his literary profession, and the parallels between his meta-position and analysis and that of author-character Zaimoglu suggest a certain congeniality between the two quasi-*Kanaken*. Memet more or less appears as Zaimoglu's alter ego.

76. This homogenising move is endorsed by the fact that 'other' Turkish-German voices – other in the sense of 'of other opinion', but also female voices and the voices of the first generation of Turkish labour migrants – do hardly sound at all. The few deviant *Kanak* voices get lost in the verbal violence of this dominant *Kanak* discourse. In this sense I do not quite agree with Christian Begemann who insists on a variety of *Kanak* self-representations as a result of the fact that *Kanak* talk 'leaves scope for numerous variations – from the jargon of the pimp to that of the Islamist' ['Spielraum für zahlreiche Varianten läßt – vom Jargon des Zuhälters bis zu dem des Islamisten'] (1999: 218).

77. I use the German '*du*' instead of the English 'you' in order to prevent confusion caused by the homonymy of the second-person pronoun in the singular and plural form in the English language.

78. Herman focuses on Edna O'Brien's novel *A Pagan Place* (1970). This novel is an example of a second-person narration, a narrative entirely told in the second person. Obviously this is not the case for *Kanak Sprak*.

79. The use of the phrase 'brand on your forehead' ['brandstempel auf der stirn'] offers another example of 'touching tales' in the *Kanak* protocols. It evokes memories of both the Holocaust (as 'burnt offering' ['Brandopfer']) and the history of slavery as two histories of violently and literally marking Otherness. For an elaboration on the idea of 'touching tales' of *Kanaken* and Jews in *Kanak Sprak* see Adelson (2000b, 2005: 95-104).

80. Throughout the protocols the use of the 'you plural' ['ihr'] as a form of address oscillates in reference between 'you other *Kanaken*' and 'you intellectual readers'.

81. When readers consider themselves as members of the *Kanak* community, the process of identification obviously proceeds differently. To my assumption, however, the majority of the German readership does not identify as *Kanake*.

82. My conclusion of *Kanak* 'mono-frequency' ['Monofrequenz'] (Zaimoglu in Tuschick 1998) contradicts Günter's discussion of *Kanak Sprak* as an example of polyphonia (Günter 1999: 18). Although I agree with her that *Kanak Sprak* claims to offer a multi-vocal representation of *Kanak* identity, I am of the opinion that the promise of diversity and differentiation is not realised.

83. The four 'discord voices' constitute an important, but in terms of media effectivity hardly audible exception. Their protocols demand further investigation.

84. *Abschaum's* ('authentic') myth of origin claims that the young Turkish-German delinquent Ertan approached Zaimoglu to write down his life story after he had heard him read *Kanak Sprak* in prison.

85. 'Mann, hab das Zeugs also geraucht, auf einmal voll breit geworden. Vielleicht kam das auch wie gerufen, weil ich so fertig war und ich nicht verkraften konnte, daß ich so allein bin und so. Jedenfalls hab ich's genommen, das war das erste Mal.'

86. 'Dann hab ich gemerkt, jetzt bist du drauf, jetzt bist du gefickt, mein junge, jetzt sieh mal zu, wie du da rauskommst. Jetzt bist du am Arsch, Alter, yarrağı yedin oğlum, aynaya bakıyodum böyle ve yarrağı yedin oğlum diyodum. Ich kuckte innen Spiegel und sagte: Jetzt bist du gefickt.' The act of looking in the mirror in combination with a situation of growing self-awareness and moments of insight is classical. In Lacanian psychoanalysis the mirror-phase is considered of crucial importance for the constitution of the subject. Ertan's moment of insight when looking at himself in the mirror, prefigures a more elaborate mirror-scene in the last, almost-apocalyptic story. Here Ertan's gaze at himself in the mirror is connected to a negative moment of self-insight: 'In the morning I look into the mirror and see myself, and that's it, that's my life' ['morgens schau ich innen Spiegel und sehe mich, und das wars dann, das is mein leben'] (AB 179). The moments that Ertan takes refuge in the Turkish language (slang and proverbs) mostly coincide with moments of growing discontent. For Ertan this move also assures a certain distance towards (the majority of) his German readership for whom the Turkish phrases remain formulaic.

87. Petra Fachinger (2001) ascertains an analogy between the political strategy of rap and Zaimoglu's imagination of criminal *Kanaken*. She argues that this depiction is a response to dominant German discourse that often associates a Turkish origin with criminal involvement of some kind: 'By appropriating notions of criminality for black identity, rappers turn delinquency into a metaphor for power. Similarly, Zaimoglu depicts *Kanaksta* involvement with drugs, prostitution, and theft to signify self-identifica-

tion and liberation from "German" attempts to contain the image of the "Turk"' (Fachinger 2001: 102).

88. Ertan recalls the situation and quotes his father in direct speech. In this quote – 'I know, nothing will ever be made of you' ['ich weiß, aus dir wird nix mehr'] (AB 114) – the deictic roles of the personal pronouns are turned around.

89. The discrepancy between this respectful representation of the 'cool' attitude of the father and the respectless representation of the father generation and their affected 'guest worker literature' in *Kanak Sprak* is remarkable.

90. 'meine letzte Story erzählen, dir, Alter, und dem Scheißgerät'.

91. 'Glaub mir, Alter, glaub mir, es gibt nur zwei Sachen in Deutschland: einmal der Dreck und einmal die Nullachtfuffzehngesellschaft. Und weißt du was, ich scheiß auf die Gesellschaft. Da, im Dreck, da war ich wenigstens wer, da war ich Abschaum, weißt du, und jetzt geh ich so unter.'

92. 'für euch Ärsche da draußen, die ihr das lest, is das wien Roman, amına koyum, ihr könnt das gar nicht nachvollziehen, das geht ja gar nicht, was ich da durchgemacht hab.' In the last story Ertan not only explicitly addresses his readers, but he also reflects on their future reception of his stories. He reproaches the readers for their 'fascination with the criminalized subject, fascination with the wild Other, fascination for those who come from the lowest of the low (...), fascination with misery' ['Faszination durchs kriminelle Subjekt, Faszination durchs wilde Andere, Faszination für die, die von ganz unten kommen (...), Faszination Elend']. He continues by pointing out the affective gap between his readers and himself: 'It might be fascination for you lot, but for me it's just shit, everything's shit' ['Für euch mag das ne Faszination sein, aber für mich ist es nur Scheiße, is alles Scheiße'] (AB 180). Translation: Cheesman (2004: 89).

93. 'Wie definiert man sowas wie mich?'

94. 'Das wars dann. Kein Bock mehr.'

95. 'Ertan Ongun lebt zur Zeit der Fertigstellung dieses Buches in Kiel, und er ist clean. Er ist 25 Jahre alt, in Deutschland geboren und aufgewachsen, und es ist seine Geschichte: Er hat sie mir erzählt, die Geschichte eines Kanaken, eines Drogenabhängigen, eines Gangsters.'

96. This phrase is a reference to the best-selling work *Wir Kinder vom Bahnhof Zoo* (1981) that tells the story of the drug-addicted teenaged prostitute Christiane F. The work uses a similar format as *Kanak Sprak*: *Stern*-reporters Kai Hermann and Horst Rieck acted as ghostwriters and wrote down the story of Christiane F.'s life at Zoo Station after recordings.

97. 'Ertans Botschaft ist: Wir sind die Kanaken, vor denen ihr Deutschen immer gewarnt habt. Jetzt gibt es uns, ganz eurem Bild und euren Ängsten entsprechend.'

98. 'Nicht Identitätspauschalen, sondern Identitätsbrüche lassen literarisches Neuland entstehen.'

VI. Abdelkader Benali
'Als de wereld gek wordt en iedereen zijn woorden kwijt is' (Benali in Peters 2004).

1. 'Dat is mijn familie, dacht Lamarat, en het komt nooit meer goed.'
2. The Geertjan Lubberhuizen Prize is awarded to the best Dutch debut of the year. The annual Libris Literature Prize is one of the most important literary prizes for prose work in the Netherlands and Belgium.
3. As I argue in the chapter on national identity, Fortuyn strongly profited from (and contributed to) the political polarisation that evolved in the wake of 9/11.
4. In fact this intermediate silence was only a partial silence, as Benali published several smaller pieces of literature (including two works of drama). Nevertheless, the period of 'waiting' for the second *novel* was publicly staged as a (symbolic) silence.
5. The 1997 Libris Literature Prize was awarded to Hugo Claus for his novel *De geruchten*.
6. Compare Minnaard (2001).
7. Among other minor prizes, Benali won the El Hizjra writing contests in the years 1994 and 1995.
8. Ton Brouwers (2004) counts nineteen impressions (hardcover and paperback) in the period between the novel's first publication in October 1996 and the summer of 2003. The novel was awarded the 'Prix du Meilleur Premier Roman Étranger' 1999 and nominated for the IMPAC International Dublin Literary Award.
9. See Anbeek (1999, 2002) and Pam (2003). When Benali actually won the Libris Literature Prize 2003 for his second novel *De Langverwachte* this critique was repeated in intensified form.
10. All translations of citations from interviews, reviews and the drama *Onrein* are my own.
11. Several reviewers present citations of 'failures' as proof of this critique, for instance, Vullings (1997).
12. In her article 'Zwartrijders in de Nederlandse literatuur: het motief van de queeste in de migrantenliteratuur' (2001) Henriëtte Louwerse offers a comparative analysis of the two travel-stories *De weg naar het Noorden* by the Moroccan-Dutch Naima El Bezaz and Benali's *Bruiloft aan zee*.
13. Benali expresses his admiration for the work of Salman Rushdie in interviews with Bel (2000), Dijkgraaf and Meijer (2002), Pos (1997), and Schutte (1997). In my opinion Dutch critics dismiss Benali's establishment of a link between his work and that of Rushdie too easily as an instance of youthful hubris. They seem to think that the listed 'failures' in Benali's work suffice to demonstrate that it belongs to another league. A more thorough analysis or substantial arguments that refute Benali's self-claimed position in the literary landscape fail to appear.
14. In his contribution to *Het beslissende boek* (Dijkgraaf and Meijer 2002), a collection of interviews with Dutch writers about the book that has been of decisive impact on their writing, Benali discusses Salman Rushdie's *The Satanic Verses*. He praises this highly contested work as a masterpiece of literature and, by doing so, takes position in an ideological debate on freedom of speech and hurtful language. He opposes the fatwa pronounced by Ayatollah Khomeini and pleads for a valuation of the work's literary qualities.

15. The distinction between postcolonial and postmodern literature is not always clear, as their boundaries are fluid and sometimes their 'territories' overlap. Studies of Dutch literature generally use a definition of postcolonial literature that restricts the field to literature by writers from or otherwise connected to the former Dutch colonies. Literature of Moroccan labour migration falls outside of this category. One exception to this can be found in an analysis by Herbert van Uffelen (2004b) in which he discusses the work of both Benali and Bouazza as representative of 'standard' (postmodern) Dutch literature of the early twenty-first century. He argues that the idea of uprootedness is not specific for literature of migration, but for literature of our time in general. All this literature focuses on the 'being in the moment' of subjects that are continually in process. Compare Cheesman's remarks on 'axialism' as common currency within international modernism and postmodernism (2006: 478/479). See also Van Uffelen (2004a).

16. The translations of the citations from Bruiloft aan zee originate from Susan Massotty's English translation of the novel: Wedding by the Sea (1999b). For citations from the two works I use the notations BZ and WS.

17. Frans Roggen (1997) suggests that the name Lamarat is a pun and can also be read as a rather negative character description: Lamarat as 'lamme rat' which means 'sluggish rat'.

18. The references to this second house function as prefigurations of the dramatic outcome of the agreed upon transaction. Already in the phase of construction the house shows the first signs of decline. The double meaning of house (as home and family) is telling in this respect. The second house in Morocco counts as a contemporary trope in literature of labour migration. It resonates the dream of prosperity and return of the first generation. Rosemarie Buikema and Maaike Meijer refer to stories on themes related to (dreams and reality of) labour migration as 'new-Dutch classics' ['nieuw-Nederlandse klassiekers'] (2004: 14).

19. As a major example of the metafictional commentaries, Louwerse (2001: 176/177) discusses the repeated reference to the metaphor of the 'doll house'. Both Lamarat and the extradiegetic narrator assume that in a doll house, relations between people are clearly structured. They long for similar convenient arrangements themselves.

20. A fitting translation of Chalid's nickname 'Chalid Blik op de Weg' is not so easy, as the Dutch use of the word 'Blik' contains a pun. The homonym can mean both 'view' and 'tin can', resulting in the simultaneous meaning of 'Chalid view/tin can on the road'. Whereas the 'View on the Road' variant indicates a trustworthy driver, the 'tin can' option constitutes a rather derogative and untrustworthy indication of the condition of Chalid's car.

21. Chalid for instance knows about the birth of Lamarat before the father himself knows about it: it is the taxi driver who informs him that he has become the father of a son (BZ 29). On the other hand, as Benali himself writes in 'Het ABC van Bruiloft aan zee' [The ABC of Wedding by the Sea], published in Berichten uit Maanzaad Stad: 'C is correct: is Bucket of Bolts Chalid a correct narrator? No, ladies and gentlemen, he is not' ['C is Correct: is Chalid Blik op de Weg een correcte verteller? Nee, dames en heren, dat is hij níet'] (2001: 7).

22. 'In die taxi zei de taxichauffeur – de iets jongere, maar al met een gebit in staat van verval, Chalid Blik op de Weg – altijd in voor een praatje, tegen de nog prille vader: "Dus jij gaat naar Duitsland, hmm"' (BZ 75).

23. The epilogue of *Bruiloft aan zee* briefly lists the 'final life destinies' of the several characters. Chalid, so the narrator, is said to have founded a magazine called 'Blik op de Wereld', literally translated as 'View on the World'. This destiny seems to do justice to his 'worldly wisdom'. The English translation as 'Bucket of Gold' clearly gives preference to the sonic contiguity to Chalid's name over the content of the wordplay. See also footnote 20.

24. The name 'Nadorp' is a playful combination of the Moroccan city named Nador and the Dutch word 'dorp' for village. The border city 'Melilliar' where Mosa visits his favourite prostitute Chatischa, is a fictive variation of the Spanish colonial city in North Morocco named Melilla.

25. 'Sesame Seed City' is the alliterating 'translation' of 'Maanzaad Stad' (BZ 55), which literally means 'poppy seed city'. 'Maanzaad Stad' appears as the literary equivalent to Rotterdam in several of Benali's works. See Vlaskamp (1997).

26. 'Hij bleef een jaar, twee jaar, tien jaar en uiteindelijk zat hij al dertig jaar bij elke vleesmaaltijd te verkondigen dat dit jaar het laatste zou zijn: "Ik ga terug, voorgoed. Weg uit dit land van *chelloef* en rotte bananen"' (BZ 27).

27. 'Ik ben jullie vader, de alfa en de omega weetjewel' (BZ 27). For example, the father repeatedly makes the following statement without any action preceding from it: 'it's darn well time for a darn bit of Islam in this house: from now on we are going to change some things' (WS 64) ['het wordt potverdorie tijd voor potverdorie wat islam in dit huis: van nu af aan gaan we een paar dingetjes veranderen' (BZ 58)].

28. 'een ijsje, een kusje en een gouden kettinkje vergezeld van een omhelzing totdat ze niets anders kon uitbrengen dan: "Ja, maar ik wil wel zelfstandig blijven. Ja, maar je moet me met respect behandelen. Ja, maar hoe weet ik dat je niet een beetje jokt"' (BZ 94).

29. Again the narrator seems to warn for that which is yet to come. His repetitive references to the house's fundamental corrosion function as hints for the reader. They symbolically prefigure the disputable status of the agreement as well as its doubtable outcome.

30. 'Im Normalismus läßt sich die Hauptfunktion von Kunst und Literatur als Bereitstellung von Applikations-Vorlagen für Denormalisierungen (z.B. 'Marginalisierungen') begreifen.'

31. The old Dutch children's song that is referred to originally goes: 'We gaan naar Zandvoort, al aan de zee. We nemen broodjes en koffie mee' ['We go to Zandvoort at the sea. We take sandwiches and coffee with us'].

32. Susan Massotty has translated the Dutch term 'jongen', literally meaning 'boy', 'youth', 'lad' (*Van Dale Nederlands-Engels* 1999), with the term 'young man'. This translation causes a considerable loss of meaning as the following analysis of the used terminology for the threesome makes clear. The German translation *Hochzeit am Meer* (1998) by Gregor Seferens retains the original meaning of the Dutch word.

33. Here again a striking shift in meaning as a result of the translation occurs. Whereas the English translation speaks of 'the sacrifice', the Dutch original reads 'your sacrifice'. The Dutch text puts more emphasis on Mosa's part in the drama.

34. Examples of similar current issues of debate are honour revenge and honour killings, (institutionalised) wife battering and the genital mutilation of girls.

35. Compare the section on the 'multicultural drama' as well as the section on Bouazza and his critique of 'Dutch blindness'.

36. In fact, Benali published several smaller pieces of work in this period in between: a collection of short prose *Berichten uit Maanzaad Stad* (2001) and two works of drama: *De Ongelukkige* (1999a) and *Jasser. Een monoloog* (2002b). The last piece was awarded the triennial Mr. H.G. van der Vlies Prize 2002 for new original Dutch theatre. *Berichten uit Maanzaad Stad* concludes with a fictive press release that parodies the public waiting for the ultimate Moroccan novel. It uses exactly the same Orientalist and strongly ethnicised language that characterised the reception of Benali's *Bruiloft aan zee*.

37. In an interview with Marije Vlaskamp in *Het Parool* six years before, Benali already used a similar argument. At that time he answered her question as to whether he could be considered 'the allochthon' of the publishing house as follows: 'The categorisation allochthonous-autochthonous is nonsensical both on a literary and a human level. I can't say anything about it that seems not said with feigned indifference. Really, I'm concerned about the credits for my book, not about my origin' ['De indeling allochtoon-autochtoon is onzinnig op literair en menselijk niveau. Ik kan er niets over zeggen zonder dat het lijkt dat ik er met gespeelde onverschilligheid over praat. Echt, het gaat mij om mijn eigen krediet voor het boek, niet om mijn afkomst'] (Benali in Vlaskamp 1997).

38. Colour obviously refers to skin colour here. The dangerously deterministic connection between colour and ethnicity is common usage in popular discourse. Benali assumes the problematic connection here as well.

39. See Peters (2004) and Scheldwacht (2002).

40. The first fundamental right in the Dutch Constitution forbids discrimination on various grounds: 'All persons in the Netherlands shall be treated equally in equal circumstances. Discrimination on the grounds of religion, belief, political opinion, race or sex or on any other grounds whatsoever shall not be permitted' ['Allen die zich in Nederland bevinden, worden in gelijke gevallen gelijk behandeld. Discriminatie wegens godsdienst, levensovertuiging, politieke gezindheid, ras, geslacht of op welke grond dan ook, is niet toegestaan'].

41. 'dringend behoefte aan originele nieuwe antwoorden op wat het betekent om Nederlander te zijn' and 'Benali's oproep staat nog recht overeind.'

42. In one of his book reviews he writes about the apparent fate of the migrant writer: 'It is bitter when an artist who has created a work of the imagination, all of a sudden realises that the public is mostly interested in the Sahara yellow and the Moroccan blue' ['Het is bitter als een kunstenaar die een werk uit de verbeelding heeft gemaakt, plotseling ziet dat men vooral oog heeft voor het Sahara-geel en Marokko-blauw'] (2004c: 26).

43. The Libris Literature Prize awards a monetary grant of 50,000 euros. The members of the 2003 jury were Onno Blom, Hugo Brems, Kees 't Hart, Ingrid Hoogervorst, and Jeltje van Nieuwenhoven as their chairwoman.
44. 'een weids panorama van de gehele gekleurde hedendaagse samenleving'.
45. See Pam (2003, 2005), Speet (2003), and Vanegeren (2003a).
46. The critic Bart Vanegeren wrote in *Humo*: 'after all, the award of the premature book of an alibi-Abdelkader is not at all meant to the greater honour and glory of the laureate, but of the jury itself' ['de bekroning van het premature boek van een alibi-Abdelkader is immers helemaal niet bedoeld ter meerdere eer en glorie van de gelauwerde, maar van de jury zelf'] (Vanegeren 2003a). See also Benali's response in Vuijsje (2003).
47. 'Een jury bekroont het beste boek, niet het boek van een prijzenswaardige allochtoon. Mocht die omstandigheid een overweging zijn geweest, dan ben ik alsnog bereid de prijs, inclusief het geld, direct in te leveren.'
48. This drama was commissioned by Braches CS and Toneelschuur Producties and was performed in several Dutch theatres in the winter of 2003/2004. The performance of the drama was directed by Ernst Braches of Toneelschuur Producties and performed by the actors Sabri Saad El Hamus (the father), Mohammed Azaay (the son) and Servaes Nelissen (the dog).
49. The *Biblion Literom* does not list any reviews of *Onrein*. Hermans (2004), Oranje (2003), and Schmitz (2003) review the performance of the drama by theatre company De Toneelschuur.
50. Benali remains a regular contributor to the ongoing discourse on the Dutch multicultural society (e.g. Benali 2004a, 2004b; Van Dam 2002; Groen 2003). After the murder of Theo van Gogh he published several articles and also performed as expert on the Dutch situation in several foreign newspapers. In the *Neue Zürcher Zeitung* he published the articles 'Hinter der Fassade der Alltäglichkeit. Junge Muslime zwischen Integration und Radikalisierung' ['Behind the Façade of the Everyday. Young Muslims between Integration and Radicalisation'] (25 July 2005) and 'Mehr Couscous und Concertgebouw. Niederländer und Marokkaner sollten neugieriger werden' ['More Couscous and Concert Hall. Dutch People and Moroccans Should become More Curious'] (13 January 2005).
51. 'Abdelkader Benali werd bij het schrijven van *Onrein* geïnspireerd door recente politieke en maatschappelijke ontwikkelingen: de emotie van de politiek, de politiek van de emoties en de wens om veiligheid in plaats van avontuur centraal te stellen in het leven.'
52. Compare Hanke (2007), McClintock (1995), Young (1995) and Zantop (1997).
53. '*Het is Vrijdag.*' For citations from the drama *Onrein* I use the notation OR.
54. Traditional Islamic jurisdiction divides the world into two (political) parts, the 'House of Islam' and the 'House of War'. The 'House of War' does not know or accept the Islamic law, the Sharia.
55. The father practices the kind of Occidentalism that Ian Buruma and Avishai Margalit describe in their work *Occidentalism: the West in the Eyes of Its Enemies* (2004): the father homogenises 'the West' as the centre of impurity, sex, individualism, money and immorality.

56. 'Door dit beest raken we het béétje respect dat we hadden helemaal kwijt! De instructies zijn duidelijk: er moet respect zijn voor de vader!'
57. For a discussion of the 'El Moumni affair' see Prins (2004: 39-42).
58. 'Man, we lijken toch meer op elkaar dan je denkt. Jij bent toch ook als een hond behandeld door deze maatschappij.'
59. 'Als jullie mij respecteren, respecteer ik jullie ook. Respect voor de vader, de zoon en de hond!'
60. 'Het is een kwestie van presentatie. Dit is belangrijk voor jouw zoon, hij moet jouw naam verderdragen. Het probleem familie Mansoer is dat jullie geen act hebben.'
61. The semantic connection of dog, mother and impurity in this scene also resonates the Islamic (and Jewish) traditional assumption that menstruating women are impure.
62. 'Je zult alleen achterblijven, net zo alleen als toen je hier aankwam, dit huis zal je asiel worden, je ziel zal tegen de ramen opklimmen, zoals mijn ziel tegen de tralies op klom. Ik waarschuw je alleen omdat ik je mag.'
63. 'We begrijpen elkaar heel goed. We zijn tenslotte Overwinnaars.'
64. 'als ik terugkom wil ik je hier nooit meer zien.'
65. Another example of Benali's combined literary and socio-political involvement is the book project *Marokko door Nederlandse ogen 1605-2005. Verslag van een reis door de tijd* [*Morocco in Dutch Eyes 1605-2005. Report on a Journey through Time*] (2005) that he wrote together with the historian Herman Obdeijn. This book was published as a part of the state-subsidised project that celebrated 400 years of Moroccan-Dutch relations. Benali contributed several fictive portraits of 'early, historical Moroccan-Dutch intermediaries'. See also Depondt (2005).

Conclusion

1. The refusal to identify oneself as German or to imagine something as German identity is also not uncommon in contemporary literature by indigenous German writers. However, in contrast to the writers discussed in this study, for these indigenous German writers, neither their personal German identity nor that of their literary work is subject to doubt.

Works Cited

Abel, Julia. (2005). Erzählte Identität. Mündliches Erzählen in der neueren deutschen 'Migrantenliteratur'. *Der Deutschunterricht*, 2, 30-39.

— (2006). Positionslichter. Die neue Generation von Anthologien der 'Migrationsliteratur'. *Text+Kritik. Zeitschrift für Literatur. Sonderband Literatur und Migration*, 9(6), 233-245.

Ackermann, Irmgard (Ed.). (1982). *Als Fremder in Deutschland: Berichte, Erzählungen, Gedichte von Ausländern*. Munich: dtv.

— (Ed.). (1983). *In zwei Sprachen leben. Berichte, Erzählungen, Gedichte von Ausländern*. Munich: dtv.

Ackermann, Irmgard and Harald Weinrich (Eds.). (1986). *Eine nicht nur deutsche Literatur. Zur Standortbestimmung der 'Ausländerliteratur'*. Munich; Zurich: Piper.

Adelson, Leslie A. (1990). Migrants' Literature or German Literature? TORKAN's *Tufan: Brief an einen islamischen Bruder. The German Quarterly*, 63(3/4), 382-389.

— (1997a). Minor chords? Migration, Murder, and Multiculturalism. In Robert Weninger and Brigitte Rossbacher (Eds.), *Wendezeiten – Zeitenwenden. Positionsbestimmungen zur deutschsprachigen Literatur 1945-1995* (pp. 115-129). Tübingen: Stauffenburg.

— (1997b). The Price of Feminism: Of Women and Turks. In Patricia Herminghouse and Magda Mueller (Eds.), *Gender and Germanness: Cultural Productions of Nation* (pp. 305-319). Providence; Oxford: Berghahn Books.

— (2000a). Coordinates of Orientation. An Introduction. In Zafer Şenocak (Ed.), *Atlas of a Tropical Germany. Essays on Politics and Culture 1990-1998* (pp. xi-xxxvii). Lincoln; London: University of Nebraska Press.

— (2000b). Touching Tales of Turks, Germans, and Jews: Cultural Alterity, Historical Narrative, and Literary Riddles for the 1990s. *New German Critique*, 80, 93-124.

— (2001). Against Between: A Manifesto. In Salah Hassan and Iftikhar Dadi (Eds.), *Unpacking Europe; Towards a Critical Reading* (pp. 244-256). Rotterdam: Museum Boijmans van Beuningen and NAi Publishers.

— (2002). The Turkish Turn in Contemporary German Literature and Memory Work. *The Germanic Review*, 77(4), 326-337.

— (2005). *The Turkish Turn in Contemporary Literature: Toward a New Critical Grammar of Migration*. New York: Palgrave Macmillan.

Aerts, Mieke and Sawitri Saharso. (1994). Sekse als etniciteit. Een beschouwing over collectieve identiteit en sociale ongelijkheid. *Tijdschrift voor Vrouwenstudies*, 15(1), 11-26.

Ahmed, Leila. (1982). Western Ethnocentrism and Perceptions of the Harem. *Feminist Studies*, 8(3), 521-534.

— (1992). *Women and Gender in Islam. Historical Roots of a Modern Debate*. New Haven; London: Yale University Press.

Akçam, Dursun. (1982). *Deutsches Heim – Glück allein: Wie Türken Deutsche sehen. Alaman Ocağı: Türkler Almanları anlatıyor*. Bornheim-Merten: Lamuv.

Alcoff, Linda Martin and Eduardo Mendieta (Eds.). (2003). *Identities. Race, Class, Gender, and Nationality*. Malden; Oxford: Blackwell.

Alphen, Ernst van. (2002). Imagined Homelands. In Ginette Verstraete and Tim Crosswell (Eds.), *Mobilizing Place, Placing Mobility. The Politics of Representation in a Globalized World*. Amsterdam; New York: Rodopi.

— (2005). *Art in Mind. How Contemporary Images Shape Thought*. Chicago; London: The University of Chicago Press.

Althusser, Louis. (1971). Ideology and Ideological State Apparatuses. In Ben Brewster (Ed.), *Lenin and Philosophy* (pp. 170-186). New York; London: Monthly Review Press.

Amirsedighi, Nasrin and Thomas Bleicher (Eds.). (1997). *Literatur der Migration*. Mainz: Kinzelbach.

Amodeo, Immacolata. (1996). *'Die Heimat heißt Babylon': Zur Literatur ausländischer Autoren in der Bundesrepublik Deutschland*. Opladen: Westdeutscher Verlag.

Anbeek, Ton. (1999). Fataal succes. Over Marokkaans-Nederlandse auteurs en hun critici. *Literatuur*, 16(6), 335-341.

— (2002). Doodknuffelen. Over Marokkaans-Nederlandse auteurs en hun critici. In Theo D'Haen (Ed.), *Europa Buitengaats. Koloniale en postkoloniale literaturen in Europese talen* (Vol. 1, pp. 289-301). Amsterdam: Bert Bakker.

Anderson, Benedict. (1986). *Imagined Communities. Reflections on the Origin and Spread of Nationalism*. London: Verso.

Anker, Robert. (2002, 28 September). Spring maar achterop. *Vrij Nederland*, 74-77.

Anthias, Floya and Nira Yuval-Davis (Eds.). (1989). *Women, Nation, State*. London: MacMillian.

— (1992). *Racialized Boundaries. Race, Nation, Gender, Colour and Class and the Anti-Racist Struggle*. London; New York: Routledge.

Appadurai, Arjun. (1997). *Modernity at Large: Cultural Dimensions of Globalization*. Minneapolis; London: University of Minnesota Press.

— (2005). The power of the imagination. In Frank Frangenberg (Ed.), *Projekt Migration* (pp. 50-53). Cologne: DuMont.

Arens, Hiltrud. (2000). *Kulturelle Hybridität in der deutschen Minoritätenliteratur der achtziger Jahre*. Tübingen: Stauffenburg.

Assmann, Aleida. (1998). Die Gleichzeitigkeit des Ungleichzeitigen. Nationale Diskurse zwischen Ethnisierung und Universalisierung. In Ulrich Bielefeld and Gisela Engel (Eds.), *Bilder der Nation. Kulturelle und politische Konstruktionen des Nationalen am Beginn der europäischen Moderne* (pp. 379-400). Hamburg: Hamburger Edition.

Attridge, Derek. (1999). Innovation, Literature, Ethics: Relating to the Other. *Publications of the Modern Language Association of America*, 114(1), 20-31.

Auslander, Leora. (2000). Bavarian Crucifixes and French Headscarves. Religious Signs and the Postmodern European State. *Cultural Dynamics*, 12(3), 283-309.

Austin, J.L. (1975). *How to Do Things with Words*. Cambridge: Harvard University Press.

Aytaç, Gürsel. (1997). Sprache als Spiegel der Kultur. Zu Emine Sevgi Özdamars Roman *Das Leben ist eine Karawanserei*. In Mary Howard (Ed.), *Interkulturelle Konfigurationen: zur deutschsprachigen Erzählliteratur von Autoren nichtdeutscher Herkunft* (pp. 171-188). Munich: Iudicium.

Bade, Klaus J. (1983). *Vom Auswanderungsland zum Einwanderungsland? Deutschland 1880-1980.* Berlin: Colloquium.

— (Ed.). (1992). *Deutsche im Ausland – Fremde in Deutschland. Migration in Geschichte und Gegenwart.* Munich: Beck.

— (Ed.). (1994). *Das Manifest der 60: Deutschland und die Einwanderung.* Munich: Beck.

— (Ed.). (1996). *Die multikulturelle Herausforderung. Menschen über Grenzen – Grenzen über Menschen.* Munich: Beck.

— (2001). Immigration, Naturalization, and Ethno-national Traditions in Germany: From the Citizenship Law of 1913 to the Law of 1999. In Larry Eugene Jones (Ed.), *Crossing Boundaries. The Exclusion and Inclusion of Minorities in Germany and America* (pp. 29-49). New York; Oxford: Berghahn Books.

Bade, Klaus J. and Jochen Oltmer. (2005). Einwanderung in Deutschland seit dem Zweiten Weltkrieg. In Frank Frangenberg (Ed.), *Projekt Migration* (pp. 72-81). Cologne: DuMont.

Bade, Klaus J., Pieter C. Emmer, Leo Lucassen, and Jochen Oltmer (Eds.). (2007). *Enzyklopädie Migration in Europa. Vom 17. Jahrhundert bis zur Gegenwart.* Paderborn; Munich; Vienna; Zurich: Ferdinand Schöningh and Wilhelm Fink.

Bal, Mieke. (2002). *Travelling concepts in the humanities: a rough guide.* Toronto; Buffalo; London: University of Toronto Press.

— (2003). Meanwhile. Literature in an Expanded Field. *Thamyris/Intersecting*, 11, 183-197.

Bal, Mieke, Jonathan Crewe, and Leo Spitzer (Eds.). (1999). *Acts of Memory. Cultural Recall in the Present.* Hanover; London: University Press of New England.

Balibar, Etienne. (1996). The Nation Form: History and Ideology. In Geoff Eley and Ronald Grigor Suny (Eds.), *Becoming National. A Reader* (pp. 132-149). New York; Oxford: Oxford University Press.

— (1998). The Borders of Europe. In Pheng Cheah and Bruce Robbins (Eds.), *Cosmopolitics: Thinking and Feeling beyond the Nation* (pp. 216-229). Minneapolis: University of Minnesota Press.

Balibar, Etienne and Immanuel Wallerstein (Eds.). (1991). *Race, Nation and Class: Ambiguous Identities.* London: Verso.

Bammer, Angelika. (1997). Interrogating Germanness: What's Literature Got to Do with It. In Scott Denham, Irene Kacandes, and Jonathan Petropoulos (Eds.), *A User's Guide to German Cultural Studies* (pp. 31-44). Ann Arbor: University of Michigan Press.

Bassnett, Susan. (1993). *Comparative Literature. A Critical Introduction.* Oxford; Cambridge: Blackwell.

Bay, Hansjörg. (1999). Der verrückte Blick. Schreibweisen der Migration in Özdamars Karawanserei-Roman. *Sprache und Literatur in Wissenschaft und Unterricht*, 83, 29-61.

Beck, Ulrich. (2000). The cosmopolitan perspective: the sociology of the second age of modernity. *British Journal of Sociology*, 51(1), 79-105.

— (2004). *Der kosmopolitische Blick oder: Krieg ist Frieden.* Frankfurt am Main: Suhrkamp.

Becker, Lars (Director) and Feridun Zaimoglu (Writer). (2000). *Kanak Attack!* [Motion Picture]. Becker & Häberle Filmproduktion.

Begemann, Christian. (1999). 'Kanakensprache'. Schwellenphänomene in der deutschsprachigen Literatur ausländischer AutorInnen der Gegenwart. In Nicholas Saul (Ed.), *Schwellen. Germanistische Erkundungen einer Metapher* (pp. 209-220). Würzburg: Königshausen & Neumann.

Beil, Hermann. (2005). In einer fremden Sprache zu schreiben, ist eine Reise. Kleist-Preis 2004 für Emine Sevgi Özdamar. In Ingo Breuer (Ed.), *Kleist Jahrbuch* (pp. 8-12). Stuttgart: J.B. Metzler.

Beitter, Ursula E. (Ed.). (2000). *Literatur und Identität: deutsch-deutsche Befindlichkeiten und die multikulturelle Gesellschaft.* New York: Lang.

Bekers, Elisabeth. (2008). Chronicling Beyond Abyssinia. African Writing in Flanders, Belgium. In Elisabeth Bekers, Sissy Helff, and Daniella Merolla (Eds.), *Transcultural Modernities: Narrating Africa in Europe.* Amsterdam; New York: Rodopi.

Bel, Jacqueline. (2000). 'Zo groot ik nu ben, ben ik nog nooit geweest'. Jacqueline Bel in gesprek met Abdelkader Benali. *Armada. Tijdschrift voor wereldliteratuur,* 5(18), 112-119.

Benali, Abdelkader. (1996). *Bruiloft aan zee.* Amsterdam: Vassallucci.

— (1998). *Hochzeit am Meer* (Gregor Seferens, Trans.). Munich; Zurich: Piper.

— (1999a). *De Ongelukkige.* Amsterdam: Vassallucci.

— (1999b). *Wedding by the Sea* (Susan Massotty, Trans.). London: Phoenix.

— (2001). *Berichten uit Maanzaad Stad.* Amsterdam: Vassallucci.

— (2002a). *De langverwachte.* Amsterdam: Vassallucci.

— (2002b). *Jasser. Een monoloog.* Amsterdam: Vassallucci.

— (2002c, 11 February). Voor de Zonnekoning is artikel 1 maar lastig. *NRC Handelsblad.*

— (2002d, 14 September). Waarom zwijgen de Nederlandse schrijvers? *Vrij Nederland,* 76-77.

— (2003). *Onrein. De vader, de zoon en de hond.* Amsterdam: Vassallucci.

— (2004a, 17 July). Het verhaal van het schoolplein, of: de vernietiging van Nederland. *De Groene Amsterdammer,* 51.

— (2004b, 24 April). Op de Gazelle ten onder. *De Groene Amsterdammer,* 50-53.

— (2004c, 14 May). Opgelost in het geel van de Sahara. Migrantenkunst tussen authenticiteit en exotisme. *NRC Handelsblad.*

— (2005a, 25 July). Hinter der Fassade der Alltäglichkeit. Junge Muslime zwischen Integration und Radikalisierung. *Neue Zürcher Zeitung.*

— (2005b, 13 January). Mehr Couscous und Concertgebouw. Niederländer und Marokkaner sollten neugieriger werden. *Neue Zürcher Zeitung.*

— (2006). *Berichten uit een belegerde stad. Beiroet, zomer 2006.* Amsterdam; Antwerp: De Arbeiderspers.

Benali, Abdelkader and Herman Obdeijn. (2005). *Marokko door Nederlandse ogen 1605-2005. Verslag van een reis door de tijd.* Amsterdam; Antwerp: De Arbeiderspers.

Benhabib, Seyla. (2002). *The Claims of Culture. Equality and Diversity in the Global Era.* Princeton; Oxford: Princeton University Press.

Benzakour, Mohammed. (2004). Een groteske woordkunstenaar in domineesland. 2 mei 1996. Hafid Bouazza debuteert met *De voeten van Abdullah.* In Rosemarie Buikema and Maaike Meijer (Eds.), *Kunsten in beweging 1980-2000* (pp. 305-322). The Hague: Sdu.

Berger, John. (1972). *Ways of Seeing.* Harmondsworth: British Broadcasting Corporation and Penguin.

Berkeljon, Sara and Hans Wansink. (2006). *De orkaan Ayaan. Verslag van een politieke carrière.* Amsterdam: Augustus.

Berlant, Lauren and Elizabeth Freeman. (1993). Queer Nationality. In Michael Warner (Ed.), *Fear of a Queer Planet. Queer Politics and Social Theory* (pp. 193-229). Minneapolis; London: University of Minnesota Press.

Bernheimer, Charles (Ed.). (1995). *Comparative Literature in the Age of Multiculturalism.* Baltimore: John Hopkins University Press.

Bhabha, Homi K. (Ed.). (1990). *Nation and Narration.* London; New York: Routledge.

— (1994). *The Location of Culture.* London; New York: Routledge.

Bielefeld, Ulrich and Gisela Engel (Eds.). (1998). *Bilder der Nation. Kulturelle und politische Konstruktionen des Nationalen am Beginn der europäischen Moderne.* Hamburg: Hamburger Edition.

Biller, Maxim. (2000). Feige das Land, schlapp die Literatur. Über die Schwierigkeiten beim Sagen der Wahrheit. *Die Zeit, 16.*

Biondi, Franco and Rafik Schami. (1981). Literatur der Betroffenheit. Bemerkungen zur Gastarbeiterliteratur. In Christian Schaffernicht (Ed.), *Zu Hause in der Fremde* (pp. 124-135).

Bird, Stephanie. (2003). *Women Writers and National Identity. Bachmann, Duden, Özdamar.* Cambridge: Cambridge University Press.

Blamberger, Günter. (2005). Carpe diem et respice finem: Emine Sevgi Özdamars Schattenspiele. Rede zur Verleihung des Kleist-Preises an Emine Sevgi Özdamar am 21.11.2004 in Berlin. In Ingo Breuer (Ed.), *Kleist Jahrbuch* (pp. 3-7). Stuttgart: J.B. Metzler.

Bleicher, Joan Kristin. (1999). Unterwegs im Dazwischen. Ein kleiner Streifzug durch die Geschichte der deutschen Migrantenliteratur. In Joachim Lottmann (Ed.), *Kanaksta. Geschichten von deutschen und anderen Ausländern* (pp. 86-95). Berlin: Quadriga.

Blioumi, Aglaia. (2000). 'Migrationsliteratur', 'interkulturelle Literatur' und 'Generationen von Schriftstellern'. Ein Problemaufriß über umstrittene Begriffe. *Weimarer Beiträge, 46,* 595-601.

— (Ed.). (2002). *Migration und Interkulturalität in neueren literarischen Texten.* Munich: Iudicium.

Blom, Ida, Karen Hagemann, and Catherine Hall (Eds.). (2000). *Gendered Nations: Nationalisms and Gender Order in the Long Nineteenth Century.* Oxford; New York: Berg.

Boa, Elizabeth. (1997). Sprachenverkehr. Hybrides Schreiben in Werken von Özdamar, Özakin und Demirkan. In Mary Howard (Ed.), *Interkulturelle Konfigurationen: zur deutschsprachigen Erzählliteratur von Autoren nichtdeutscher Herkunft* (pp. 115-138). Munich: Iudicium.

— (2006). Özdamar's Autobiographical Fictions: Trans-National Identity and Literary Form. *German Life and Letters,* 59(4), 526-539.

Böcker, Anita and Kees Groenendijk. (2004). Einwanderungs- und Integrationsland Niederlande: Tolerant, liberal und offen? In Friso Wielenga and Ilona Taute (Eds.), *Länderbericht Niederlande. Geschichte – Wirtschaft – Gesellschaft* (pp. 303-361). Bonn: Bundeszentrale für politische Bildung.

Böcker, Anita and Dieter Thränhardt. (2003a). Einbürgerung und Mehrstaatigkeit in Deutschland und den Niederlanden. In Dieter Thränhardt and Uwe Hunger (Eds.), *Migration in Spannungsfeld von Globalisierung und Nationalstaat* (pp. 117-134). Wiesbaden: Westdeutscher Verlag.

— (2003b). Is het Duitse integratiebeleid succesvoller, en zo ja, waarom? *Migrantenstudies*, 19(1), 33-44.

Boehncke, Heiner and Harald Wittich (Eds.). (1991). *Buntesdeutschland. Ansichten zu einer multikulturellen Gesellschaft*. Reinbek bei Hamburg: Rowohlt.

Boer, Inge E. (1996). The World beyond our Window: Nomads, Travelling Theories and the Function of Boundaries. *Parallax. A journal of metadiscursive theory and cultural practices, 3*, 7-26.

— (2006). *Uncertain Territories: Boundaries in Cultural Analysis*. Amsterdam: Rodopi.

Bogdal, Klaus-Michael. (2000). Wo geht's denn hier nach Kanakstan? Deutsch-türkische Schriftsteller auf der Suche nach Identität. In Christoph Parry, Liisa Voßschmidt, and Detlev Wilske (Eds.), *Literatur und Identität. Beiträge auf der 10. internationalen Arbeitstagung 'Germanistische Forschungen zum literarischen Text'* (pp. 225-234). Vaasa: Vaasan Yliopiston Julkaisuja.

Bolkestein, Frits. (1991, 12 September). Integratie van minderheden moet met lef worden aangepakt. *de Volkskrant.*

— (1994). *Islam en de democratie. Een ontmoeting*. Amsterdam: Contact.

— (2003). Nederlandse identiteit in Europa. *Ons Erfdeel, 47*(4), 485-497.

— (2004). De noodzaak van een Leitkultur. *Liberales*. Retrieved from the World Wide Web: http://www.liberales.be

Botman, Maayke, Nancy Jouwe, and Gloria Wekker (Eds.). (2001). *Caleidoscopische visies. De zwarte, migranten- en vluchtelingenvrouwenbeweging in Nederland*. Amsterdam: Koninklijk Instituut voor de Tropen.

Bouazza, Hafid. (1996). *De voeten van Abdullah*. Amsterdam: Arena.

— (1998a). *Apollien, een toneelstuk*. Amsterdam: Prometheus.

— (1998b). *Momo*. Amsterdam: Prometheus.

— (2000). *Abdullah's Feet* (Ina Rilke, Trans.). London: Review Books.

— (2001). *De slachting in Parijs. Toneel*. Amsterdam: Prometheus.

— (2001). *Een beer in bontjas*. Amsterdam: Prometheus.

— (2001). *Salomon*. Amsterdam: Prometheus.

— (2002). *De voeten van Abdullah*. (revised ed.). Amsterdam: Prometheus.

— (2002, 2 March). Moslims kwetsen Nederland. *NRC Handelsblad.*

— (2002, 20 February). Nederland is blind voor moslimextremisme. *NRC Handelsblad.*

— (2002, 20 September). Nederland slikt te veel onzin van moslims. Mosse lezing 'Homoseksualiteit en Islam'. *NRC Handelsblad.*

— (2003, 19 February). Demonstreer voor vrijheid moslima's. *NRC Handelsblad.*

— (2004, 13 November). Angstige mannen, afvallige vrouwen en het voorbeeld van de profeet – een gevaarlijke combinatie. *NRC Handelsblad.*

— (2004). *Een beer in bontjas. Autobiografische beschouwingen/schetsen*. Amsterdam: Prometheus.

— (2004). Islam in Europa. 'Winking dark thoughts into a little tiddle cup'. In Henk Pröpper (Ed.), *Dromen van Europa. Hafid Bouazza, Bas Heijne en Michaël Zeeman over het nieuwe Europa* (pp. 28-34). Amsterdam: Bert Bakker.

— (2004). *Paravion*. Amsterdam: Prometheus.

Bourdieu, Pierre. (1993). *The Field of Cultural Production. Essays on Art and Literature*. New York: Columbia University Press.

Brady, John. (2004). Dangerous Foreigners: The Discourse of Threat and the Contours of Inclusion and Exclusion in Berlin's Public Sphere. In Deniz Göktürk and Barbara Wolbert (Eds.), *New German Critique. Multicultural Germany: Art, Performance, and Media* (Vol. 92, pp. 194-224).

Brah, Avtar. (1996). *Cartographies of Diaspora: Contesting Identities*. London: Routledge.

Braidotti, Rosi. (1994). *Nomadic Subjects. Embodiment and Sexual Difference in Contemporary Feminist Theory*. New York: Columbia University Press.

Brandt, Bettina. (2004). Collecting Childhood Memories of the Future: Arabic as Mediator Between Turkish and German in Emine Özdamar's *Mutterzunge. The Germanic Review*, 79 (4), 295-315.

Brecht, Bertolt. (1968). *Schriften zum Theater 2* (Vol. 16). Frankfurt am Main: Suhrkamp.

Breger, Claudia. (1999a). 'Meine Herren, spielt in meinem Gesicht ein Affe?' Strategien der Mimikry in Texten von Emine S. Özdamar und Yoko Tawada. In Cathy S. Gelbin, Kader Konug, and Peggy Piesche (Eds.), *Aufbrüche: Kulturelle Produktionen von Migrantinnen, Schwarzen und jüdischen Frauen in Deutschland* (pp. 30-59). Königstein/Taunus: Ulrike Helmer.

— (1999b). Mimikry als Grenzverwirrung. Parodistische Posen bei Yoko Tawada. In Claudia Benthien and Irmela Marei Krüger-Fürhoff (Eds.), *Über Grenzen. Limitation und Transgression in Literatur und Ästhetik* (pp. 176-206). Stuttgart: J.B. Metzler.

— (2003). Narratives of Nomadism or Copying German Culture. In Barbara Kosta and Helga Kraft (Eds.), *Writing against Boundaries. Nationality, Ethnicity and Gender in the German-speaking Context* (pp. 47-60). Amsterdam; New York: Rodopi.

Brennan, Timothy. (1997). *At Home in the World: Cosmopolitanism Now*. Cambridge, Mass.; London: Harvard University Press.

— (2001). Cosmo-Theory. *The South Atlantic Quarterly*, 100(3), 659-691.

Breure, Marnel and Liesbeth Brouwer. (2004). Een reconstructie van het debat rond migrantenliteratuur in Nederland. 14 maart 2001. Schrijven tussen twee culturen wordt het thema van de Boekenweek. In Rosemarie Buikema and Maaike Meijer (Eds.), *Kunsten in beweging 1980-2000* (pp. 381-396). The Hague: Sdu.

Brinker-Gabler, Gisela and Sidonie Smith (Eds.). (1997). *Writing New Identities: Gender, Nation and Immigration in Contemporary Europe*. Minneapolis; London: University of Minnesota Press.

Brouwers, Jeroen. (1996). *Feuilletons*. (Vol. I). Zutendaal: Noli me tangere.

Brouwers, Ton. (2004). Bruiloft aan Zee. Abdelkader Benali, *Lexicon van literaire werken*. (43 ed., pp. 1-13). Groningen: Martinus Nijhoff.

Brubaker, Rogers. (1992). *Citizenship and Nationhood in France and Germany*. Cambridge: Harvard University Press.

Brumlik, Micha and Claus Leggewie. (1992). Konturen der Einwanderungsgesellschaft. Nationale Identität, Multikulturalismus und 'Civil Society'. In Klaus J. Bade (Ed.), *Deutsche im Ausland – Fremde in Deutschland. Migration in Geschichte und Gegenwart* (pp. 430-442). Munich: Beck.

Brunt, Emma. (2003, 1 February). Driften. *Het Parool.*

Buikema, Rosemarie and Maaike Meijer (Eds.). (2003). *Kunsten in beweging 1900 – 1980*. The Hague: Sdu.

— (Eds.). (2004). *Kunsten in beweging 1980 – 2000*. The Hague: Sdu.

Buruma, Ian. (2006). *Murder in Amsterdam. The Death of Theo van Gogh and the Limits of Tolerance*. London: Atlantic Books.

Buruma, Ian and Avishai Margalit. (2004). *Occidentalism: the West in the Eyes of its Enemies*. New York: Penguin.

Butler, Judith. (1990). *Gender trouble. Feminism and the Subversion of Identities*. New York: Routledge.

— (1993). *Bodies That Matter: On the Discursive Limits of 'Sex'*. New York; London: Routledge.

— (1997). *Excitable Speech. A Politics of the Performative*. New York: Routledge.

— (2004). *Undoing Gender*. New York; London: Routledge.

Çağlar, Ayşe. (1998). Verordnete Rebellion. Deutsch-türkischer Rap und türkischer Pop in Berlin. In Ruth Mayer and Mark Terkessidis (Eds.), *Globalkolorit. Multikulturalismus und Populärkultur* (pp. 41-56). St. Andrä; Wördern: Hannibal.

Captain, Esther and Halleh Ghorashi. (2001). 'Tot behoud van mijn identiteit'. Identiteitsvorming binnen de zmv-vrouwenbeweging. In Maayke Botman, Nancy Jouwe, and Gloria Wekker (Eds.), *Caleidoscopische visies. De zwarte, migranten- en vluchtelingenvrouwenbewegingin Nederland* (pp. 153-185). Amsterdam: KIT Publishers.

Casanova, Pascale. (2005). Literature as a World. *New Left Review*, 31, 71-90.

Chambers, Iain. (1994). *Migrancy, Culture, Identity*. London: Routledge.

Cheah, Pheng. (1999). Grounds of Comparison. *Diacritics*, 29(4), 3-18.

Cheah, Pheng and Bruce Robbins (Eds.). (1998). *Cosmopolitics: Thinking and Feeling beyond the Nation*. Minneapolis: University of Minnesota Press.

Cheesman, Tom. (2002). Akçam – Zaimoglu – 'Kanak Attak': Turkish Lives and Letters in German. *German Life and Letters*, 55(2), 180-194.

— (2004). Talking 'Kanak': Zaimoglu contra Leitkultur. *New German Critique*, 92, 82-99.

— (2006). Juggling Burdens of Representation: Black, Red, Gold and Turquoise. *German Life and Letters*, 59(4), 471-487.

— (2007). *Novels of Turkish Settlement. Cosmopolite Fictions*. Rochester: Camden House.

Chervel, Thierry and Anja Seeliger (Eds.). (2007). *Islam in Europa. Eine internationale Debatte*. Frankfurt am Main: Suhrkamp.

Chiellino, Carmine (Ed.). (2000). *Interkulturelle Literatur in Deutschland: Ein Handbuch*. Stuttgart: J.B. Metzler.

Chorus, Jutta and Ahmet Olgun. (2005). *In godsnaam: Het jaar van Theo van Gogh*. Amsterdam: Contact.

Christiane F. (1981). *Wir Kinder vom Bahnhof Zoo*. Hamburg: Gruner + Jahr.

Cohen, Joshua, Matthew Howard, and Martha C. Nussbaum (Eds.). (1999). *Is Multiculturalism Bad for Women? Susan Moller Okin with Respondents*. Princeton: Princeton University Press.

Collins, Patricia Hill. (1990). *The Social Construction of Black Feminist Thought: Knowledge, Consciousness and the Politics of Empowerment*. Boston: Unwin Hyman.

Couwenberg, S.W. (1992). Onze culturele identiteit vergeleken met die van Duitsland. *Neerlandia*, 5, 171-176.

— (1996). Een omstreden zelfbesef. De Nederlandse identiteit in ontwikkeling. In Koen Koch and Paul Scheffer (Eds.), *Het nut van Nederland: opstellen over soevereiniteit en identiteit* (pp. 130-147). Amsterdam: Bert Bakker.

— (2001). Nationale identiteit: van Nederlands probleem tot Nederlandse uitdaging. In S.W. Couwenberg (Ed.), *Nationale identiteit: van Nederlands probleem tot Nederlandse uitdaging. Civis Mundi jaarboek* (pp. 9-61). Budel: DAMON.

Crenshaw, Kimberlé Williams. (1995). Mapping the Margins: Intersectionality, Identity, and Violence against Women of Color. In Kimberlé Williams Crenshaw, Neil Gotanda, Gary Peller, and Kendal Thomas (Eds.), *Critical Race Theory: The Key Writings That Formed the Movement* (pp. 357-383). New York: New Press.

Crewe, Jonathan. (1999). Recalling Adamastor: Literature as Cultural Memory in 'White' South Africa. In Mieke Bal, Jonathan Crewe, and Leo Spitzer (Eds.), *Acts of Memory. Cultural Recall in the Present* (pp. 75-86). Hanover; London: University Press of New England.

Culler, Jonathan. (1988). *Framing the Sign. Criticism and its Institutions.* Oxford: Basil Blackwell.

— (1997). *Literary Theory. A Very Short Introduction.* Oxford: Oxford University Press.

— (1998). *On Deconstruction: Theory and Criticism after Structuralism.* London: Routledge.

— (2000). Philosophy and Literature: The Fortunes of the Performative. *Poetics Today*, 21(3), 503-518.

Dam, Jan van. (2002, 5 December). Wat gij niet wilt dat u geschiedt. *Contrast*, pp. 26-27.

Damrosch, David. (2003). *What is World Literature?* Princeton; Oxford: Princeton University Press.

Daum, Denise, Andrea Geier, Iulia-Karin Patrut, and Kea Wienand. (2005). Einleitung. In Graduiertenkolleg Identität und Differenz (Ed.), *Ethnizität und Geschlecht. (Post-)Koloniale Verhandlungen in Geschichte, Kunst und Medien* (pp. 3-20). Cologne; Weimar; Vienna: Böhlau.

Dayıoğlu-Yücel, Yasemin. (2005). *Von der Gastarbeit zur Identitätsarbeit. Integritätsverhandlungen in türkisch-deutschen Texten von Şenocak, Özdamar, Agaoglu und der Online-Community vaybee!* Göttingen: Universitätsverlag Göttingen.

Deleuze, Gilles and Félix Guattari. (1976). *Kafka. Eine kleine Literatur.* Frankfurt am Main: Suhrkamp.

— (2004). *A thousand plateaus. Capitalism and Schizophrenia* (Brian Massumi, Trans.). London; New York: Continuum.

Depondt, Paul. (2005, 21 January). Tolerantie heeft iets heel neerbuigends. *de Volkskrant.*

Derrida, Jacques. (1997). *Of Grammatology* (Gayatri Chakravorty Spivak, Trans. Corrected ed.). Baltimore; London: John Hopkins University Press.

D'Haen, Theo (Ed.). (2002). *Europa Buitengaats. Koloniale en postkoloniale literaturen in Europese talen.* Amsterdam: Bert Bakker.

Dietrich, Helmut. (2005). Ausländerpolitik in der Bundesrepublik Deutschland. In Frank Frangenberg (Ed.), *Projekt Migration* (pp. 290-297). Cologne: DuMont.

Dijkgraaf, Margot and Martin Meijer. (2002). Abdelkader Benali. In Margot Dijkgraaf and Martin Meijer (Eds.), *Het beslissende boek. Nederlandse en Vlaamse schrijvers over het boek dat hun leven veranderde* (pp. 18-22). Amsterdam: Prometheus.

Dresselhuys, Cisca. (2004). 'Pak emancipatie moslimvrouwen revolutionair aan'. Hafid Bouazza langs de Feministische Meetlat. *Opzij. Feministisch Maandblad*, 32(11), 72-79.

Dros, Nico. (2003). Over schrijverschap en politiek. *Tirade*, 47(3/4), 48-55.

Dunk, H.W. von der. (1994). *Twee buren, twee culturen.* Amsterdam: Prometheus.

Dürr, Tobias. (2000). Der Leitkulturwart. Die Union beruft sich auf Bassam Tibi. Zu Unrecht. *Die Zeit*, 45.

Duyvené de Wit, Thom and Ruud Koopmans. (2001). Die politisch-kulturelle Integration ethnischer Minderheiten in den Niederlanden und Deutschland. *Forschungsjournal Neue Soziale Bewegungen*, 14(1), 26-41.

Eley, Geoff and Ronald Grigor Suny (Eds.). (1996). *Becoming National. A Reader*. New York; Oxford: Oxford University Press.

El-Tayeb, Fatima. (2001). Foreigners, Germans and German Foreigners; Constructions of National Identity in Early Twentieth Century Germany. In Salah Hassan and Iftikhar Dadi (Eds.), *Unpacking Europe; Towards a critical reading* (pp. 72-81). Rotterdam: Museum Boijmans Van Beuningen and NAi Publishers.

El-Tayeb, Fatima, Encarnación Gutiérrez Rodríguez, Hito Steyerl, and Kien Nghi Ha. (2005). Das hippe Verlangen nach Otherness. In Frank Frangenberg (Ed.), *Projekt Migration* (pp. 226-235). Cologne: DuMont.

Entzinger, Han. (2006). Changing the Rules While the Game Is On: From Multiculturalism to Assimilation in the Netherlands. In Y. Michal Bodemann and Gökce Yurdakul (eds.), *Migration, Citizenship, Ethnos* (pp. 121-44). New York: Palgrave Macmillan.

'Erbe und Auftrag – Bemerkungen zu einem rassistischen Auftritt', Aufzeichnungen aus der Talkshow 'Drei nach Neun' mit Feridun Zaimoglu, Heide Simonis, Harald Juhnke, Wolf Biermann und Norbert Blüm, N3, 8.5.98, 22.00 – 24.00 Uhr. (1999). *Karoshi. Zeitschrift gegen die innere Sicherheit des Subjekts*, 4, 22-26.

Ergün, Ayfer (Ed.). (1996). *Het land in mij*. Amsterdam: Arena.

Ernst, Thomas. (2005). *Popliteratur*. Hamburg: Europäische Verlagsanstalt.

Esselborn, Karl. (2004). Der Adelbert-von-Chamisso-Preis und die Förderung der Migrationsliteratur. In Klaus Schenk, Almut Todorow, and Milan Tvrdík (Eds.), *Migrationsliteratur. Schreibweisen einer interkulturelle Moderne* (pp. 317-325). Tübingen; Basel: Francke.

Fachinger, Petra. (2001). *Rewriting Germany from the margins: 'Other' German literature of the 1980s and 1990s*. Montreal: McGill-Queen's University Press.

Fennell, Barbara A. (1997). *Language, Literature and the Negotiation of Identity*. Chapel Hill; London: University of North Carolina Press.

Ferron, Louis. (2002, 21 September). Van oude en nieuwe volkscommissarissen. *Vrij Nederland*, 98-99.

Fischer, Sabine and Moray McGowan. (1995). From 'Pappkoffer' to Pluralism: Migrant Writing in the German Federal Republic. In Russell King, John Connell, and Paul White (Eds.), *Writing across Worlds: Literature and Migration* (pp. 39-56). London: Routledge.

— (1996). From 'Pappkoffer' to Pluralism: on the Development of Migrant Writing in the Federal Republic of Germany. In David Horrocks and Eva Kolinsky (Eds.), *Turkish culture in German society today* (pp. 1-21). Providence; Oxford: Berghahn Books.

— (Eds.). (1997). *Denn du tanzt auf einem Seil. Positionen deutschsprachiger MigrantInnenliteratur*. Tübingen: Stauffenburg.

Flotow, Luise von. (2000). Life is a caravanserai: Translating Translated Marginality, a Turkish-German *Zwittertext* in English. *Meta*, XLV(1), 65-72.

Förschler, Silke. (2005). Die orientalische Frau aus der hellen Kammer. Zur kolonialen Postkarte. In Graduiertenkolleg Identität und Differenz (Ed.), *Ethnizität und Geschlecht*.

(Post-)Koloniale Verhandlungen in Geschichte, Kunst und Medien (pp. 77-94). Cologne; Weimar; Vienna: Böhlau.

Fortuin, Arjen. (2003, 24 October). Donderwolk aan de heilige horizon: Hafid Bouazza proeft de roes en ontnuchtering van het paradijs. *NRC Handelsblad.*

Fortuyn, Pim. (1997). *Tegen de islamisering van onze cultuur. Nederlandse identiteit als fundament.* Utrecht: Bruna.

— (2001). *De islamisering van onze cultuur. Nederlandse identiteit als fundament. Het woord als wapen.* (actualised and revised ed.). Uithoorn; Rotterdam: Karakter & Speakers Academy.

Foucault, Michel. (1976). *De orde van het vertoog.* Meppel: Boom.

— (1986). Of Other Spaces. *Diacritics,* 16(1), 22-27.

— (2003). *The Archeology of Knowledge.* London: Routledge.

Francken, Eep. (1999). Hafid Bouazza. De Voeten van Abdullah. In A.G.H Anbeek van der Meijden, Jaap Goedegebuure, and M. Janssens (Eds.), *Lexicon van literaire werken* (43 ed., pp. 1-8). Groningen: Martinus Nijhoff.

Frangenberg, Frank (Ed.). (2005). *Projekt Migration.* Cologne: DuMont.

Frankenberg, Ruth. (1993). *White Women, Race Matters. The Social Construction of Whiteness.* London: Routledge.

Freidank, Michael. (2001). *Grund- und Aufbauwortschatz Kanakisch.* Frankfurt am Main: Eichborn.

— (2001). *Kanakisch-Deutsch: Dem krassesten Sprakbuch ubernhaupt.* Frankfurt am Main: Eichborn.

Frölich, Margrit. (1997). Reinventions of Turkey: Emine Sevgi Özdamar's *Life is a Caravanserai.* In Karen Jankowsky and Carla Love (Eds.), *Other Germanies. Questioning Identity in Women's Literature and Art* (pp. 56-73). New York: State University of New York Press.

— (2003). Aufbrüche in geteilten Welten: Emine Sevgi Özdamars transkulturelle Spurensuche. In Margrit Frölich, Astrid Messerschmidt, and Jörg Walther (Eds.), *Migration als biografische und expressive Ressource. Beiträge zur kulturellen Produktion in der Einwanderungsgesellschaft* (pp. 45-65). Frankfurt am Main: Brandes & Apsel.

Gaonkar, Dilip Parameshwar. (2002). Towards New Imaginaries: An Introduction. *Public Culture: Society for Transnational Cultural Studies,* 14(1), 1-19.

Gaschke, Susanne. (2003, 21 August). Nie mehr Migrations-Ali. Hier zu Hause, hier erfolgreich: Die neue Mittelschicht. Vier Porträts. *Die Zeit,* 35.

Geier, Jens, Klaus Ness, and Muzaffer Perik (Eds.). (1991). *Vielfalt in der Einheit. Auf dem Weg in die multikulturelle Gesellschaft.* Marburg: Schüren.

George, Rosemary Marangoly. (1996). *The Politics of Home. Postcolonial Relocations and Twentieth Century Fiction.* Cambridge: Cambridge University Press.

Gelbin, Cathy S., Kader Konug, and Peggy Piesche (Eds.). (1999). *Aufbrüche: Kulturelle Produktionen von Migrantinnen, Schwarzen und jüdischen Frauen in Deutschland.* Königstein/Taunus: Ulrike Helmer.

Gellner, Ernest. (1983). *Nations and Nationalism.* Oxford: Blackwell.

Gemünden, Gerd. (1999). Nostalgia for the Nation: Intellectuals and National Identity in Unified Germany. In Mieke Bal, Jonathan Crewe, and Leo Spitzer (Eds.), *Acts of Memory. Cultural Recall in the Present* (pp. 120-133). Hanover; London: University Press of New England.

Gerhard, Ute and Jürgen Link. (1991). Kleines Glossar neorassistischer Feindbild-Begriffe. In Heiner Boehncke and Harald Wittich (Eds.), *Buntesdeutschland. Ansichten zu einer multikulturellen Gesellschaft* (pp. 138-147). Reinbek bei Hamburg: Rowohlt.

Gerstenberger, Katharina. (2004). Writing by ethnic minorities in the age of globalisation. In Stuart Taberner (Ed.), *German literature in the age of globalisation* (pp. 209-228). Birmingham: University of Birmingham Press.

Geuijen, C.H.M. (Ed.). (1998). *Multiculturalisme. Werken aan ontwikkelingsvraagstukken.* Utrecht: LEMMA.

Ghaussy, Sohelia. (1999). Das Vaterland verlassen: Nomadic Language and 'Feminine Writing' in Emine Sevgi Özdamar's *Das Leben ist eine Karawanserai. The German Quarterly,* 72(1), 1-16.

Ghorashi, Halleh. (2004). Ayaan Hirsi Ali: dapper of dogmatisch? *Gender. Tijdschrift voor Genderstudies,* 7(1), 58-62.

— (2006, 14 October). Nederlander, ga eens opzij met je dikke identiteit. *de Volkskrant.*

— (2006). *Paradoxen van culturele erkenning.* Amsterdam: Vrije Universiteit.

Gilroy, Paul. (1991). It Ain't Where You're From, It's Where You're At... The Dialectics of Diasporic Identification. *Third Text,* 13(Winter), 3-15.

Ginkel, Rob van. (1999). *Op zoek naar eigenheid. Denkbeelden en discussie over cultuur en identiteit in Nederland.* The Hague: Sdu.

Glastra van Loon, Karel. (2002, 7 December). Abdelkader en de kaaskoppen. *Vrij Nederland,* 84-85.

Glick Schiller, Nina, Data Dea, and Markus Höhne. (2005). *African Culture and the Zoo in the 21st Century. The 'African Village' in the Augsburg Zoo and Its Wider Implications* (Report to the Max Planck Institute for Social Anthropology). Halle/Saale.

Glissant, Édouard. (1997). *Poetics of Relation* (Betsy Wing, Trans.). Ann Arbor: University of Michigan Press.

Göckede, Regina and Alexandra Karentzos (Eds.). (2006). *Der Orient, die Fremde. Positionen zeitgenössischer Kunst und Literatur.* Bielefeld: transcript.

Goedegebuure, Jaap. (1996, 16 August). De exotica van het gezochte woord. *HP/De Tijd.*

— (1998, 1 May). Morsen met woorden. *HP/De Tijd.*

Goedkoop, Hans. (1996, 25 October). Een borrelende smeltkroes van stijlen. *NRC Handelsblad.*

— (1998, 8 May). Een taal graaft haar eigen graf. *NRC Handelsblad.*

Gogh, Theo van (Director) and Ayaan Hirsi Ali (Writer). (2004). *Submission Part One* [Television Broadcast]. Amsterdam: Column Productions.

Gökberk, Ülker. (1991). Understanding Alterity: *Ausländerliteratur* between Relativism and Universalism. In David Perkins (Ed.), *Theoretical Issues in Literary History.* Cambridge: Harvard University Press.

— (1997a). *Culture Studies* und die Türken. Sten Nadolnys *Selim oder Die Gabe der Rede* im Lichte einer Methodendiskussion. *The German Quarterly,* 70(2), 97-122.

— (1997b). Encounters with the Other in German Cultural Discourse: Intercultural Germanistik and Aysel Özakin's Journeys of Exile. In Karen Jankowsky and Carla Love (Eds.), *Other Germanies. Questioning Identity in Women's Literature and Art* (pp. 19-55). New York: State University of New York Press.

Göktürk, Deniz, David Gramling, and Anton Kaes (Eds.). (2007). *Germany in Transit. Nation and Migration 1955-2005.* Berkeley; Los Angeles: University of California Press.

Gosewinkel, Dieter. (1998). Citizenship and Nationhood: The Historical Development of the German Case. In Ulrich K. Preuss and Ferran Requejo (Eds.), *European Citizenship, Multiculturalism, and the State* (pp. 125-135). Baden-Baden: Nomos Verlagsgesellschaft.

Gowricharn, Ruben S. (Ed.). (1993). *Binnen de grenzen. Immigratie, etniciteit en integratie in Nederland.* Utrecht: De Tijdstroom.

Graef, Ortwin de and Henriëtte Louwerse. (2000). The Alteration of Amsterdam: Hafid Bouazza's Entertainment of Cultural Identity. In Andy Hollis (Ed.), *Beyond Boundaries – Textual Representations of European Identities* (Vol. 15, pp. 35-51).

— (2001). De alteratie van Amsterdam. Hafid Bouazza's liefdesgeschiedenissen, *Onverwerkt Europa. Jaarboek voor literatuurwetenschap* (Vol. 1, pp. 169-190).

Grewal, Inderpal and Caren Kaplan. (1994). *Scattered Hegemonies. Postmodernity and Transnational Feminist Practices.* Minneapolis; London: University of Minnesota Press.

Groen, Mieke. (2003). De bewogenheid van Benali. *Socialisme en Democratie, 60(5/6),* 6-7.

Grünefeld, Hans-Dieter. (1995). Deutsche Literatur oder Literatur in Deutschland? Rezeption und Bedeutung literarischer Texte der Migration. *Sirene: Zeitschrift für Literatur, 14,* 88-104.

Grüttemeier, Ralf. (2001). Migrantenliteratuur in de Nederlandse en Duitse letteren. *Neerlandica extra muros, 39(3),* 13-25.

— (2005). Nederlandse migrantenliteratuur in Duitse vertaling. *Neerlandica extra muros, 43* (1), 1-11.

Günter, Manuela. (1999). 'Wir sind bastarde, freund...' Feridun Zaimoglus Kanak Sprak und die performative Struktur von Identität. *Sprache und Literatur in Wissenschaft und Unterricht, 83,* 15-28.

Ha, Kien Nghi. (1999). *Ethnizität und Migration.* Münster: Westfällisches Dampfboot.

— (2003a). Die kolonialen Muster deutscher Arbeitsmigrationspolitik. In Hito Steyerl and Encarnación Gutiérrez Rodríguez (Eds.), *Spricht die Subalterne deutsch? Migration und postkoloniale Kritik* (pp. 56-107). Münster: UNRAST.

— (2003b). Sprechakte – SprachAttakken: Rassismus, Konstruktion kultureller Differenz und Hybridität in einer TV-Talkshow mit Feridun Zaimoglu. In Margrit Frölich, Astrid Messerschmidt, and Jörg Walther (Eds.), *Migration als biografische und expressive Ressource. Beiträge zur kulturellen Produktion in der Einwanderungsgesellschaft* (pp. 123-149). Frankfurt am Main: Brandes & Apsel.

— (2005). *Hype um Hybridität. Kultureller Differenzkonsum und postmoderne Verwertungstechniken im Spätkapitalismus.* Bielefeld: transcript.

Habermas, Jürgen. (1995). Citizenship and National Identity: Some Reflections on the Future of Europe. In Ronald Beiner (Ed.), *Theorizing Citizenship* (pp. 255-283). Albany: State University of New York Press.

— (1998). *Die postnationale Konstellation.* Frankfurt am Main: Suhrkamp.

Hall, Stuart. (1990). Cultural Identity and Diaspora. In Jonathan Rutherford (Ed.), *Identity. Community, Culture, Difference* (pp. 222-237). London: Lawrence & Wishart.

— (1993). The Question of Cultural Identity. In Stuart Hall, David Held, and Tony McGrew (Eds.), *Modernity and its Futures* (Vol. 4, pp. 273-316). Cambridge: Polity Press.

— (1996a). Introduction: Who Needs 'Identity'. In Stuart Hall and Paul du Gay (Eds.), *Questions of Cultural Identity* (pp. 1-17). London: Sage.

— (1996b). New Ethnicities. In David Morley and Kuan-Hsing Chen (Eds.), *Stuart Hall. Critical Dialogues in Cultural Studies* (pp. 441-449). London; New York: Routledge.

— (Ed.). (1997). *Representation: Cultural Representations and Signifying Practices*. London: Sage.

— (2005). Europe's other self. In Frank Frangenberg (Ed.), *Projekt Migration* (pp. 182-187). Cologne: DuMont.

Hall, Stuart and Paul du Gay (Eds.). (1996). *Questions of Cultural Identity*. London: Sage.

Hammelehle, Sebastian. (2006, 26 February). 'Meine Leute sind die Deutschen'. *Welt am Sonntag*.

Handke, Peter. (1972). Publikumsbeschimpfung, *Stücke 1* (pp. 9-47). Frankfurt am Main: Suhrkamp.

Hanke, Christine. (2007). *Zwischen Auflösung und Fixierung. Zur Konstitution von 'Rasse' und 'Geschlecht' in der physischen Anthropologie um 1900*. Bielefeld: transcript.

Haraway, Donna. (1991). *Simians, Cyborgs and Women. The Reinvention of Nature*. London: Free Associations Books.

Harding, Sandra. (1987). *Feminism and methodology*. Bloomington; Indianapolis: Indiana University Press.

Hardt, Michael and Antonio Negri. (2000). *Empire*. Cambridge: Harvard University Press.

Harlow, Barbara. (1987). *Resistance Literature*. New York; London: Methuen.

Hartung, Harald. (2003, 26 June). Wir sind nur Hospitant auf Erden. V-Affekte: Emine Sevgi Özdamar lernt das Brecht-Theater. *Frankfurter Allgemeine Zeitung*.

Haselbach, Dieter. (1998). Multicultural Reality and the Problem of German Identity. In Dieter Haselbach (Ed.), *Multiculturalism in a World of Leaking Boundaries* (pp. 210-228). Münster: Lit.

Hassan, Salah and Iftikhar Dadi (Eds.). (2001). *Unpacking Europe; Towards a critical reading*. Rotterdam: Museum Boijmans Van Beuningen and NAi Publishers.

Hedetoft, Ulf and Mette Hjort. (2002). *The Postnational Self: Belonging and Identity*. Minneapolis: University of Minnesota Press.

Heidelberger Manifest. (1982). In Klaus Staeck and Inge Karst (Eds.), *Macht Ali deutsches Volk kaputt?* (pp. 59-61). Göttingen: Steidl.

Heijne, Bas. (2003, 7 June). 'Een moskee is geen cultuur, het is folklore'. *NRC Handelsblad*.

Heijs, Eric. (1995). *Van vreemdeling tot Nederlander. De verlening van het Nederlanderschap aan vreemdelingen 1813-1992*. Amsterdam: Het Spinhuis.

Heitmeyer, Wilhelm (Ed.). (2005). *Deutsche Zustände. Folge 4*. Frankfurt am Main: Suhrkamp.

— (Ed.). (2006). *Deutsche Zustände. Folge 5*. Frankfurt am Main: Suhrkamp.

— (Ed.). (2007). *Deutsche Zustände. Folge 6*. Frankfurt am Main: Suhrkamp.

Hendriksma, Martin. (2004, 22 January). Reacties van moslims kan ik dromen. *Noordhollands Dagblad*.

Herbert, Ulrich. (1986). *Geschichte der Ausländerbeschäftigung in Deutschland 1880 bis 1980*. Berlin; Bonn: J.H.W. Dietz.

— (2001). *Geschichte der Ausländerpolitik in Deutschland. Saisonarbeiter, Zwangsarbeiter, Gastarbeiter, Flüchtlinge*. Munich: Beck.

Herman, David. (2002). *Story Logic. Problems and Possibilities of Narrative*. Lincoln; London: University of Nebraska Press.

Hermans, Katherine. (2004, 5 February). Liever Katja dan al-Jazeera. *Mare*, 19.

Herminghouse, Patricia and Magda Mueller (Eds.). (1997). *Gender and Germanness: Cultural Productions of Nation*. Providence; Oxford: Berghahn Books.

Herrmann, Britta and Walter Erhart. (2002). XY ungelöst: Männlichkeit als Performance. In Therese Steffen (Ed.), *Masculinities – Maskulinitäten. Mythos – Realität – Repräsentation – Rollendruck* (pp. 33-53). Stuttgart; Weimar: J.B. Metzler.

Hessel, Franz. (1968). *Spazieren in Berlin. Mit einem Nachwort von Janos Frecot und 24 Photographien der Zeit*. Munich: Rogner & Bernhard.

Hestermann, Sandra. (2003). The German-Turkish Diaspora and Multicultural German Identity. Hyphenated and Alternative Discourses of Identity in the Works of Zafer Şenocak and Feridun Zaimoglu. In Monika Fludernik (Ed.), *Diaspora and Multiculturalism* (pp. 329-373). Amsterdam: Rodopi.

Heynders, Odile. (1999). Ten geleide. *Literatuur*, 6, 322-323.

Hirsi Ali, Ayaan. (2004). *Submission. De tekst, de reacties en de achtergronden*. Amsterdam; Antwerp: Augustus.

Hobsbawm, Eric J. (1990). *Nations and nationalism since 1780. Programme, myth, reality*. Cambridge: Cambridge University Press.

Hobsbawm, Eric J. and Terence Ranger (Eds.). (1983). *The Invention of Tradition*. Cambridge: Cambridge University Press.

Hofmann, Marit. (1999). Kanak-Attak! *Cinema*, 3, 188-189.

Holquist, Michael (Ed.). (1981). *The dialogic Imagination. Four essays by M.M. Bakhtin*. Austin: University of Texas Press.

Honneth, Axel. (2003). *Unsichtbarkeit. Stationen einer Theorie der Intersubjektivität*. Frankfurt am Main: Suhrkamp.

hooks, bell. (1981). *Ain't I a Woman: Black Women and Feminism*. Boston: South End Press.

— (1984). *Feminist Theory: From Margin to Center*. Boston: South End Press.

— (1990). *Yearning. Race, gender and cultural politics*. Boston: South End Press.

Horrocks, David. (1996). In Search of a Lost Past: A Reading of Emine Özdamar's novel *Das Leben ist eine Karawanserai, hat zwei Türen, aus einer kam ich rein aus der anderen ging ich raus*. In David Horrocks and Eva Kolinsky (Eds.), *Turkish culture in German society today* (pp. 23-43).

Horrocks, David and Eva Kolinsky (Eds.). (1996). *Turkish culture in German society today*. Providence; Oxford: Berghahn Books.

Hoving, Isabel. (2001). Een leeg graf, een boze man, en een spraakmakende foto. De brokstukken van een Nederlandstalige reflectie over interculturaliteit. In Elisabeth Leijnse and Michiel van Kempen (Eds.), *Tussenfiguren. Schrijvers tussen de culturen* (pp. 47-61). Amsterdam: Het Spinhuis.

— (2005). Circumventing Openness: Creating New Senses of Dutchness. *Transit*, 1(1), Article 50909.

Howard, Mary (Ed.). (1997). *Interkulturelle Konfigurationen: zur deutschsprachigen Erzählliteratur von Autoren nichtdeutscher Herkunft*. Munich: Iudicium.

Huggan, Graham. (2001). *The Postcolonial Exotic. Marketing the Margins*. New York: Routledge.

Huizinga, Johan. (1946). *Nederland's geestesmerk*. Leiden: Sijthoff.

Hunn, Karin. (2005). *'Nächstes Jahr kehren wir zurück ...' Die Geschichte der türkischen 'Gastarbeiter' in der Bundesrepublik*. Göttingen: Wallstein.

Huntington, Samuel. (1996). *The Clash of Civilisations and the Remaking of World Order*. New York: Simon and Schuster.

Huyssen, Andreas. (1980). The Politics of Identification: 'Holocaust' and West-Germany. *New German Critique*, 19(1), 117-136.

— (1995a). The Inevitability of Nation: Germany after Unification. In John Rajchman (Ed.), *The Identity in Question* (pp. 73-83). New York; London: Routledge.

— (1995b). *Twilight Memories. Marking Time in a Culture of Amnesia*. New York; London: Routledge.

— (2003). Diaspora and Nation: Migration Into Other Pasts. *New German Critique*, 88, 147-164.

Ingleby, David. (2000). *Psychologie en de multiculturele samenleving: Een gemiste aansluiting*. Utrecht: CERES.

Jäger, Siegfried. (2004). Paradoxe Entschärfungen im Interesse der Nation. Der deutsche Einwanderungsdiskurs im Umfeld der Terroranschläge vom 11.9.01 und sein Beitrag zur Verfestigung eines völkischen Verständnisses deutscher Identität. In Alfred Schobert and Siegfried Jäger (Eds.), *Mythos Identität. Fiktion mit Folgen* (pp. 167-189). Münster: UNRAST.

Jankowsky, Karen. (1997). 'German' Literature Contested: The 1991 Ingeborg-Bachmann-Prize Debate, 'Cultural Diversity,'and Emine Sevgi Özdamar. *The German Quarterly*, 70(3), 261-276.

Johnson, Barbara. (1992). *The Critical Difference. Essays in the Contemporary Rhetoric of Reading*. Baltimore; London: John Hopkins University Press.

Johnson, Sheila. (2001). Transnational Ästhetik des türkischen Alltags: Emine Sevgi Özdamar's *Das Leben ist eine Karawanserei. The German Quarterly*, 74(1), 37-57.

Jonge, Stefanie de. (2004, 10 February). Ik ben mijn moeder heel dankbaar dat ik niet zo'n macho ben als de andere Marokkanen. *Humo*.

Joppke, Christian. (1999). How Immigration is Changing Citizenship: A Comparative View. *Ethnic and Racial Studies*, 22(4), 629-652.

Joppke, Christian and Eva Morawska (Eds.). *Toward Assimilation and Citizenship. Immigration in Liberal Nation-States*. London: Palgrave Macmillan, 2003.

Jordan, Jim. (2006). More Than a Metaphor: the Passing of the Two Worlds Paradigm in German-Language Diasporic Literature. *German Life and Letters*, 59(4), 488-499.

Kanak Attak. (1999). Kanak Attak und basta! [Manifesto, November 1998]. *Parapluie*. Retrieved from the World Wide Web: http://parapluie.de/archiv/generation/manifest/

Kaplan, Caren. (1996). *Questions of Travel. Postmodern Discourses of Displacement*. Durham; London: Duke University Press.

Keiner, Sabine. (1999). Von der Gastarbeiterliteratur zur Migranten- und Migrationsliteratur – literaturwissenschaftliche Kategorien in der Krise? *Sprache und Literatur in Wissenschaft und Unterricht*, 83, 3-13.

Kellerhuis, Tom. (2003, 7 February). Verlichte visioenen. *HP/De Tijd*.

Kempen, Michiel van. (1999). Vindingrijke zwervers. Een woord vooraf. *Armada. Tijdschrift voor wereldliteratuur*, 'Migranten' 4(16), 3-7.

Kempen, Yves van. (1998, 3 June). Geschuifel en geguichel. *De Groene Amsterdammer*.

Kersting, Ruth. (2007). *Fremdes Schreiben. Yoko Tawada*. Trier: Wissenschaftlicher Verlag Trier.

Kieskamp, Wilma. (1997, 21 January). Bekroonde Hafid Bouazza gebruikt archaïsch Nederlands in sprookjesachtige verhalen. *Trouw*.

Kluge Etymologisches Wörterbuch der deutschen Sprache. *(23 ed.)(1999). Berlin; New York: Walter de Gruyter.*

Koch, Koen and Paul Scheffer (Eds.). (1996). *Het nut van Nederland: opstellen over soevereiniteit en identiteit*. Amsterdam: Bert Bakker.

Koelemeijer, Judith. (1997, 10 May). Literatuur moet ernstig zijn, dacht ik toen nog: Benali's 'Bruiloft aan zee' is 'best wel een Marokkaans boek geworden'. *de Volkskrant*.

Kohl, Karl-Heinz. (1987). Cherchez la femme d'Orient. In Hermann Pollig, Susanne Schlichtenmayer, and Gertrud Baur-Burkath (Eds.), *Exotische Welten, europäische Phantasien* (pp. 356-367). Stuttgart: Cantz.

Konuk, Kader. (1997). Das Leben ist eine Karawanserei: Heimat bei Emine Sevgi Özdamar. In Gisela Ecker (Ed.), *Kein Land in Sicht. Heimat – Weiblich?* (pp. 143-157). Munich: Fink.

— (1999). 'Identitätssuche ist ein [sic!] private archäologische Gräberei': Emine Sevgi Özdamars inszeniertes Sprechen. In Cathy S. Gelbin, Kader Konug, and Peggy Piesche (Eds.), *Aufbrüche: Kulturelle Produktionen von Migrantinnen, Schwarzen und jüdischen Frauen in Deutschland* (pp. 60-74). Königstein/Taunus: Ulrike Helmer.

Koopmans, Ruud. (2001). Duitsland en het rechtsextremisme: hoe de blik op het verleden leidt tot verblinding in het heden. In Joost Kleuters and Erika Poettgens (Eds.), *Duitsland in beweging* (pp. 70-75). Nijmegen: Centrum voor Duitsland Studies [Centre for German Studies].

— (2002). Zachte heelmeesters... Een vergelijking van de resultaten van het Nederlandse en het Duitse integratiebeleid en wat de WRR daaruit niet concludeert. *Migrantenstudies*, 18(2), 87-92.

— (2003a). Good Intentions Sometimes Make Bad Policy. A Comparison of Dutch and German Integration Policies. In René Cuperus, Karl A. Duffek, and Johannes Kandel (Eds.), *The Challenge of Diversity: European social democracy facing migration, integration, and multiculturalism* (pp. 163-169). Innsbruck: Studien Verlag.

— (2003b). Uitvluchten kan niet meer... Een repliek op Böcker en Thränhardt. *Migrantenstudies*, 19(1), 45-56.

Koopmans, Ruud and Paul Statham. (2001). How national citizenship shapes transnationalism. A comparative analysis of migrant Claims-making in Germany, Great Britain and the Netherlands. *Revue Européenne des Migrations Internationales*, 17(2), 63-100.

Koopmans, Ruud, Paul Statham, Marco Giugni, and Florence Passy. (2005). *Contested Citizenship. Immigration and Cultural Diversity in Europe.* Minnesota: University of Minnesota Press.

Kossmann, E.H. (1994). Hoe Nederlands is de Nederlandse literatuur? *Literatuur*, 11(1), 2-10.

— (1996). Verdwijnt de Nederlandse identiteit? Beschouwingen over natie en cultuur. In Koen Koch and Paul Scheffer (Eds.), *Het nut van Nederland: opstellen over soevereiniteit en identiteit* (pp. 56-69). Amsterdam: Bert Bakker.

Kosta, Barbara and Helga Kraft (Eds.). (2003). *Writing against Boundaries. Nationality, Ethnicity and Gender in the German-speaking Context.* Amsterdam; New York: Rodopi.

Kottmann, Hans. (2004, 19 February). Een heerlijk stadje om binnen te zitten. *Noordhollands Dagblad*.

Kouters, Steffie. (2002, 7 March). Genoeg van het gesus. *de Volkskrant*.

Krause, Frank. (2000). Shadow Motifs in Emine Sevgi Özdamar's die Brücke vom goldenen Horn. A Corrective to the Limitations of Current Debates on Intercultural Issues. *Debatte*, 8(1), 71-86.

Kreuzer, Helmut. (1984). Gastarbeiter-Literatur, Ausländer-Literatur, Migranten-Literatur? Zur Einführung. *Zeitschrift für Literaturwissenschaft und Linguistik LiLi*, 14(56), 7-11.

Kristeva, Julia. (1993). *Nation without nationalism*. New York: Columbia University Press.

Krusche, Dietrich. (1985). *Literatur und Fremde. Zur Hermeneutik kulturräumlicher Distanz*. Munich: Iudicium.

Kuipers, Willem. (1998, 1 May). Ik ben een Nederlandse schrijver. *de Volkskrant*.

Kuitert, Lisa. (1999). Niet zielig, maar leuk. Nederlandse uitgevers van multiculturele literatuur. *Literatuur*, 6, 355-364.

Kurthen, Hermann. (1995). Germany at the Crossroads: National Identity and the Challenges of Immigration. *International Migration Review*, 29(4), 914-938.

LaCapra, Dominick. (1997). The Historians' Debate (Historikerstreit) takes place over the status and representation of the Nazi period, and more specifically of the Holocaust, in Germany's past. In Sander L. Gilman and Jack Zipes (Eds.), *Yale Companion to Jewish Writing and Thought in German Culture, 1096-1996* (pp. 812-819). New Haven: Yale University Press.

— (2004). *History in Transit: Experience, Identity, Critical Theory*. Ithaca: Cornell University Press.

Lammert, Norbert (Ed.). (2006). *Verfassung, Patriotismus, Leitkultur. Was unsere Gesellschaft zusammenhält*. Hamburg: Hoffmann & Campe.

Laroui, F. (2001). *Vreemdeling: aangenaam*. Amsterdam: G.A. van Oorschot.

Leeuw, Marc de and Sonja van Wichelen. (2005). 'Please, Go and Wake Up!' Submission, Hirsi Ali and the 'War on Terror' in the Netherlands. *Feminist Media Studies*, 5(3), 325-340.

Leggewie, Claus (Ed.). (1990). *Multi Kulti: Spielregeln für die Vielvölkerrepublik*. Berlin: Rotbuch.

Leijnse, Elisabeth and Michiel van Kempen (Eds.). (2001). *Tussenfiguren; Schrijvers tussen de culturen*. Amsterdam: Het Spinhuis.

Lewis, Reina. (1996). *Gendering Orientalism. Race, Femininity and Representation*. London; New York: Routledge.

Link, Jürgen. (1999). *Versuch über den Normalismus. Wie Normalität produziert wird*. (2 rev. ed.). Opladen; Wiesbaden: Westdeutscher Verlag.

Linthout, Dik. (2006). *Onbekende buren: Duitsland voor Nederlanders, Nederland voor Duitsers*. Amsterdam: Atlas.

Lionnet, Francoise. (1995). *Postcolonial Representations; Women, Literature, Identity*. Ithaca; London: Cornell University Press.

Literaturen. (2005). 'Ich bin ein Teil der deutschen Literatur, so deutsch wie Kafka'. *Literaturen*, 4, 26-31.

Littler, Margaret. (2002). Diasporic Identity in Emine Sevgi Özdamar's Mutterzunge. In Stuart Taberner and Frank Finlay (Eds.), *Recasting German Identity. Culture, Politics and Literature in the German Republic* (pp. 219-234). Rochester: Camden House.

Lorde, Audre. (1993). *Sister Outsider: Essays and Speeches*. New York: Quality Paperback Book Club.

Lottmann, Joachim. (1997, 14 November). Kanak Attack! Ein Wochenende in Kiel mit Feridun Zaimoglu, dem Malcolm X der deutschen Türken. *Die Zeit*, 47.

— (Ed.). (1999). *Kanaksta. Geschichten von deutschen und anderen Ausländern*. Berlin: Quadriga.

Louwerse, Henriëtte. (1997). The Way to the North. The Emergence of Turkish and Moroccan Migrant Writers in the Dutch Literary Landscape. *Dutch Crossing*, 21(1), 69-88.

— (2000). Dutch Distorted: Hafid Bouazza's Momo. *Dutch Crossing*, 24(1), 29-37.

— (2001). Zwartrijders in de Nederlandse literatuur: het motief van de queeste in de migrantenliteratuur. In Gerard Elshout, Carel ter Haar, Guy Janssens, Marja Kristel, Anneke Prins, and Roel Vismans (Eds.), *Perspectieven voor de internationale neerlandistiek in de 21e eeuw. Handelingen Veertiende Colloquium Neerlandicum*. Münster: Nodus-Publ.

— (2004a). Het mijne is het uwe. Culturele integriteit in Hafid Bouazza's 'De verloren zoon'. In Michiel van Kempen, Piet Verkruijsse, and Adrienne Zuiderweg (Eds.), *Wandelaar onder de palmen. Opstellen over koloniale en postkoloniale literatuur en cultuur* (pp. 43-51). Leiden: KITLV.

— (2004b). 'Sweet is the music of yon whispering pine'. Migration and the pastoral in Hafid Bouazza's 'Paravion'. *Dutch Crossing*, 28(1-2), 105-120.

— (2007a). Authenticiteitshelers? De 'on-Nederlandse' auteur in een tijd van onbehagen. *Neerlandica extra muros*, 1, 1-10.

— (2007b). *Homeless Entertainment. On Hafid Bouazza's Literary Writing*. Bern: Peter Lang.

Lucassen, Jan and Rinus Penninx. (1985). *Nieuwkomers. Immigranten en hun nakomelingen in Nederland 1550-1985*. Amsterdam: Meulenhoff Informatief.

— (1994). *Nieuwkomers, nakomelingen, Nederlanders: immigranten in Nederland 1550-1993*. Amsterdam: Het Spinhuis.

Lutz, Helma. (1996). Doeken des aanstoots. Een beschouwing over hoofddoeken en genderverhoudingen in de multiculturele samenleving. In Gloria Wekker and Rosi Braidotti (Eds.), *Praten in het donker. Multiculturalisme en anti-racisme in feministisch perspectief* (pp. 119-148). Kampen: Kok Agora.

— (2002). Zonder blikken of blozen. Het standpunt van de (nieuw-)realisten. *Tijdschrift voor Genderstudies*, 5(3), 7-17.

Lutz, Helma, Ann Phoenix, and Nira Yuval-Davis (Eds.). (1995). *Crossfires. Nationalism, Racism and Gender in Europe*. London; East Haven: Pluto Press.

Mandel, Ruth. (1989). Turkish Headscarves and the 'Foreigner Problem': Constructing Difference Through Emblems of Identity. *New German Critique*, 46(Winter), 27-46.

Mani, B. Venkat (2002). Phantom of the 'Gastarbeiterliteratur'. Aras Ören's Berlin Savignyplatz. In Aglaia Blioumi (Ed.), *Migration und Interkulturalität in neueren literarischen Texten* (pp. 112-129). Munich: Iudicium.

McClintock, Anne. (1993). Family Feuds: Gender, Nationalism and the Family. *Feminist Review*, 44(2), 61-80.

— (1995). *Imperial Leather: Race, Gender and Sexuality in the Colonial Contest*. New York; London: Routledge.

McFalls, Laurence. (1997). Living with Which Past? National Identity in Post-Wall, Postwar Germany. In Scott Denham, Irene Kacandes, and Jonathan Petropoulos (Eds.), *A User's Guide to German Cultural Studies* (pp. 297-308). Ann Arbor: University of Michigan Press.

McGowan, Moray. (2000a). 'The Bridge of the Golden Horn': Istanbul, Europe and the 'Fractured Gaze from the West' in Turkish Writing in Germany. In Andy Hollis (Ed.), *Beyond Boundaries – Textual Representations of European Identities* (Vol. 15, pp. 53-68).

— (2000). Some Turkish-German Views and Visions of 'Europa'. In Barry Axford, Daniela Berghahn, and Nick Hewlett (Eds.), *Unity and Diversity in the New Europe* (pp. 339-354). Oxford; Bern: Peter Lang.

— (2001). Multiple Masculinities in Turkish-German Men's Writing. In Roy Jerome (Ed.), *Conceptions of Postwar German Masculinity* (pp. 289-312). New York: State University of New York Press.

Mecklenburg, Norbert. (1990). Über kulturelle und poetische Alterität: Kultur- und literaturtheoretische Grundprobleme einer interkulturellen Germanistik. In Dietrich Krusche and Alois Wierlacher (Eds.), *Hermeneutik der Fremde* (pp. 80-103). Munich: Iudicium.

— (2006). Ein türkischer Literaturskandal in Deutschland? Kritischer Kommentar zum Streit um Feridun Zaimoglus 'Leyla' und Emine Sevgi Özdamars 'Das Leben ist eine Karawanserei'. *literaturkritik.de*, 7. Retrieved from the World Wide Web: http://www.literaturkritik.de

Meier-Braun, Karl-Heinz (Ed.). (1995). *40 Jahre 'Gastarbeiter' in Deutschland*. Baden-Baden: Nomos.

— (2002). *Deutschland, Einwanderungsland*. Frankfurt am Main: Suhrkamp.

Meijer, Sietse. (2003, 10 May). Je hoorde overal: Oek, Oek, Oek. *Het Parool*.

Mein, Georg. (2004). Die Migration entlässt ihre Kinder. Sprachliche Entgrenzungen als Identitätskonzept. In Clemens Kammler and Torsten Pflugmacher (Eds.), *Deutschsprachige Gegenwartsliteratur seit 1989: Zwischenbilanzen – Analysen – Vermittlungsperspektiven* (pp. 201-217). Heidelberg: Synchron.

Melas, Natalie. (1995). Versions of incommensurability. *World Literature Today*, 69(2), 275-288.

Merz, Friedrich. (2000, 25 October). Einwanderung und Identität. *Die Welt*.

Meyer, Jörg. (2001). 'Durchgeknallt gibt es überall'. JW sprach mit Feridun Zaimoglu. *Junge Welt*.

Miller, J. Hillis. (2001). *Speech acts in literature*. Stanford: Stanford University Press.

Minh-ha, Trin T. (2005). *The Digital Film Event*. London: Routledge.

Minnaard, Liesbeth. (2001). Kennisachterstand. Interculturalisatie aan de universiteit. *Pandora*, 2, 20-21.

— (2004). Playing Kanak Identity: Feridun Zaimoglu's rebellious Performances. In H. Arlt (Ed.), *Das Verbindende der Kulturen / The Unifying Aspects of Cultures / Les points commun des cultures*. Vienna: INST.

— (2005). Hafid Bouazzas fliegender Teppich. Die Imagination eines niederländischen Arkadiens. In Graduiertenkolleg Identität und Differenz (Ed.), *Ethnizität und Geschlecht. (Post-)Koloniale Verhandlungen in Geschichte, Kunst und Medien* (pp. 263-280). Cologne; Weimar; Vienna: Böhlau.

— (2006a). De succesvolle wisselwerking tussen parodie en performance. Voorstellingen van Moreaanse mannelijkheid in Hafid Bouazza's *Paravion*. *Gender. Tijdschrift voor Genderstudies*, 8(3), 49-62.

— (2006b). Mein Istanbul, mein Berlin. Emine Sevgi Özdamar's literary re-negotiations of Turkish-German division. In Alexandra Karentzos and Regina Göckede (Eds.), *Der Ori-*

ent, die Fremde. Positionen zeitgenössischer Kunst und Literatur (pp. 83-100). Bielefeld: transcript.

Mohanty, Satya P. (1993). The Epistemic Status of Cultural Identity: On 'Beloved' and the Postcolonial Condition. Cultural Critique, 24, 41-80.

Moretti, Franco. (2000). Conjectures on World Literature. New Left Review, 1, 54-68.

Mosse, George L. (1996). The Image of Man: The Creation of Modern Masculinity. New York; Oxford: Oxford University Press.

Mouffe, Chantal. (1992). Feminism, Citizenship, and Radical Democratic Politics. In Judith Butler and Joan W. Scott (Eds.), Feminists theorize the political (pp. 369-384). London: Routledge.

Moya, Paula M.L. and Michael R. Hames-García (Eds.). (2000). Reclaiming Identity. Realist Theory and the Predicament of Postmodernism. Berkeley: University of California Press.

Müller, Regula. (1997). 'Ich war Mädchen, war ich Sultanin': Weitgeöffnete Augen betrachten türkische Frauengeschichten. In Sabine Fischer and Moray McGowan (Eds.), Denn du tanzt auf einem Seil. Positionen deutschsprachiger MigrantInnenliteratur (pp. 133-149). Tübingen: Stauffenburg.

Naficy, Hamid. (2001). An Accented Cinema. Exilic and Diasporic Filmmaking. Princeton; Oxford: Princeton University Press.

Neubert, Isolde. (1997). Searching for Intercultural Communication. Emine Sevgi Özdamar – A Turkish Woman Writer in Germany. In Chris Weedon (Ed.), Postwar Women's Writing in German (pp. 153-168). Providence; Oxford: Berghahn.

Neumann, Olaf. (2004, 3 March). 'Ich bezeichne mich nicht als Europäer'. Interview mit Feridun Zaimoglu. Jungle World, 11.

Nochlin, Linda. (1989). The Imaginary Orient, The Politics of Vision. Essays on Nineteenth-Century Art and Society (pp. 33-59). New York: Harper & Row.

Nord, Christina. (2004, 20 December). Das Lachen des Tricksters. Die Tageszeitung.

Nussbaum, Martha. (1996). Patriotism and Cosmopolitanism. In Joshua Cohen (Ed.), For Love of Country. Debating the Limits of Patriotism. Martha C. Nussbaum with Respondents (pp. 12-17). Boston: Beacon Press.

Oostindie, Gert (Ed.). (2001). Facing Up to the Past: Perspectives on the Commemoration of Slavery from Africa, the Americas and Europe. Jamaica: Ian Randle Publishers.

— (2001). Woord vooraf. Verbannen in de letteren. In Elisabeth Leijnse and Michiel van Kempen (Eds.), Tussenfiguren. Schrijvers tussen de culturen (no pagination). Amsterdam: Het Spinhuis.

Opitz, Michael. (2003, 6 August). Stern über geteilter Stadt. Emine Sevgi Özdamar entführt ins Berlin der 70er Jahre. Neues Deutschland.

Oranje, Hans. (2003, 11 December). Brutale hond in Marokkaans gezin. Trouw.

Overdijk-Francis, J.E. and H.M.A.G. Smeets (Eds.). (2000). Bij nader inzien: het integratiedebat op afstand bekeken. Houten; Diegen: Bohn Stafleu Van Loghum.

Özdamar, Emine Sevgi. (1992). Das Leben ist eine Karawanserei hat zwei Türen aus einer kam ich rein aus der anderen ging ich raus. Cologne: Kiepenheuer & Witsch.

— (1998a). Die Brücke vom Goldenen Horn. Cologne: Kiepenheuer & Witsch.

— (1998b). Mutterzunge. Cologne: Kiepenheuer & Witsch.

— (2001). Der Hof im Spiegel. Erzählungen. Cologne: Kiepenheuer & Witsch.

— (2003). *Seltsame Sterne starren zur Erde. Wedding – Pankow 1976/77.* Cologne: Kiepenheuer & Witsch.

— (2005). Kleist-Preis-Rede. In Ingo Breuer (Ed.), *Kleist Jahrbuch* (pp. 13-18). Stuttgart: J.B. Metzler.

Paasman, Bert. (1999). Een klein aardrijkje op zichzelf, de multiculturele samenleving en de etnische literatuur. *Literatuur, 16*(6), 324-333.

— (2002). *Wandelen onder de palmen. De morele actualiteit van het koloniale verleden.* Amsterdam: Vossiuspers UvA.

Pam, Max. (2003, 12 December). Een Dorrestijn uit Arabië. *HP/De Tijd.*

— (2005, 25 February). Bergen in het vlakke land. *HP/De Tijd.*

Pautz, Hartwig. (2005). The politics of identity in Germany: the *Leitkultur* debate. *Race & Class, 46*(4), 39-52.

Pazarkaya, Yüksel. (1986). Literatur ist Literatur. In Irmgard Ackermann and Harald Weinrich (Eds.), *Eine nicht nur deutsche Literatur. Zur Standortbestimmung der 'Ausländerliteratur'* (pp. 59-64). Munich; Zurich: Piper.

Peck, Jeffrey M. (1996). Rac(e)ing the Nation: Is There a German 'Home'? In Geoff Eley and Ronald Grigor Suny (Eds.), *Becoming National. A Reader* (pp. 481-492). New York; Oxford: Oxford University Press.

Pels, Dick. (2003). *De geest van Pim. Het gedachtegoed van een politieke dandy.* Amsterdam: Anthos.

Persch, Patricia. (2004). 'Identität ist Tofu für Lemminge'. Interview mit dem Kieler Schriftsteller Feridun Zaimoglu. *Der Deutschunterricht, 5,* 87-89.

Peters, Arjan. (2003, 17 October). 'Meer een westerse projectie dan werkelijkheid'. *de Volkskrant.*

— (2004, 28 January). Ik zeg liever op papier dat man en vrouw gelijk zijn. Zoiets roepen in een moskee werkt niet. *De Morgen.*

Pfaff, Carol W. (2005). 'Kanaken in Alemannistan': Feridun Zaimoglu's representation of migrant language. In Volker Hinnenkamp and Katharina Meng (Eds.), *Sprachgrenzen überspringen. Sprachliche Hybridität und polykulturelles Selbstverständnis* (pp. 195-223). Tübingen: Gunter Narr.

Piryns, Piet. (2003, 29 October). 'Ik zie voornamelijk domheid en fanatisme om me heen'. Piet Piryns interviewt Hafid Bouazza. *Knack.*

Pos, Gert Jan. (1997, 28 June). Zonen van Scheherazade: verfrissende literatuur van de marokkaans-nederlandse schrijvers Hafid Bouazza en Abdelkader Benali. *Elsevier.*

Potter, Russell A. (1995). *Spectacular vernaculars: hip-hop and the politics of postmodernism.* Albany: State University of New York Press.

Pratt, Mary Louise. (1977). *Toward a Speech Act Theory of Literary Discourse.* Bloomington: Indiana University Press.

Preter, Jeroen de. (2004, 22 March). Nederland boven op Vlaams literair feest. *De Morgen.*

Prins, Baukje. (2002). Het lef om taboes te doorbreken. Nieuw realisme in het Nederlandse discours over multiculturalisme. *Migrantenstudies, 4,* 241-254.

— (2004). *Voorbij de onschuld. Het debat over integratie in Nederland* (2 rev. ed.). Amsterdam: Van Gennep.

Prins, Baukje and Boris Slijper. (2002). Inleiding. *Migrantenstudies, 4,* 194-210.

Radhakrishnan, R. (2003). Postcoloniality and the Boundaries of Identity. In Linda Martin Alcoff and Eduardo Mendieta (Eds.), *Identities. Race, Class, Gender, and Nationality* (pp. 312-329). Malden; Oxford: Blackwell.

Radisch, Iris (Ed.). (2003). *Die besten 2003. Klagenfurter Texte. Die 27. Tage der deutschsprachigen Literatur in Klagenfurt.* Munich; Zurich: Piper.

Rajchman, John (Ed.). (1995). *The Identity in Question.* New York; London: Routledge.

Ramdas, Anil. (1997, 14 March). Niemand heeft oog voor het vreemde. Moedwil en kwade trouw bij blanke schrijvers. *NRC Handelsblad.*

Räthzel, Nora. (1997). *Gegenbilder. Nationale Identität durch Konstruktion des Anderen.* Opladen: Leske & Budrich.

Renan, Ernest. (1996). What is a Nation? In Geoff Eley and Ronald Grigor Suny (Eds.), *Becoming National. A Reader* (pp. 42-55). New York; Oxford: Oxford University Press.

Roggen, Frans. (1997, 18 July). Bezeten Burleske. *De Morgen.*

Römhild, Regina. (2000). Europäisierung als Transnationalisierung. *Anthropolitan, 8,* 15-27.

— (2005). Global Heimat Germany. Migration and the Transnationalization of the Nation state. *Transit, 1(1),* No. 50903.

Rommelspacher, Birgit. (2002). *Anerkennung und Ausgrenzung; Deutschland als multikulturelle Gesellschaft.* Frankfurt am Main: Campus.

Ronneberger, Klaus and Vassilis Tsianos. (2001). Abschied von der postmodernen Kulturgesellschaft. Nachlese zur 'Leitkultur'-Debatte. *Texte zur Kunst, 11(41),* 91-97.

Rushdie, Salman. (1991). *Imaginary Homelands: Essays and Criticism 1981-1991.* London: Granta Books.

Rutherford, Jonathan (Ed.). (1990). *Identity. Community, Culture, Difference.* London: Lawrence & Wishart.

Ryan, Marie-Laure. (2002). Fiction and its other: How trespassers help defend the border. *Semiotica, 138(1/4),* 351-369.

Saharso, Sawitri. (2000). *Feminisme versus multiculturalisme?* Utrecht: Forum.

Said, Edward W. (1995). *Orientalism. Western Conceptions of the Orient.* Harmondsworth: Penguin.

Sanders, Stephan and Xandra Schutte. (2003, 22 February). 'We waren blind van barmhartigheid'. Het multiculturele drama door negen denkers verklaard. *Vrij Nederland, 64,* 32-41.

Sassen, Saskia. (1998). *Globalization and Its Discontents: Essays on the New Mobility of People and Money.* New York: The New Press.

Saussy, Haun (Ed.). (2006). *Comparative Literature in an Age of Globalization.* Baltimore: The John Hopkins University Press.

Schami, Rafik. (1986). Selbstverständnis und Stellenwert der 'Ausländerliteratur'. Eine Literatur zwischen Minderheit und Mehrheit. In Irmgard Ackermann and Harald Weinrich (Eds.), *Eine nicht nur deutsche Literatur. Zur Standortbestimmung der 'Ausländerliteratur'* (pp. 55-58). Munich; Zurich: Piper.

Scheffer, Paul. (2000, 29 January). Het multiculturele drama. *NRC Handelsblad.*

Scheldwacht, Ricci. (2002, 22 February). Interview met Abdelkader Benali. *HP/De Tijd.*

Schmitz, Jowi. (2003, 8 December). Benali's warrige 'Onrein' mist plot. *NRC Handelsblad.*

Schnabel, Paul. (2000, 17 februari). De multiculturele samenleving is een illusie. *de Volkskrant.*

Schneider, Jens. (2001). *Deutsch Sein. Das Eigene, das Fremde und die Vergangenheit im Selbstbild des vereinten Deutschland.* Frankfurt am Main; New York: Campus.

Schobert, Alfred and Siegfried Jäger (Eds.). (2004). *Mythos Identität. Fiktion mit Folgen.* Münster: UNRAST.

Schouten, Rob. (2003, 1 November). Amsterdam: een fata morgana. Bouazza mengt lyriek en ironie. *Trouw.*

Schut, Lies. (2003, 24 October). Hafid Bouazza schrijft nieuwe roman. *De Telegraaf.*

Schutte, Xandra. (1996, 14 May). Ik ben net een voddenraper. *De Groene Amsterdammer.*

Scott, Joan W. (1995). Multiculturalism and the Politics of Identity. In John Rajchman (Ed.), *The Identity in Question* (pp. 3-12). New York; London: Routledge.

— (2001). Fantasy Echo: History and the Construction of Identity. *Critical Inquiry, 27,* 284-304.

Seidel-Arpacı, Annette. (2003). Kant in 'Deutsch-Samoa' und Gollwitz: 'Hospitalität' und Selbst-Positionierung in einem deutschen Kontext. In Hito Steyerl and Encarnación Gutiérrez Rodríguez (Eds.), *Spricht die Subalterne deutsch? Migration und postkoloniale Kritik* (pp. 195-212). Münster: UNRAST.

Şenocak, Zafer. (1992). *Atlas des tropischen Deutschland. Essays.* Berlin: Babel.

— (1998). *Gefährliche Verwandtschaft.* Munich: Babel.

— (2001). *Zungenentfernung. Bericht aus der Quarantänestation. Essays.* Berlin: Babel.

— (2005, 7 October). Dunkle deutsche Seele. Warum ist es so schwierig, die Erfolgsgeschichte des eigenen Landes zu erkennen. *Die Welt.*

— (2006, 10/11 June). Authentische Türkinnen. *Die Tageszeitung.*

Seyhan, Azade. (1996). Lost in Translation: Re-Membering the Mother Tongue in Emine Sevgi Özdamar's Das Leben ist eine Karawanserei. *The German Quarterly, 69*(4), 414-426.

— (2001). *Writing Outside the Nation.* Princeton; Oxford: Princeton University Press.

Sieg, Katrin. (2002). *Ethnic Drag: Performing Race, Nation and Sexuality in West Germany.* Ann Arbor: University of Michigan Press.

Silverman, Kaja. (1992). *Male Subjectivity at the Margins.* New York; London: Routledge.

— (1996). *The Threshold of the Visible World.* New York; London: Routledge.

Skiba, Dirk. (2004). Ethnolektale und literarisierte Hybridität in Feridun Zaimoglus Kanak Sprak. In Klaus Schenk, Almut Todorow, and Milan Tvrdík (Eds.), *Migrationsliteratur. Schreibweisen einer interkulturelle Moderne* (pp. 183-204). Tübingen; Basel: Francke.

Smith, Anthony D. (1993). *National Identity.* Reno; Las Vegas: University of Nevada Press.

Smith, Joy. (2005, 31 March). In the Shadow of Slavery: Monuments, Cultural Memory and Dutch Geographies of Time, Space and Morality. Paper presented at the conference Sonic Interventions. Pushing the Boundaries of Cultural Analysis, Amsterdam.

Şölçün, Sargut. (1992). *Sein und Nichtsein: Zur Literatur in der multikulturellen Gesellschaft.* Bielefeld: Aisthesis.

— (2002). Gespielte Naivität und ernsthafte Sinnlichkeit der Selbstbegegnung – Inszenierungen des Unterwegsseins in Emine Sevgi Özdamars Roman 'Die Brücke vom Goldenen Horn'. In Aglaia Blioumi (Ed.), *Migration und Interkulturalität in neueren literarischen Texten* (pp. 92-111). Munich: Iudicium.

Sollors, Werner. (2005). Good-bye, Germany! *Transit,* 1(1), No. 50902.

Soysal, Yasemin Nuhoğlu. (1994). *Limits of Citizenship. Migrants and Postnational Membership in Europe.* Chicago: The University of Chicago.

— (2000). Citizenship and identity: Living in diasporas in postwar Europe? *Ethnic and Racial Studies*, 23(1), 1-15.

Speet, Fleur. (2003, 10 May). Het wringt en wurgt en dat is zonde. *Het Financieel Dagblad*.

Spijkerboer, Thomas. (1993). Het toelatingsbeleid: verkeerde prioriteiten. In Ruben S. Gowricharn (Ed.), *Binnen de grenzen. Immigratie, etniciteit en integratie in Nederland* (pp. 36-49). Utrecht: De Tijdstroom.

Spivak, Gayatri Chakravorty. (2003). *Death of a Discipline*. New York: Columbia University Press.

Stephan, Inge. (2003). Im toten Winkel. Die Neuentdeckung des 'ersten Geschlechts' durch *men's studies* und Männlichkeitsforschung. In Claudia Benthien and Inge Stephan (Eds.), *Männlichkeit als Maskerade. Kulturelle Inszenierungen vom Mittelalter bis zur Gegenwart* (pp. 11-35). Cologne: Böhlau.

Sterck, Marita de. (1997). Schoonheid en betekenis. Hafid Bouazza en de grenzen van taal en verlangen. *Kultuurleven*, 4, 94-99.

Sterk, Garjan. (2004). Uitzicht op kruispunten vanuit de witte toren. Een reconstructie van het debat over gender en etniciteit. *Gender. Tijdschrift voor Genderstudies*, 7(4), 49-60.

Steyerl, Hito and Encarnación Gutiérrez Rodríguez (Eds.). (2003). *Spricht die Subalterne deutsch? Migration und postkoloniale Kritik*. Münster: UNRAST.

Stolcke, Verena. (1995). Talking Culture: New Boundaries, New Rhetorics of Exclusion in Europe. *Current Anthropology*, 36(1), 1-24.

Suhr, Heidrun. (1989). Ausländerliteratur: Minority Literature in the Federal Republic of Germany. *New German Critique*, 46(Winter), 71-103.

Taberner, Stuart and Frank Finlay (Eds.). (2002). *Recasting German Identity. Culture, Politics and Literature in the German Republic*. Rochester: Camden House.

Taylor, Charles. (1992). *Multiculturalism and 'The Politics of Recognition'. An Essay*. Princeton: Princeton University Press.

Teipel, Jürgen. (2001). Unser türkischer Nigger. Der 'Malcolm X' der Türken in Deutschland. *Rolling Stone Deutschland*, 2, 40.

Teraoka, Arlene A. (1987). Gastarbeiterliteratur: The Other speaks back. *Cultural Critique*, 7, 77-101.

— (1989). Talking 'Turk': On Narrative Strategies and Cultural Stereotypes. *New German Critique*, 46(Winter), 104-128.

— (1997). Multiculturalism and the Study of German Literature. In Scott Denham, Irene Kacandes, and Jonathan Petropoulos (Eds.), *A User's Guide to German Cultural Studies* (pp. 63-78). Ann Arbor: University of Michigan Press.

Terkessidis, Mark. (2000). *Migranten*. Hamburg: Europäische Verlagsanstalt and Rotbuch.

Thränhardt, Dieter. (2002). Inclusie of exclusie: Discoursen over migratie in Duitsland. *Migrantenstudies*, 4, 225-240.

Tibi, Bassam. (1998). *Europa ohne Identität. Die Krise der multikulturellen Gesellschaft*. Munich: Bertelsmann.

Trojanow, Ilija (Ed.). (2000). *Döner in Walhalla. Texte aus der anderen deutschen Literatur*. Cologne: Kiepenheuer & Witsch.

Tubergen, Frank van and Ineke Maas (Eds.). (2006). *Allochtonen in Nederland in Internationaal Perspectief. Jaarboek Mens & Maatschappij* (Vol. 81). Amsterdam: Amsterdam University Press.

Tuschick, Jamal. (1998). 'Auf die Ethnie beziehen sich die Ausgebremsten'. Ein Gespräch mit dem Literaturagitator Feridun Zaimoglu. *Junge Welt*.

— (2000a). 'Bruder, du bist meine Stimme'. Feridun Zaimoglu, Kombattant im Kulturkampf. In Thomas Kraft (Ed.), *aufgerissen. Zur Literatur der 90er*. Munich: Piper.

— (Ed.). (2000b). *Morgen Land. Neueste deutsche Literatur*. Frankfurt am Main: Fischer.

Uerlings, Herbert. (1997). *Poetiken der Interkulturalität. Haiti bei Kleist, Seghers, Müller, Buch und Fichte*. Tübingen: Niemeyer.

— (2001). Das Subjekt und die Anderen. Zur Analyse sexueller und kultureller Differenz. In Herbert Uerlings, Karl Hölz, and Viktoria Schmidt-Linsenhoff (Eds.), *Das Subjekt und die Anderen. Interkulturalität und Geschlechterdifferenz vom 18. Jahrhundert bis zur Gegenwart* (pp. 19-53). Berlin: Erich Schmidt.

— (2006). *'Ich bin von niedriger Rasse' (Post-)Kolonialismus und Geschlechterdifferenz in der deutschen Literatur*. Cologne; Weimar; Vienna: Böhlau.

Uerlings, Herbert, Karl Hölz, and Viktoria Schmidt-Linsenhoff (Eds.). (2001). *Das Subjekt und die Anderen. Interkulturalität und Geschlechterdifferenz vom 18. Jahrhundert bis zur Gegenwart*. Berlin: Erich Schmidt.

Uffelen, Herbert van. (2004a). Fremd sein unter Fremden. Über die Rezeption der niederländischen Literatur von Allochthonen im deutschen Sprachraum. In M. Elisabeth Weissebböck, Leopold Decloedt, and Herbert van Uffelen (Eds.), *Rezeption, Interaktion und Integration* (pp. 209-230). Vienna: Edition Praesens.

— (2004b). Geboren worden is een vorm van herinneren. Over de Nederlandstalige literatuur van de allochtonen. In Agata Kowalska-Szubert and Stefan Kiedron (Eds.) (pp. 691-708). Wroclaw: Oficyna Wydawnicza ATUT.

— (2006). Wie zoekt, die vindt... Nederlandse migrantenliteratuur in Duitse vertaling, zum Zweiten! *Neerlandica extra muros*, 44(1), 10-20.

Ullmaier, Johannes. (2001). *Von Acid nach Adlon und zurück. Eine Reise durch die deutschsprachige Popliteratur*. Mainz: Ventil.

Valk, Arno van der. (2004). Abdelkader Benali. In Hugo Brems, Tom van Deel, and Ad Zuiderent (Eds.), *Kritisch lexicon van de Nederlandstalige literatuur na 1945* (92 ed., pp. 1-7; A1; B1-2). Alphen aan de Rijn: Samson.

Van Dale. Groot woordenboek Nederlands-Engels. (3 ed.) (1999). Utrecht; Antwerp: Van Dale Lexicografie.

Vanegeren, Bart. (2003a, 20 May). Benali: Alibi-Abdelkader. *Humo*.

— (2003b, 28 October). Het herdersuurtje. *Humo*.

Veer, Peter van der. (2000). Nederland bestaat niet meer. *De Gids*, September, 742-749.

Vertovec, Steven. (2000). *Fostering Cosmopolitanisms: A Conceptual Survey and A Media Experiment in Berlin*. Retrieved from the World Wide Web: http://www.transcomm.ox.ac.uk

— (2001). *Transnational Challenges to the 'New' Multiculturalism*. Retrieved from the World Wide Web: http://www.transcomm.ox.ac.uk

Visser, Harm. (2003). Hafid Bouazza: Ik ben brandstof voor de hel. In Harm Visser (Ed.), *Leven zonder god. Elf interviews over ongeloof* (pp. 11-27). Amsterdam; Antwerp: L.J. Veen.

Vlaskamp, Marije. (1997, 5 April). Hier is de model-Marokkaan. *Het Parool*.

Von Dirke, Sabine. (1994). Multikulti: The German Debate on Multiculturalism. *German Studies Review*, 17(3), 513-536.

Vromen, Suzanne. (1993). The Ambiguity of Nostalgia. *YIVO Annual*, 21, 69-86.

Vuijsje, Herman. (1986). *Vermoorde onschuld. Etnisch verschil als Hollands taboe.* Amsterdam: Bert Bakker.

Vuijsje, Marja. (2003, 3 July). 'Les één: zeg wat je denkt'. *Contrast*, pp. 25-27.

Vullings, Jeroen. (1997, 5 April). We zien wel waar het uitkomt. *Vrij Nederland*.

— (2003, 22 November). De eeuwige schoolstrijd. *Vrij Nederland*.

Wahrig deutsches Wörterbuch. (2000). Gütersloh: Bertelsmann Lexikon Verlag.

Wallraff, Günter. (1985). *Ganz Unten.* Cologne: Kiepenheuer & Witsch.

Webeling, Pieter. (2004). Hafid Bouazza: 'Ik leef met grote gulzigheid. En ik flirt met de dood.' *Rails*, 14-20.

Weigel, Sigrid. (1992). Literatur der Fremde – Literatur in der Fremde. In Klaus Briegleb and Sigrid Weigel (Eds.), *Gegenwartsliteratur seit 1968* (pp. 182-229). Munich: Deutscher Taschenbuch Verlag.

— (2002). Zum 'topographical turn'. Kartographie, Topographie und Raumkonzepte in den Kulturwissenschaften. *KulturPoetik. Zeitschrift für kulturgeschichtliche Literaturwissenschaft*, 2(2), 151-165.

Wekker, Gloria. (2002). *Nesten bouwen op een winderige plek. Denken over gender en etniciteit in Nederland.* Utrecht: Universiteit Utrecht.

Wenk, Silke. (2000). Gendered Representations of the Nation's Past and Future. In Ida Blom, Karen Hagemann, and Catherine Hall (Eds.), *Gendered Nations: Nationalisms and Gender Order in the Long Nineteenth Century* (pp. 63-77). Oxford; New York: Berg.

Wertheimer, Jürgen. (2002). Kanak / wo / man contra Skinhead – zum neuen Ton jüngerer AutorInnen der Migration. In Aglaia Blioumi (Ed.), *Migration und Interkulturalität in neueren literarischen Texten* (pp. 131-135). Munich: Iudicium.

White, Paul. (1995). Geography, Literature and Migration. In Russell King, John Connell, and Paul White (Eds.), *Writing across Worlds: Literature and Migration* (pp. 1-19). London: Routledge.

Wierlacher, Alois (Ed.). (1985). *Das Fremde und das Eigene. Prologomena zu einer interkulturellen Germanistik.* Munich: Iudicium.

Wierlacher, Alois and Andrea Bogner (Eds.). (2003). *Handbuch interkulturelle Germanistik.* Stuttgart; Weimar: J.B. Metzler.

Wierschke, Annette. (1996). *Schreiben als Selbstbehauptung: Kulturkonflikt und Identität in den werken von Aysel Özakin, Alev Tekinay und Emine Sevgi Özdamar.* Frankfurt am Main: IKO – Verlag für Interkulturelle Kommunikation.

— (1997). Auf den Schnittstellen kultureller Grenzen tanzend: Aysel Özakin und Emine Sevgi Özdamar. In Sabine Fischer and Moray McGowan (Eds.), *Denn du tanzt auf einem Seil. Positionen deutschsprachiger MigrantInnenliteratur* (pp. 179-194). Tübingen: Stauffenburg.

Wise, Gail E. (1995). *Ali in Wunderland. German representations of foreign workers.* Diss. University of California, Berkeley.

Yeğenoğlu, Meyda. (1998). *Colonial fantasies. Towards a feminist reading of Orientalism.* Cambridge: Cambridge University Press.

Yeşilada, Karin E. (2000). Topographien im 'tropischen Deutschland' – Türkisch-deutsche Literatur nach der Wiedervereinigung. In Ursula E. Beitter (Ed.), *Literatur und Identität: deutsch-deutsche Befindlichkeiten und die multikulturelle Gesellschaft* (pp. 303-339). New York: Lang.

Yildiz, Yasemin. (2004). Critically 'Kanak': A Reimagination of German Culture. In Andreas Gardt and Bernd Hüppauf (Eds.), *Globalization and the future of German* (pp. 319-340). Berlin; New York: Mouton de Gruyter.

Young, Robert J. C. (1995). *Colonial Desire. Hybridity in Theory, Culture and Race*. London; New York: Routledge.

Yue, Ming-Bao. (2000). On not looking German. Ethnicity, diaspora and the politics of vision. *European Journal of Cultural Studies*, 3(2), 173-194.

Yuval-Davis, Nira. (1997). *Gender and Nation*. London: Sage.

Zaimoglu, Feridun. (1995). *Kanak Sprak. 24 Mißtöne vom Rande der Gesellschaft*. Hamburg: Rotbuch.

— (1997). *Abschaum. Die wahre Geschichte des Ertan Ongun*. Hamburg: Rotbuch.

— (1998a). Gastarbeiterliteratur. Ali macht Männchen. In Ruth Mayer and Mark Terkessidis (Eds.), *Globalkolorit. Multikulturalismus und Populärkultur* (pp. 85-97). St. Andrä; Wördern: Hannibal.

— (1998b). *Koppstoff: Kanaka Sprak vom Rande der Gesellschaft*. Hamburg: Rotbuch.

— (1999a). An Stelle eines Vorworts. In Joachim Lottmann (Ed.), *Kanaksta. Geschichten von deutschen und anderen Ausländern* (pp. 7-9). Berlin: Quadriga.

— (1999b). Knabenwindelprosa. Überall wird von deutscher Popliteratur geschwärmt. Aber sie ist nur reaktionäres Kunsthandwerk. Eine Abrechnung. *Die Zeit*, 47.

— (2000). *Liebesmale, scharlachrot*. Hamburg: Rotbuch.

— (2001). *Kopf und Kragen. Kanak-Kultur-Kompendium*. Frankfurt am Main: Fischer Taschenbuch.

— (2002). *German Amok*. Cologne: Kiepenheuer & Witsch.

— (2003a, 11 October). Häute. *Frankfurter Allgemeine Zeitung*.

— (2003b). *Leinwand*. Hamburg: Rotbuch.

— (2004). *Zwölf Gramm Glück*. Cologne: Kiepenheuer & Witsch.

— (2005, 26 November). Meine kleine Geschichte der Einwanderung. *Neue Zürcher Zeitung*.

— (2006a). *Der Liebe zu Deutschland nicht schämen* [Broadcast Deutschlandfunk]. Retrieved from the World Wide Web: http://www.dradio.de/dlf/sendungen/schwarzrotgold/546709/

— (2006b, 5 October). 'Für all das liebe ich Deutschland' Doppelte Einheit: Feridun Zaimoglu über Ost, West und Deutschtürken, Ethnohysteriker und den Berliner Islamgipfel. *Der Tagesspiegel*.

— (2006c). *Leyla*. Cologne: Kiepenheuer & Witsch.

— (2006d, 12 April). Mein Deutschland. Warum die Einwanderer auf ihre neue Heimat stolz sein können. *Die Zeit*.

Zaimoglu, Feridun and Jamal Tuschick. (2000). 'Ihr habt Angst vor unserem Sperma'. Kollaboration. In Jamal Tuschick (Ed.), *Morgen Land. Neueste deutsche Literatur* (pp. 9-20). Frankfurt am Main: Fischer.

Zantop, Susanne. (1997). *Colonial Fantasies. Conquest, Family and Nation in Precolonial Germany, 1770-1870*. Durham; London: Duke University Press.

Zimmermann, Peter (Ed.). (1989). *'Interkulturelle Germanistik'. Dialog der Kulturen auf Deutsch?* Frankfurt am Main: Lang.

Index

NEW GERMANS, NEW DUTCH